Essays on Knowledge
and Justification

Essays on Knowledge and Justification

Edited by

GEORGE S. PAPPAS *and*
MARSHALL SWAIN

Cornell University Press ITHACA AND LONDON

First published 1978 by Cornell University Press.
Published in the United Kingdom by Cornell University Press Ltd., 2-4 Brook Street, London W1Y 1AA.

International Standard Book Number (cloth) 0-8014-1086-X
International Standard Book Number (paper) 0-8014-9865-1
Library of Congress Catalog Card Number 77-10299
Printed in the United States of America by Vail-Ballou Press, Inc.
Librarians: Library of Congress cataloging information appears on the last page of the book.

Preface

The readings selected for this book depict the main lines of research surrounding the problem of knowledge during the past decade. Most of the readings deal directly with the analysis of knowledge, but we have also included some recent essays concerned more directly with justification and scepticism, for work on these problems has been intimately connected with, indeed often inseparable from, work on the more central problem. Most of these essays have appeared in journals, but several are printed here for the first time. While the essay by Roderick Chisholm has been published previously, it has been revised in several important respects for inclusion in the present volume. Two of the essays are excerpts from books that have recently been published, Gilbert Harman's *Thought* (Princeton University Press) and Keith Lehrer's *Knowledge* (Oxford University Press). In both cases, the selections were made with particular topics in mind, and are not intended to be condensations of the books. In the introductory essay we have surveyed the positions and problems represented in our collection, and we have attempted to locate many of the specific arguments on the epistemological map.

We are most grateful to the authors of these essays and to the various editors and publishers who have kindly permitted us to reprint their work. We are grateful also to James Twiggs of Cornell University Press for his patience, help, and encouragement. Our special thanks go to Mary Lee Raines, who man-

aged to produce neatly typed order from a jumble of notes
and manuscripts.

GEORGE S. PAPPAS
MARSHALL SWAIN

Columbus, Ohio

Contents

Introduction   11

1. Conclusive Reasons   *Fred Dretske*   41

2. Some Conclusive Reasons against "Conclusive Reasons"   *George S. Pappas and Marshall Swain*   61

3. A Causal Theory of Knowing   *Alvin I. Goldman*   67

4. Knowledge, Causality, and Justification   *Marshall Swain*   87

5. Professor Swain's Account of Knowledge   *Thomas D. Paxson, Jr.*   100

6. On Swain's Causal Analysis of Knowledge   *Joseph T. Tolliver*   106

7. Some Revisions of "Knowledge, Causality, and Justification"   *Marshall Swain*   109

8. Discrimination and Perceptual Knowledge   *Alvin I. Goldman*   120

9. Knowledge: Undefeated Justified True Belief   *Keith Lehrer and Thomas D. Paxson, Jr.*   146

10. Knowledge and Defeasibility   *David Annis*   155

11. Epistemic Defeasibility   *Marshall Swain*   160

12. How Do You Know?   *Ernest Sosa*   184

13. Selections from *Thought*   *Gilbert H. Harman*   206

14. Foundational versus Nonfoundational Theories of Empirical Justification   *James W. Cornman*   229

15. On the Nature of Empirical Evidence
                                    Roderick M. Chisholm   253

16. Modest Foundationalism and Self-Warrant
                                          Mark Pastin   279

17. Systematic Justification: Selections from *Knowledge*
                                         Keith Lehrer   289

18. Some Forms of Epistemological Scepticism
                                      George S. Pappas   309

19. A Defense of Skepticism   *Peter Unger*   317

20. In Reply to "A Defense of Skepticism" *James Cargile*   337

21. Why Not Scepticism?   *Keith Lehrer*   346

22. Why Scepticism?   *Dan Turner*   364

    Selected Bibliography   370

    Index   375

*Essays on Knowledge
and Justification*

Introduction

Many philosophers have agreed that a person knows a proposition only if that proposition is true, the person in question believes the proposition, and the proposition is justified for that person. According to a number of important philosophers, these three features are not only necessary conditions for knowledge, but also jointly sufficient for knowledge. Thus, if a true proposition is believed by some person, and the belief is justified, then that person is said to know the proposition in question. This account of knowledge is often referred to, somewhat misleadingly, as the 'traditional analysis' of knowledge. The view in question has its roots, perhaps, in Plato's *Theatetus*. In more recent times, it has been endorsed by a number of influential philosophers, including C. I. Lewis, A. J. Ayer, and Roderick Chisholm. But during the past decade, this tripartite analysis of knowing has been the subject of intensive scrutiny. The beginning of this controversy can be dated at the publication, in 1963, of a brief paper by Edmund Gettier, titled "Is Justified True Belief Knowledge?"[1] In this paper, Gettier proposed two original counterexamples to the sufficiency of the conditions in the traditional analysis of knowledge. Consideration of Gettier's examples has led epistemologists to question virtually every aspect of the traditional analysis. The greatest effort has gone into the attempt to revise the traditional analysis in ways that will render it immune to the problems raised by

1. *Analysis* 23.6 (1963), 121–123.

Gettier (and to other problems that have since been discovered). But some philosophers have been led to question the necessity of the three conditions in the traditional analysis, others have been led to question Gettier's examples themselves; some philosophers have been prompted to investigate theories concerning the nature of epistemic justification, and still others have been inspired by the controversy to new arguments for radical forms of scepticism concerning knowledge and justification. In this volume are collected a set of essays representative of the most important developments in the Gettier-inspired controversy about knowledge, justification, and scepticism.

1. The Gettier Problems

One of Gettier's examples concerns a man, Smith, who has adequate evidence for the conjunction,

(1) Jones is the man who will get the job, and Jones has ten coins in his pocket.

Smith is justified in believing (1) since the President of the company, a thoroughly reliable person, has told him that Jones will get the job, and Smith has just counted the number of coins in Jones' pocket. Now, Gettier notes, (1) entails

(2) The man who will get the job has ten coins in his pocket.

Moreover, Smith sees that (1) entails (2), reasons from (1) to (2), and accepts (2) as a result of this reasoning. Thus, Gettier claims, Smith is justified in believing (2). It happens, however, that Smith himself will get the job and, coincidentally, but unknown to Smith, he has ten coins in his pocket. Thus, (2) is true and Smith justifiably believes (2). However, Smith does not know (2), so, Gettier argues, the traditional justified-true-belief analysis of knowledge is inadequate.

Gettier also suggests a second example, in which a person, S, justifiably believes a false proposition q, infers from this that $p \lor q$, and where the disjunctive proposition $p \lor q$ is true. Since S has no evidence for p, S does not know that $p \lor q$, even though S justifiably believes $p \lor q$. Since the essential structure of this example is no different from that of the first, we shall concentrate on the first example. Many philosophers, perhaps most, have agreed that the Gettier examples defeat the traditional analysis. Other philosophers, however, have maintained on various grounds that the Gettier examples fail. We shall briefly consider four significant points raised in criticism of Gettier.

In Gettier's example, Smith is justified in accepting (1) despite the fact that (1) is false. It has been argued, however, that if a person is justified in accepting a proposition h, then h is true.[2] If this contention is correct, Gettier's examples would be effectively short-circuited. But the contention is dubious. First, people often have what would normally be regarded as excellent evidence for propositions that turn out to be false. For instance, at one time some people had good evidence for believing the Ptolemaic account of the universe and so had excellent evidence for the false proposition that the planets travel in circular orbits. The kind of justification involved in such a case is what we typically call *inductive*. One feature of such cases is that the evidence which constitutes the justification is compatible with the denial of the proposition justified (otherwise, the justification would be deductive). If the contention under question were correct, then it appears that many inductive justifications would simply not qualify as *justifications* at all, and this surely flies in the face of accepted views about justification. Second, it is easy to imagine two cases which are identical in all respects, i.e., same evidence and same circumstances, except that the proposition justified is true in one case and false in the other. For instance, we might suppose another example just like Gettier's in which (1) is true, rather than false. If the contention in question were correct, we should have to say in the one case that the belief is justified, but in the other that it is not. What explanation could there be for this difference? Surely not simply that the proposition justified is true in the one case, but false in the other!

A related response to Gettier's example is that part of the evidence Smith has for accepting (2) is false, and this violates a

2. R. Almeder, "Truth and Evidence," *Philosophical Quarterly*, 24.97 (1974), 365–368.

general principle that if a proposition, q, justifies a person in believing a proposition, h, then q is true.[3] Part of Smith's evidence for (2) is the false proposition (1). If (1) justifies (2) for Smith, (1) would have to be true given the principle just stated. Since (1) is not true, Gettier's example fails.

There is an effective reply to this argument.[4] Suppose S has a great deal of evidence bearing on some proposition, h, where the evidence justifies S in accepting h. We may suppose that the evidence consists of the conjunction c of many propositions, all of which are true. Now, suppose S *also* has some evidence for h which is *false*, and let us call the conjunction of c with this evidence, c^*. The conjunction c^* is false. The conjunction c^* justifies h for S, however, since the true propositions included in the conjunction c suffice to justify h. Thus, the principle that q justifies h for S only if q is true, is too restrictive.

The following principle does seem right, however: If h is justified for S on the basis of evidence, e, then no elements of e that are *essential* for that justification are false. A proposition, p, is essential in this context, let us say, just in case S would no longer be justified in accepting h if p were deleted from his evidence, and no other changes were made. Gettier's actual examples do run afoul of this highly plausible principle. We shall see, however, that it is possible to construct other examples that do not violate this principle.

Another related objection to Gettier's example is that Smith *reasons through* a false step. That is, Smith sees that (1) entails (2), reasons from (1) to (2) and accepts (2) as a result of this deduction. But he has reasoned through the false premise (1) and, the objection goes, no proposition is justified for a person if he has reasoned to that proposition through some false step.[5]

A slight modification of the argument presented against the preceding objection suffices to undercut this objection. We may imagine that S reasons through the conjunction c^* which con-

3. R. Meyers and K. Stern, "Knowledge without Paradox," *Journal of Philosophy*, 70 (1973), 147–160.

4. R. Dees and J. Hart, "Paradox Regained: A Reply to Meyers and Stern," *Journal of Philosophy*, 71 (1974), 367–372.

5. Cf. Meyers and Stern, *op. cit.*, and G. Harman, "Selections from *Thought*," Chapter 13 below.

tains the conjunction c of true propositions. He has, thus, reasoned through a false step; yet, for reasons similar to those cited above, we would still hold that his belief is justified. The above principle concerning reasoning through a false step is too strong. Again, a modified principle is much more plausible: If an *essential* part of the reasoning from the evidence to the accepted proposition, h, proceeds through a false step, then acceptance of h is not justified.[6] Gettier's example does seem to violate this principle, for Smith's reasoning through the false proposition, (1), would appear to be essential to his justification for accepting proposition (2).

If Gettier's two examples do violate each of these plausible principles, then, to that extent, his examples are defective. Nevertheless, there are Gettier-like examples that avoid these problems. Consider, first, an example proposed by Keith Lehrer.[7] He supposes that a person, Smith, observes two men, Mr. Nogot and Mr. Havit, enter his office. Smith knows both of these men, and each is known by Smith to be reliable and honest. Smith observes Mr. Nogot getting out of a new Ford automobile, and Nogot tells Smith that he (Nogot) has just purchased the new Ford. In this situation, Smith is completely justified in accepting,

P1: Mr. Nogot, who is in my office, owns a Ford.

From *P1* Smith then deduces

H: Someone in my office owns a Ford.

So, according to Lehrer, Smith is completely justified in believing *H*. However, this time Nogot has deceived Smith for some reason; Nogot does not own a Ford. Thus, *P1* is false. *H*, however, is true, since Havit, who is in the office, does own a Ford. Lehrer says, "Though *H* is true, and (Smith is) completely justified in (his) belief that it is true, (Smith) does not know that it is true. For the reason that *H* is true is that Mr. Havit owns a Ford, and (Smith) has no evidence that this is so."[8]

This example is very much like Gettier's, except for one im-

6. R. Chisholm, "On The Nature of Empirical Evidence," Chapter 15 below.

7. K. Lehrer, "Knowledge, Truth and Evidence," *Analysis*, 25.5 (1965), 168–175.

8. Ibid., p. 170.

portant difference. As Lehrer notes, Smith has adequate evidence for H that consists entirely of true statements, viz., all of the evidence he has for $P1$. All of that evidence is true and is, by itself, sufficient to justify Smith in believing H. Hence, even though Smith reasons through the false statement $P1$, and bases his belief that H, in part, on this reasoning, his doing so is *inessential* to his justification for believing H. Hence, we have a counterexample to the traditional analysis, even when that analysis is buttressed by the two plausible principles discussed above.

One might take issue with this example on the grounds that Smith does in fact reason through a false step, $P1$. What is crucial here is whether such reasoning is essential to Smith's justification. One might hold that this reasoning *is* essential to Smith's justification; however, the following alternative line of reasoning in the Nogot-Havit case suggests that reasoning through a false step is not essential.[9]

Suppose that m is Smith's evidence for $P1$ and that m is true and known by Smith to be so. Imagine that Smith deduces from m its existential generalization,

> n: There is someone in the office who told Smith that he owns a Ford and even showed him a certificate to that effect, and who up till now has always been reliable and honest in his dealings with Smith.

Now n is true and, it is plausible to hold, known by Smith. He has, after all, deduced n from m which he knows to be true. Further, imagine that on the basis of n, Smith believes that H, viz., that someone in the office owns a Ford. In this case, Smith has an inductively justified true belief that H; his reasoning does not proceed through any false steps; and no part of his evidence for H is false. Yet, Smith does not know that H, since he has no evidence bearing on the reason that H is true, namely that Havit owns a Ford.

The above examples avoid the three objections we have discussed to Gettier's original argument. There is, however, an-

9. Cf. R. Feldman, "An Alleged Defect in Gettier-Counterexamples," *Australasian Journal of Philosophy*, 52.1 (1974), 68–69.

other objection which, if correct, undercuts both Gettier's examples and Lehrer's Nogot-Havit example.

The objection is aimed at a principle of justification used by Gettier. The principle is this: (PDJ = Principle of Deduction for Justification):[10]

> PDJ: For any proposition P, if S is justified in believing P, and P entails Q, and S deduces Q from P, and accepts Q as a result of this deduction, then S is justified in accepting Q.[11]

It is clear that Gettier's examples utilize PDJ; so does Lehrer's Nogot-Havit example. Hence, if PDJ is implausible, the examples in question will be weakened, and the traditional analysis will not be refuted by them. According to Irving Thalberg, PDJ is implausible.

In Gettier's example, Smith deduces (2) from the false but nonetheless justified proposition, (1). Of proposition (2) ("The man who will get the job has ten coins in his pocket"), Thalberg observes that it is *general*, in the sense that (2) "can be true in many different ways." Proposition (1), by contrast, is not general since it can be true in just one way, viz., when Jones is the man who will get the job and he has ten coins in his pocket. Similar remarks apply to the general proposition used in the Nogot-Havit examples, viz., someone in the office owns a Ford. Thalberg's point seems to be that Smith has no evidence bearing on the way that (2) is in fact made true; and, similarly, he has no evidence bearing on the way that H is in fact made true. For, (2) is made true by the fact that Smith himself has ten coins in his pocket and will get the job; and, H is made true by the fact that Havit is in the office and owns a Ford. But, Smith has no evidence that *these* facts obtain, and so has no evidence that what makes (2) and H true obtains. Hence, Thalberg reasons, Smith also lacks evidence that (2) and H are true, or at least he lacks evidence sufficient to justify belief in those propositions. But, since Smith surely is justified in believing those propositions from which he deductively infers (2) and H, re-

10. This term is introduced by I. Thalberg in "In Defense of Justified True Belief," *Journal of Philosophy*, 66.22 (1969), 796.
11. The principle is stated first by Gettier, *op. cit.*

spectively, then one instantiation of PDJ is incorrect. Hence, Thalberg concludes PDJ is also incorrect.

We will restrict matters to two observations on Thalberg's argument.[12] First, it seems clear that his argument succeeds only if a principle such as the following is correct:

> P: A person, S, is justified in believing a proposition, h, only if S is justified in believing that the state of affairs that does, or would, make h true, obtains.

Thalberg does not argue for such a principle, though some of his remarks suggest he has it in mind. Principle P, though, seems no more obvious than PDJ. Second, there are examples similar to Gettier's which do not utilize PDJ, but which seem to effectively defeat the traditional analysis of knowledge. We need only cite the example given above, from Feldman, in which S inductively bases his belief that H on n. In Feldman's case, S lacks knowledge that H.

Thus far we have been discussing some elementary attempts to revise the traditional analysis by taking into account the role of false propositions in one's evidence, or in one's reasoning from the evidence. Two of the selections in this book (those by Roderick Chisholm and Gilbert Harman) suggest considerably more sophisticated approaches along these lines. Chisholm's paper concerns, among other things, the role of false propositions in the structure of one's justification. In the selections from *Thought*, Gilbert Harman introduces some considerations concerning the role of false premises in one's reasoning. Perhaps these more sophisticated emendations of the traditional analysis will serve to rescue it from Gettier-type counterexamples.

2. Conclusive Reasons

We have seen that the problems presented by Gettier-style examples cannot easily be dealt with by requirements to the ef-

---

12. Cf. M. Hooker, "In Defense of a Principle of Deducibility for Justification," *Philosophical Studies,* 24 (1973), 402–406; J. Saunders, "Thalberg's Challenge to Justification via Deduction," *Philosophical Studies,* 23 (1972) 358–364; and I. Thalberg, "Is Justification Transmissible through Deduction?" *Philosophical Studies,* 25.5 (1974), 347–356.

fect that all of one's evidence must be true, nor by requirements to the effect that one's reasoning must involve only true
premises and lemmas. Some philosophers have reacted to this
by suggesting that a different approach must be taken if one's
evidence is to provide one with knowledge. They note, correctly, that the evidence, e, that a person has for some proposition, h, may support h to any degree along a continuum rang-
ing from virtually worthless to conclusive. Then it is noted that
if a person's evidence is less than conclusive, it always seems
possible that the proposition for which the evidence provides
support is only coincidentally true. This characterization seems
to hold, for example, in the cases provided by Gettier; in those
cases, the subject has excellent but not conclusive evidence for
the believed proposition h, and it seems merely a coincidence
that h is true. It is tempting and natural to conclude that a person can have knowledge on the basis of evidence e only if e is
sufficiently strong to rule out the possibility of coincidence; that
is, S has knowledge that h only if S has conclusive reasons for
believing that h.

How might we formulate a conclusive reasons requirement
in a way that will elevate that notion from the level of vagueness? In a paper titled "The Analysis of Factual Knowledge,"[13]
Peter Unger noted that in the Gettier cases there is an element
of accident involved in S's being right about the fact that h is
true. In the example where S comes to correctly believe that
the man who will get the job has ten coins in his pocket, it
seems accidental that he is right about this. If it is thus accidental that S is right in these cases, then S's evidence, we might say,
cannot be *conclusive*. For, S could just as well have been *wrong* if
it is accidental that S is right. Unger suggests that the following
will handle such cases and will suffice as an analysis of knowledge:

    A person, S, has knowledge that h if and only if it is not at
    all accidental that S is right about its being the case that h.
Unfortunately, this suggestion of Unger's does not advance us
much beyond the level of vagueness from which we started.

13. *Journal of Philosophy,* 65.6 (1968), 157–170.

When is it correct to say that it is not at all accidental that S is right about its being the case that h? Unger says that he does not intend the notion of accidentality to include the sort of thing we talk about when discussing automobile accidents, but he does not tell us precisely what he does intend. Let us return to the Gettier example involving the person who believes that the man who will get the job has ten coins in his pocket. As Gettier presents the example, it does seem to be accidental in some sense that S is right about the conclusion drawn, but we can easily imagine a more complicated example in which it is not at all accidental that S is right about this conclusion, even though he still does not know. Suppose that someone has cleverly staged the entire set of circumstances described by Gettier. The employer has been bribed to mislead S, ten coins have been placed purposefully in Smith's pocket, etc. Then, it would seem, in whatever sense it *is* accidental that S is right in the case described by Gettier, it is in the same sense *not* accidental in this revised case that S is right. This would seem to suggest that Unger's notion of nonaccidentality is too weak to serve the purpose. Unger himself provides some examples that also suggest this.

But perhaps we have missed the point about accidentality. The notion of conclusive evidence seems to point to some relation between the evidence and the proposition for which it is evidence. Even in the revised Gettier case suggested above, the fact that h is true does not seem to be connected in any appropriate way with the facts that are described by the evidence. Since the evidence does not guarantee that h is true, there is room for coincidence, even though, as we have supposed, someone has cleverly arranged for S to be misled. At this point it is natural to think of exceedingly strong relations between the evidence e and the believed proposition h. The strongest of these seems to be logical implication. If a person's evidence logically guarantees that the proposition h is true, then it hardly seems accidental that S is right about its being the case that h. In a perfectly clear sense, S could not be mistaken about h, and so it is no accident that S is right. We might suggest then, that a person knows that h on the basis of evidence only if it is logically impossible that S's evidence e be true while h is false. Unfortunately, this straightforward proposal concerning conclusiveness of one's reasons is both too weak and too strong as a requirement for knowledge.

To see that it is too strong, we need only consider the fact, already illustrated in section 1, that there are many propositions that virtually everyone agrees are known but where the evidence we have is ultimately only inductive. To see that the proposal is also too weak, we can consider the following situation. Suppose you justifiably believe some set of axioms A for arithmetic, and suppose that T is a theorem of arithmetic which is incredibly complex. Theorem T is so complex that no one has been able to prove it. However, the famous mathematician Abernathy has constructed what he thinks is a proof of T, and all of his colleagues agree that it is a proof of T. Even so, there is a subtle flaw in his reasoning which no one is clever enough to detect. Abernathy tells you, with complete confidence, that T is a theorem. You come to believe this, and of course your belief is correct. But, you do not know that T is a theorem of arithmetic. Nevertheless, your evidence e contains the axioms of arithmetic, which *alone* entail T. So, it is logically impossible that your evidence be true but T be false.

It does not help much if we move to the somewhat weaker notion of physical or causal possibility. That is, we might suggest that a person knows that h only if it is causally, or physically, impossible that S's evidence be true while it is false that h. (A variation on this would be the view that a person knows that h only if it is causally or physically impossible that S should be in the state of *believing* that h when h is false.)[14] If we assume that causal or physical impossibility is to be explicated in terms of compatibility with laws of nature, then this proposal suffers from defects similar to its predecessor; it is both too weak and too strong. If the believed proposition h is a contingent proposition describing some event or state of affairs H, then in many situations where a person does have knowledge that h we can nevertheless imagine that the circumstances had

14. Cf. D. Armstrong, *Belief, Truth and Knowledge* (London: Cambridge University Press, 1973).

been different in such a way that h was false but S had the same evidence for believing that h, even though no laws of nature had been violated. This shows the proposal to be too strong. To see that the proposal is also too weak, we may suppose that h is a law of nature. S is justified in believing h because an eminent scientist has told him that h is true. The scientist's belief, however, is in turn based upon defective evidence. Then, since h is a law of nature, it is physically impossible that S should have the evidence that he does and that h should be false, but S does not know that h.

These two proposals concerning a 'conclusive' connection between one's evidence and the believed proposition will not work, but perhaps a still weaker kind of conclusive connection will suffice. In his contribution to this volume, titled "Conclusive Reasons," Fred Dretske proposes a conclusive reasons analysis of knowledge which is weaker than either of the above. According to Dretske, a person's reasons for believing that h are conclusive if and only if, given the situation that S is in, S would not have had those reasons if the situation had been different in the following way: if h had been false, and the situation had otherwise been different only in whatever ways are required causally or logically by the supposition that h is false. Dretske's proposal is both powerful and promising. However, as we argue in our paper "Some Conclusive Reasons against 'Conclusive Reasons,'" Dretske's proposal still appears to be too strong. We suggest a case in which there are two alternative ways in which S could have come to have his evidence, so that S's evidence is not conclusive in Dretske's sense, but where the person would appear to have knowledge anyway.

Another problem with Dretske's proposal is that it is not clear in what sense a person who satisfies Dretske's conditions as sketched above would be said to have conclusive reasons. In thinking of conclusive reasons, we seem to have in mind some reasons which guarantee the truth of what they are reasons for, in some appropriate sense of 'guarantee.' Dretske's proposal requires that S would not have had the reasons he does for believing that h if h had been false (along with other constraints). But, it does not seem to follow from this that S's *reasons* are conclusive *evidence* for h. However, it does follow that S's *having* his reasons is dependent in some way upon it being true that h (or, upon the fact that h). Perhaps this is where the real value of Dretske's proposal is to be found. We began this section by considering the suggestion that a person knows that h only if it is not accidental that S is right about its being the case that h. If S's *having* of his reasons for believing that h is dependent in some appropriate way on the fact that h is true, perhaps the nonaccidentality of S's being right about h can be accounted for in terms of this dependency. Such considerations lead naturally to another major approach to the analysis of knowledge, namely, the causal theory of knowing.

3. Knowledge and Causality

In "A Causal Theory of Knowing," Alvin Goldman suggests that a person can be said to have knowledge that h only if the fact that h is causally connected in an "appropriate" way with S's believing that h. This suggestion has a great deal in common with Dretske's proposal considered in the previous section. In some cases, S's believing that h is causally connected with the fact that h, because S's believing that h is causally dependent upon its being the case that h. If S's believing that h is causally dependent upon its being the case that h, then S would not have believed that h had it not been the case that h (assuming that nothing else was causally sufficient for S's believing that h). This much sounds very similar to what Dretske had proposed.

What sorts of causal connections between the fact that h and S's believing that h are "appropriate" for knowledge? Goldman develops a list of several types of causal connections, without claiming that the list is exhaustive. The principal kinds are what he calls "Pattern 1" and "Pattern 2" causal chains. A causal chain of Pattern 1 is a situation in which the fact that h is a causal ancestor of S's believing that h (for instance, when the fact that a red ball is before S is a causal ancestor of S's belief that a red ball is before him). A causal chain of Pattern 2 is a situation in which the fact that h and S's belief that h are both effects of some common cause. Goldman also singles out perception and memory as appropriate knowledge-producing causal processes, but it seems likely that either of these will be a special instance of one of the two basic patterns. Goldman provides a number of very clear cases exemplifying these kinds of causal situations. He notes, in addition, that it is at best a necessary condition of knowing that one's belief be causally connected in one of these appropriate ways with the fact that h, for the causal chain might be a very unusual one. Consequently, Goldman complicates his proposal by an additional requirement to the effect that S must correctly reconstruct the "important" links in the relevant causal chain(s). Again, the reasons for this complication are amply illustrated in Goldman's paper.

But there are problems facing Goldman's proposal, and two of them are major. First, Goldman's account of knowledge is intended to be fully general, that is, it is intended as an account of knowledge for any S and h. But, there are many known propositions that do not fit easily into the causal schemata; for example, knowledge of universal propositions. We know that all men are mortal, but our belief in this proposition does not seem to be causally connected with the fact that all men are mortal, for this fact is not the sort of fact that can be a cause of anything. To account for such cases, Goldman suggests that logical (as well as inferential) connections should be included among the 'links' of appropriate causal chains. However, this suggestion appears to be both *ad hoc* and counterintuitive. Second, Goldman's requirement that S must correctly reconstruct the important links in the relevant causal chains is too vague to be serviceable. What links are the important ones? And, in what sense must S *reconstruct* those links? Some of these problems facing Goldman's proposals are discussed in the selections from *Thought* by Gilbert Harman.

In "Knowledge, Causality, and Justification," Marshall Swain suggests a causal theory of knowing which is intended in part as an improvement on Goldman's proposal. Swain requires that there be a causal connection of an appropriate type between the event or state of affairs designated by h and S's having of his local reasons for believing that h. This differs from Goldman's account in that it is S's having his *reasons*, rather than S's believing h that must be causally connected with the event or state of affairs designated by h (recall Dretske's requirement that S would not have had his reasons for believing that h had h been false). Moreover, Swain restricts the scope of his analysis to primary knowledge, which is knowledge of specific events and states of affairs that can be parts of causal chains. This limitation avoids the problem mentioned above concerning universal generalizations and other propositions that do not fit the causal mold, but it does so at the expense of leaving open the question how we are to analyze knowledge of those propositions. Swain attempts to avoid the 'correct reconstruction' problem by adding a condition which requires that there not be any defeating counterevidence that is true because of events or states of affairs in the relevant causal chains involved in a given case. (The notion of defeating evidence is discussed in the next section.)

There are difficult problems facing Swain's proposal, one of which is also a problem for the view suggested by Goldman. In their commentaries on Swain's paper, Thomas D. Paxson, Jr., and Joseph T. Tolliver outline these problems clearly. Paxson attacks the defeasibility clause by providing counterexamples to the condition formulated by Swain. Tolliver provides a most interesting example which shows the proposals of both Goldman and Swain to be too weak. In this example a person is fully warranted in believing that a causal connection obtains, the causal connection does in fact obtain, but the person's background evidence consists of a grotesquely biased sample. Goldman's conditions as well as Swain's are satisfied in this case, but the person in question obviously does not have knowledge.

In "Some Revisions of Knowledge, Causality, and Justification," Swain attempts to modify his earlier proposals to meet the various problems confronting it. In "Discrimination and Perceptual Knowledge," Goldman presents a theory of noninferential perceptual knowledge which is a descendant of his earlier paper. Goldman and Swain both attempt to account for knowledge by reference to causal antecedents of the belief that h (Goldman) or the reasons one has for believing that h (Swain). And both of them utilize counterfactual considerations concerning the manner in which the subject's beliefs or reasons would have been affected by different causal antecedents. In at least this respect, both authors have moved closer to the kind of suggestion made by Dretske in his conclusive reasons theory discussed above. The analyses suggested in these two papers reach levels of considerable complexity, and each of them contains a variety of interesting examples. No attempt will be made to summarize the proposals here.

Not everyone will agree that the causal approach to the analysis of knowledge is viable, even in principle. Some will argue that it is a mistake to introduce what is essentially a nonepistemic consideration (causation) into the analysis of an epistemic notion, especially when that concept has a history of difficulty at least as great as the concept of knowledge itself. Others will argue that the causal ancestry of a person's beliefs, or of a person's reasons, is simply irrelevant to the question whether that person has knowledge. What *is* relevant is the evidence a person has, and whether that evidence provides the appropriate kind of support for the belief in question. Still others will argue that even if causal considerations are relevant to knowledge, the variety of causal situations is so complex that any effort to account for all of them is doomed to failure. Whether one agrees with any of these objections or not, it must be granted that the issues raised are fundamental ones. Anyone who would seriously defend a causal theory must ultimately provide a defense against them.

4. Defeasibility Analyses

We have noted that a natural response to the Gettier-style examples is to require one's evidence for *h* to be sufficiently strong that it allows no room for error, or at least no room for coincidence. But this response seems to conflict with the equally strong desire to allow for inductive or nonconclusive justification in many instances of knowledge. One way in which we might try to meet both of these natural demands is to impose a completeness requirement on our evidence; this would result in a version of what is called a *total evidence* requirement. In a normal situation, with respect to a given proposition *h*, a person will have at his disposal a certain body of evidence *e* which is relevant to h. But, typically, this body of evidence is incomplete in the sense that there are many additional facts relevant to h that the person does not have in his possession. Now let us consider someone who is in an ideal position epistemically with respect to h: he has in his possession every bit of information that is relevant to the question whether h is true or not. We might say that such a person is h-omniscient; there is absolutely nothing that this person could come to know that would be relevant to h. Of course, such a person would either know that h is true or know that h is false, whichever is the case, for if not there would have to be something relevant to h that this person did not know. We could define an extremely strong notion of total evidence in the following way: S's evidence for h is total if and only if S is h-omniscient. It is a safe assumption, however, that no person is h-omniscient with respect to any h, not even where h is some proposition that the person knows to be true. Even when we know some proposition h there will always be some information relevant to h that we do not have in our possession.

These considerations point the way to a weaker kind of total evidence requirement. We might say that when a person knows that h on the basis of some body of evidence e, then the evidence e must be sufficiently complete that no further additions to e would result in a loss of justification, and hence a loss of knowledge that h. We may express this by saying that if a person has knowledge, then that person's justification must be sufficiently strong that it is not capable of being *defeated* by evidence that he does not possess. Hence, such a view may be called a *defeasibility analysis* of knowledge. This approach to the analysis of knowledge has emerged as one of the most promising and popular responses to the Gettier problems. In our selections, this approach is represented in "Knowledge and Defeasibility," by David Annis, "Selections from *Thought*," by Harman, "Knowledge: Undefeated Justified True Belief," by Lehrer and Paxson, "How Do You Know?" by Ernest Sosa, and "Epistemic Defeasibility," by Swain.

One attractive feature of the defeasibility approach, as suggested above, is that it allows us to indulge in two apparently conflicting intuitions concerning requirements for knowledge.

On the one hand, it is compatible with the defeasibility analysis that one's evidence for h be inductive. On the other hand, the defeasibility analysis also yields a result which appeals to our intuition concerning conclusive reasons. For, if a person's justification for h is not capable of defeat, then h is true. If h were false, then any justification that S might have for h would be defeasible, since there would then be a true proposition such that if it were added to S's evidence then S would lose his justification for h. This proposition is, of course, the denial of h!

But, how shall we characterize the conditions under which a person's justification is defeasible? Obviously, it will not do to simply require that the justification of h by e is indefeasible only if it is either logically or physically impossible that e be true and h false. This suggestion would collapse into the strong versions of the conclusive reasons requirement that we have already considered, and would be subject to precisely the same criticisms. Perhaps the most straightforward suggestion concerning defeasibility is expressed in the following way:

> Where e is S's evidence for h, and where e justifies S in believing that h, this justification is defeasible if and only if there is some true statement q such that if S were to come to have q as additional evidence, then S would no longer be justified in believing that h.

Unfortunately, this straightforward proposal is much too strong, as is shown in some of the reprinted papers just referred to. Indeed, Harman argues that for any (inductive) justification of a proposition h by some evidence e there will always be *some* true proposition such that if the person came to have that true proposition as additional evidence then the justification would be lost. Suppose that e inductively justifies h for S. Then, let k be any true proposition that is irrelevant to h but such that k is antecedently very improbable, given what S knows. Then, let q be the proposition that either k is true or h is false. If S were to learn that q is true (without also learning that k is true), then S would no longer be justified in believing that h. Given that S is justified in believing that k is false, the only way in which S could come to be justified in believing that q is true (without learning that k is true) is for S to be justified in believing that h is false.

Whether one agrees with the general claim just considered, there are clear examples which run counter to the proposal under consideration. Lehrer and Paxson suggest an example in which S sees a man named Tom Grabit steal a book from a library. We may suppose that S has whatever justification we like for believing that Grabit stole the book. However, suppose that, entirely unknown to S, Tom Grabit's mother has said that Tom was not in the library, but that Tom's twin brother Tim was in the library. Let q be the statement that Tom Grabit's mother has said these things. This statement is such that if S came to have it as additional evidence, then S's justification would be lost. But, suppose that Tom Grabit's mother is demented, that Tom has no twin brother, and that the mother's remarks are thus completely wrong, all of which is unknown to S. Lehrer and Paxson suggest that under these circumstances, S can still be said to know that Tom Grabit stole the book, even though there is a true statement q that would sully his justification if he were to gain it as evidence. If this example is not convincing, there are many others that have been advanced.

These considerations point to an extremely important distinction that the defeasibility analyst must take into account. Since no person is h-omniscient, no matter how good his evidence e might be for some proposition h, there will always be some evidence relevant to h that the person does not possess. Some of this unpossessed evidence may be positive, but typically, perhaps even always, there will be evidence that is negatively relevant to the justification in question. Let us say that unpossessed evidence that would sully a justification is *counterevidence*. Then, the point of the above examples is that not all counterevidence serves to render a justification defeasible. And so, with respect to a justification we must distinguish between counterevidence which also serves to defeat that justification and counterevidence that does not. Providing an account of this distinction is the main problem for the defeasibility theorist.

The papers mentioned above attempt in one way or another to incorporate an indefeasibility requirement in an analysis of knowledge, and to do so in a way that takes account of the important distinction just discussed. Lehrer and Paxson suggest that the difference between defeating and nondefeating counterevidence has to do with whether the subject is justified in believing that evidence to be false. David Annis notes that in those examples where we would not consider a fragment of counterevidence to be defeating it seems natural to say that the counterevidence is merely misleading, and he suggests that evidence which is merely misleading counterevidence should be ruled out of court. Gilbert Harman expresses despair over finding any adequate way of drawing the distinction, and takes it as given. He then imposes a requirement for knowledge to the effect that a person knows that h only if that person is warranted in inferring that there is no defeating counterevidence (for Harman this is called "undermining" evidence) to the justification involved. Marshall Swain suggests that whether a justification is defeasible depends upon whether that justification would survive if the person were to become ideally situated in an appropriate way with respect to the proposition h. Ernest Sosa imbeds an indefeasibility requirement in his account of the conditions under which a set of propositions can be said to fully and nondefectively render a proposition evident for a person. Sosa's suggestion appears to be that a fragment of counterevidence does not defeat a justification provided that there is yet further evidence which nullifies the potentially defeating effect of that counterevidence.

5. Theories of Epistemic Justification

Implicit in our discussion of attempts to explicate the concept of knowledge has been an assumed understanding of the concept of epistemic justification. Indeed, several of the analyses that we have discussed have been attempts to restrict the circumstances under which a *justified* true belief is to count as an instance of knowledge. On one view, such a belief is an instance of knowledge only if the justification does not involve any false propositions; on another, the justification must be conclusive;

and on yet another, the justification must be indefeasible. It can hardly be said, however, that the concept of epistemic justification is clearly understood. Indeed, there are many who would argue that the provision of an adequate theory of epistemic justification is even more problematic than the problem of explicating the concept of knowledge. Whether that is true or not, it certainly cannot be denied that our understanding of knowledge will not be complete until we have come to grips with the problem of epistemic justification. Happily, this is an area in which considerable work is being done, and it appears that some progress is being made. In an attempt to represent some of the main lines of current research on epistemic justification, we have included in this volume several recent papers that are directed specifically to that problem. These are the papers by Chisholm, James Cornman, Mark Pastin, and Lehrer. In addition, several of the papers in this volume (Harman, Sosa, Swain, Annis) that are concerned primarily with the analysis of knowledge also contain interesting reflections on the nature of epistemic justification.

Most epistemologists will grant that some propositions h are justified for a person because that person has evidence, consisting of other justified propositions, such that this evidence provides justification for h. For anyone who holds that some propositions are thus *inferentially* justified a crucial question is: what are the conditions under which one proposition, or set of propositions, e, can be said to justify another proposition h, for a person S at a time t? Many epistemologists will argue that a necessary *part* of an adequate answer to this question is that e must *itself* be justified for S if e is to justify h for S. Suppose we hold, then, that a given e is justified for S. But how is e justified for S? Is it only because there is some further proposition, or set of propositions e' such that e' justifies e for S? Then, once again we must ask, how is e' justified for S? This kind of questioning gives rise to what is known as the *regress argument*. If e must be justified in order that it justify h for S, then either e is itself justified only by some other proposition e' or it is justified but not justified only by some other proposition e'. If e is justified only because it is justified by some other proposition e', then we are involved in what we may call an *ancestral chain* of justification for *h*. An ancestral chain of justification for *h* is a series of propositions (or sets of propositions) *e, e', e'', . . . ,* such that *e* justifies *h, e'* justifies *e,* and so forth. There are two possibilities for such an ancestral chain of justification: either (A) the chain does not come to an end, in which case it either goes to infinity or forms a circle, or (B) the chain does come to an end. According to the regress argument, the first possibility is absurd; hence, the ancestral chain must come to an end. But, if the chain comes to an end, and if each proposition in the chain must be justified if it is to justify its successor, then the last proposition (or set of propositions) in the chain must be justified. But the last proposition (or set of propositions) in the chain does not have an ancestor. So the question arises, how is the last member justified? Those who give the regress argument often respond at this point by saying that the last member of such a chain is *noninferentially* justified. In addition, those who give the regress argument, and hold that the last member of the chain is noninferentially justified are usually foundationalists. According to the foundationalist, the following two theses are true:

(1) Some propositions are noninferentially justified
(2) Every proposition *h* that is justified but not noninferentially justified is such that there is at least one ancestral chain of justifications leading from *h* to a proposition (or set of propositions) which is noninferentially justified.

On this view, those propositions that are noninferentially justified form the basis, or the foundation, upon which all inferential justifications 'ultimately' rest (through ancestral chains).

But now we are faced with some new questions. If your epistemology is committed to a class of noninferentially justified propositions, then we must ask, how are *these* propositions justified; and we must ask, which propositions are so justified for a person at a time? In his paper "Modest Foundationalism and Self-Warrant," Mark Pastin points out that foundationalists fall into two groups with respect to such questions. On the one hand, there are foundationalists who hold that the noninferen-

tially justified propositions must be absolutely certain, or incorrigible, or infallible. Pastin calls such philosophers radical foundationalists. On the other hand, a foundationalist may hold
that the noninferentially justified propositions need only be
(noninferentially) justified to some slight degree; that is, such
propositions need only be what Pastin calls *self-warranted.* On either of these variations, we still need specific answers to the
questions posed above. Pastin attempts to provide an account
of self-warrant, and many philosophers have attempted to provide an account of the stronger notion of incorrigibility. In his
essay, "On the Nature of Empirical Evidence," Roderick Chisholm provides an account of *self-presentation* in accordance with
which basic propositions are noninferentially *evident,* but where
the notion of being evident is not as strong as the notion of incorrigibility. It seems generally agreed now that efforts at iso-
lating a relevant class of contingent incorrigible propositions
are doomed to failure, and most contemporary foundationalists
appear to be modest foundationalists. Even so, there is considerable room for disagreement concerning the degree of justification required of self-warranted propositions, and considerable disagreement concerning the class of propositions that
are thus noninferentially justified. In general, the stronger the
degree of justification required, the narrower the class of propositions countenanced as noninferentially justified. For Chisholm, whose notion of the self-presenting requires the fairly
strong status of being evident, the class of basic propositions is
restricted to descriptions of immediate experiential states ("I
seem to perceive something to be F"). On a weaker view, perhaps one that only requires some slight degree of justification,
the class of basic propositions may well include more ordinary
perceptual claims ("I see something red").

Until recently, epistemologists tended to assume without
serious argument that some form of foundationalism is correct.
However, many contemporary epistemologists, discouraged
perhaps by the failure of attempts to clearly define a class of
basic statements, have begun to take seriously some alternatives
to foundationalism. Intuitively, anyone who denies either of
the two theses (1) and (2) suggested above as characteristic of

foundationalism will qualify as a nonfoundationalist. In his essay, "Foundational versus Nonfoundational Theories of Epistemic Justification," James Cornman considers a variety of versions of foundational and nonfoundational theories. He attempts to characterize what he calls minimal versions of each type of theory, and then engages in a comparative study of these minimal versions. According to Cornman, the minimal nonfoundational thesis should be formulated as a contrary of the foundational thesis, where the latter can be taken to be the conjunction of (1) and (2). This minimal nonfoundational thesis allows that (1) may be true (that is, that there are some noninferentially justified propositions), and holds a contrary of thesis (2). Hence, on Cornman's suggested minimal version of nonfoundationalism, for a theory to be nonfoundational it must hold that *all* propositions h that are justified but not noninferentially justified for a person S are such that S has at least one ancestral chain of justification leading from h to a proposition or set of propositions no member of which is noninferentially justified for S. But on this classification, there will be possible, and not implausible theories of justification that are neither foundational nor nonfoundational. For example, any theory that holds that *some* inferentially justified propositions have ancestral justification chains leading only to propositions that are noninferentially justified, while holding that others do not, will not qualify either as foundational or nonfoundational. Whether it is advisable to introduce a new classification to cover such theories, or weaken the conditions for nonfoundationalist theories to cover them is, as far as we can see, merely a terminological matter. If we adopt Cornman's classification, however, then it is important to realize that in rejecting varieties of (what he calls) nonfoundational theories one is not thereby committing oneself to any form of (what he calls) foundational theory.

No matter how we classify things, there are difficult problems facing any theory that denies the basic tenets of foundationalism. For if we want to say that all or even some propositions that are justified but not noninferentially justified are not 'ultimately' justified by basic propositions, then we must ask, how *are* these propositions justified? If we assume that any such proposition will have an ancestral chain of justification, then we seem forced back into the first possibility (A) above concerning such chains. That is, the ancestral justification chain for any such proposition would either have to run on to infinity or it would have to form some sort of circle. There is, actually, a third possibility here, namely, that the ancestral chain for such a proposition comes to an end in a set of propositions that are *un*justified for *S*. As Cornman suggests in his essay, however, this option does not seem to have much *prima facie* plausibility, so we shall not consider it a serious option. Moreover, most philosophers would not consider the possibility of an infinite ancestral justification chain to be a serious possibility. But, this possible view has had its defenders. Cornman considers and rejects one line of argument (Bruce Aune) that such a regress need not be vicious.

The variation according to which some ancestral justification chains can form some sort of a circle is the one that appears to be most popular among nonfoundationalists. And, the version of this that has been most vigorously defended is known as the *coherence* theory of justification. In the selection from *Knowledge* reprinted in this book, Keith Lehrer presents a coherence theory. According to him, a (noninferentially) justified belief is so justified because it coheres with other beliefs in a system of specified kind *K*. Lehrer explains in detail the sort of coherence that he has in mind, and what sort of system a given belief must cohere with if it is to be justified. The resulting picture of justification is one in which the ancestral justification chains for a given proposition (belief) is 'circular,' since every belief in the system will be in the ancestral chain of every other, and hence will be one of its own ancestors. The primary question that such a view must face is whether the circularity involved is vicious or virtuous?

6. *Epistemological Scepticism*

We have already noted that many philosophers were spurred by Gettier's short article to try either to amend the traditional analysis, or to propose new analyses of knowledge. Others, however, have proposed more radical doctrines, such as different forms of epistemological scepticism. One natural explanation of this development is that philosophers construed the continuing spate of counterexamples to proposed analyses of knowledge as indicating that more restrictive conditions had to be met if knowledge was to be achieved. Proponents of different analyses of knowledge (e.g. conclusive reasons and defeasibility analyses) have also been moved by the same considerations, as we pointed out above. The difference is that advocates of epistemological scepticism have reckoned the conditions for knowledge, or justification, to be so strict that it becomes reasonable to hold that the conditions are never met. Thus, the conclusion is drawn that there is no knowledge, or that no propositions are epistemically justified.

We can be somewhat more precise regarding sceptical doctrines. Epistemological scepticism (as opposed, say, to ethical or aesthetic scepticisms) may be construed as a thesis about a specific set of propositions. Thus, with respect to the class of putatively known propositions, it might be held that each such proposition is suspect in some fashion, perhaps because there are reasons for believing that none of those propositions is in fact known. We will say that epistemological scepticism construed as a sceptical thesis about putatively known (or knowable) propositions is *knowledge*-scepticism. And, similarly, construed as a thesis about the class of putatively justified (or justifiable) propositions, epistemological scepticism is *justification*-scepticism.

As might be suspected, there are many varieties of each form of epistemological scepticism. In the essay by Pappas, some of these different varieties are classified as *global;* each, that is, concerns *all* putatively known or knowable, justified or justifiable propositions. In "Why Not Scepticism?" for example, Lehrer defends a global version of knowledge-scepticism, viz., the view that no person knows any proposition at all. (We should point out, though, that Lehrer would no longer accept such a sceptical doctrine.) Unger's thesis is just slightly less global, namely, that hardly any proposition is known. Global forms of epistemological scepticism, in Pappas' terminology, contrast with *local* versions of scepticism. An example of the latter is scepticism concerning the external world; another would be scepticism regarding the existence of other minds. It is clear that globality is a degree-concept, at its strongest extreme when the sceptical thesis concerns all propositions (as in the essay by Lehrer). Traditionally, slightly less global theses have been advanced, since necessarily true propositions have often been reckoned as exempt from sceptical doubt and argument.

In addition to degree of globality, both knowledge- and justification-scepticism admit of different degrees of what Pappas terms *strength*. For example, one version of knowledge-scepticism is the thesis that no proposition is *knowable*. A considerably weaker sceptical thesis is one in which it is held that no proposition is in fact known. Weaker still is the view that no proposition is ever known with certainty.[15] This same notion of strength is applicable to different versions of justification-scepticism. Thus, one extreme thesis would be that no proposition is even justifiable, while a more moderate doctrine would be the thesis defended by Lehrer, viz., that no proposition is ever in fact completely justified. Each major form of epistemological scepticism, then, will admit of a great many variations depending on how different degrees of globality and strength are combined.

Two further matters pertain to each form of epistemological scepticism. The first concerns the epistemic status of the relevant sceptical thesis itself. For example, it seems that some ancient sceptics held the thesis that no proposition is known; but they also maintained that they knew this sceptical thesis to be true![16] A much less ambitious epistemic status needs to be ascribed to this sceptical thesis, perhaps that it is reasonable to believe that no proposition is known, as both Lehrer and Unger claim. In general, then, the epistemic status of a given sceptical thesis, T, concerns whether it is claimed that T is known to be true, completely justified, evident, reasonable to

15. K. Lehrer, "Scepticism and Conceptual Change," in R. Chisholm and R. Swartz, eds., *Empirical Knowledge* (Englewood Cliffs: Prentice-Hall, 1973).

16. See St. Augustine, *Against the Academicians,* tr. Garvey (Milwaukee: Marquette University Press, 1957).

believe, or the like. In his paper, Pappas suggests that the epistemic status of a given global sceptical thesis must be weaker than the degree of strength of that thesis. It is in some sense absurd or self-defeating to maintain that it is known that no proposition is known, or that it is reasonable to believe that no proposition is reasonable to believe.

A related point, secondly, is that it is not easy to present cogent arguments in support of scepticism. For example, consider the sceptical thesis that no person knows any proposition to be true, and suppose that some philosopher (e.g., Lehrer) defends this thesis. In offering reasons for the thesis, of course, it cannot be claimed plausibly that any of the reasons is itself known to be true. Hence, the strength of the arguments used in behalf of a given global sceptical thesis will vary with the strength of the thesis. The claimed epistemic status of individual premises used to support global sceptical positions, in the sense of 'epistemic status' indicated above, will have to be no stronger than the sceptical thesis being supported. Naturally, the same must be said for the statement that the argument used in behalf of scepticism is deductively valid or inductively strong.

Unger and Lehrer, in their respective essays on scepticism reprinted in this book, are well aware of the matters just discussed. Their respective sceptical positions, and the support each adduces for those positions, are claimed to be just reasonable to accept.

Unger maintains that a person knows some proposition, p, only if the person is absolutely certain that p, and that no person is ever certain of (hardly) any proposition; so, he concludes that no person ever knows (hardly) any proposition. Unger claims for each of his two premises, however, that it is reasonable to believe, or at least that neither is unreasonable.

Even so, each of the premises in Unger's argument is open to debate. The first, that knowledge implies certainty, is subject to a number of interpretations depending on how the term 'certainty' is explicated. The premise seems clearly false if a proposition is certain for some person only if it is logically impossible for the person to mistakenly believe that proposition. But

Unger does not have this traditional concept of certainty in mind. A proposition, p, is certain for a person, S, on his account, just in case "within the bounds of nuance, it is not at all doubtful [that p]."[17] Even so construed, however, Unger's first premise seems dubious. For consider a person who has some lingering doubts concerning some proposition, h, even though he knows that these doubts are totally irrational and baseless. In such a case, given appropriate other conditions, this person might well know that h even though he was not certain that h in Unger's sense.

Unger's second premise, that hardly any proposition is ever certain, is criticized at some length by James Cargile. He cites a number of propositions that surely seem to qualify as certain in Unger's sense so that Unger's argument appears to be effectively undercut. Of course, it is open to Unger to reply by strengthening the notion of certainty, but this would have the immediate effect of making his first premise even more dubious.

In one form or another, Unger's form of argument for knowledge-scepticism has been used in epistemological literature for some time. The major differences come in differing accounts of the notion of certainty. Lehrer, however, in the selection reprinted here, argues instead for a version of justification-scepticism, viz., that no proposition is ever completely justified for a person, and infers from this that no person knows any proposition to be true. He assumes, of course, that a person knows that a proposition h is true only if he is completely justified in believing h. The central notion in Lehrer's paper, then, is that of complete justification. Unfortunately, he does little to explicate this concept, so it is difficult to evaluate his case for either justification-scepticism or knowledge-scepticism. However, in his essay, Dan Turner notes that Lehrer does cite specific necessary conditions for a person's being completely justified in believing a proposition. And, Turner argues that given these necessary conditions, Lehrer's overall argument for global justification-scepticism faces serious problems.

17. See Unger's "In Defense of Scepticism," Chapter 19 below.

There are other ways in which one might try to support global scepticism of one sort or another; [18] however, we will not consider such attempts here. The essays reprinted here by Unger and Lehrer, we feel, are respresentative of the main types of arguments normally used in defense of global scepticism.

18. See I. Oakley, "An Argument for Scepticism concerning Justified Belief," *American Philosophical Quarterly*, 13.3 (1976), 221–228; and J. Kekes, "The Case for Scepticism," *Philosophical Quarterly*, 25.98 (1975), 28–39.

1

Conclusive Reasons

FRED DRETSKE

Conclusive reasons have a modal as well as an epistemic character. In having conclusive reasons to believe that P is the case one's epistemic credentials are such as to eliminiate the possibility of mistake. This, at least, is how I propose to understand them for the remainder of this paper. Letting the symbol '<>' represent the appropriate modality (a yet to be clarified sense of *possibility*), I shall say, then, that R is a conclusive reason for P if and only if, given R, $\sim <> \sim$ P (or, alternatively, $\sim <>$ (R . $\sim$ P)). This interpretation allows us to say of any subject, S, who believes that P and who has conclusive reasons for believing that P, that, given these reasons, he *could not be wrong* about P or, given these reasons, *it is false that he might be mistaken* about P.

Suppose, then, that

(1) S knows that P and he knows this on the basis (simply) of R entails

(2) R would not be the case unless P were the case.[1]

The latter formula expresses a connection between R and P

Reprinted from *The Australasian Journal of Philosophy,* 49 (1971), 1–22, by kind permission of the author and editor.

An early version of this paper was read to the Philosophy Department at The University of Illinois, Chicago Circle. More recently it was read at The University of North Carolina's Colloquium in Philosophy with Professor Robert Sleigh commenting.

1. I shall be using 'R' and 'P' to replace a variety of related grammatical units. Depending on the sentential context, they sometimes serve as noun phrases, sometimes as full indicative sentences, sometimes for appropriate transformations of the indicative.

which is strong enough, I submit, to permit us to say that if (2) is true, then R is a conclusive reason for P. For if (2) is true, we are entitled, not only to deny that, given R, not-P *is* the case, but also that, given R, not-P *might* be the case. That is to say, (2) eliminates R and not-P as a possible (joint) state of affairs and, when we are *given* R, it eliminates not-P as a possible state of affairs. This is so because (2) entails the falsity of,

(3) Although R is the case P might not be the case.

If we express (3) as 'Given R, $<> \sim$ P', then (2) entails that it is false that, given R, $<> \sim$ P which is equivalent to, given R, $\sim <> \sim$ P; and this is precisely the required feature of conclusive reasons given above. Hence, when (2) is true, R is a conclusive reason for P.

What follows is an amplification of the above sketch—hence, an argument for the view that in those cases where knowledge that P rests on evidence, grounds, or reasons, when the question 'How does S know?' can sensibly be asked and answered, the evidence, grounds, or reasons must be conclusive. Anything short of conclusive reasons, though it may provide one with justified true beliefs, fails to give the kind of support requisite to knowledge.

1. Knowing P on the Basis of R:
The Connection between (1) and (2)

Suppose S, in order to assure himself that his child's temperature is normal (no fever), places a thermometer in the child's mouth, extracts it after several minutes, and observes a reading of 98.6°F. In remarking to the doctor that his child's temperature is normal S is asked how he knows. S responds, naturally enough, by saying, 'I just took his temperature.' Let us assume, then, that we have an instantiation of (1):

(1a) S knows that his child's temperature is normal and he knows this on the basis of the (normal) reading on the thermometer (which he has just placed in the child's mouth, etc.).

Can one consistently affirm (1a) and deny the corresponding instantiation of (2)?

(2a) The thermometer would not have read 98.6° unless
the child's temperature was normal.

If it is not already obvious that one cannot consistently affirm
(1a) and deny (2a), I think it can be made obvious by considering the kind of thing which would show (2a) to be false. For example, if Charles, familiar with the particular thermometer in
question, should say, 'Oh, I know that termometer; it is fairly
accurate for temperatures below 98° but it sticks at 98.6 for almost any higher temperature,' we have been given solid
grounds for rejecting (2a). Simultaneously, however, we have
been given solid grounds for rejecting (1a). If it is *that* kind of
thermometer, then if S's only basis for thinking his child's temperature normal is a 98.6 reading on it, then he does not *know*
that his child's temperature is normal. It *might* be normal, of
course, but if S knows that it is, he must have more to go on
than the reading on this (defective) thermometer.

Other attempts to show (2a) false have the same effect; they
immediately undermine R (the reading on the thermometer) as
an adequate basis for someone's knowing that the child's temperature is normal (P). For in rejecting (2a) we reject the thermometer as a reliable device for discovering whether a person's
temperature is normal, and knowledge is not acquired by relying on what is unreliable in precisely those respects in which we
rely on it.

We frequently purport to know things on the basis of testimony. James has a large stamp collection and, after giving a detailed description of it, invites S to his home to see it. S declines,
but he later refers to James' stamp collection in conversation. It
is easy enough to imagine circumstances in which it would be
natural for someone to ask S how he knew, what reasons he
had for thinking, that James had such a collection. And it is just
as easy to imagine S, in reponse to such a query, referring to
his conversation with James. Let us assume, then, that

(1b) S knows that James has a stamp collection and he
knows this on the basis of James' description (and invitation)

is true. I am not now concerned to argue that one can know

something of this sort in this way; the question is, rather, whether (2b) must be true *if* (1b) is true.

> (2b) James would not have said he had a stamp collection, described it in such detail, and issued an invitation unless he had a stamp collection.

If James is the sort of fellow about which (2b) cannot be truly asserted, then he is not the sort of fellow who can be trusted on such matters as this. If James is the sort of fellow who sometimes says such things as a joke, who would (or might) concoct such elaborate stories for his own amusement (or whatever), who would (or might) whimsically issue an invitation of this sort under totally false pretexts, then, despite the fact that he is (by hypothesis) telling the truth on this occasion, his testimony is hardly the sort on which one can rest a claim to know. In denying (2b) one is conceding that James would, or might, have said what he did without possessing a stamp collection, and in the light of this concession one cannot go on to insist that, nonetheless, S *knows* he has a stamp collection on the basis, simply, of what James said.

In a recent article Gilbert Harman contrasts two cases, *the lottery case* and *the testimony case*.[2] Although S, say, has only one among thousands of tickets in a lottery and, hence, has an extremely slender chance of winning, we naturally reject the idea that S could know what he was going to lose on the basis of a correct probability estimate (well over 99.9%) of his losing. Even if S correctly predicts that he is going to lose, we would deny that he knew he was going to lose if the *only* basis he had for this belief was the fact that his chances of winning were so slight.[3] Harman compares this case with the situation in which we often seem prepared to say that S knows that P when he is

2. 'Knowledge, Inference, and Explanation', in *American Philosophical Quarterly*, 5.3 (1968), 164–173.

3. Of course S may have said 'I know I am going to lose' and he may say now, after he has lost, 'I knew I was going to lose', but these expressions are normally accepted without epistemological quibbling because they are taken as little more than expressions of resignation or despair. With this use of the verb 'to know', one can know one is going to lose and *still* spend a dollar for a ticket and a chance at the prize—a fact about human beings which is puzzling if they believe they know (in any epistemologically relevant sense) that they are going to lose.

told that P is the case by some other person (testimony case). Although probability estimates are not altogether appropriate here, we do know that people sometimes lie, sometimes they are honestly mistaken, and so on. There always seems to be a chance that what a person tells us is not the case however sincere or credible he may appear, and the order of magnitude of this chance seems to be comparable to the chance we might win in some appropriate lottery situation. Why, then, are we prepared to say that we know in the one case but not in the other? I think this contrast strengthens the view that (2) is normally accepted as a necessary consequence of (1), that when we are unwilling to endorse the corresponding instantiation of (2) we are unwilling to talk of anyone knowing that P is the case on the basis of the evidence expressed by R. In many testimony situations we are, I believe, willing to affirm (2): the person would not have said it unless it was so. In the lottery case, however, the connection between R and P expressed by this subjunctive conditional fails to be realized, and it fails no matter how great the probabilities become. Adjusting the wording of (2) to suit the example in question[4] we have

>   (2c) If S were going to win the lottery, his chances of winning would not be 1/m (m being the number of tickets sold).

4. The wording of (2) will sometimes have to be adjusted to suit the particular instantiation in question. The chief factors determining this adjustment are the relative temporal locations of R, P and the time of utterance and also the causal connections, if any, which are believed to hold between R and P. The particular wording I have given (2) is most appropriate when P is some state of affairs antecedent to (or contemporaneous with) both R and the time of utterance. This, of course, is the result of the fact that (2) is most often used when P is some state of affairs causally responsible for the present condition R. When P is a future state we might express (2) as: R would not be the case unless P were going to happen. For example, he would not have registered unless he were going to vote. I do not wish to preclude the possibility of knowing that something *will* occur on the basis of present evidence by restricting the wording of (2). The difficulty, of course, is that when P is some future state, the subjunctive relating it to R generally becomes somewhat questionable. We prefer to say, in our more cautious moods, that if he were not *planning* to vote, he would not have registered (acknowledging, thereby, the fact that contingencies may interfere with the execution of his plans). But in the same cautious moods we prefer to say, not that we know he is going to vote (because he registered), but that we know he plans or intends to vote.

Whatever (finite) value we give to 'm,' we know this is false
since someone whose chances of winning are 1/m *will* win, and
since there is nothing special about S which would require him
to have a better chance of winning than anyone else in order to
win, we reject (2c) as false. Hence, we reject the idea that S can
know he is going to lose on the basis of the fact that his chances
of losing are $(m-1)/m$.

Alvin Goldman, in developing a causal account of knowledge, constructs a situation in which S is said to know that a
nearby mountain (I will call it M) erupted many years ago. He
knows this on the basis of the presence of solidified lava
throughout the countryside surrounding the mountain.[5] According to Goldman, a necessary condition for S's knowing that
M erupted many years ago on the basis of the present existence
and distribution of the lava is that there be a causal connection
between the eruption of the mountain and the present existence and distribution of the lava. I do not wish to dispute this
claim at the moment since the view I am advancing is even
stronger: *viz.* that a necessary condition for S to know that M
erupted on this basis is that

    (2d) The lava would not be here, and distributed in this
           manner, unless M erupted

is true. (2d) is a stronger claim than that the eruption of M is
causally connected with the present existence and distribution
of the lava. (2d) requires, in addition, that M's eruption be necessary for the present state of affairs. To illustrate, consider the
following embellishment on Goldman's example. Not far from
M is another mountain, N. The geology of the area is such that
at the point in time at which M erupted something, so to speak,
was bound to give; if M had not erupted, N would have. Furthermore, the location of N is such that if it, rather than M,
had erupted, the present distribution of lava would have been,
in all respects relevant to S's taking it as a reason for believing
M erupted, the same. In such circumstances Goldman's necessary condition is satisfied, but mine is not. (2d) is false; it is false
that the lava would not be here, and distributed in this fashion,

5. 'A Causal Theory of Knowing', *Journal of Philosophy* [Chapter 3 in the
present volume].

unless M had erupted. For if, contrary to hypothesis, M had not erupted, N would have; leaving the very same (relevant) traces.

In such circumstances I do not think we could say that S knew that M erupted on the basis of the present existence and distribution of lava. For, by hypothesis, *this* state of affairs would have obtained whether M erupted or not and, hence, there is nothing about this state of affairs which favours one hypothesis (M erupted) over a competing hypothesis (N erupted). S is still correct in supposing that M did erupt, still correct in supposing that it was M's eruption which is causally responsible for the present existence and distribution of lava, but he does not know it was M that erupted—not unless he has some additional grounds which preclude N. If he has such additional grounds, call them Q, then we can say that he knows that M erupted and he knows this on the basis of R *and* Q. In this case, however, the corresponding instantiation of (2) is also satisfied: R *and* Q would not be the case unless M erupted. As things stand, the most that S could know, on the basis simply of the present existence and distribution of lava, is that *either* M *or* N *erupted*. (2) permits us to say this much, and no more, about what can be known on the basis of lava flow.

The case becomes even clearer if we exploit another of Harman's examples.[6] Harold has a ticket in a lottery. The odds against his winning are 10,000 to 1. The prize, call it an X, is something that Harold does not now have nor could he reasonably expect to obtain one by means other than winning the lottery. Enter a philanthropic gentleman, Rockaford, who decides to give Harold an X if (as seems likely) he should fail to win one in the lottery. Things go as one would expect; Harold holds a losing ticket. Rockaford keeps his word and gives Harold an X. S, familiar with the above circumstances but unaware of whether Harold won or lost in the lottery, finds Harold with his newly acquired X. S infers that Harold received his X from Rockaford. He concludes this because he knows that the only other way Harold might have acquired an

6. In 'Knowledge, Inference, and Explanation', pp. 168–169. I have adapted the example somewhat.

X is by winning the lottery and the odds against that happening are enormous. The following conditions are satisfied: (a) Harold received his X from Rockaford; (b) S believes that Harold received his X from Rockaford; (c) S is warranted in believing this since the chances of his having received it in any other way are negligible; (d) Rockaford's generous gift of an X to Harold is the (causal?) explanation of Harold's present possession of an X; and, finally (e) S correctly reconstructs (to use Goldman's language) the causal chain of events which brought about Harold's possession of an X. Yet, why does it seem clear (at least to myself—and apparently to Harman) and S does *not* know that Rockaford gave Harold his X. Because

> (2e) Harold would not have an X unless Rockaford gave
>   him one

is plainly false.[7] If Rockaford had not given him an X, it would have been because Harold already possessed one as a winner in the lottery. Hence, Harold would possess an X even if Rockaford had not given him one. It is not true that R would not be the case *unless* P; hence, not true that S knows that P on the basis of R.[8]

(2), therefore, expresses something stronger than a causal relationship between R and P. It should be pointed out, however, that it expresses something which is, in certain important respects, weaker than a universal association between states or conditions similar to R and states or conditions similar to P. When 'R' and 'P' are expressions which stand for particular conditions or states of affairs, as will often be the case when we

---

7. There is a way of reading (2e) which makes it sound true—*viz.*, if we illicitly smuggled in the fact that Harold *has lost* the lottery. That is, (2e') 'Harold, having lost the lottery, would not have an X unless Rockaford had given him one,' is true. But this version of (2) makes R, the reason S has for believing Rockaford gave him an X, not only Harold's possession of an X but also *his having lost the lottery*. This, by hypothesis, is not part of S's reason; hence, not properly included in (2e). (2e) must be read in something like the following fashion: Harold would not have an X, whatever the outcome of the lottery, unless Rockaford had given him one. With this reading it is clearly false.

8. It is difficult to say whether this is a counterexample to Goldman's analysis. I think it satisfies all the conditions he catalogues as sufficient for knowledge, but this depends on how strictly Goldman intends the condition that S must be warranted in inferring that P is the case from R.

know one thing on the basis of something else, (2) expresses a connection between more *determinate* states of affairs than those described by talking about states similar to R and P. If someone remarks, mid-way through a poker hand, that if his neighbour had not folded (dropped from the game) he (the speaker) would have been dealt a royal flush, he is obviously not maintaining that *whenever* his neighbour remains in the game, he (the speaker) is rewarded with a royal flush. Rather, he is talking about *this* hand (already holding four cards to the royal flush), *this particular* distribution of cards in the remainder of the deck, *this particular* seating arrangement, and so on. He is not saying that his neighbour's remaining in the game is, quite generally, sufficient for his receipt of a royal flush. Rather, he is saying that *in the particular circumstances which in fact prevailed on this occasion*, circumstances which include such things as card distribution, arrangement of players, etc., an occurrence of the first sort (neighbour remains in game) will invariably be followed by one of the second sort (his receipt of a royal flush). One cannot falsify his claim by showing that he would not have received a royal flush, despite his neighbour's remaining in the game, if the card distribution in the deck had been different from what it in fact was. For his claim was a claim about the inevitable sequence of events *with that distribution of cards.*

Statements such as (2), then, even when R and P are expressions for particular states of affairs, express a general uniformity, but this general uniformity is not that whenever a state similar to R is the case, then a state similar to P will also be (or have been) the case. The uniformity in question concerns the relationship between states similar to R and P *under a fixed set of circumstances*. Whenever (a state such as) R *in circumstances* C then (a state such as) P where the circumstances C are defined in terms of those circumstances which actually prevail on the occasion of R and P. But does C include all the circumstances that prevail on the occasion in question or only *some* of these? Clearly not all the circumstances since this would trivialize every subjunctive conditional of this sort. Even if we restrict C to only those circumstances logically independent of R and P we still obtain a trivilization. For, to use Goldman's mountain example (as embellished), C would still include the fact that N did not erupt (since this is logically independent of both R and P), and this is obviously one of the circumstances *not* held fixed when we say that the lava would not be here unless M erupted. For in asserting his subjunctive we mean to be asserting something which would be *false* in the situation described (N would have erupted if M had not) whereas if we hold this circumstance (N did not erupt) fixed, the uniformity between the presence of lava and M's eruption would *hold*.

I think that our examples, not to mention an extensive literature on the subject, point the way to a proper interpretation of C. The circumstances which are assumed constant, which are tacitly held fixed, in conditionals such as (2), are those circumstances prevailing on the occasion in question (the occasion on and between which the particular states R and P obtain) which are logically and causally independent of the state of affairs expressed by P.[9] When we have a statement in the subjunctive which (unlike (2)) is counterfactual (the antecedent gives expression to a state of affairs which does or did not obtain), then C includes those circumstances prevailing on the occasion which are logically and causally independent of the state of affairs (or lack of such state) expressed by the *antecedent* of the conditional. In our poker game, for example, we can say that S's statement (I would have got a royal flush if my neighbour had stayed in the game) *fixes* that set of circumstances which are logically and causally independent of his neighbour's staying in the game (i.e. the antecedent since the statement is counterfactual). Hence, if there is another player in the game (whose

9. This characterization of the circumstances 'C' has interesting and, I believe, significant repercussions for subjunctives having the form of (2) in which R expresses some present (or past) state of affairs and P expresses some future state of affairs. Although I lack the space to discuss the point here, I believe an important asymmetry is generated by a shift in the relative temporal locations of R and P. I also believe, however, that this asymmetry is faithfully reflected in the difference between knowing what *will* happen on the basis of present data and knowing what *did* happen on the basis of present data. In other words, I feel that an asymmetry in (2), arising from a shift in the relative temporal locations of R and P, helps one to understand the difference we all feel between knowing, on the one hand, what did happen or is happening, and, on the other hand, what will happen.

presence or absence affects the cards dealt to S) who would
have dropped if S's neighbour had not dropped, then this person's remaining in the game is *not* held fixed, not included in C,
because it is causally connected to the state of affairs expressed
by the antecedent in S's statement. Therefore, we can show S's
statement to be false if we can show that such a circumstance
prevailed, and it is along these lines that one would surely
argue in attempting to show S that he was wrong, wrong in saying that he would have received a royal flush if his neighbour
had stayed in the game.

On the other hand, one cannot show that S's statement is
false by showing that, were the cards differently arranged in
the remainder of the deck, he would not have received his
royal flush; for the arrangement of cards in the remainder of
the deck (unlike the presence or absence of our other player) is
(presumably) independent of S's neighbour's departure from
the game. Hence, it is one of the conditions held fixed, included in C, by S's statement, and we are not allowed to consider alterations in it in assessing the general implication of S's
statement.

Or consider our original thermometer example. Recall, the
statement in question was: 'The thermometer would not have
read 98.6° unless the child's temperature was normal.' Suppose
someone responds, 'Oh, it would have (or might have) if the
thermometer was broken.' It is important to understand that
one can grant the truth of this response without abandoning
the original assertion; for the original assertion had, as its general implication, *not* a statement expressing a uniform relationship between states of affairs similar to the child's temperature (normal body temperature) and states of affairs similar to
the thermometer reading (a reading of 98.6), but, rather, a
uniformity between such states *under a fixed set of circumstances*.
And, if I am right, this fixed set of circumstances includes *the
actual state of the thermometer* (defective or accurate); it is one of
those circumstances prevailing on the occasion in question
which is causally and logically independent of the child's temperature. Hence, this circumstance cannot be allowed to vary as
it is in the above response by the words 'if the thermometer was

broken.' To determine the truth of the original assertion we must suppose that the thermometer is accurate (or defective) *whatever the actual condition is*. If, therefore, the thermometer was not broken or otherwise defective on that occasion, then the suggestion that it would (or might) have read the same despite a feverish child if it were broken or defective is, although quite true, irrelevant to the truth of the statement: 'It would not have read 98.6 unless the child's temperature was normal.'

One final important feature of (2). I have said that, generally speaking, the place-holders 'R' and 'P' represent expressions designating *specific* states of affairs or conditions. When this is so, (2) still has a general implication, but the general implication, expressing a uniform relationship between states of affairs similar to R and P, *has its scope restricted* to situations in which the circumstances C (as specified above) obtain. Since we are talking about specific states of affairs in most instantiations of (2), it becomes extremely important to observe the sorts of referring expressions embodied within both 'R' and 'P.' For example, when I say, 'John would not have said it was raining unless it was raining' I am talking bout *John* and about a *particular utterance* of his. *Someone else* might have said this without its being true; John may have said *something else* without its being true. Nonetheless, *John* would not have said *it was raining* unless it was. An incurable liar about most things, John has a pathological devotion to accuracy on matters concerning the weather. In such a case, although John is, admittedly, a most unreliable informant on most matters, we can say that he would not have said it was raining unless it was so. This is only to say that the referring expressions to be found in 'R' and 'P' *help to define the scope* of the implied genralization. Recall, the implied generalization was about states of affairs *similar* to (the particular states) R and P. Similar in what respect? The sort of referring expressions to be found within 'R' and 'P' help us to answer this question. In the case of John above, the general implication involved, not *a person's saying something* (under circumstances C), not *John's saying something* (under circumstances C), but John's saying something about the weather (under circumstances C).

2. *The Possibility of Mistake: The Connection between* (2) *and* (3)

Taking a cue from the fact that (2) expresses some form of necessary relationship between R and P, I have (in my opening remarks) expressed (2) as: Given R, $\sim$ <> $\sim$ P (or, alternatively, $\sim$ <>(R. $\sim$ P)). I think the full justification for expressing (2) in this fashion lies in the fact that (2) and (3) are contradictories, and since (3) may be rendered as:

(3) Given R, <> $\sim$ P (or, alternatively, <>(R . $\sim$ P)

(2) may be represented as 'Given R, $\sim$ <> $\sim$ P.'

To see that this is so, it should be noticed that in denying the connection between R and P expressed by (2) we do not commit ourselves to anything as strong as:

(4) R would be the case even though not-P were the case.

(4) is the *contrary* of (2), not its contradictory, since both (2) and (4) may turn out false. For example, suppose S asserts,

(2g) I would have won the lottery if I had bought two tickets (instead of only one).

We may deny the truth of this contention without committing ourselves to the truth of

(4g) You would have lost even if you had bought two tickets.

All that is intended in denying (2g) is that the purchase of two tickets is connected with winning in the alleged manner, that the purchase of two tickets would have assured him of winning. Its failing to be connected in the manner alleged is, however, quite consistent with *his winning* with two tickets. What we commit ourselves to in denying (2g) is:

(3g) You *might* have lost even with two tickets.

(3g) asserts what (2g) denies; *viz.* that even with two tickets it is *still* a matter of chance, the possibility of losing is *not* eliminated by holding two tickets instead of one.

As a matter of common practice, of course, we often employ something similar to (4) in denying (2). This is understandable enough since the truth of (4) does entail the falsity of (2). The point I am driving at, however, is that we need not affirm anything as strong as (4) in denying (2); all we are required to affirm is that R and not-P *might* both be the case or that, even though R is given, P *might not* be the case. That is to say, the proper expression for the negation of (2) is (3); and if we understand (3) as affirming 'Given R, <> ~ P' (alternatively <>(R . ~ P)), then we are justified in representing (2) as 'Given R , ~ <> ~ P' (alternatively, ~ <>(R . ~ P)). If someone says, 'James would not have come without an invitation,' we can deny this without supposing that James would have come without an invitation. For suppose we know that if James had not received an invitation, he would have flipped a coin to decide whether to go or not. In such a case, it is not true that he would not have come without an invitation, but neither is it true that he would have come without an invitation. The fact is that *he might have come* (depending on the outcome of the toss) without an invitation.

The modal term appearing in (3) is meant to be understood in an objective sense. (3) is meant to be a statement about the possibilities for the joint realization of two states of affairs (R and not-P) independent of what the speaker happens to know about the actual realization of P (R being given). Drawing from our discussion in the preceding section, we can say that if (2) is true, if R would not be the case unless P were the case, then *in these circumstances* (specified earlier) P is a state of affairs which is necessary to the realization of R. Hence, in these circumstances it is false to say that R and not-P might both be the case or that, given R, not-P might be the case, and it is false whether or not anyone appreciates the fact that it is false.

We have here a more or less *particularized* impossibility; (3), as well as (2), is tied to the circumstances, C, specified earlier. Nothing else but (a state such as) P could have brought about (a state such as) R *in these circumstances*. Often, of course, our statements about what could be the case, about what is possible, are broader in scope. They do not restrict themselves to the particular set of circumstances prevailing on some specific occasion. They are statements to the effect that, whatever the circumstances on this occasion happened to be, there are (nonetheless) circumstances in which a state relevantly similar to R is, or might easily be, brought about without a state relevantly similar to P. S may admit, for example, that the thermometer would not have read 98.6 unless the child's temperature was normal—

hence, concede that it would be false to say that in these circumstances (given the thermometer reading) the child might
(nonetheless) have a fever. Yet, he may go on to insist that one
can get a normal reading on a thermometer with a feverish
child. One can do so when one has a defective thermometer,
when the child is sucking an ice cube, and so on. That is, one
can have R without P in *other* circumstances. These 'general'
possibilities are, however, quite consistent with the 'particularized' impossibilities expressed by (3). Most genuine impossibilities can be made possible by enlarging the frame of reference, by relaxing the conditions tacitly taken as fixed in the
original statement of impossibility. I can't swim the English
Channel; this despite the fact that I could *if* I had trained since
a boy, been endowed with the requisite endurance, etc.

If I may summarize the argument up to this point in preparation for the following section: (1) entails (2), if S knows that
P, and he knows this on the basis (simply) of R, then R would
not be the case unless P were the case. Furthermore, (2) gives
expression to a connection between R and P which permits us
to say that when R is given, in the kind of circumstances which
actually prevailed on the occasion in question, the possibility of
not-P is eliminated. The sense of the word 'possible' that is op-
erative here is, I submit, the *same* sense of this word that is
operating in our strongest statements about what is phyically
possible; the difference between the possibility expressed in (3)
and other, apparently stronger, statements of what is possible
and impossible is simply a shift in the set of circumstances
which is taken as fixed. The impossibility expressed by (3) is an
impossibility relative to those circumstances, C, held fixed in
(2), and it is this fact which makes (3) the contradictory of (2)
and, hence, which makes its negation a logical consequence of
(1).

3. Conclusive Reasons

Let us call R a conclusive reason for P if and only if R would
not be the case unless P were the case.[10] This makes logically

10. Recall footnote 4 concerning the particular wording of (2); I intend
those remarks to apply to this definition of 'conclusive reasons.'

conclusive reasons (LCR) a subclass of conslusive reasons. Conclusive reasons depend, simply, on the truth of (2); logically conclusive reasons require that the truth of (2) be demonstrable on purely logical and definitional grounds. When the conditional is true, but not logically true, we can speak of the conclusive reasons as being *empirically conclusive* (ECR).

Of course, R may *be* a conclusive reason for believing P without anyone believing P, much less having R as their reason for believing. I shall say, therefore, that S *has conclusive reasons*, R, for believing P if and only if:

(A) R is a conclusive reason for P (i.e. (2) is true),
(B) S believes, without doubt, reservation, or question, that P is the case and he believes this on the basis of R,
(C) (i) S knows that R is the case or
      (ii) R is some experimental state of S (about which it may not make sense to suppose that S *knows* that R is the case; at least it no longer makes much sense to ask *how* he knows).

With only minor embellishments, to be mentioned in a moment, I believe that S's having conclusive reasons for believing P is *both* a necessary and sufficient condition for his knowing that P is the case. The appearance of the word 'know' in this characterization (in Ci)) does not render it circular as a characterization of knowledge since it can be eliminated by a recursive application of the three conditions until (Cii) is reached.

If S has conclusive reasons for believing P, then it is *false* to say that, given these grounds for belief, and the circumstances in which these grounds served as the basis for his belief, *S might be mistaken about P*. Having conclusive reasons, as I have just defined it, not only implies that P is the case, it not only implies that S believes that P is the case, but it also implies that, in the circumstances in which he came to believe that P, his basis for believing that P was sufficiently secure to eliminate the possibility of his being mistaken about P. This goes a long way toward capturing everything that philosophers have traditionally required of knowledge. Indeed, in certain respects it goes beyond it in requiring a stronger connection between one's

reasons or grounds and what one believes (on the basis of these
reasons or grounds) than has normally been demanded by
those wishing to preserve our ordinary knowledge claims from
sceptical criticism.[11]

It may be thought that in arguing for the impossibility of
mistake as a necessary condition for knowing that P I have
been wasting my time. It may be thought that if S knows that P,
then P *cannot* be false since S's knowing that P entails P; hence
S *cannot* be mistaken in believing that P. In answer to this objection it should be pointed out that the impossibility of mistake
which I have been talking about is an impossibility which arises
in virtue of a *special connection* between S's reasons, R, and what
he consequently believes, P. It is not the trivial impossibility of
being wrong about something which (by hypothesis) you know.
When philosophers concern themselves with the possibility of
mistake in putative cases of knowledge, they are not concerned
with the possibility of mistake which is trivially avoidable by saying that *if* you do know that P, then you cannot be mistaken
about P. They are concerned, rather, with that possibility as it

11. It is this stronger connection which blocks the sort of counterexample
which can be generated to justified-true-belief analyses of knowledge. Gettier's
(and Lehrer's) examples, for instance, are directed at those analyses which construe knowledge in terms of a *degree* of justification which is compatible with
being justified in believing something false (both Gettier and Lehrer mention
this feature at the beginning of their discussion). The counterexamples are
then constructed by allowing S to believe that P (which is false) *with the appropriate degree of justification,* letting P entail Q (which is true), and letting S believe
that Q on the basis of its logical relationship to P. We have, then, a case where S
truly believes that Q *with the appropriate degree of justification* (this degree of justification is allegedly preserved through the entailment between P and Q), but a
case where S does *not know* that Q (since his means of arriving at it were so
clearly defective). On the present analysis, of course, the required connection
between S's evidence and P is strong enough to *preclude* P's being false. One
cannot have *conclusive* reasons for believing something which is false. Hence,
this sort of counterexample cannot be generated. Part of the motivation for the
present analysis is the conviction (supported by Gettier-like examples) that
knowledge, if it embodies an evidential relation at all, must embody a strong
enough one to eliminate the *possibility* of mistake. See Edmund Gettier's 'Is Justified True Belief Knowledge?' *Analysis,* 23.6 June 1963, and Keith Lehrer,
'Knowledge, Truth and Evidence', *Analysis,* 25.5, April 1965. I should also
mention here that these same sorts of considerations seemed to move Brian
Skyrms toward a similar analysis; see especially pp. 385–86 in his 'The Explication of "X knows that *p*" ', *The Journal of Philosophy,* 64.12, June 22, 1967.

exists in relation to one's evidence or grounds for believing P, and *that* is the possibility with which (2) is concerned.

The point may be put in another way. Both

    I. R would not be the case unless P were the case

       R is the case

and

    II. R ⊃ P (when it is *not* true that R would not be the case unless P)

       R

constitute conclusive grounds, logically conclusive grounds, for believing P. Neither set of premises would be true unless P were true, and this fact is in both cases demonstrable on purely logical and definitional grounds. But the significant difference between I and II is that in I, but *not* in II, the second premise *alone* turns out to be a *conclusive* reason (ECR). If we were searching for conclusive reasons to believe P, then in the second case we would require as our reasons *both premises,* and this would require that we knew that both premises were true (see clause (C) in having conclusive reasons). In case I, however, the second premise alone is a conclusive reason and, hence, to have conclusive reasons it is required *only that we know that R is the case.* We need not (as in case II) know that the first premise is true. All that is required in case I for R alone to be a conclusive reason is that the first premise be true; there is nothing that requires S to know that the first premise is true in order to have R as his conclusive reason for believing P. For if the first premise is true (regardless of whether S knows it is true or not) then (3) is false; hence, the possibility of S's being mistaken about P has been successfully avoided—and it has been successfully avoided *whether or not S knows it has been avoided.*

In speaking of conclusive reasons I do not wish to suggest that in having R as a conclusive reason S must be in a position to *give* R as his reason. R may simply be a certain experience which S has undergone and, having undergone this experience, come to the belief that P was the case on the basis of (as a result of) this experience. He may find it difficult, or impossible, to give verbal expression to R. He may have forgotten R. Or R may consist in something's looking a particular way to

him which he finds difficult to describe. Still, if the way the
thing looks to S is such that it would not look that way unless it
had the property Q, then its looking that way to S is a conclusive reason for S's believing that it has the property Q; and if S
believes that it is Q *on this basis,* then he has, in the way the
thing looks to him, a conclusive reason for believing it Q.

Also, there are a number of things which people commonly
profess to know (Sacramento is the capital of California, the
earth is roughly spherical) for which there is no definite piece
of evidence, no single state of affairs or easily specifiable set of
such states, which even approximates a conclusive reason. In
such cases, although we can site no single piece of data which is
clinching and, hence, are at a loss for conclusive reasons when
asked to give reasons (or when asked 'How do you know?') we,
nonetheless, often enough have conclusive reasons in a vast
spectrum of experiences which are too diverse to admit of convenient citation. Countless experiences converge, so to speak,
on the truth of a given proposition, and this variety of experience may be such that although one *may* have had any *one* of
these experiences without the proposition in question being
true, one *would not* have had *all* of them unless what one consequently believes was true. The fallibility of source A and the
fallibility of source B does not automatically entail that when A
and B *agree* about P's being the case, that, nonetheless, P might
still be false. For it may be that A and B *would not* both have indicated that P was the case unless P was the case although neither A nor B, taken by themselves, provide conclusive reasons
for P. For example, although any single newspaper account
may be in error on a particular point, several independent versions (wire services, of course, tend to eliminate this indepen-
dence) may be enough to say that we know that something is so
on the basis of the newspaper accounts. All of them would not have
been in such close agreement unless their account was substantially correct.[12]

12. The fact that all newspapers sometimes print things which are false does
not mean that we cannot know that something is true on the basis of a single
newspaper account. The relevant question to ask (as in the case of a person's
testimony—see section 1) is not whether *newspapers* sometimes print false

Finally, I do not wish to suggest by my use of the word 'reason' that when S has conclusive reasons for believing P, S has *reasoned* his way to the conclusion that P is the case from premises involving R or that S has conciously used R as a reason in arriving at the belief that P. I am inclined to think (but I shall not now argue it) that when one knows that P, on whatever basis this might be, little or no reasoning is involved. I would prefer to describe it as follows: sometimes a person's conviction that P is the case can be traced to a state of affairs (or cluster of situations) which satisfies the three conditions defining the possession of conclusive reasons. When it can be so traced, then he knows; when it cannot be so traced, then we say he does not know although he may be right about P's being the case. Of course, his belief may be *traceable* to such a source without our being able to trace it. In such a case we are mistaken in saying that he does not know.[13]

---

stories, not even whether *this newspaper* sometimes print false stories, but whether *this newspaper* would have printed *this story* if it were not true. The *Midville Weekly Gazette's* story about dope addiction on the campus may not correspond with the facts, but would *The Times* have printed this story about the President's visit to Moscow if it were not true?

13. [Editors' Note: Dretske's paper has been abridged. In the omitted sections, Professor Dretske argues that his conditions are jointly sufficient for knowledge.]

2

Some Conclusive Reasons against "Conclusive Reasons"

GEORGE S. PAPPAS *and* MARSHALL SWAIN

According to Dretske,[1] a person has knowledge that P only if he has conclusive reasons for believing that P. A reason, R, is a conclusive reason for believing that P, in a specific situation, if and only if, given R, and given the circumstances in that situation that are causally and logically independent of P, it is not physically possible that not-P (p. 55). A person, S, is said to *have* conclusive reasons, R, for believing that P if and only if (i) R is a conclusive reason for believing that P, (ii) S believes, without doubt, reservation, or question, that P is the case and believes this on the basis of R, and (iii) either S knows that R is the case or R is [a description of] some experimental state of S about which it may not make sense to suppose that S knows that R is the case (p. 56). In what follows we shall argue that, given Dretske's characterization of conclusive reasons, it is a mistake for him to claim that, (see p. 41)

(1) S knows that P

entails

(2) S has conclusive reasons for believing that P.

Before turning to these arguments, however, let us consider what might have led Dretske to think that (1) does entail (2).

In recent literature on the analysis of knowing, a variety of cases have been concocted in which a person appears to be fully justified in some belief of his but falls short of knowledge be-

Reprinted from *The Australasian Journal of Philosophy*, 51 (1973), 72–76, by kind permission of the editor.

1. "Conclusive Reasons." All page references are to Chapter 1 above.

cause of a subtle defect in his justification. Perhaps the best
known of these cases are those proposed by Edmund Gettier.[2]
In Gettier's examples, the subject, S, has knowledge that E, and
E provides excellent reason for believing that Q, which in turn
entails P. S believes that P on the basis of his knowledge of
these facts. However, Q is false, and even though P is true, it is
not true for the reasons provided by S's evidence E. It is only
coincidental that S's evidence E provides him with convincing
justification for belief that P. In Gettier's examples, and in
many others that are fashioned after them, it is entirely possible that P might have been false, instead of true, and S's justification would have remained precisely the same. It is not difficult to see that Dretske's requirement of conclusive reasons is
strong enough to render his conditions for knowing immune to
such examples.

This immunity to the Gettier problems, and to similar problems, is a merit of Dretske's proposal. It is a merit that is
shared, however, with many other proposals that have been
made recently. These other proposals for analysing knowledge
are, like Dretske's, attempts to strengthen the 'justified true
belief' analysis in order to rule out instances of defective justification. Many of these suggestions have proven to be too
weak for the task; that is, they involve a strengthening of the
conditions for knowing that is sufficient to rule out Gettier-style
examples, but not sufficient to rule out other, more subtle, examples of defective justification.[3] Given this, it is tempting to
think that the only way in which we can avoid examples of
defective justification is to require that, in order for a person to
know something, he must have such a strong justification that
he *cannot be mistaken in* his belief. It is clear that Dretske has
taken this tempting line, for at one point in his essay he re-

2. Edmund L. Gettier: "Is Justified True Belief Knowledge?" *Analysis* 23.6
(1963), 121–123; reprinted in Roth and Galis, eds., *Knowing: Essays in the Analysis of Knowledge*, (New York: Random House, 1970), pp. 35–38.
3. For example, see Brian Skyrms: "The Explication of "X knows that p,'"
Journal of Philosophy, 64.12 (1967), 373–389; reprinted in Roth and Galis, pp.
89–111. For problems with Skyrms's proposal, see M. Swain, "Skyrms on Non-
derivative Knowledge," *Nous* 3.2 (1969), 227–231. The Roth-Galis book contains further essays and a useful bibiliography.

marks, "If S has conclusive reasons for believing P, then it is *false* to say that, given these grounds for belief, and the circumstances in which these grounds served as the basis for his belief, S *might be mistaken about P*" (p. 56). Others have also taken this tempting approach, but their suggestions prove to be *too* strong.[4] We will now show that, like other suggestions of this sort, Dretske's requirement of conclusive reasons is simply too strong to serve as a necessary condition for knowing.

As we have seen above, if we let 'C' stand for all of the actually obtaining circumstances that are logically and causally independent of the state of affairs referred to by 'P', then the conclusive reasons requirement (2) can be formulated as:

   (2a) In circumstances, C, R would not be the case unless P were the case.

Like most subjunctives, this one is vague on the question of what precisely we are allowed to imagine in considering whether R would be the case if P were not. We are told only that we must hold the circumstances C fixed. Are we allowed, then, to imagine situations in which C remains fixed, but in which everything else is radically different from the circumstances which actually obtain? If so, then (2a) would clearly not be a necessary condition for the truth of (1). It is easy to see why this is so.

Suppose that S is having visual experiences of a cup on a table, he has all the relevant concepts (knows what cups and tables are), he is attentive, the lighting is adequate, and there is nothing wrong with his sensory or neural mechanisms. In such a case it would seem clear that S knows that there is a cup on the table (P), on the basis of the visual experiences he is then having and his background knowledge (R). Now imagine the situation having been different so that all of the circumstances

4. Some authors have, for example, recently defended the view that knowledge requires *indefeasibly* justified true belief, and have imposed such strict requirements on indefeasible justification that the results approach the very strong requirements of Dretske. See Risto Hilpinen, "Knowledge and Justification," *Ajatus*, 33.1 (1971), 7–39, for an example and further references. A considerably weaker defeasibility analysis is given by M. Swain, "An Alternative Analysis of Knowing," *Synthese*, 23.4 (1972), 423–442, and in "Epistemic Defeasibility" [Chapter 11 of this volume].

C are the same, but instead of there being a cup on the table, there is a cleverly disguised hologram image of a cup being projected to the appropriate point on the table. Now consider the subjunctive conditional,

> (a) S would not be having the visual experiences he is having in these circumstances, C, unless there were a cup on the table.

If we suppose, as we may, that S would be having the same visual experiences if there were only a cup-hologram on the table, then (a) is plainly false. Moreover, the statement "There is only a cup-hologram on the table" is not logically independent of P, since the latter entails the falsity of the former. We thus have a case in which S does know that P (i.e. that there is a cup on the table) on the basis of R (his visual experiences plus background knowledge) in the relevant circumstances, but the corresponding conditional of the form (2a) is false.

This example shows that we cannot read the subjunctive conditional (2a) in a thoroughly unrestricted fashion if it is to express a necessary condition of the truth of (1). There is, however a considerably more restricted way of reading (2a) which avoids the above example. There is also some reason to think that this restricted way of reading the conditional is what Dretske has in mind, although his remarks are far from clear on this and similar matters.[5] The restricted way of reading (2a) can be stated as follows:

> (2a′) In circumstances C, R would not have been the case if the circumstances other than C had been different in only the following way: P is false, and whatever other changes in truth-values are required logically or causally by the falsity of P.

---

5. In discussing one of his examples, Dretske remarks, "Nothing else but (a state such as) P could have brought about (a state such as) R *in these circumstances*. Often, of course, our statements about what would be the case, about what is possible, are broader in scope. They do not restrict themselves to the particular set of circumstances prevailing on some specific occasion. They are statements to the effect that, whatever the circumstances on this occasion happened to be, there are (nonetheless) circumstances in which a state relevantly similar to R is, or might easily be, brought about without a state relevantly similar to P" (p. 54).

This way of reading (2a) rules out the possibility of imagining circumstances other than C as being radically different from what they in fact are when determining whether R would have been the case if P had not.

If (2) is interpreted in accordance with (2a′) then, obviously, the example presented above is not a counterexample to Dretske's thesis. The following, however, is a counterexample. Let us suppose that S works for the local electric company, and is thoroughly knowledgeable concerning the way in which the company's generators are responsible for the transmission of electricity to homes in the area. He knows that the company equipment has just been inspected and found to be in good working order, and he knows that the equipment has always been reliable in the past. One evening he visits at the home of a friend. On the way he notices that the street lights are burning, homes have lights on inside of them, and so forth. When he arrives at his friend's home, he notes that the lights are on there as well. He concludes that his company's generators are at that time causing the lights to be on in his friend's home (P). He is, of course, correct in his belief, and he has impeccable evidence, R, upon which he bases his belief. His reasons, R, include not only his presently perceiving that the lights are on in his friend's home, but also his considerable background knowledge. It seems uncontroversial to say that S knows that P in this example. Moreover, the conditional instantiating the conclusive reasons requirement (2a′) is clearly true:

(b)   Given the circumstances that are causally and logically independent of P, it would not have been the case that S perceives the lights to be on in his friend's home, etc., if the circumstances other than C had been different in just the following way: it is false that (P) the company's generators are causing the lights to be on in his friend's home, and whatever other changes in truth-values are required causally or logically by the falsity of P.

It is not difficult, however, to complicate the situation in such a way that the subjunctive conditional (b) would turn out to be false, but such that this fact has *no effect whatever on* S's knowledge that P. Suppose, for example, that entirely unknown to S, his friend has a private generator in the basement of his home, and the generator is rigged in such a way that it will automatically produce electricity for his home if there should be an electric company failure. This aspect of the situation is not one of those that is to be included in the circumstances, C, for it is not causally independent of P (if P were false, then that would be causally sufficient for the generator to begin producing electricity.) So, even though the generator is off, it would have been on if the electric company had been witnessing a failure. This is *one* of the changes in the circumstances other than C that is *required* by the supposition that P is false in the conditional (b). It is not difficult to see that, if we amend the case in this fashion, then (b) is no longer true. Even if P were false, S would still have the same reasons, R, for believing that P. His background evidence would remain exactly the same, and his present perceptual evidence, although misleading, would be the same. Moreover, all of his reasons, R, would remain *true* as we have described the situation. He would not, of course, know that P if P were false, but his reasons for believing that P would be the same. And, surely, we do not want to say that the fact that his friend has a generator in his basement *prevents* S from having knowledge that the company's generators are causing the lights to be on.

We can conclude, then, that Dretske's claim that knowledge requires conclusive reasons is mistaken. We have given examples that show this on the assumption that either (2a) or (2a′) is the intended interpretation of the conclusive reasons requirement. Possibly neither of these interpretations is what Dretske has in mind. If not, it would be interesting to know what his intended interpretation is. We suspect, however, that *any* interpretation of the conclusive reasons requirement will yield a conception of knowledge that is too strong, for the having of conclusive reasons is supposed to guarantee that one cannot be mistaken in beliefs that are based on those reasons. We suggest that the examples presented above illustrate not only that (1) does not entail (2a) or (2a′), but also that a person can know something even though he *might* be mistaken.

3

A Causal Theory of Knowing

ALVIN I. GOLDMAN

Since Edmund L. Gettier reminded us recently of a certain important inadequacy of the traditional analysis of "S knows that p," several attempts have been made to correct that analysis.[1] In this paper I shall offer still another analysis (or a sketch of an analysis) of "S knows that p," one which will avert Gettier's problem. My concern will be with knowledge of empirical propositions only, since I think that the traditional analysis is adequate for knowledge of nonempirical truths.

Consider an abbreviated version of Gettier's second counterexample to the traditional analysis. Smith believes

(q) Jones owns a Ford

and has very strong evidence for it. Smith's evidence might be that Jones has owned a Ford for many years and that Jones has just offered Smith a ride while driving a Ford. Smith has another friend, Brown, of whose whereabouts he is totally igno-

Reprinted from *The Journal of Philosophy*, 64, 12 (1967), 355–372, by kind permission of the author and editor.

I wish to thank members of the University of Michigan Philsophy Department, several of whom made helpful comments on earlier versions of this paper.

1. "Is Justified True Belief Knowledge?" *Analysis,* 23.6 (1963), 121–123. I say "reminded" because essentially the same point was made by Russell in 1912. Cf. *The Problems of Philosophy* (Oxford, 1912), ch. 13, pp. 132 ff. New analyses have been proposed by Michael Clark, "Knowledge and Grounds: A Comment on Mr. Gettier's Paper," *Analysis* 24.2 (1963), 46–48; Ernest Sosa, "The Analysis of 'Knowledge that P'," ibid., 25.1 (1964): 1–8; and Keith Lehrer, "Knowledge, Truth and Evidence," ibid., 25.5 (1965), 168–175.

rant. Choosing a town quite at random, however, Smith constructs the proposition

(p) Either Jones owns a Ford or Brown is in Barcelona.

Seeing that q entails p, Smith infers that p is true. Since he has adequate evidence for q, he also has adequate evidence for p. But now suppose that Jones does *not* own a Ford (he was driving a rented car when he offered Smith a ride), but, quite by coincidence, Brown happens to be in Barcelona. This means that p is true, that Smith believes p, and that Smith has adequate evidence for p. But Smith does not know p.

A variety of hypotheses might be made to account for Smith's not knowing p. Michael Clark, for example, points to the fact that q is false, and suggests this as the reason why Smith cannot be said to know p. Generalizing from this case, Clark argues that, for S to know a proposition, each of S's grounds for it must be *true*, as well as his grounds for his grounds, etc.[2] I shall make another hypothesis to account for the fact that Smith cannot be said to know p, and I shall generalize this into a new analysis of "S knows that p."

Notice that what *makes* p true is the fact that Brown is in Barcelona, but that this fact has nothing to do with Smith's believing p. That is, there is no *causal* connection between the fact that Brown is in Barcelona and Smith's believing p. If Smith had come to believe p by reading a letter from Brown postmarked in Barcelona, then we might say that Smith knew p. Alternatively, if Jones did own a Ford, and his owning the Ford was manifested by his offer of a ride to Smith, and this in turn resulted in Smith's believing p, then we would say that Smith knew p. Thus, one thing that seems to be missing in this example is a causal connection between the fact that makes p true [or simply: the fact that p] and Smith's belief of p. The requirement of such a *causal connection* is what I wish to add to the traditional analysis.

To see that this requirement is satisfied in all cases of (empirical) knowledge, we must examine a variety of such causal connections. Clearly, only a sketch of the important kinds of cases is possible here.

2. *Op. cit.* Criticisms of Clark's analysis will be discussed below.

Perhaps the simplest case of a causal chain connecting some fact p with someone's belief of p is that of *perception*. I wish to espouse a version of the causal theory of perception, in essence that defended by H. P. Grice.[3] Suppose that S sees that there is a vase in front of him. How is this to be analyzed? I shall not attempt a complete analysis of this, but a necessary condition of S's seeing that there is a vase in front of him is that there be a certain kind of causal connection between the presence of the vase and S's believing that a vase is present. I shall not attempt to describe this causal process in detail. Indeed, to a large extent, a description of this process must be regarded as a problem for the special sciences, not for philosophy. But a certain causal process—viz. that which standardly takes place when we say that so-and-so *sees* such-and-such—must occur. That our ordinary concept of sight (i.e., knowledge acquired by sight) includes a causal requirement is shown by the fact that if the relevant causal process is absent we would withhold the assertion that so-and-so *saw* such-and-such. Suppose that, although a vase is directly in front of S, a laser photograph[4] is interposed between it and S, thereby blocking it from S's view. The photograph, however, is one of a vase (a different vase), and when it is illuminated by light waves from a laser, it looks to S exactly like a real vase. When the photograph is illuminated, S forms the belief that there is a vase in front of him. Here we would deny that S *sees* that there is a vase in front of him, for his view of the real vase is completely blocked, so that it has no causal role in the formation of his belief. Of course, S might *know* that there was a vase in front of him even if the photograph is blocking his view. Someone else, in a position to see the vase, might tell S that there is a vase in front of him. Here the presence of the vase might be a causal ancestor of S's belief, but the

3. "The Causal Theory of Perception," *Proceedings of the Aristotelian Society,* supp. vol. 35 (1961).
4. If a laser photograph (hologram) is illuminated by light waves, especially waves from a laser, the effect of the hologram on the viewer is exactly as if the object were being seen. It preserves three-dimensionality completely, and even gives appropriate parallax effects as the viewer moves relative to it. Cf. E. N. Leith and J. Upatnieks, "Photography by Laser," *Scientific American* (June 1965), p. 24.

causal process would not be a (purely) *perceptual* one. *S could not be said to see* that there is a vase in front of him. For this to be true, there must be a causal process, but one of a very special sort, connecting the presence of the vase with *S*'s belief.

I shall here assume that perceptual knowledge of facts is noninferential. This is merely a simplifying procedure, and not essential to my account. Certainly a percipient does not *infer* facts about physical objects from the state of his brain or from the stimulation of his sense organs. He need not know about these goings-on at all. But some epistemologists maintain that we directly perceive only sense data and that we infer physical-object facts from them. This view could be accommodated within my analysis. I could say that physical-object facts cause sense data, that people directly perceive sense data, and that they infer the physical object facts from the sense data. This kind of process would be fully accredited by my analysis, which will allow for knowledge based on inference. But for purposes of exposition it will be convenient to regard perceptual knowledge of external facts as independent of any inference.

Here the question arises about the *scope* of perceptual knowledge. By perception I can know noninferentially that there is a vase in front of me. But can I know noninferentially that the painting I am viewing is a Picasso? It is unnecessary to settle such issues here. Whether the knowledge of such facts is to be classed as inferential or noninferential, my analysis can account for it. So the scope of noninferential knowledge may be left indeterminate.

I turn next to memory, i.e., knowledge that is based, in part, on memory. Remembering, like perceiving, must be regarded as a causal process. *S* remembers *p* at time *t* only if *S*'s believing *p* at an earlier time is a cause of his believing *p* at *t*. Of course, not every causal connection between an earlier belief and a later one is a case of remembering. As in the case of perception, however, I shall not try to describe this process in detail. This is a job mainly for the scientist. Instead, the kind of causal process in question is to be identified simply by example, by "pointing" to paradigm cases of remembering. Whenever causal processes are of that kind—whatever that kind is, precisely—they are cases of remembering.[5]

A causal connection between earlier belief (or knowledge) of p and later belief (knowledge) of p is certainly a necessary ingredient in memory.[6] To remember a fact is not simply to believe it at t_0 and also to believe it at t_1. Nor does someone's knowing a fact at t_0 and his knowing it at t_1 entail that he remembers it at t_1. He may have perceived the fact at t_0, forgotten it, and then relearned it at t_1 by someone's telling it to him. Nor does the inclusion of a memory "impression"—a feeling of remembering—ensure that one really remembers. Suppose S perceives p at t_0, but forgets it at t_1. At t_2 he begins to believe p again because someone tells him p, but at t_2 he has no memory impression of p. At t_3 we artificially stimulate in S a memory impression of p. It does not follow that S remembers p at t_3. The description of the case suggests that his believing p at t_0 has no causal effect whatever on his believing p at t_3; and if we accepted this fact, we would deny that he remembers p at t_3.

Knowledge can be acquired by a combination of perception and memory. At t_0, the fact p causes S to believe p, by perception. S's believing p at t_0 results, via memory, in S's believing p at t_1. Thus, the fact p is a cause of S's believing p at t_1, and S can be said to know p at t_1. But not all knowledge results from perception and memory alone. In particular, much knowledge is based on *inference*.

As I shall use the term 'inference', to say that S knows p by "inference" does not entail that S went through an explicit, conscious process of reasoning. It is not necessary that he have "talked to himself," saying something like "Since such-and-such is true, p must also be true." My belief that there is a fire in the neighborhood is based on, or inferred from, my belief that I

5. For further defense of this kind of procedure, with attention to perception, cf. Grice, *op. cit.*

6. Causal connections can hold between states of affairs, such as believings, as well as between events. If a given event or state, in conjunction with other events or states, "leads to" or "results in" another event or state (or the same state obtaining at a later time), it will be called a "cause" of the latter. I shall also speak of "facts" being causes.

hear a fire engine. But I have not gone through a process of explicit reasoning, saying "There's a fire engine; therefore there must be a fire." Perhaps the word 'inference' is ordinarily used only where explicit reasoning occurs; if so, my use of the term will be somewhat broader than its ordinary use.

Suppose S perceives that there is solidified lava in various parts of the countryside. On the basis of this belief, plus various "background" beliefs about the production of lava, S concludes that a nearby mountain erupted many centuries ago. Let us assume that this is a highly warranted inductive inference, one which gives S adequate evidence for believing that the mountain did erupt many centuries ago. Assuming this proposition is true, does S know it? This depends on the nature of the causal process that induced his belief. If there is a continuous causal chain of the sort he envisages connecting the fact that the mountain erupted with his belief of this fact, then S knows it. If there is no such causal chain, however, S does not know that proposition.

Suppose that the mountain erupts, leaving lava around the countryside. The lava remains there until S perceives it and infers that the mountain erupted. Then S does know that the mountain erupted. But now suppose that, after the mountain has erupted, a man somehow removes all the lava. A century later, a different man (not knowing of the real volcano) decides to make it look as if there had been a volcano, and therefore puts lava in appropriate places. Still later, S comes across this lava and concludes that the mountain erupted centuries ago. In this case, S cannot be said to know the proposition. This is because the fact that the mountain did erupt is not a cause of S's believing that it erupted. A necessary condition of S's knowing p is that his believing p be connected with p by a causal chain.

In the first case, where S knows p, the causal connection may be diagrammed as in Figure 1. (p) is the fact that the mountain erupted at such-and-such a time. (q) is the fact that lava is (now) present around the countryside. 'B' stands for a belief, the expression in parentheses indicating the proposition believed, and the subscript designating the believer. (r) is a "background" proposition, describing the ways in which lava is produced and how it solidifies. Solid arrows in the diagram represent causal connections; dotted arrows represent inferences. Notice that, in Figure 1, there is not only an arrow connecting (q) with S's belief of (q), but also an arrow connecting (p) with (q). In the suggested variant of the lava case, the latter arrow would be missing, showing that there is no continuous causal chain connecting (p) with S's belief of (p). Therefore, in that variant case, S could not be said to know (p).

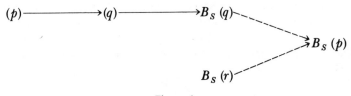

Figure 1

I have said that p is causally connected to S's belief of p, in the case diagrammed in Figure 1. This raises the question, however, of whether the inferential part of the chain is itself a causal chain. In other words, is S's belief of q a cause of his believing p? This is a question to which I shall not try to give a definitive answer here. I am inclined to say that inference *is* a causal process, that is, that when someone *bases* his belief of one proposition on his belief of a set of other propositions, then his belief of the latter propositions can be considered a cause of his belief of the former proposition. But I do not wish to rest my thesis on this claim. All I do claim is that, if a chain of inferences is "added" to a causal chain, then the entire chain is causal. In terms of our diagram, a chain consisting of solid arrows plus dotted arrows is to be considered a causal chain, though I shall not take a position on the question of whether the dotted arrows represent causal connections. Thus, in Figure 1, p is a cause of S's belief of p, whether or not we regard S's belief of q a cause of his belief of p.[7]

7. A fact can be a cause of a belief even if it does not *initiate* the belief. Suppose I believe that there is a lake in a certain locale, this belief having started in

Consider next a case of knowledge based on "testimony." This too can be analyzed causally. p causes a person T to believe p, by perception. T's belief of p gives rise to (causes) his asserting p. T's asserting p causes S, by auditory perception, to believe that T is asserting p. S infers that T believes p, and from this, in turn, he infers that p is a fact. There is a continuous causal chain from p to S's believing p, and thus, assuming that each of S's inferences is warranted, S can be said to know p.

This causal chain is represented in Figure 2. 'A' refers to an act of asserting a proposition, the expression in parentheses indicating the proposition asserted and the subscript designating the agent. (q), (r), (u), and (v) are background propositions. (q) and (r), for example, pertain to T's sincerity; they help S conclude, from the fact that T asserted p, that T really believes p.

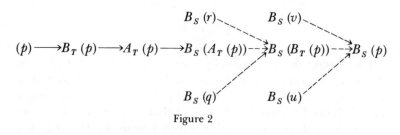

Figure 2

In this case, as in the lava case, S knows p because he has correctly reconstructed the causal chain leading from p to the evidence for p that S perceives, in this case, T's asserting (p). This correct reconstruction is shown in the diagram by S's inference "mirroring" the rest of the causal chain. Such a correct reconstruction is a necessary condition of knowledge based on inference. To see this, consider the following example. A newspaper reporter observes p and reports it to his newspaper. When

---

a manner quite unconnected with the existence of the lake. Continuing to have the belief, I go to the locale and perceive the lake. At this juncture, the existence of the lake becomes a cause of my believing that there is a lake there. This is analogous to a table top that is supported by four legs. When a fifth leg is inserted flush beneath the table top, it too becomes a cause of the table top's not falling. It has a causal role in the support of the table top even though, before it was inserted, the table top was adequately supported.

printed, however, the story contains a typographical error so that it asserts not-p. When reading the paper, however, S fails to see the word 'not', and takes the paper to have asserted p. Trusting the newspaper, he infers that p is true. Here we have a continuous causal chain leading from p to S's believing p; yet S does not know p. S thinks that p resulted in a report to the newspaper about p and that this report resulted in its printing the statement p. Thus, his reconstruction of the causal chain is mistaken. But, if he is to know p, his reconstruction must contain no mistakes. Though he need not reconstruct *every* detail of the causal chain, he must reconstruct all the important links.[8] An additional requirement for knowledge based on inference is that the knower's inferences be warranted. That is, the propositions on which he bases his belief of p must genuinely confirm p very highly, whether deductively or inductively. Reconstructing a causal chain merely by lucky guesses does not yield knowledge.

With the help of our diagrams, we can contrast the traditional analysis of knowing with Clark's analysis (*op. cit.*) and contrast each of these with my own analysis. The traditional analysis makes reference to just three features of the diagrams. First, it requires that p be true; i.e., that (p) appear in the diagram. Secondly, it requires that S believe p; i.e., that S's belief of p appear in the diagram. Thirdly, it requires that S's inferences, if any, be warranted; i.e., that the sets of beliefs that are at the tail of a dotted arrow must jointly highly confirm the belief at the head of these arrows. Clark proposes a further requirement for knowledge. He requires that *each* of the beliefs in S's chain of inference be *true*. In other words, whereas the traditional analysis requires a fact to correspond to S's belief of p, Clark requires that a fact correspond to *each* of S's beliefs on which he based his belief of p. Thus, corresponding to each belief on the right side of the diagram there must be a fact on

---

8. Clearly we cannot require someone to reconstruct every detail, since this would involve knowledge of minute physical phenomena, for example, of which ordinary people are unaware. On the other hand, it is difficult to give criteria to identify which details, in general, are "important." This will vary substantially from case to case.

the left side. (My diagrams omit facts corresponding to the
"background" beliefs.)

As Clark's analysis stands, it seems to omit an element of the
diagrams that my analysis requires, viz., the arrows indicating
causal connections. Now Clark might reformulate his analysis
so as to make implicit reference to these causal connections. If
he required that the knower's beliefs include *causal beliefs* (of
the relevant sort), then his requirement that these beliefs be
true would amount to the requirement that there *be* causal
chains of the sort I require. This interpretation of Clark's analysis would make it almost equivalent to mine, and would enable
him to avoid some objections that have been raised against him.
But he has not explicitly formulated his analysis this way, and it
therefore remains deficient in this respect.

Before turning to the problems facing Clark's analysis, more
must be said about my own analysis. So far, my examples may
have suggested that, if S knows p, the fact that p is a cause of
his belief of p. This would clearly be wrong, however. Let us
grant that I can know facts about the future. Then, if we
required that the known fact cause the knower's belief, we
would have to countenance "backward" causation. My analysis,
however, does not face this dilemma. The analysis requires that
there be a causal *connection* between p and S's belief, not necessarily that p be a *cause* of S's belief. p and S's belief of p can also
be causally connected in a way that yields knowledge if both p
and S's belief of p have a *common* cause. This can be illustrated
as follows.

T intends to go downtown on Monday. On Sunday, T tells S
of his intention. Hearing T say he will go downtown, S infers
that T really does intend to go downtown. And from this S
concludes that T *will* go downtown on Monday. Now suppose
that T fulfills his intention by going downtown on Monday. Can
S be said to know that he would go downtown? If we ever can
be said to have knowledge of the future, this is a reasonable
candidate for it. So let us say S did know that proposition. How
can my analysis account for S's knowledge? T's going downtown on Monday clearly cannot be a cause of S's believing, on
Sunday, that he would go downtown. But there is a fact that is

the *common* cause of T's going downtown and of S's belief that
he would go downtown, viz., T's intending (on Sunday) to go
downtown. This intention resulted in his going downtown and
also resulted in S's believing that he would go downtown. This
causal connection between S's belief and the fact believed
allows us to say that S *knew* that T would go downtown.

The example is diagrammed in Figure 3. (p) = T's going
downtown on Monday. (q) = T's intending (on Sunday) to go
downtown on Monday. (r) = T's telling S (on Sunday) that he
will go downtown on Monday. (u) and (v) are relevant background propositions pertaining to T's honesty, resoluteness,
etc. The diagram reveals that q is a cause both of p and of S's
belief of p. Cases of this kind I shall call *Pattern 2* cases of
knowledge. Figures 1 and 2 exemplify *Pattern 1* cases of knowledge.

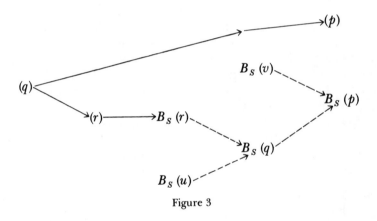

Figure 3

Notice that the causal connection between q and p is an essential part of S's knowing p. Suppose, for example, that T's intending (on Sunday) to go downtown does not result in, or
cause, T's going downtown on Monday. Suppose that T, after
telling S that he would go downtown, changes his mind. Nevertheless, on Monday he is kidnapped and forced, at the point of
a gun, to go downtown. Here both q and p actually occur, but
they are not causally related. The diagram in Figure 3 would

have to be amended by deleting the arrow connecting (q) with (p). But if the rest of the facts of the original case remain the same, S could not be said to know p. It would be false to say that S knew, on Sunday, that T would go downtown on Monday.

Pattern 2 cases of knowledge are not restricted to knowledge of the future. I know that smoke was coming out of my chimney last night. I know this because I remember perceiving a fire in my fireplace last night, and I infer that the fire caused smoke to rise out of the chimney. This case exemplifies Pattern 2. The smoke's rising out of the chimney is not a causal factor of my belief. But the fact that there was a fire in the fireplace was a cause both of my belief that smoke was coming out of the chimney and of the fact that smoke was coming out of the chimney. If we supplement this case slightly, we can make my knowledge exemplify *both* Pattern 1 and Pattern 2. Suppose that a friend tells me today that he perceived smoke coming out of my chimney last night and I base my continued belief of this fact on his testimony. Then the fact was a cause of my current belief of it, as well as an *effect* of another fact that caused my belief. In general, numerous and diverse kinds of causal connections can obtain between a given fact and a given person's belief of that fact.

Let us now examine some objections to Clark's analysis and see how the analysis presented here fares against them. John Turk Saunders and Narayan Champawat have raised the following counterexample to Clark's analysis:[9]

Suppose that Smith believes
(p) Jones owns a Ford
because his friend Brown whom he knows to be generally reliable and honest yesterday told Smith that Jones had always owned a Ford. Brown's information was correct, but today Jones sells his Ford and replaces it with a Volkswagen. An hour later Jones is pleased to find that he is the proud owner of two cars: he has been lucky enough to win a Ford in a raffle. Smith's belief in p is not only justified and true, but is fully grounded, e.g., we suppose that each link in the . . . chain of Smith's grounds is true (8).

9. "Mr. Clark's Definition of 'Knowledge'," *Analysis*, 25.1 (1964), 8–9.

Clearly Smith does not know p; yet he seems to satisfy Clark's analysis of knowing.

Smith's lack of knowledge can be accounted for in terms of my analysis. Smith does not know p because his believing p is not causally related to p, Jones's owning a Ford *now*. This can be seen by examining Figure 4. In the diagram, (p) = Jones's owning a Ford now; (q) = Jones's having always owned a Ford (until yesterday); (r) = Jones's winning a Ford in a raffle today. (t), (u), and (v) are background propositions. (v), for example, deals with the likelihood of someone's continuing to own the same car today that he owned yesterday. The subscript 'B' designates Brown, and the subscript 'S' designates Smith. Notice the absence of an arrow connecting (p) with (q). The absence of this arrow represents the absence of a causal relation between (q) and (p). Jones's owning a Ford in the past (until yesterday) is not a cause of his owning one now. Had he continued owning the same Ford today that he owned yesterday, there would be a causal connection between q and p and, therefore, a causal connection between p and Smith's believing p.. This causal connection would exemplify Pattern 2. But, as it happened, it is purely a coincidence that Jones owns a Ford today as well as yesterday. Thus, Smith's belief of p is not connected with p by Pattern 2, nor is there any Pattern 1 connection between them. Hence, Smith does not know p.

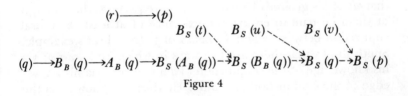

Figure 4

If we supplement Clark's analysis as suggested above, it can be saved from this counterexample. Though Saunders and Champawat fail to mention this explicitly, presumably it is one of Smith's beliefs that Jones's owning a Ford yesterday would *result* in Jones's owning a Ford now. This was undoubtedly one of his grounds for believing that Jones owns a Ford now. (A complete diagram of S's beliefs relevant to p would include this belief.) Since this belief is false, however, Clark's analysis would yield the correct consequence that Smith does not know p. Unfortunately, Clark himself seems not to have noticed this point, since Saunders and Champawat's putative counterexample has been allowed to stand.

Another sort of counterexample to Clark's analysis has been given by Saunders and Champawat and also by Keith Lehrer. This is a counterexample from which his analysis cannot escape. I shall give Lehrer's example (*op. cit.*) of this sort of difficulty. Suppose Smith bases his belief of

(p) Someone in his office owns a Ford

on his belief of four propositions

(q) Jones owns a Ford

(r) Jones works in his office

(s) Brown owns a Ford

(t) Brown works in his office

In fact, Smith knows q, r, and t, but he does not know s because s is false. Since s is false, not *all* of Smith's grounds for p are true, and, therefore, on Clark's analysis, Smith does not know p. Yet clearly Smith does know p. Thus, Clark's analysis is *too strong*.

Having seen the importance of a causal chain for knowing, it is fairly obvious how to amend Clark's requirements without making them too weak. We need not require, as Clark does, that *all* of S's grounds be true. What is required is that enough of them be true to ensure the existence of at least *one* causal connection between p and S's belief of p. In Lehrer's example, Smith thinks that there are two ways in which he knows p: via his knowledge of the conjunction of q and r, and via his knowledge of the conjunction of s and t. He does not know p via the conjunction of s and t, since s is false. But there is a causal connection, via q and r, between p and Smith's belief of p. And this connection is enough.

Another sort of case in which one of S's grounds for p may be false without preventing him from knowing p is where the false proposition is a dispensable background assumption. Suppose S bases his belief of p on 17 background assumptions, but only 16 of these are true. If these 16 are strong enough to confirm p, then the 17th is dispensable. S can be said to know p though one of his grounds is false.

Our discussion of Lehrer's example calls attention to the necessity of a further clarification of the notion of a "causal chain." I said earlier that causal chains with admixtures of inferences are causal chains. Now I wish to add that causal chains with admixtures of logical connections are causal chains. Unless we allow this interpretation, it is hard to see how facts like "Someone in the office owns a Ford" or "All men are mortal" could be *causally* connected with beliefs thereof.

The following principle will be useful: *If x is logically related to y and if y is a cause of z, then x is a cause of z.* Thus, suppose that q causes S's belief of q and that r causes S's belief of r. Next suppose that S infers q & r *from his belief of q and of r.* Then the facts q and r are causes of S's believing q & r. But the fact q & r is logically related to the fact q and to the fact r. Therefore, using the principle enunciated above, the fact q & r is a cause of S's believing q & r.

In Lehrer's case another logical connection is involved: a connection between an existential fact and an instance thereof. Lehrer's case is diagrammed in Figure 5. In addition to the usual conventions, logical relationships are represented by dou-

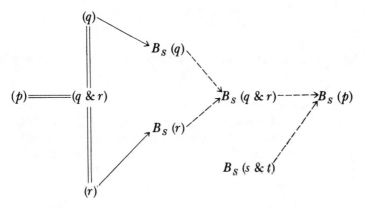

Figure 5

ble solid lines. As the diagram shows, the fact p—someone in Smith's office owning a Ford—is logically related to the fact q & r—Jones's owning a Ford and Jones's working in Smith's office. The fact q & r is, in turn, logically related to the fact q and to the fact r. q causes S's belief of q and, by inference, his belief of q & r and of p. Similarly, r is a cause of S's belief of p. Hence, by the above principle, p is a cause of S's belief of p. Since Smith's inferences are warranted, even setting aside his belief of s & t, he knows p.

In a similar way, universal facts may be causes of beliefs thereof. The fact that all men are mortal is logically related to its instances: John's being mortal, George's being mortal, Oscar's being mortal, etc. Now suppose that S perceives George, John, Oscar, etc. to be mortal (by seeing them die). He infers from these facts that all men are mortal, an inference which, I assume, is warranted. Since each of the facts, John is mortal, George is mortal, Oscar is mortal, etc., is a cause of S's believing that fact, each is also a cause of S's believing that all men are mortal. Moreover, since the universal fact that all men are mortal is logically related to each of these particular facts, this universal fact is a cause of S's belief of it. Hence, S can be said to know that all men are mortal. In analogous fashions, S can know various other logically compound propositions.

We can now formulate the analysis of knowing as follows:

S knows that p if and only if

the fact p is causally connected in an "appropriate" way with S's believing p.

"Appropriate," knowledge-producing causal processes include the following:

(1) perception
(2) memory
(3) a causal chain, exemplifying either Pattern 1 or 2, which is correctly reconstructed by inferences, each of which is warranted (background propositions help warrant an inference only if they are true) [10]
(4) combinations of (1), (2), and (3)

10. Perhaps background propositions that help warrant S's inference must be *known* by S, as well as true. This requirement could be added without making our analysis of "S knows that p" circular. For these propositions would not

We have seen that this analysis is *stronger* than the traditional analysis in certain respects: the causal requirement and the correct-reconstruction requirement are absent from the older analysis. These additional requirements enable my analysis to circumvent Gettier's counterexamples to the traditional one. But my analysis is *weaker* than the traditional analysis in another respect. In at least one popular interpretation of the traditional analysis, a knower must be able to justify or give evidence for any proposition he knows. For S to know p at t, S must be able, at t, to *state* his justification for believing p, or his grounds for p. My analysis makes no such requirement, and the absence of this requirement enables me to account for cases of knowledge that would wrongly be excluded by the traditional analysis.

I know now, for example, that Abraham Lincoln was born in 1809.[11] I originally came to know this fact, let us suppose, by reading an encyclopedia article. I believed that this encyclopedia was trustworthy and that its saying Lincoln was born in 1809 must have resulted from the fact that Lincoln was indeed born in 1809. Thus, my original knowledge of this fact was founded on a warranted inference. But now I no longer remember this inference. I remember that Lincoln was born in 1809, but not that this is stated in a certain encyclopedia. I no longer have any pertinent beliefs that highly confirm the proposition that Lincoln was born in 1809. Nevertheless, I know this proposition now. My original knowledge of it was preserved until now by the causal process of memory.

Defenders of the traditional analysis would doubtlessly deny that I really do know Lincoln's birth year. This denial, however, stems from a desire to protect their analysis. It seems clear that many things we know were originally learned in a way that we no longer remember. The range of our knowledge would be drastically reduced if these items were denied the status of knowledge.

Other species of knowledge without explicit evidence could

---

include p. In other words, the analysis of knowledge could be regarded as recursive.

11. This kind of case is drawn from an unpublished manuscript of Gilbert Harman.

also be admitted by my analysis. Notice that I have not closed the list of "appropriate" causal processes. Leaving the list open is desirable, because there may be some presently controversial causal processes that we may later deem "appropriate" and, therefore, knowledge-producing. Many people now doubt the legitimacy of claims to extrasensory perception. But if conclusive evidence were to establish the existence of causal processes connecting physical facts with certain persons' beliefs without the help of standard perceptual processes, we might decide to call such beliefs items of knowledge. This would be another species of knowledge in which the knower might be unable to justify or defend his belief. My analysis allows for the possibility of such knowledge, though it doesn't commit one to it.

Special comments are in order about knowledge of our own mental states. This is a very difficult and controversial topic, so I hesitate to discuss it, but something must be said about it. Probably there are some mental states that are clearly distinct from the subject's belief that he is in such a state. If so, then there is presumably a casual process connecting the existence of such states with the subject's belief thereof. We may add this kind of process to the list of "appropriate" causal processes. The more difficult cases are those in which the state is hardly distinguishable from the subject's believing that he is in that state. My being in pain and my believing that I am in pain are hardly distinct states of affairs. If there is no distinction here between the believing and the believed, how can there be a causal connection between them? For the purposes of the present analysis, we may regard identity as a "limiting" or "degenerate" case of a causal connection, just as zero may be regarded as a "limiting" or "degenerate" case of a number. It is not surprising that knowledge of one's own mental state should turn out to be a limiting or degenerate case of knowledge. Philosophers have long recognized its peculiar status. While some philosophers have regarded it as a paradigm case of knowledge, others have claimed that we have no "knowledge" of our mental states at all. A theory of knowledge that makes knowledge of one's own mental states rather different from garden-variety species of knowledge is, in so far forth, acceptable and even welcome.

In conclusion, let me answer some possible objections to my analysis. It might be doubted whether a causal analysis adequately provides the meaning of the word 'knows' or of the sentence (-schema) "S knows p." But I am not interested in giving the *meaning* of "S knows p"; only its *truth conditions*. I claim to have given one correct set of truth conditions for "S knows p." Truth conditions of a sentence do not always provide its meaning. Consider, for example, the following truth-conditions statement: "The sentence 'Team T wins the baseball game' is true if and only if team T has more runs at the end of the game than the opposing team." This statement fails to provide the meaning of the sentence 'Team T wins the baseball game'; for it fails to indicate an essential part of the meaning of that sentence, viz., that to win a game is to achieve the presumed goal of playing it. Someone might fully understand the truth conditions given above and yet fail to understand the meaning of the sentence because he has no understanding of the notion of "winning" in general.

Truth conditions should not be confused with verification conditions. My analysis of "S knows p" does not purport to give procedures for *finding out* whether a person (including oneself) knows a given proposition. No doubt, we sometimes do know that people know certain propositions, for we sometimes know that their beliefs are causally connected (in appropriate ways) with the facts believed. On the other hand, it may often be difficult or even impossible to find out whether this condition holds for a given proposition and a given person. For example, it may be difficult for me to find out whether I really do remember a certain fact that I seem to remember. The difficulties that exist for *finding out* whether someone knows a given proposition do not constitute difficulties for my analysis, however.

In the same vein it should be noted that I have made no attempt to answer skeptical problems. My analysis gives no answer to the skeptic who asks that I start from the content of my own experience and then prove that I know there is a material world, a past, etc. I do not take this to be one of the jobs of giving truth conditions for "S knows that p."

The analysis presented here flies in the face of a well-

established tradition in epistemology, the view that epistemological questions are questions of logic or justification, not
causal or genetic questions. This traditional view, however,
must not go unquestioned. Indeed, I think my analysis shows
that the question of whether someone knows a certain proposition is, in part, a causal question, although, of course, the question of what the correct analysis is of "S knows that p" is not a
causal question.

4

Knowledge, Causality, and Justification

MARSHALL SWAIN

One of the pillars of empiricism is the thesis that the primary source of our knowledge about the world is experience. More precisely, to say that we have knowledge of the world means, in part, that our beliefs about the world are justified by some true body of evidence that we have gained through experience. A distinction is commonly made between knowledge about the world which is basic, and knowledge that is nonbasic. Roughly speaking, basic knowledge is knowledge that is not dependent, from the point of view of justification, on other knowledge, and nonbasic knowledge is dependent on other knowledge. Many empiricists have wanted to say that all nonbasic knowledge is ultimately dependent, from the point of view of justification, on basic knowledge. Whether this is so or not, surely some of our knowledge is dependent upon other things that we know. We surely do have some nonbasic knowledge. On the one hand, we sometimes have knowledge of specific events and states of affairs in the world. For example, we sometimes know that there is a table in front of us, that a particular house is on fire, or that one thing is larger than another. I shall call such knowledge *primary* nonbasic knowledge. On the other hand, we sometimes have knowledge about the world that is not knowledge of specific events and states of affairs. For example, we

Reprinted from *The Journal of Philosophy*, 69.11 (1972), 291–300, by kind permission of the editor.

A shorter version of this paper was read at the Western Division APA meetings in St. Louis, May 4, 1972. Thomas D. Paxson, Jr., commented.

know that all men are mortal, that some horses are not thoroughbreds, that it is possible that it will rain tomorrow, and that knowledge is hard to come by. I shall call this type of knowledge *secondary* nonbasic knowledge. Both of these types of nonbasic knowledge are genuinely empirical. We have such knowledge only if our justification consists of evidence we have gained through experience. Moreover, primary and secondary knowledge are related in an important way—secondary knowledge is dependent, from the point of view of justification, on primary knowledge. For any instance of secondary knowledge, our justification will always ultimately consist of propositions of which we have primary knowledge (that is, of propositions about specific events and states of affairs). Hence, a clear analysis of primary knowledge is of considerable importance for an adequate general theory of empirical knowledge. In this paper, I shall present an analysis of the concept of primary nonbasic knowledge.

I

Whether a man has nonbasic knowledge, primary or secondary, depends on the structure of his justification. In order for a man's justification to be sufficient for knowledge, it is necessary that his justification be strong enough to render the known proposition evident for him. However, even if a man's justification renders some true proposition evident for him, he may still fail to have knowledge because his justification is defective from the point of view of knowing. In his well-known article, "Is Justified True Belief Knowledge?"[1] Edmund Gettier has shown that a man may have an evident true belief but not have knowledge. In the cases Gettier provides it is clear that what prevents knowledge is some defect in the structure of the justification involved. One way of characterizing this defect is to say that, even though the justification involved is sufficiently strong to render the proposition evident, the justification is nevertheless *defeated* by some special counterevidence.[2] We

---

1. *Analysis,* 23.6 (1963), 121–123.
2. The most comprehensive attempt at formulating a defeasibility analysis is Keith Lehrer and Thomas Paxson, "Knowledge: Undefeated Justified True Belief" [Chapter 9 in this volume]. A similar approach was taken earlier by Er-

might, then, define what it is to have nonbasic knowledge in the following manner:

(K) S has nonbasic knowledge that p if and only if

(i) p is true;

(ii) S believes that p;

(iii) S's justification renders p evident for S;

(iv) There is no special counterevidence q such that q defeats S's justification.

I believe that the defeasibility approach, as exemplified in (K) is essentially correct as an analysis of nonbasic knowledge. The analysis as stated in (K) is not very illuminating, however, since we do not have any characterization of the conditions under which a man's justification renders some proposition evident for him, nor of the conditions under which "special" coun-terevidence defeats such a justification. I shall not attempt here to give a precise characterization of the notion of justification. Informally we can say that S's justification renders a proposi-tion h evident for him just in case there is some body of propo-sitions E such that each member of E is known by S and such that the expression 'h is evident for S' is epistemically derivable from the members of E in accordance with appropriate epis-temic rules.[3]

In what follows I shall attempt to clarify condition (iv) of def-inition (K). I shall argue that with respect to primary nonbasic knowledge the defeasibility condition can be replaced by condi-tions that refer to facts about the *causal connections* that obtain between a man's evidential beliefs and the events or states of af-fairs about which he has knowledge.[4]

---

nest Sosa in "The Analysis of 'Knowledge that P'," *Analysis*, 25.1 (1964), 1–8. Discussions relevant to this approach can be found in Gilbert Harman, "Induc-tion," in Marshall Swain, ed., *Induction, Acceptance, and Rational Belief* (Dor-drecht: Reidel, 1970), pp. 83–99; J. R. Kress, "Lehrer and Paxson on Nonbasic Knowledge," *Journal of Philosophy*, 68.3 (1971), 78–82; and Sosa, "Two Concep-tions of Knowledge," ibid., 67.3 (1970), 59–66.

3. For some clarification of the notion of epistemic rules see Roderick Chis-holm, *Theory of Knowledge* (Englewood Cliffs, N.J.: Prentice-Hall, 1966), chs. 2 and 3; and Sosa, "Propositional Knowledge," *Philosophical Studies*, 20.3 (1969), 33–43, and "Two Conceptions of Knowledge," *op. cit.*

4. The approach that I shall take is similar in some respects to the proposal made by Alvin Goldman in "A Causal Theory of Knowing" [Chapter 3 in this volume].

II

Let us begin by considering an example of the type proposed by Gettier.[5] Suppose that S is looking into a field, and in the distance he sees an object that has the shape of a sheep. In addition to seeing an object that looks like a sheep, he hears bleating noises, is aware of sheeplike odors in the air, and so forth. On the basis of this experience he comes to believe (truly) that he seems to see a sheep in the field. This evidence, in the context of the other relevant propositions that he believes, renders it evident for him that he does see a sheep in the field, and this latter evidence then renders it evident for him that there is a sheep in the field $(=p)$. Suppose that, on the basis of his evidence, he comes to believe that there is a sheep in the field. Thus, conditions (ii) and (iii) are satisfied. Now, suppose there is in fact a sheep in the field, but the sheep is in some far corner of the field where S cannot see. The object that S sees is a cement replica of a sheep placed in the field by the farmer for decorative purposes. Thus, S has a true belief that there is a sheep in the field, and his justification renders this evident for him. Yet S does not *know* that there is a sheep in the field, for his justification is defective. In the case at hand, there is some special counterevidence q, namely "S does not see a sheep, but rather a cement replica of one" such that q defeats the justification of p. Hence, condition (iv) of (K) is not satisfied—a desired result.

There is, however, also a causal condition that could replace (iv) in (K) and would yield exactly the same result. This condition can be formulated as follows:

(iva) The causal chain leading to S's belief in e contains the event or state of affairs referred to by p.

In this condition, and in the remainder of the paper, 'e' will refer to that portion of S's total body of evidence (E) that is immediately relevant to the justification of p. The remaining part of E may be labeled 'background evidence'. In the particular case we are considering, S's belief that e (he seems to see a

---

5. *Op. cit.* The particular example I am using here is derived from one used by Chisholm, *op. cit.*, p. 23.

sheep in the field) is caused by his seeing a cement replica of a sheep, and not by the presence of the real sheep that is in the field. The state of affairs referred to by p plays no part in the causal chain leading to his belief that e. Thus, given (iva), we also get the desired result that S does not know that there is a sheep in the field.

Conditions (iv) and (iva) thus accomplish the same thing with respect to this example. Moreover, these conditions point to the same aspect of the situation; that there is some special defeating counterevidence can be *explained* in terms of the lack of a causal chain connecting S's belief that e with the state of affairs referred to by p. As the examples that follow will illustrate, whether a man's justification is defeated or undefeated is in general a function of the characteristics of such causal chains, with respect to knowledge of specific events or states of affairs.

III

Even though the causal condition (iva) and the defeasibility condition (iv) yield the same results in the above example, the adoption of (iva) would not result in an adequate analysis of primary nonbasic knowledge. For we can sometimes be said to have knowledge of specific events and states of affairs even though our evidential beliefs are not caused by those events or states of affairs. An example will help to make this clear. Suppose that you have set about blasting a hole in the side of a mountain. You have planted TNT in the appropriate place, and have wired the TNT to a detonator box. The detonator box has a timer on it. Having carefully checked the wiring, the batteries, and the TNT, you set the timer, remove yourself to a safe distance, and wait for the explosion that you *know* will occur. Before the occurrence of the explosion, it seems clear that you can be said to know it will occur, and even when it will occur. However, the above conditions of knowledge, with condition (iva) replacing (iv), are not satisfied, because the event referred to by p (the future explosion) is not a member of the causal chain leading to your evidential beliefs. It could hardly be so, since it has not occurred yet.

Nevertheless, there is a clear causal *connection* between the chain of events that caused you to have your evidential beliefs and the occurrence of the explosion, namely, that the events that caused you to believe your evidence (for example, turning the switch on the detonator box) are among the events that caused the explosion to occur. We might, then, consider revising condition (iva) in the following way:

> (ivb) The causal chain leading to S's belief in e either (1) contains the event or state of affairs referred to by p, or (2) contains some other event that is also a member of the causal chain leading to the occurrence of the event referred to by p.

The replacement of (iva) by (ivb) will allow us to say that S knows that the explosion will occur in this example. The resulting conditions are similar in some respects to the causal theory of knowledge put forward by Alvin Goldman.[6] He distinguishes two basic types of causal chains that can enter into a cognitive situation, and these two basic types are reflected in parts (1) and (2) of condition (ivb). However, Brian Skyrms[7] has raised a telling example against analyses that involve clauses formulated in the manner of (ivb).

Suppose that, as you are walking down the street, you chance upon an unfortunate soul lying in the gutter with his head severed from his body. As a result of perceiving this unhappy scene you come to believe that the man is dead on the basis of your (evidential) belief that his head has been severed from his body, and your evidence surely renders this evident for you. The man is, of course, dead; thus, conditions (i), (ii), and (iii) of (K) are satisfied. Moreover, you can be said to *know* that the man is dead. But, condition (ivb) need not be satisfied. Skyrms invites us to imagine that, before your arrival on the scene, the

6. *Op. cit.* One major difference between Goldman's proposal and (ivb) is that Goldman wishes his analysis to cover all cases of empirical knowledge, including what I have called "secondary" nonbasic knowledge. But it is difficult to see how, for example, the fact that all men are mortal could enter into a causal chain. This leads Goldman to reckon logical connections as well as inferential connections among the "links" of causal chains—a proposal that seems at best counterintuitive. Gilbert Harman has discussed some of these problems in "Induction," *op. cit.*

7. *Brian Skyrms, "The Explication of 'X knows that p',"* Journal of Philosophy 64.12 (1967), 373–389.

following grisly sequence of events occurred. The man in the gutter died sometime before of a heart attack. After he had lain in the gutter for a time, a demented fiend came along and severed his head from his body. Then, some time after that, you came along. Even though you know that he is dead, condition (ivb) is not satisfied because there is no event in the causal chain leading to your belief that his head has been severed from his body which is also in fact causally responsible for his death, nor is his being dead causally responsible for your belief that his head has been severed from his body.

Notice, however, that in this example there is an event in the causal chain leading to your belief that his head has been severed from his body which is *causally relevant* to whether the man is dead or not, namely, the event of his head having been severed from his body. We can say that, had this unfortunate man not died of a heart attack and had his head been severed from his body *anyway,* then he would (still) be dead. The severing of his head from his body, even though it was not in fact the cause of his death, was causally *sufficient* for his death.

In order to allow for knowledge in situations of this sort we can replace (ivb) with the following condition.

> (ivc) The causal chain leading to S's belief that e either (1) contains the event or state of affairs referred to by p, or (2) contains some other event or state of affairs that is causally sufficient for the occurrence of the event referred to by p.

In this condition, the phrase 'causally sufficient for' is intended to include those situations where one event is *in fact* the cause of another.

This condition will rule out the problem raised by the latest example. However, there is a class of cases which are similar in structure to Skyrms's example and which do not appear to be overcome by condition (ivc). Consider the following.[8] Suppose that you attend a wedding ceremony in which your friends Bob and Sally appear to go through the motions of getting married. And suppose that the ceremony you witness is perfectly cor-

---

8. This example is similar to one that I proposed in "Skyrms on Non-Derivative Knowledge," *Noûs,* 3.2 (1969), 227–231.

rect, legal, etc., and is performed by the Bishop, who has previously married hundreds of people in exactly the same ceremony. However, unknown to you, Bob and Sally were secretly married two weeks earlier in a civil ceremony; they are only going through the present ceremony to please their parents. It seems clear, in this case, that you can be said to know that Bob and Sally are in a state of wedlock, even though they were not in fact married in the ceremony that you witnessed. Had they not been married previously, then they would have been married in the witnessed ceremony. However, the relationship between the events referred to in your evidence (the witnessing of the ceremony) and the fact that Bob and Sally are married does not appear to be one of *causal* sufficiency. It is odd, in my opinion, to say that performing a certain ceremony causes two people to be married, just as it would be odd to say that uttering the words 'I promise' causes you to be in a state of obligation. In general, performative acts and utterances can be said to *constitute* making a promise or getting married, but the making of the promise or the performing of the act does not cause one to be in a state of wedlock or promissory obligation. If so, condition (ivc) will not guarantee that you know that Bob and Sally are married.

However, if performance of a ceremony such as the one you have witnessed *constitutes* getting married (provided you are not already married), then it is plausible to say that S's evidence is, in the context presented, *logically* sufficient for the truth of the statement 'Bob and Sally are married'. Thus, we can replace (ivc) with the following:

(ivd) The causal chain leading to S's belief in e either (1) contains the event or state of affairs referred to by p, or (2) contains some other event or state of affairs that is, in the context of the evidence possessed by S, either causally or logically sufficient for the occurrence of the state of affairs referred to by p.

If (ivd) is added to the other conditions, then we shall be assured of knowledge in situations like the one under consideration.

These examples illustrate the claim that, in many cases,

whether a man has empirical knowledge is dependent upon the presence or lack of a causal (or sometimes logical) connection between events that he has experienced, and through which he has gained certain crucial evidential beliefs, and the event of which he is said to have knowledge. These cases are, however, cases in which the causal connections are quite straightforward, where there is nothing unusual or peculiar about the causal chains involved. As long as we stay with cases where the causal connections are more or less what we would expect, the conditions above will suffice to account for empirical knowledge of specific events and states of affairs.

Unfortunately, there are many cases in which the causal connections between one's evidential beliefs and the events of which one is claiming to have knowledge are very peculiar. Such cases provide ample evidence that the conditions presented thus far will not suffice. I shall consider two such cases, and then present a solution to the problems they pose.

Imagine the following variation on the first of the above examples. Suppose that S is looking into a field as before, and sees an object that he takes to be a sheep. And, as before, he hears bleating noises and is aware of sheeplike odors in the air. This time, however, he is seeing not a cement replica of a sheep, but rather a very cleverly engineered television image of a sheep. Someone, for reasons on which we need not speculate, has placed an invisible glass projection screen out in the field and with hidden projection equipment is projecting the image of a sheep on the screen. Moreover, the sheep whose image is being projected is off in some far corner of the field, where S cannot see. We may suppose that S's evidential beliefs, etc., are in this case just as they were in the previous example. Of course, in this case, as in the previous example, S does not know that there is a sheep in the field.

However, in this case the conditions for knowing postulated thus far are satisfied. It is clear that conditions (i), (ii), and (iii) are satisfied; unhappily, so is condition (ivd). For in the present case the state of affairs referred to by p (there being a sheep in the field) is a member of the causal chain leading to S's evidential belief that he seems to see a sheep in the field. This yields the result that S knows there is a sheep in the field, which is unsatisfactory.

Let us consider another situation that poses a similar problem. This example is a variation on the second of the above examples. Imagine, again, that you have set about blasting a hole in a mountainside, have checked the wiring, TNT, and other things as before. However, this time, shortly before you set the timer, one of the wires connected to the TNT becomes severed. When the timer sets off the detonator, the explosion occurs as expected, but only because of a stroke of luck. The battery in the detonator was just strong enough to cause the current to arc between the severed ends of the wire. We should conclude that you do not have knowledge that the explosion will occur, since the current passed through the wires only as a result of good fortune. And yet the conditions above will yield the conclusion that you do have knowledge. For the events that cause you to have your evidential beliefs are in fact the beginning of the (unusual) causal chain that leads to the explosion.

These examples show us that it will not do in an analysis of primary empirical knowledge simply to require that there be *some* causal connection between your evidential beliefs and the state of affairs of which you have knowledge. We need somehow to guarantee that the causal chains referred to in condition (ivd) are unproblematic; that is, we need to guarantee that the causal chains involved are roughly what one would expect them to be if one's evidence is to provide one with knowledge.

In the latest of our examples, as in those previously considered, the key to solving the problem lies in the fact that the justification provided by S's evidential belief e is defeated by some special counterevidence in just the manner specified in our original condition (iv). Moreover, this special counterevidence consists of certain statements that are true because of events in the unusual causal chains that have resulted in S's evidential beliefs. In the penultimate case, S's evidential belief is his belief that he seems to see a sheep in the field. This belief, in the context of his other relevant beliefs, justifies him in believing that there is a sheep in the field. However, this justification is defeated by the true counterevidence that the object seen by S is in fact a televised image of a sheep. This counterevidence, when conjoined with S's evidential beliefs, fails to justify the belief that there is a sheep in the field. Similarly, in the last case, S has evidential beliefs about the detonator box which completely justify him in believing that the explosion will occur (in the context of his other true beliefs). But this justification is defeated by the true counterevidence that the wires connecting the TNT and the detonator are broken.

One way, then, of guaranteeing that the causal chains referred to in (ivd) are not peculiar is to stipulate that those causal chains may not contain any events or series of events such that the occurrence of these events is a source of special defeating counterevidence. Since we have located the type of evidence that will have a defeating effect in these circumstances, we can drop the vague term 'special defeating counterevidence' and formulate our condition as follows:

(v) There is no true statement q such that q in conjunction with S's evidence E fails to render p evident for S and such that q is true because of events in the causal chains referred to in (ivd).

This completes the list of conditions that I shall offer as an analysis of our knowledge of specific events and states of affairs; the final set consists of (i), (ii), (iii), (ivd), and (v). The explicandum of (K) must, of course, be revised to read 'S has primary nonbasic knowledge that p'. I shall conclude my discussion of primary nonbasic knowledge by attempting to ward off some potential misunderstandings.

IV

First, the cases I have considered in illustration of my analysis have all been quite simple; that is, the causal connections and the epistemic relations involved have been relatively uncomplicated. The analysis will apply, however, in cases where these factors are considerably more complex. For example, in situations where we have knowledge of events that occurred either long ago or far away the causal chains connecting those events and the experienced events that provide us with our crucial evidence *e* will be enormously complicated. This complexity need not prevent us from having knowledge, however, unless the causal chains involved contain events that provide defeating evidence. Whether our justification is in fact defeated through evidence provided by such events is dependent upon the *strength* of our total evidential beliefs (that is, upon the weight and content of our evidence). In general, the strength our evidence must have in order to render some proposition evident without being defeated will be a function largely of the complexity of the causal chains involved. I cannot at this time offer any general analysis of the exact nature of this functional relationship.

Second, I have emphasized in some of the above cases that a man can fail to have knowledge because of some peculiarity in the causal chain connecting his crucial evidential beliefs with the event in question. This is, of course, not the only way in which a man can fail to have knowledge. One important type of example is that in which the causal chain involved is quite normal and uncomplicated and yet knowledge is lacking because one's justification is not strong enough. For example, when a ball is thrown onto a moving roulette wheel, a fairly straightforward causal chain is inaugurated which results in the ball landing on a specific number. We do not generally know which number it will land upon, however, because our evidence is simply inadequate to render evident any such belief. This point is closely related to the first. Just as it is true that causal complexity and evidential strength are functionally related, it is also true that knowledge of specific events and states of affairs is a function of both causal and epistemic considerations, and claims to knowledge can be vitiated by defects of either type.

Finally, although my analysis requires that certain causal connections obtain if one is to have knowledge, we must not suppose that one must *know* that such connections obtain. Indeed, one need not have any conception of causation whatever in order to qualify as cognizant in accordance with my conditions. To suppose otherwise would be to suppose that persons utterly lacking in "scientific" sophistication are incapable of empirical knowledge, and this is surely false. It may be that, in some ideal world, knowing implies knowing that you know, and perhaps knowing what it means to have knowledge, but in this real world of ours no such implication obtains.

5

Professor Swain's Account of Knowledge

THOMAS D. PAXSON, JR.

The Gettier type counter-examples to justified-true-belief analyses of knowledge employ cases in which the evidence, completely justifying some person S in believing that *p,* is not causally connected with the state of affairs that *p.* In these cases it is causally possible, *ceteris paribus,* that S possess the evidence that he or she does possess, but that not *p.* Given this possibility, the argument runs, S cannot be said to know that *p.* To stipulate that there must be a causal connection between one's being justified in believing that *p* and *p*'s being the case, then, ought to block the counter-examples. Armstrong, Barker, Goldman, and Unger are among those who have attempted causal analyses of knowledge in line with this strategy.[1] However, such attempted analyses have generally proven to be too weak also, but in a different way. Counter-examples have employed anomalies in causal chains and non-rational, non-epistemic causes of belief. Professor Swain's article 'Knowledge, Causality, and Justification' is particularly interesting in that it

Reprinted from *Philosophical Studies,* 25 (1974), 57–61, by kind permission of the author and publisher. Copyright © 1974 by D. Reidel Publishing Company, Dordrecht, Holland.

1. D. M. Armstrong, 'Max Deutscher and Perception', *Australasian Journal of Philosophy,* 41 (1963), 247–249; and *A Materialist Theory of Mind,* 1968, Ch. 9 (London: Humanities Press); John Barker, 'Knowledge and Causation' presented to the Southern Society for Philosophy and Psychology, April 2, 1972; Alvin Goldman, 'A Causal Theory of Knowing' [Chapter 3 in this volume]; Peter Unger, 'An Analysis of Factual Knowledge', *Journal of Philosophy,* 65 (1968), 157–170.

presents an analysis combining justified true belief and causal connection as conditions of knowledge, each designed to complement the other.[2] What I shall consider in the following is whether Swain's analysis is successful in employing the two sorts of analyses to correct the weaknesses of one another and, if not, whether his analysis can be modified to give a satisfactory analysis:

Swain's analysis is as follows:

S has primary non-basic knowledge that p iff

    (i) p is true;

    (ii) S believes that p;

    (iii) S's justification e renders p evident for S;

    (iv) the causal chain leading to S's belief in e either

        (a) contains the event or state of affairs referred to by p

or   (b) contains some other event or state of affairs which is, in the context of the evidence possessed by S, either causally or logically sufficient for the occurrence of the state of affairs referred to by p;

    (v) there is no true statement q such that q in conjunction with S's total evidence, E, fails to render p evident for S and such that q is true because of events in the causal chains referred to in (iv).

I

Causal analyses of knowledge have usually been found to be too weak rather than too strong, and therefore we ought, perhaps, to begin by asking whether there are cases satisfying Prof. Swain's five conditions which we would not admit to be cases of primary non-basic knowledge. Surprisingly, his own example about blasting a hole in a mountainside seems to provide just such a counter-example. Suppose Smith plants TNT in a hole in the side of a mountain, wires it to a detonator with a timing mechanism, sets the timer for thirty minutes, and withdraws to watch the spectacle. Suppose also that the explosion occurs on schedule.

2. [Chapter 4 in this volume.]

Smith believes that p, the TNT will explode at t_{30}, 'p' is true, and his justification renders p evident for Smith. Conditions (i) through (iii) are satisfied. Further, the causal chain leading to S's belief in e contains some other event or state of affairs which is, in the context of the evidence possessed by S, causally sufficient for the occurrence of the state of affairs referred to by 'p'. However, unknown to Smith one of the two wires running to the TNT breaks, is gnawed through or whatever (and here I let you construct the example to your liking) and the two ends fall either (1) into a small pool of brine or (2) onto a small piece of steel or anything else that you wish so that the circuit is fortuitously completed once again. Now, there is a true statement, q, such that q in conjunction with S's evidence E fails to render p evident for Smith, namely that one of the wires which Smith used to complete the circuit connecting the timer, detonator, and TNT, breaks at some time t_{30-r}. However, it is false that q is true *because of* events in the causal chain leading to Smith's belief in his evidence or *because of* events in the causal chain which, in the context of the evidence possessed by Smith, renders some event or state in the first chain causally sufficient for the explosion at t_{30}. Thus conditions (iv) and (v) are satisfied even though, as we would all agree, Smith does not know that the explosion will occur at t_{30}. His evidence has been defeated by q. No q can be found, I think, that will defeat e according to (v).

Let us examine the fourth and fifth conditions carefully. In the fourth, the clause 'in the context of the evidence possessed by S' seems to introduce the following conditions: The logical chains are restricted to those whose premises are contained in S's total evidence, E, or are logical consequences of propositions contained in E. The causal chains referred to in (iv) are restricted to those which lead to S's belief in e and which either contain the state of affairs referred to by 'p' or some other event which, in conjunction with the states of affairs that are evidence for S, is causally sufficient for, though perhaps not causally responsible for, the state of affairs p. But the causal sufficiency must be subject to temporal *ceteris paribus* limitations. In our example, e contains a state of affairs causally sufficient at t_0 for p at t_{30}. But this causal sufficiency obtains subject to *ceteris paribus* conditions since the temporal gap precludes direct causal sufficiency. No states of affairs which would be included in the evidence possessed by an ordinary mortal would be fully causally sufficient for the explosion thirty minutes hence. Furthermore, to require complete causal sufficiency without a *ceteris paribus* clause would be too severe. Smith's evidence need not, surely, causally preclude some rodent's gnawing through the wire at t_{30-r} or its being severed by a tree felled in a lightning storm, and so forth. Thus a *ceteris paribus* reading of causal sufficiency in the case of future events is necessary for (iv) in order that ordinary cases of knowledge of future events are not ruled out. But this interpretation of (iv) raises difficulties for (v) since it requires the defeating statement to be true as a result of state of affairs which may not turn out to be causally insufficient for p given the state of the universe. The remedy which best accords with Swain's intentions may be to substitute the following condition for (v):

(v′) There is no true statement 'q' such that 'q' in conjunction with S's evidence E fails to render 'p' evident for S and such that either 'q' is true because of events in the causal chains referred to in (iv) or because of events in the causal chain actually yielding p.

It seems to me that we can count the breaking of the wire as an element in the causal chain which led to the occurrence of p.

II

Having strengthened the analysis of knowledge, we must now consider whether it is not too strong. The following counter-example seems to show that it is. Suppose that Robinson, seeing a farmer pointing into a field, looks, and sees something distinctly sheep-like, hears bleating noises, and so forth. As a result he comes to believe correctly that there is a sheep in the field right there, that what he sees is in fact a sheep. Robinson has justified true belief and the causal chain leading to his belief that he seems to see something distinctly sheep-like, seems to hear bleating noises, etc. contains the sheep that he sees and hears. Conditions (i) through (iv) are satisfied. But

now suppose that the farmer has been chatting by the fence
with a city-slicker and is enjoying himself at the other's expense. "Now that ram," he was saying, as he pointed to the mo-
tionless sheep, "is a carefully contrived wooden replica covered
with wool and containing an electronic bleater. Aye, the ewes
eat more and thus produce more wool now that I've installed
my artificial ram." Robinson, we may suppose, is too far away
from the farmer to overhear the conversation, but not so far
from the sheep that he could confuse it with any other familiar
farm animal.

What are we to say of this case? It seems to me that we would
say of Robinson that he knows that there is a sheep in the field
despite the farmer's joshing with the poor city slicker down the
road. Yet by teasing the city slicker the farmer is, on Swain's
analysis, preventing poor Robinson from knowing. After all,
the farmer's assertion that the sheep is an artificial ram is part
of the state of affairs causally responsible for Robinson's seeing
the sheep. The farmer's pointing causes Robinson to see the
sheep and was an integral part of the testimony whereby he
sought to mislead the city slicker. Let 'q' be "the farmer said, as
he pointed, 'Now that ram is a carefully contrived wooden replica. . . .' " This 'q' is true because of the causal chain leading to
Robinson's belief. Furthermore, q in conjunction with Robinson's total evidence, E, lacking as it does any information
regarding animal husbandry, would fail to render it evident to
Robinson that there is a sheep in the field. Swain's analysis,
then is too strong.

Swain had claimed that "with respect to primary non-basic
knowledge the defeasibility condition can be replaced by conditions that refer to facts about the *causal connections* that obtain
between a man's evidential beliefs and the events or states of affairs about which he has knowledge."[3] But we have seen that
the importation of causal conditions into an essentially justified
true belief analysis has failed to save it. It seems clear that it is
often causally possible that there be some misleading counterevidence that obtains because of the causal chains leading to S's

3. Ibid., p. 89; italics are Swain's.

belief in the evidence or those leading to the state of affairs to be known. If this is so, causal connections between the state of affairs designated by the defeating statement 'q' and either S's belief in e or the state of affairs p, no matter how carefully restricted, are not sufficient to guarantee the appropriate epistemic relation.

An earlier version of this paper was presented as a commentary on Swain's address at the APA convention, Western Division, held in St. Louis May 4–6, 1972. I wish to thank him and my colleague Kenneth Collier for discussions that have influenced the final formulation of the paper.

6

On Swain's Causal
Analysis of Knowledge

JOSEPH T. TOLLIVER

In his paper "Knowledge, Causality, and Justification,"[1] Marshall Swain presents an analysis of the concept of primary, nonbasic knowledge. It is essentially a causal account under which knowledge is gained only if certain causal relations obtain between a person's evidential beliefs and the event or state of affairs known.

(K) S has nonbasic knowledge that p if and only if:

(i) p is true;

(ii) S believes that p;

(iii) S's justification renders p evident for S;

(ivd) The causal chain C leading to S's belief in evidence e (1) contains the event or state of affairs referred to by p, or (2) contains some other event or state of affairs that is, in the context of the evidence possessed by S, either causally or logically sufficient for the occurrence of the state of affairs referred to by p.

(v) There is no true statement q such that q in conjunction with S's evidence fails to render p evident for S and such that q is true because of events in the causal chains referred to in (ivd).

Swain intends clause (v) of the foregoing definition to specify the conditions under which there might be 'special defeating

1. [Chapter 4 in the present volume.]

counterevidence.' Thus (v) functions as a defeasibility component in analysis (K). Swain states that

> We need to guarantee that the causal chains referred to in condition (ivd) are unproblematic, that is, we need to guarantee that the causal chains involved are roughly what one would expect them to be if one's evidence is to provide one with knowledge. [P. 96]

I agree that if analysis (K) is to be adequate, then something of this sort is necessary; we do not want the causal chains involved to generate defeating counterevidence. However, Swain also says that these causal chains are the only source of possible defeating counterevidence, and it is with this claim that I wish to take issue.

Suppose S is a hunter of some experience who comes across some tracks on the ground. He is very good at discriminating tracks, and realizes that he has seen tracks like these before. Every time he has followed tracks like these, and discovered an animal at the end of them, that animal has been a deer. Let all this past observational evidence be part of S's background evidence b. In virtue of b, S correctly believes that

(h) One hundred percent of times when S has observed tracks like these have been times when S subsequently found deer at the end of them.

On the basis of b, h, and his current observations, S believes that

(e) These tracks are deer tracks.

He follows the tracks and they eventually disappear into a thicket behind which he hears some noise. On the basis of these observations and e, S concludes that

(p) The animal behind the thicket made these tracks and it is a deer.

Now suppose p is true but that, unknown to S, there exists a strange species of animal that are extremely shy, and with such keen senses that, even though they exist in numbers far exceeding the number of deer, they have avoided human detection. But their most remarkable feature is that they leave tracks that are indistinguishable from deer tracks. Suppose there are enough of these animals that

(*r*) Ninety-nine percent of tracks that look like the ones observed by *S* are in fact left by those strange animals.

In these circumstances, we have a case where *p* is true, *S* believes that *p*, *S*'s evidence renders *p* evident for *S*, the causal
chain *C* leading to *S*'s belief that *e* contains some other state of
affairs (the deer's having made the tracks leading into the
thicket) that is, in the context of the evidence possessed by *S*,
causally sufficient for the occurrence of the state of affairs referred to by 'p', and there is no true statement *q* such that *q* in
conjunction with *S*'s evidence fails to render *p* evident for *S* and
such that *q* is true *because of events in the causal chains* referred to
in (ivd).

But *S* does not know that *p*. *S* is clearly justified in believing
that a deer left the tracks, for he is warranted in making a singular predictive inference of the form:

(I) One hundred percent of observed *A*'s are *B*'s (and
many *A*'s have been observed); therefore, this *A* is a *B*.

However, (T) is true.

(T) Ninety-nine percent of *A*'s are not *B*'s.

And we can reasonably say that a person does not know by
means of an inference of type (I) if a sentence of the form of
(T) is true. Thus, we must regard analysis (K) as inadequate,
since *r* does seem to constitute defeating counterevidence to *S*'s
justification but *r* is not true because of events in the causal
chains involved, as required by clause (v).

7

Some Revisions of "Knowledge, Causality, and Justification"

MARSHALL SWAIN

Paxson, Tolliver, and others have provided convincing arguments to show that the causal theory of knowing suggested in
my paper "Knowledge, Causality, and Justification" (hereafter,
KCJ)[1] is inadequate. However, I believe that the basic intuition
behind the view suggested in that paper is correct, and in this
discussion I shall provide a sketch of an improved version of
the theory.

The theory of primary knowledge presented in KCJ attempts
to combine causal and defeasibility considerations, the idea
being that whether a person's justification is defeasible or indefeasible is dependent upon considerations concerning the
causal chains involved in the ancestry of his evidential beliefs.
Since the writing of that paper, a good deal of work has been
done on defeasibility.[2] This work has revealed an important
distinction, one that is exemplified in the examples discussed in
KCJ and by Paxson and Tolliver. When a person has evidence
which justifies a belief, there will almost always be some additional evidence that the person does not possess. Sometimes
fragments of this unpossessed evidence are such that if the person came to have that fragment as additional evidence, then his
belief would no longer be justified. Let us call any fragment of

1. My paper, as well as the critical discussions by Paxson and Tolliver, are
reprinted in the present volume. Because of space considerations, I shall in this
discussion assume familiarity with these papers.
2. See the essays in this volume by Annis, Sosa, Lehrer and Paxson, Harman,
and Swain.

unpossessed evidence which has this characteristic *undermining counterevidence*. There has been a great temptation to suppose that if there is *any* undermining counterevidence with respect to a particular justification, then that justification is defeasible. However, one of Paxson's examples shows that this is a mistake. Consider his example of a person who sees a sheep in a field. In that example, as Paxson correctly notes, S does have knowledge but there is some undermining counterevidence which S does not possess (having to do with what the farmer is saying to the city slicker). This evidence, even though undermining, does not defeat S's justification. But, in the example provided by Tolliver, there is undermining counterevidence (his proposition (T)) which also renders the justification defeasible. Both of these are counterexamples to my conditions in KCJ; hence, those conditions fail to adequately take this important distinction between defeating and merely undermining counterevidence into account.

In order to rectify this situation, I shall introduce yet another distinction, namely, the distinction between a *defective* and a *nondefective causal chain* with respect to a particular justification. Intuitively, a defective causal chain is one that provides undermining counterevidence, while a nondefective causal chain is one that does not provide such counterevidence. Hence, when I say that a causal chain is defective, I mean that it is defective insofar as it plays a role in some epistemic situation; I do not mean that it is defective from the causal point of view. What I want to do is replace conditions (ivd) and (v) of the theory suggested in KCJ with the following single condition (iv*). In presenting this condition, I shall adopt the following notation: capital letters '*P*,' '*L*,' and so forth shall be names for the specific events or states of affairs referred to by '*p*,' '*l*,' etc. '*BSe*' shall be used to designate the state of affairs of S's believing that *e*.

> (iv*) Where '*e*' designates the portion of S's total evidence *E* that is immediately relevant to the justification of *p*, *either*
>
> (A) there is a *nondefective* causal chain from *P* to *BSe;*
>
> or   (B) there is some event or state of affairs *Q* such that

> (i) there is a *nondefective* causal chain from Q to *BSe;* and
>
> (ii) there is a *nondefective* causal chain from Q to *P;*

or (C) there is some event or state of affairs H such that

> (i) there is a *nondefective* causal chain from H to *BSe;* and
>
> (ii) H is a *nondefective* pseudo-overdeterminant of *P.*

I shall now provide an account of the defective/nondefective causal chain distinction, as well as an account of the notion of a nondefective pseudo-overdeterminant introduced in (ii) of clause (C).

As a beginning, let us consider one of the examples in KCJ. In this example, S sees a televised image of a sheep in the field projected onto a cleverly disguised television screen. The sheep whose image is being projected is actually in the field, but S cannot directly see the sheep. S comes to believe correctly that there is a sheep in the field, but does not know that there is a sheep there. This is one of the kinds of situations covered by clause (A) of (iv*). It is a situation in which S's justification is defeasible, and hence I want to say that the causal chain from the sheep's being in the field to S's believing his evidence e is defective. What does the defect consist in? There is an event in the causal chain from the sheep to *BSe* such that S would be justified in believing that this event did *not* occur. For an example, consider the event of there being a televised image of a sheep out there in the field. Is this sufficient generally for a causal chain to be defective with respect to a person's justification? We can see that it is not by considering the following example.

Suppose that the president of Harvard writes a letter to an old friend. The president has just recently learned how to type, and so he types the letter himself, rather than having his secretary type it for him. His friend receives the letter, reads it, and comes to know all sorts of things about the president of Harvard as a result. However, the president's friend does not know

that he has just learned how to type, and assumes justifiably
that the letter was typed by the secretary. Then, there is an
event in the causal chain leading to his having his evidence *e*
such that his believing that this event did not occur is justified.
But, there is nothing defective about this causal chain with respect to his justification and his justification is indefeasible. It is,
moreover, clear why this causal chain is not defective; the fact
that the president's friend justifiably believes that the president
did not type the letter is not at all *essential* to his justifiably believing what is said in the letter. If we take this into account,
then I believe that the defectiveness of the causal chain in our
televised sheep example can be accounted for. In the following
condition, I shall use 'X' and 'Y' as variables for event-names,
and a solid arrow '→' to designate a causal chain. So, 'X→Y'
will take names of causal chains from X to Y.

   (D) Where S justifiably believes that p on the basis of[3]
       evidence *e*, causal chain $X→Y$ is defective with respect
       to this justification *if* (a) there is some event or state of
       affairs U in $X→Y$ such that S would be justified in be-
       lieving that U did not occur and (b) it is essential to S's
       justifiably believing that p on the basis of the evidence
       e that S would be justified in believing that U did not
       occur.

In the televised sheep example, then, (D) gives us the result
that the causal chain from the sheep to *BSe* is defective with respect to S's believing that there is a sheep in the field. Let us
compare this result with Paxson's sheep-in-the-field example
mentioned earlier. In that example, S does directly see a sheep,
and knows that there is a sheep in the field (no television, etc.).
The causal chain from the sheep to *BSe* is nondefective. However, as Paxson constructs the example, there *is* a defective
causal chain involved, namely, the causal chain which initially
resulted in S's looking at the sheep. In *that* causal chain, the
event of the farmer's saying to the city slicker that the object is

---

3. The phrase 'on the basis of' used here does not appear in my earlier
paper. I would revise my earlier conditions (i)–(iii) to guarantee that S's belief
that p is *based upon* his evidential belief that *e*. Otherwise, a person's belief that p
might be held for irrational reasons having nothing to do with his evidence.

a mechanical ram provides undermining counterevidence. But this fact no longer presents a problem for my conditions, for the causal chain in question is not part of the causal chain referred to in condition (a) of (iv*), and thus the fact that it is defective with respect to S's justification is irrelevant to whether S knows.

Let me turn now to the example suggested by Tolliver, in which a hunter comes to believe correctly that there is a deer in the thicket on the basis of perceiving deerlike tracks which lead therein. This situation is one of those handled by clause (B) of (iv*). We may let Q be the event of the deer walking into the thicket. To handle this example, we must go beyond the conditions for defectiveness presented in (D), for those conditions will not give us the result that the hunter does *not* know. The causal chain from Q to BSe in that example is defective. But in what respect is it defective? There is no specific event or state of affairs in $Q \rightarrow BSe$ which renders it defective in accordance with (D), and even if we take the entire chain to be a single event, it is not defective in accordance with (D). It is defective, I believe, in the following sense. If we consider all of the actual and possible situations which are relevantly similar to the situation being considered, we can see that within that class of cases the proportion of cases in which a causal chain relevantly similar to $Q \rightarrow BSe$ would obtain is exceedingly small. There are different ways in which a person relevantly similar to the hunter could be caused to have evidence relevantly similar to the hunter's; the two most salient ones are cases in which a deer has made the tracks and cases in which one of Tolliver's clever little animals makes the tracks, but there are others as well. If you were to pick at random one from among this total class of cases (actual and possible), it is *unlikely* that you would pick a case in which a deer has made the tracks. Hence, even though $Q \rightarrow BSe$ did occur, and even though the hunter's *actual sample* from among the total class of relevant cases has always consisted of similar cases, I shall say that it is *objectively unlikely* that $Q \rightarrow BSe$ should have occurred. These considerations will provide us with some of what we need to characterize the defectiveness of $Q \rightarrow BSe$ in this example. Let me note in passing that exactly similar considerations will apply concerning the causal chain $Q \rightarrow P$.

Generally, when a causal chain occurs there will be possible alternative causal chains with respect to some specific events or state of affairs in that causal chain. More precisely,

(CA) C^* is an alternative to causal chain $X \rightarrow Y$ with respect to Y if and only if:

(i) C^* is exactly like $X \rightarrow Y$ except that for some event Z, or set of events $Z_1, Z_2, \ldots, Z_n$, which are in $X \rightarrow Y$, there is instead some event Z^* or set of events $Z^*_1, Z^*_2, \ldots, Z^*_m$ in C^*, and

(ii) had C^* occurred instead of $X \rightarrow Y$, then Y would still have occurred, and would have been an effect in C^*.

In our example, had the animal that caused the tracks been one of Tolliver's clever little animals *rather* than a deer, then there would have occurred an alternative to the actual causal chain $Q \rightarrow BSe$ that resulted in the hunter's having his evidence. The idea that I want to develop is that *one* way in which a causal chain can be defective with respect to a justification is that there be some alternative of this sort to that causal chain. I shall call alternatives 'of this sort' *significant* alternatives.

Not every alternative to a causal chain is a significant one with respect to a particular justified belief. For example, in the case described above where the president of Harvard writes a letter to a friend, the actual causal chain from P to BSe contains the event of the president typing the letter himself. One alternative to that causal chain is the causal chain in which the president has his secretary type the letter instead. But the mere fact that there *is* this alternative does not render $P \rightarrow BSe$ defective in that case. Another, and more important consideration is this: in almost *any* situation in which there is a causal chain to BSe it will be *possible* that the person is hallucinating instead. But, to hallucinate would merely mean that there is some causal chain occurring which is an alternative to the actual causal chain which results in BSe. Surely we do not want the *mere* possibility of hallucination to provide a significant alternative to a causal chain, thereby rendering that causal chain defective.[4] With these things in mind, I propose the following as a partial explication of the notion of a significant alternative:

(S) C^* is a significant alternative to $X \to Y$ with respect to S justifiably believing that p on the basis of evidence e if:

    (a) it is objectively likely that C^* should have occurred rather than $X \to Y$; and

    (b) if C^* had occurred instead of $X \to Y$, then there would have been an event or state of affairs U in C^* such that S would not be justified in believing that p if S were justified in believing that U occurred.

I suggest the conditions in (S) as a *partial* explication of significance because it is not clear that the objective likelihood of an alternative is *necessary* for significance.

Consider the following example, which is based on one suggested by Goldman.[5] Henry is driving through the countryside, and comes across a barn, which he sees from the front. He comes to believe that there is a barn there on the basis of his evidence, e, and there is a straightforward causal chain from the barn to his belief that e. Now suppose that someone has, unknown to Henry, constructed a number of barn facsimiles in the area. These are papier-mâché constructions which look like the barns from the front, but consist of only that facade, propped up by sticks behind. If Henry had seen one of these facsimiles from the front, he would have come to believe that it is a barn and his perceptual evidence would have been similar to e. Hence, there are alternatives to the causal chain $P \to BSe$. Are they significant alternatives? Does Henry know that there is a barn? Goldman suggests that Henry does *not* know, and I confess that my intuitions are on Goldman's side here. But, since there are many more barns around than there are facsim-

---

4. Of course, if a person's situation is such that it is *likely* that an hallucination is occurring (drugs, fever, etc.), then we may want to call the possibility of hallucination a *significant* alternative.

5. This example is found in Goldman's "Discrimination and Perceptual Knowledge," Chapter 8 in the present volume.

iles, it seems clear that it is not objectively likely that one of the alternatives to $P \rightarrow BSe$ should have obtained. If you were to pick at random from among the relevantly similar cases, actual and possible, it is unlikely that you would pick a case in which the person in question was looking at a barn facsimile.

This example strongly suggests that the conditions of (S) are not necessary for significance of an alternative causal chain. However, I do not know of any considerations that show them not to be sufficient. Unfortunately, I do not have any very interesting suggestions to make at this time concerning the correct way to complete my account of significance. I shall simply have to admit that this is an unsolved (major) problem for the theory that I am defending.

With the notion of significance only partially explicated, I propose the following as a full explication of the defectiveness of a causal chain:

(D*) Where S justifiably believes that p on the basis of e, causal chain $X \rightarrow Y$ is defective with respect to this justification if and only if:
Either (I) (a) and (b) as in (D);
Or (II) there is some significant alternative C* to $X \rightarrow Y$ with respect to S justifiably believing that p on the basis of e.

In the hunter example, then, we get the result that $Q \rightarrow BSe$ is a defective causal chain by clause (II) of (D*). There is an alternative to $Q \rightarrow BSe$ (namely, that one of Tolliver's little animals causes the tracks) which is objectively likely, and which is such that if that alternative causal chain had occurred, then there would have been a state of affairs U (namely, the presence of the animal) such that the hunter would not have been justified in believing that p had he been justified in believing that this state of affairs obtained. Similarly, in the barn example just considered, the causal chain $P \rightarrow BSe$ is defective because of the significant alternatives involved, although those alternatives do not qualify as significant in accordance with (S). These examples are of the types covered by clauses (A) and (B) of (iv*), and in both of them we get the appropriate result by (iv*) that S does not know that p. I must now turn to a consideration of the situation covered by clause (C) of (iv*), for that clause contains the as yet unexplicated notion of a nondefective pseudo-overdeterminant.

Situations of the type covered by clause (C) of (4*) are those in which there is an event H which is a member of a causal chain resulting in S's having his evidence e such that H is a pseudo-overdeterminant, although not an actual cause of p. What is a pseudo-overdeterminant? There are two kinds of causal overdetermination.[6] In any case of overdetermination, two or more events or states of affairs are related to a single effect in such a way that, *ceterus paribus*, if either of them alone had occurred, then the effect in question would still have occurred. When each of the overdetermining events is appropriately called *a cause* of the effect in question, we have *genuine* overdetermination. But, when one of the overdeterminants is *not* properly called a cause, then it is a *pseudo-overdeterminant*. In KCJ I give two examples of pseudo-overdetermination; one is the severed head case originally suggested by Skyrms, and the other is the marriage example, wherein two people go through a wedding ceremony even though they are already married. Situations involving genuine overdetermination are handled by clauses (A) and (B) of (iv*).

As in the situations covered by clauses (A) and (B), the causal chain beginning with H and ending with BSe must be nondefective. But at this point our considerations become somewhat complicated because of the fact that there is no *actual* causal chain occurring between H and P. To say that H is a pseudo-overdeterminant of P is to say that H *would* have been a cause of P had the causal chain that actually results in P not occurred. Had the causal chain that actually results in P not occurred, then, as a matter of fact, some other specific causal chain involving H would have occurred. Let us call this latter chain '$H*$.' Then, $H*$ is an alternative to $H \rightarrow P$ in the sense

---

6. I have discussed causal overdetermination at some length in my paper "A Counterfactual Analysis of Event-Causation" (forthcoming, *Philosophical Studies*). For a very useful discussion of this notion, see Louis E. Loeb, "Causal Theories and Causal Overdetermination," *Journal of Philosophy*, 71 (1974), 525–544.

defined earlier. Generally, when one event X is a pseudo-over-determinant of another event Y, there will be a nonactual causal chain from X to Y which is an alternative to the actual causal chain $W \rightarrow Y$, where W is an actual cause of Y. I shall designate this nonactual causal chain with a dotted arrow, as in '$X \dashrightarrow Y$.' Then, I shall introduce the following definition of defectiveness for pseudo-overdeterminants:

> (DPO) For any event or states of affairs X and Y, X is a defective pseudo-overdeterminant of Y with respect to S's justifiably believing that p on the basis of e iff:
> If $X \dashrightarrow Y$ had occurred, then the causal chain $X \rightarrow Y$ would have been defective with respect to S's justifiably believing that p on the basis of e.

Let me now provide an example to show why we must require, in cases of the sort covered by clause (C), that H be a nondefective pseudo-overdeterminant of P.

Suppose that I observe Mr. Dunfor taking a clearly fatal dose of poison. On the basis of this I come to believe that he will soon die. Moreover, he does soon die, but unknown to me this is a result of his being run over by a truck. Normally we would say that I know he will die, even though he will not die of poisoning; had he not been run over by the truck, he surely would have died as a result of taking the poison. However, it might be that the taking of the poison is a pseudo-overdeterminant of his death in a way that has nothing to do with the fact that it is a *poison*. Thus, we might suppose that had Dunfor not been run over by a truck, then the poison would have been a cause of his death, but not by poisoning him. Suppose that an unusual chemical reaction between the poison and something Dunfor had eaten for lunch would have nullified the effect of the poison and also would have caused Dunfor to go insane and commit suicide had he not been run over by the truck. Now if *that* is what actually would have happened, then I cannot be said to know that Dunfor will die, since my being justified in believing this depends essentially on my observation that it is a fatal dose of *poison* that Dunfor has imbibed. Even though the imbibing of this poison is in fact a pseudo-overdeterminant of death, my belief is defectively justified. Letting P be the event of Dunfor's taking the poison, and H the event of his death, we can see that P is a defective pseudo-overdeterminant of H in accordance with (DPO). Given (C) of (4*), we get the correct result concerning knowledge.

This concludes my presentation of the revisions to KCJ. The resulting theory of primary knowledge is considerably more complicated than that originally envisioned. I hope that the few examples considered will sufficiently illustrate the merits of the theory, even though the complexity of the theory clearly calls for more illustrative discussion. There are other very interesting examples to consider, and further problems as well. One problem concerns *basic* knowledge, and how it can be accounted for on this causal approach. Another concerns the extension of this view to cover instances of secondary knowledge. Unfortunately, I do not have space here to enter into a discussion of these further matters.[7]

7. The views sketched in this paper are set forth at great length, with more examples, and a discussion of basic and secondary knowledge in my paper "Reasons, Causes, and Knowledge."

8

Discrimination and
Perceptual Knowledge

ALVIN I. GOLDMAN

This paper presents a partial analysis of perceptual knowledge, an analysis that will, I hope, lay a foundation for a general theory of knowing. Like an earlier theory I proposed,[1] the envisaged theory would seek to explicate the concept of knowledge by reference to the causal processes that produce (or sustain) belief. Unlike the earlier theory, however, it would abandon the requirement that a knower's belief that p be causally connected with the fact, or state of affairs, that p.

What kinds of causal processes or mechanisms must be responsible for a belief if that belief is to count as knowledge? They must be mechanisms that are, in an appropriate sense, "reliable." Roughly, a cognitive mechanism or process is reliable if it not only produces true beliefs in actual situations, but would produce true beliefs, or at least inhibit false beliefs, in relevant counterfactual situations. The theory of knowledge I envisage, then, would contain an important counterfactual component.

To be reliable, a cognitive mechanism must enable a person to *discriminate* or *differentiate* between incompatible states of affairs. It must operate in such a way that incompatible states of the world would generate different cognitive responses. Perceptual mechanisms illustrate this clearly. A perceptual mechanism is reliable to the extent that contrary features of the envi-

Reprinted from *The Journal of Philosophy*, 73.20 (1976), 771–791, by kind permission of the author and editor.
1. "A Causal Theory of Knowing" [Chapter 3 in this volume].

ronment (e.g., an object's being red, versus its being yellow) would produce contrary perceptual states of the organism, which would, in turn, produce suitably different beliefs about the environment. Another belief-governing mechanism is a reasoning mechanism, which, given a set of antecedent beliefs, generates or inhibits various new beliefs. A reasoning mechanism is reliable to the extent that its functional procedures would generate new true beliefs from antecedents true beliefs.

My emphasis on discrimination accords with a sense of the verb 'know' that has been neglected by philosophers. The O.E.D. lists one (early) sense of 'know' as *"to distinguish* (one thing) *from* (another)," as in "I know a hawk from a handsaw" (*Hamlet*) and "We'll teach him to know Turtles from Jayes" (*Merry Wives of Windsor*). Although it no longer has great currency, this sense still survives in such expressions as "I don't know him from Adam," "He doesn't know right from left," and other phrases that readily come to mind. I suspect that this construction is historically important and can be used to shed light on constructions in which 'know' takes propositional objects. I suggest that a person is said to know that *p* just in case he *distinguishes* or *discriminates* the truth of *p* from relevant alternatives.

A knowledge attribution imputes to someone the discrimination of a given state of affairs from possible alternatives, but not necessarily all logically possible alternatives. In forming beliefs about the world, we do not normally consider all logical possibilities. And in deciding whether someone knows that *p* (its truth being assumed), we do not ordinarily require him to discriminate *p* from all logically possible alternatives. Which alternatives are, or ought to be considered, is a question I shall not fully resolve in this paper, but some new perspectives will be examined. I take up this topic in section i.

I

Consider the following example. Henry is driving in the countryside with his son. For the boy's edification Henry identifies various objects on the landscape as they come into view. "That's a cow," says Henry, "That's a tractor," "That's a silo,"

"That's a barn," etc. Henry has no doubt about the identity of these objects; in particular, he has no doubt that the last-mentioned object is a barn, which indeed it is. Each of the identified objects has features characteristic of its type. Moreover, each object is fully in view, Henry has excellent eyesight, and he has enough time to look at them reasonably carefully, since there is little traffic to distract him.

Given this information, would we say that Henry *knows* that the object is a barn? Most of us would have little hesitation in saying this, so long as we were not in a certain philosophical frame of mind. Contrast our inclination here with the inclination we would have if we were given some additional information. Suppose we are told that, unknown to Henry, the district he has just entered is full of papier-mâché facsimiles of barns. These facsimiles look from the road exactly like barns, but are really just façades, without back walls or interiors, quite incapable of being used as barns. They are so cleverly constructed that travelers invariably mistake them for barns. Having just entered the district, Henry has not encountered any facsimiles; the object he sees is a genuine barn. But if the object on that site were a facsimile, Henry would mistake it for a barn. Given this new information, we would be strongly inclined to withdraw the claim that Henry *knows* the object is a barn. How is this change in our assessment to be explained?

Note first that the traditional justified-true-belief account of knowledge is of no help in explaining this change. In both cases Henry truly believes (indeed, is certain) that the object is a barn. Moreover, Henry's "justification" or "evidence" for the proposition that the object is a barn is the same in both cases. Thus, Henry should either know in both cases or not know in both cases. The presence of facsimiles in the district should make no difference to whether or not he knows.

My old causal analysis cannot handle the problem either. Henry's belief that the object is a barn is caused by the presence of the barn; indeed, the causal process is a perceptual one. Nonetheless, we are not prepared to say, in the second version, that Henry knows.

One analysis of propositional knowledge that might handle the problem is Peter Unger's non-accidentality analysis.[2] According to this theory, S knows that p if and only if it is not at all accidental that S is right about its being the case that p. In the initial description of the example, this requirement appears to be satisfied; so we say that Henry knows. When informed about the facsimiles, however, we see that it is accidental that Henry is right about its being a barn. So we withdraw our knowledge attribution. The "non-accidentality" analysis is not very satisfying, however, for the notion of "non-accidentality" itself needs explication. Pending explication, it isn't clear whether it correctly handles all cases.

Another approach to knowledge that might handle our problem is the "indefeasibility" approach.[3] On this view, S knows that p only if S's true belief is justified and this justification is not defeated. In an unrestricted form, an indefeasibility theory would say that S's justification j for believing that p is defeated if and only if there is some true proposition q such that the conjunction of q and j does not justify S in believing that p. In slightly different terms, S's justification j is defeated just in case p would no longer be evident for S if q were evident for S. This would handle the barn example, presumably, because the true proposition that there are barn facsimiles in the district is such that, if it were evident for Henry, then it would no longer be evident for him that the object he sees is a barn.

The trouble with the indefeasibility approach is that it is too strong, at least in its unrestricted form. On the foregoing account of "defeat," as Gilbert Harman shows,[4] it will (almost) always be possible to find a true proposition that defeats S's justification. Hence, S will never (or seldom) know. What is

2. "An Analysis of Factual Knowledge," *Journal of Philosophy*, 65.6 (1968), 157–170. Reprinted in M. Roth and L. Galis, eds., *Knowing* (New York: Random House, 1970), 113–130.

3. See, for example, Keith Lehrer and Thomas Paxson, Jr., "Knowledge: Undefeated Justified True Belief" [Chapter 9 in this volume], and Peter D. Klein, "A Proposed Definition of Propositional Knowledge," *Journal of Philosophy*, 68.16 (1971), 471–482.

4. *Thought* (Princeton: Princeton University Press, 1973), p. 152.

needed is an appropriate restriction on the notion of "defeat," but I am not aware of an appropriate restriction that has been formulated thus far.

The approach to the problem I shall recommend is slightly different. Admittedly, this approach will raise problems analogous to those of the indefeasibility theory, problems which will not be fully resolved here. Nevertheless, I believe this approach is fundamentally on the right track.

What, then, is my proposed treatment of the barn example? A person knows that *p*, I suggest, only if the actual state of affairs in which *p* is true is *distinguishable* or *discriminable* by him from a relevant possible state of affairs in which *p* is false. If there is a relevant possible state of affairs in which *p* is false and which is indistinguishable by him from the actual state of affairs, then he fails to know that *p*. In the original description of the barn case there is no hint of any relevant possible state of affairs in which the object in question is not a barn but is indistinguishable (by Henry) from the actual state of affairs. Hence, we are initially inclined to say that Henry knows. The information about the facsimiles, however, introduces such a relevant state of affairs. Given that the district Henry has entered is full of barn facsimiles, there is a relevant alternative hypothesis about the object, viz., that it is a facsimile. Since, by assumption, a state of affairs in which such a hypothesis holds is indistinguishable by Henry from the actual state of affairs (from his vantage point on the road), this hypothesis is not "ruled out" or "precluded" by the factors that prompt Henry's belief. So, once apprised of the facsimiles in the district, we are inclined to deny that Henry knows.

Let us be clear about the bearing of the facsimiles on the case. The presence of the facsimiles does not "create" the possibility that the object Henry sees is a facsimile. Even if there were no facsimiles in the district, it would be possible that the object on that site is a facsmile. What the presence of the facsimiles does is make this possibility *relevant;* or it makes us *consider* it relevant.

The qualifier 'relevant' plays an important role in my view. If knowledge required the elimination of all logically possible alternatives, there would be no knowledge (at least of contingent truths). If only *relevant* alternatives need to be precluded, however, the scope of knowledge could be substantial. This depends, of course, on which alternatives are relevant.

The issue at hand is directly pertinent to the dispute—at least one dispute—between skeptics and their opponents. In challenging a claim to knowledge (or certainty), a typical move of the skeptic is to adduce an unusual alternative hypothesis that the putative knower is unable to preclude: an alternative compatible with his "data." In the skeptical stage of his argument, Descartes says that he is unable to preclude the hypothesis that, instead of being seated by the fire, he is asleep in his bed and dreaming, or the hypothesis that an evil and powerful demon is making it appear to him as if he is seated by the fire. Similarly, Bertrand Russell points out that, given any claim about the past, we can adduce the "skeptical hypothesis" that the world sprang into being five minutes ago, exactly as it then was, with a population that "remembered" a wholly unreal past.[5]

One reply open to the skeptic's opponent is that these skeptical hypotheses are just "idle" hypotheses, and that a person can know a proposition even if there are "idle" alternatives he cannot preclude. The problem, of course, is to specify when an alternative is "idle" and when it is "serious" ("relevant"). Consider Henry once again. Should we say that the possibility of a facsimile before him is a serious or relevant possibility if there are no facsimiles in Henry's district, but only in Sweden? Or if a single such facsimile once existed in Sweden, but none exist now?

There are two views one might take on this general problem. The first view is that there is a "correct" answer, in any given situation, as to which alternatives are relevant. Given a complete specification of Henry's situation, a unique set of relevant alternatives is determined: either a set to which the facsimile alternative belongs or one to which it doesn't belong. According to this view, the semantic content of 'know' contains (implicit)

---

5. *The Analysis of Mind* (London: George Allen and Unwin, 1921), pp. 159–160.

rules that map any putative knower's circumstances into a set of relevant alternatives. An analysis of 'know' is incomplete unless it specifies these rules. The correct specification will favor either the skeptic or the skeptic's opponent.

The second view denies that a putative knower's circumstances uniquely determine a set of relevant alternatives. At any rate, it denies that the semantic content of 'know' contains rules that map a set of circumstances into a single set of relevant alternatives. According to this second view, the verb 'know' is simply not so semantically determinate.

The second view need not deny that there are *regularities* governing the alternative hypotheses a speaker (i.e., an attributer or denier of knowledge) thinks of, and deems relevant. But these regularities are not part of the semantic content of 'know'. The putative knower's circumstances do not *mandate* a unique selection of alternatives; but psychological regularities govern which set of alternatives are in fact selected. In terms of these regularities (together with the semantic content of 'know'), we can explain the observed use of the term.

It is clear that some of these regularities pertain to the (description of the) putative knower's circumstances. One regularity might be that the more *likely* it is, given the circumstances, that a particular alternative would obtain (rather than the actual state of affairs), the more probable it is that a speaker will regard this alternative as relevant. Or, the more *similar* the situation in which the alternative obtains to the actual situation, the more probable it is that a speaker will regard this alternative as relevant. It is not only the circumstances of the putative knower's situation, however, that influence the choice of alternatives. The speaker's own linguistic and psychological context are also important. If the speaker is in a class where Descartes's evil demon has just been discussed, or Russell's five-minute-old-world hypothesis, he may think of alternatives he would not otherwise think of and will perhaps treat them seriously. This sort of regularity is entirely ignored by the first view.

What I am calling the "second" view might have two variants. The first variant can be imbedded in Robert Stalnaker's framework for pragmatics.[6] In this framework, a proposition is a function from possible words into truth values; the determinants of a proposition are a sentence and a (linguistic) context. An important contextual element is what the utterer of a sentence presupposes, or takes for granted. According to the first variant of the second view, a sentence of the form 'S knows that p' does not determine a unique proposition. Rather, a proposition is determined by such a sentence together with the speaker's presuppositions concerning the relevant alternatives.[7] Skeptics and nonskeptics might make different presuppositions (both presuppositions being "legitimate"), and, if so, they are simply asserting or denying different propositions.

One trouble with this variant is its apparent implication that, if a speaker utters a knowledge sentence without presupposing a fully determinate set of alternatives, he does not assert or deny any proposition. That seems too strong. A second variant of the second view, then, is that sentences of the form 'S knows that p' express vague or indeterminate propositions (if they express "propositions" at all), which can, but need not, be made more determinate by full specification of the alternatives. A person who *assents* to a knowledge sentence says that S discriminates the truth of p from relevant alternatives; but he may not have a distinct set of alternatives in mind. (Similarly, according to Paul Ziff, a person who says something is "good" says that it answers to *certain* interests;[8] but he may not have a distinct set of interests in mind.) Someone who *denies* a knowledge sentence more commonly has one or more alternatives in mind as relevant, because his denial may stem from a particular alternative S cannot rule out. But even the denier of a knowledge sentence need not have a full set of relevant alternatives in mind.

I am attracted by the second view under discussion, especially its second variant. In the remainder of the paper, how-

6. "Pragmatics," in D. Davidson and G. Harman, eds., *Semantics of Natural Language* (Dordrecht: Reidel, 1972).
7. Something like this is suggested by Fred Dretske, in "Epistemic Operators," *Journal of Philosophy,* 67.24 (1970), 1022.
8. That 'good' means *answers to certain interests* is claimed by Ziff in *Semantic Analysis* (Ithaca, N.Y.: Cornell University Press, 1960), chap. 6.

ever, I shall be officially neutral. In other words, I shall not try
to settle the question of whether the semantic content of 'know'
contains rules that map the putative knower's situation into a
unique set of relevant alternatives. I leave open the question of
whether there is a "correct" set of relevant alternatives, and if
so, what it is. To this extent, I also leave open the question of
whether skeptics or their opponents are "right." In defending
my analysis of 'perceptually knows', however, I shall have to
discuss particular examples. In treating these examples I shall
assume some (psychological) regularities concerning the selection of alternatives. Among these regularities is the fact that
speakers do not *ordinarily* think of "radical" alternatives, but are
caused to think of such alternatives, and take them seriously, if
the putative knower's circumstances call attention to them.
Since I assume that radical or unusual alternatives are not *ordinarily* entertained or taken seriously, I may appear to side with
the opponents of skepticism. My official analysis, however, is
neutral on the issue of skepticism.

II

I turn now to the analysis of 'perceptually knows'. Suppose
that Sam spots Judy on the street and correctly identifies her as
Judy, i.e., believes she is Judy. Suppose further that Judy has
an identical twin, Trudy, and the possibility of the person's
being Trudy (rather than Judy) is a relevant alternative. Under
what circumstances would we say that Sam *knows* it is Judy?

If Sam regularly identifies Judy as Judy and Trudy as Trudy,
he apparently has some (visual) way of discriminating between
them (though he may not know how he does it, i.e., what cues
he uses). If he does have a way of discriminating between them,
which he uses on the occasion in question, we would say that he
knows it is judy. But if Sam frequently mistakes Judy for Trudy,
and Trudy for Judy, he presumably does not have a way of discriminating between them. For example, he may not have sufficiently distinct (visual) memory "schemata" of Judy and
Trudy. So that, on a particular occasion, sensory stimulation
from either Judy *or* Trudy would elicit a Judy-identification

from him. If he happens to be right that it is Judy, this is just accidental. He doesn't *know* it is Judy.

The crucial question in assessing a knowledge attribution, then, appears to be the truth value of a counterfactual (or set of counterfactuals). Where Sam correctly identifies Judy as Judy, the crucial counterfactual is: "If the person before Sam were Trudy (rather than Judy), Sam would believe her to be Judy." If this counterfactual is true, Sam doesn't know it is Judy. If this counterfactual is false (and all other counterfactuals involving relevant alternatives are also false), then Sam may know it is Judy.

This suggests the following analysis of (noninferential) perceptual knowledge.

S (noninferentially) *perceptually knows that p* if and only if

    (1) S (noninferentially) perceptually believes that p,

    (2) p is true, and

    (3) there is no relevant contrary q of p such that, if q were true (rather than p), then S would (still) believe that p.

Restricting attention to relevant possibilities, these conditions assert in effect that the only situation in which S would believe that p is a situation in which p is true. In other words, S's believing that p is sufficient for the truth of p. This is essentially the analysis of noninferential knowledge proposed by D. M. Armstrong in *A Materialist Theory of the Mind* (though without any restriction to "relevant" alternatives), and refined and expanded in *Belief, Truth, and Knowledge*.[9]

This analysis is too restrictive. Suppose Oscar is standing in an open field containing Dack the daschund. Oscar sees Dack and (noninferentially) forms a belief in (P):

(P) The object over there is a dog.

Now suppose that (Q):

(Q) The object over there is a wolf.

is a relevant alternative to (P) (because wolves are frequenters

9. *A Materialist Theory of the Mind* (New York: Humanities Press, 1968), pp. 189 ff., and *Belief, Truth and Knowledge* (Cambridge: Cambridge University Press, 1973), chaps. 12 and 13.

of this field). Further suppose that Oscar has a tendency to mistake wolves for dogs (he confuses them with malamutes, or
German shepherds). Then if the object Oscar saw were Wiley
the wolf, rather than Dack the dachshund, Oscar would (still)
believe (P). This means that Oscar fails to satisfy the proposed
analysis with respect to (P), since (3) is violated. But surely it is
wrong to deny—for the indicated reasons—that Oscar *knows* (P)
to be true. The mere fact that he would erroneously take a wolf
to be a dog hardly shows that he doesn't know a *dachshund* to be
a dog! Similarly, if someone looks at a huge redwood and correctly believes it to be a tree, he is not disqualified from knowing it to be a tree merely because there is a very small plant he
would wrongly believe to be a tree, i.e., a bonsai tree.

The moral can be formulated as follows. If Oscar believes
that a dog is present because of a certain way he is "appeared
to," then this true belief fails to be knowledge if there is an alternative situation in which a non-dog produces the same belief
by means of the same, or a very similar, appearance. But the
wolf situation is not such an alternative: although it would produce in him the same belief, it would not be by means of the
same (or a similar) appearance. An alternative that disqualifies
a true perceptual equivalent" of the actual state of affairs.[10] A
perceptual equivalent of an actual state of affairs is a possible state
of affairs that would produce the same, or a sufficiently similar,
perceptual experience.

The relation of perceptual equivalence must obviously be
relativized to *persons* (or organisms). The presence of Judy and
the presence of Trudy might be perceptual equivalents for
Sam, but not for the twins' own mother (to whom the twins
look quite diferent). Similarly, perceptual equivalence must be
relativized to *times,* since perceptual discriminative capacities
can be refined or enhanced with training or experience, and
can deteriorate with age or disease.

How shall we specify alternative states of affairs that are can-

10. My notion of a perceptual equivalent corresponds to Hintikka's notion of
a "perceptual alternative." See "On the Logic of Perception," in N. S. Care and
R. H. Grimm, eds., *Perception and Personal Identity* (Cleveland: The Press of Case
Western Reserve University, 1969).

didates for being perceptual equivalents? First, we should specify the *object* involved. (I assume for simplicity that only one object is in question.) As the Judy-Trudy case shows, the object in
the alternative state of affairs need not be identical with the
actual object. Sometimes, indeed, we may wish to allow non-ac-
tual possible objects. Otherwise our framework will be unable
in principle to accommodate some of the skeptic's favorite alternatives, e.g., those involving demons. If the reader's ontological sensibility is offended by talk of possible objects, I invite
him to replace such talk with any preferred substitute.

Some alternative states of affairs involve the same object but
different properties. Where the actual state of affairs involves a
certain ball painted blue, an alternative might be chosen involving the same ball painted green. Thus, specification of an alternative requires not only an object, but properties of the object
(at the time in question). These should include not only the
property in the belief under scrutiny, or one of its contraries,
but other properties as well, since the property in the belief (or
one of its contraries) might not be sufficiently determinate to
indicate what the resultant percept would be like. For full gen-
erality, let us choose a *maximal set of* (nonrelational) *properties*.
This is a set that would exhaustively characterize an object (at a
single time) in some possible world.[11]

An object plus a maximal set of (nonrelational) properties
still does not fully specify a perceptual alternative. Also needed
are relations between the object and the perceiver, plus conditions of the environment. One relation that can affect the resultant percept is *distance*. Another relational factor is *relative orientation,* both of object vis-à-vis perceiver and perceiver vis-à-vis
object. The nature of the percept depends, for example, on
which side of the object faces the perceiver, and on how the
perceiver's bodily organs are oriented, or situated, vis-à-vis the

11. I have in mind here purely qualitative properties. Properties like *being
identical with Judy* would be given by the selected object. If the set of qualitative
properties (at a given time) implied which object it is that has these properties,
then specification of the object would be redundant, and we could represent
states of affairs by ordered pairs of maximal sets of (qualitative) properties and
DOE relations. Since this is problematic, however, I include specification of the
object as well as the set of (qualitative) properties.

object. Thirdly, the percept is affected by the current state of the *environment,* e.g., the illumination, the presence or absence of intervening objects, and the direction and velocity of the wind.

To cover all such elements, I introduce the notion of a *distance-orientation-environment* relation, for short, a *DOE relation.* Each such relation is a conjunction of relations or properties concerning distance, orientation, and environmental conditions. One DOE relation is expressed by the predicate 'x is 20 feet from y, the front side of y is facing x, the eyes of x are open and focused in y's direction, no opaque object is interposed between x and y, and y is in moonlight.'

Since the health of sensory organs can affect percepts, it might be argued that this should be included in these relations, thereby opening the condition of these organs to counterfactualization. For simplicity I neglect this complication. This does not mean that I don't regard the condition of sensory organs as open to counterfactualization. I merely omit explicit incorporation of this factor into our exposition.

We can now give more precision to our treatment of perceptual equivalents. Perceptual states of affairs will be specified by ordered triples, each consisting of (1) an object, (2) a maximal set of nonrelational properties, and (3) a DOE relation. If S perceives object b at t and if b has all the properties in a maximal set J and bears DOE relation R to S at t, then the actual state of affairs pertaining to this perceptual episode is represented by the ordered triple $\langle b,J,R \rangle$. An alternative state of affairs is represented by an ordered triple $\langle c,K,R^* \rangle$, which may (but need not) differ from $\langle b,J,R \rangle$ with respect to one or more of its elements.

Under what conditions is an alternative $\langle c,K,R^* \rangle$ a perceptual equivalent of $\langle b,J,R \rangle$ for person S at time t? I said that a perceptual equivalent is a state of affairs that would produce "the same, or a very similar" perceptual experience. That is not very committal. Must a perceptual equivalent produce exactly the same percept? Given our intended use of perceptual equivalence in the analysis of perceptual knowledge, the answer is clearly No. Suppose that a Trudy-produced percept would be qualitatively distinct from Sam's Judy-produced percept, but similar enough for Sam to mistake Trudy for Judy. This is sufficient grounds for saying that Sam fails to have knowledge. Qualitative identity of percepts, then, is too strong a requirement for perceptual equivalence.

How should the requirement be weakened? We must not weaken it too much, for the wolf alternative might then be a perceptual equivalent of the dachshund state of affairs. This would have the unwanted consequence that Oscar doesn't know Dack to be a dog.

The solution I propose is this. If the percept produced by the alternative state of affairs would not differ from the actual percept in any respect that is causally relevant to S's belief, this alternative situation is a perceptual equivalent for S of the actual situation. Suppose that a Trudy-produced percept would differ from Sam's Judy-produced percept to the extent of having a different eyebrow configuration. (A difference in shape between Judy's and Trudy's eyebrows does not ensure that Sam's percepts would "register" this difference. I assume, however, that the eyebrow difference would be registered in Sam's percepts.) But suppose that Sam's visual "concept" of Judy does not include a feature that reflects this contrast. His Judy-concept includes an "eyebrow feature" only in the sense that the absence of eyebrows would inhibit a Judy-classification. It does not include a more determinate eyebrow feature, though: Sam hasn't learned to associate Judy with distinctively shaped eyebrows. Hence, the distinctive "eyebrow shape" of his actual (Judy-produced) percept is not one of the percept-features that is causally responsible for his believing Judy to be present. Assuming that a Trudy-produced percept would not differ from his actual percept in any *other* causally relevant way, the hypothetical Trudy-situation is a perceptual equivalent of the actual Judy-situation.

Consider now the dachshund wolf case. The hypothetical percept produced by a wolf would differ from Oscar's actual percept of the dachshund in respects that *are* causally relevant

to Oscar's judgment that a dog is present. Let me elaborate.
There are various kinds of objects, rather different in shape,
size, color, and texture, that would be classified by Oscar as a
dog. He has a number of visual "schemata," we might say, each
with a distinctive set of features, such that any percept that
"matches" or "fits" one of these schemata would elicit a "dog"
classification. (I think of a schema not as a "template," but as a
set of more-or-less abstract—though iconic—features.[12]) Now,
although a dachshund and a wolf would each produce a dog-
belief in Oscar, the percepts produced by these respective stimuli would differ in respects that are causally relevant to Oscar's
forming a dog-belief. Since Oscar's dachshund-schema includes
such features as having an elongated, sausagelike shape, a
smallish size, and droopy ears, these features of the percept are
all causally relevant, when a dachshund is present, to Oscar's
believing that a dog is present. Since a hypothetical wolf-
produced percept would differ in these respects from Oscar's
dachshund-produced percept, the hypothetical wolf state of affairs is not a perceptual equivalent of the dachshund state of
affairs for Oscar.

The foregoing approach requires us to relativize perceptual
equivalence once again, this time to the belief in question, or
the property believed to be exemplified. The Trudy-situation is
a perceptual equivalent for Sam of the Judy-situation *relative to
the property of being* (identical with) *Judy*. The wolf-situation is
not a perceptual equivalent for Oscar of the dachshund-situa-
tion *relative to the property of being a dog*.

I now propose the following definition of perceptual equivalence:

If object b has the maximal set of properties J and is in
DOE relation R to S at t, if S has some percept P at t that is
perceptually caused by b's having J and being in R to S at t,
and if P noninferentially causes S to believe (or sustains S
in believing) of object b that it has property F, then
$\langle c,K,R^* \rangle$ is a perceptual equivalent of $\langle b,J,R \rangle$ *for S at t relative to property F* if and only if

12. For a discussion of iconic schemata, see Michael I. Posner, *Cognition: An
Introduction* (Glenview, Ill.: Scott, Foresman, 1974), chap. 3.

(1) if at t object c had K and were in R^* to S, then this would perceptually cause S to have some percept P^* at t,

(2) P^* would cause S noninferentially to believe (or sustain S in believing) of object c that it has F, and

(3) P^* would not differ from P in any respect that is causally relevant to S's F-belief.

Since I shall analyze the *de re, relational*, or *transparent* sense of 'perceptually knows', I shall want to employ, in my analysis, the *de re* sense of 'believe'. This is why such phrases as 'believe . . . of object b' occur in the definition of perceptual equivalence. For present purposes, I take for granted the notion of (perceptual) *de re* belief. I assume, however, that the object *of which* a person perceptually believes a property to hold is the object he perceives, i.e., the object that "perceptually causes" the percept that elicits the belief. The notion of *perceptual causation* is another notion I take for granted. A person's percept is obviously caused by many objects (or events), not all of which the person is said to perceive. One problem for the theory of perception is to explicate the notion of perceptual causation, that is, to explain which of the causes of a percept a person is said to perceive. I set this problem aside here.[13] A third notion I take for granted is the notion of a (noninferential) *perceptual belief,* or perceptual "taking." Not all beliefs that are noninferentially caused by a percept can be considered perceptual "takings"; "indirectly" caused beliefs would not be so considered. But I make no attempt to delineate the requisite causal relation.

Several other comments on the definition of perceptual equivalence are in order. Notice that the definition is silent on whether J or K contains property F, i.e., whether F is exemplified in either the actual or the alternative states of affairs. The relativization to F (in the definiendum) implies that an F-*belief* is produced in both situations, not that F is exemplified (in either or both situations). In applying the definition to cases of putative knowledge, we shall focus on cases where F belongs to J (so S's belief is true in the actual situation) but does not

---

13. I take this problem up in "Perceptual Objects," forthcoming in *Synthese.*

belong to K (so S's belief is false in the counterfactual situation). But the definition of perceptual equivalence is silent on these matters.

Though the definition does not say so, I assume it is possible for object c to have all properties in K, and possible for c to be in R^* to S while having all properties in K. I do not want condition 1 to be vacuously true, simply by having an impossible antecedent.

It might seem as if the antecedent of (1) should include a further conjunct, expressing the supposition that object b is absent. This might seem necessary to handle cases in which, if c were in R^* to S, but b remained in its actual relation R to S, then b would "block" S's access to c. (For example, b might be an orange balloon floating over the horizon, and c might be the moon.) This can be handled by the definition as it stands, by construing R^*, where necessary, as including the absence of object b from the perceptual scene. (One cannot *in general* hypothesize that b is absent, for we want to allow object c to be identical with b.)

The definition implies that there is no temporal gap between each object's having its indicated properties and DOE relation and the occurrence of the corresponding percept. This simplification is introduced because no general requirement can be laid down about how long it takes for the stimulus energy to reach the perceiver. The intervals in the actual and alternative states may differ because the stimuli might be at different distances from the perceiver.

III

It is time to turn to the analysis of perceptual knowledge, for which the definition of perceptual equivalence paves the way. I restrict my attention to perceptual knowledge of the possession, by physical objects, of nonrelational properties. I also restrict the analysis to *noninferential* perceptual knowledge. This frees me from the complex issues introduced by inference, which require separate treatment.

It may be contended that all perceptual judgment is based on inference and, hence, that the proposed restriction reduces the scope of the analysis to nil. Two replies are in order. First, although cognitive psychology establishes that percepts are affected by cognitive factors, such as "expectancies," it is by no means evident that these causal processes should be construed as inferences. Second, even if we were to grant that there is in fact no noninferential perceptual belief, it would still be of epistemological importance to determine whether noninferential perceptual knowledge of the physical world is conceptually possible. This could be explored by considering merely possible cases of noninferential perceptual belief, and seeing whether, under suitable conditions, such belief would count as knowledge.

With these points in mind, we may propose the following (tentative) analysis:

At t S noninferentially perceptually knows of object b that it has property F if and only if
  (1) for some maximal set of nonrelational properties J and some DOE relation R, object b has (all the members of) J at t and is in R to S at t,
  (2) F belongs to J,
  (3) (A) b's having J and being in R to S at t perceptually causes S at t to have some percept P,[14]

14. Should (3A) be construed as implying that *every* property in J is a (perceptual) cause of P? No. Many of b's properties are exemplified in its interior, or at its backside. These are not causally relevant, at least in visual perception. (3A) must therefore be construed as saying that P is (perceptually) caused by b's having (jointly) *all* the members of J, and leaving open which, among these members, are individually causally relevant. It follows, however, that (3A) does not require that *b's-having-F*, in particular, is a (perceptual) cause of P, and this omission might be regarded as objectionable. "Surely," it will be argued, "S perceptually knows b to have F only if *b's-having-F* (perceptually) causes the percept." The reason I omit this requirement is the following. Suppose F is the property of being a dog. Can we say that *b's-being-a-dog* is a cause of certain light waves' being reflected? This is very dubious. It is the molecular properties of the surface of the animal that are causally responsible for this transmission of light, and hence for the percept.

One might say that even if the percept needn't be (perceptually) caused by *b's-having-F*, it must at least be caused by micro-structural properties of b that *ensure* *b's-having-F*. As the dog example again illustrates, however, this is too strong. The surface properties of the dog that reflect the light waves do not *ensure* that the object is a dog, either logically or nomologically. Something could

(B) P noninferentially causes S at T to believe (or sustains S in believing) of object b that it has property F, and

(C) there is no alternative state of affairs $\langle c,K,R^* \rangle$ such that

　　(i) $\langle c,K,R^* \rangle$ is a relevant perceptual equivalent of $\langle b,J,R \rangle$ for S at t relative to property F, and

　　(ii) F does not belong to K.

Conditions 1 and 2 jointly entail the truth condition for knowledge: S knows b to have F (at t) only if b does have F (at t). Condition 3B contains the belief condition for knowledge, restricted, of course, to (noninferential) perceptual belief. The main work of the conditions is done by 3C. It requires that there be no relevant alternative that is (i) a perceptual equivalent to the actual state of affairs relative to property F, and (ii) a state of afairs in which the appropriate object lacks F (and hence S's F-belief is false).

How does this analysis relate to my theme of a "reliable discriminative mechanism"? A perceptual cognizer may be thought of as a two-part mechanism. The first part constructs percepts (a special class of internal states) from receptor stimulation. The second part operates on percepts to produce beliefs. Now, in order for the conditions of the analysans to be satisfied, each part of the mechanism must be sufficiently discriminating, or "finely tuned." If the first part is not sufficiently discriminating, patterns of receptor stimulation from quite different sources would result in the same (or very similar) percepts, percepts that would generate the same beliefs. If the second part is not sufficiently discriminating, then even if different percepts are constructed by the first part, the same beliefs will be generated by the second part. To be sure, even an undiscriminating bipartite mechanism may produce a belief

---

have that surface (on one side) and still have a non-dog interior and backside. The problem should be solved, I think, by reliance on whether there are relevant perceptual equivalents. If there are no relevant perceptual equivalents in which K excludes being a dog, then the properties of the actual object that are causally responsible for the percept suffice to yield knowledge. We need not require either that the percept be (perceptually) caused by b's-having-F, nor by any subset of J that "ensures" b's-having-F.

that, luckily, is true; but there will be other, counterfactual, situations in which such a belief would be false. In this sense, such a mechanism is unreliable. What our analysis says is that S has perceptual knowledge if and only if not only does his perceptual mechanism produce true belief, but there are no relevant counterfactual situations in which the same belief would be produced via an equivalent percept and in which the belief would be false.

Let me now illustrate how the analysis is to be applied to the barn example, where there are facsimiles in Henry's district. Let S = Henry, b = the barn Henry actually sees, and F = the property of being a barn. Conditions 1 through 3B are met by letting J take as its value the set of all nonrelational properties actually possessed by the barn at t, R take as its value the actual DOE relation the barn bears to Henry at t, and P take as its value the actual (visual) percept caused by the barn. Condition 3C is violated, however. There *is* a relevant triple that meets subclauses (i) and (ii), i.e., the triple where c = a suitable barn facsimile, K = a suitable set of properties (excluding, of course, the property of being a barn), and R^* = approximately the same DOE relation as the actual one. Thus, Henry does not (noninferentially) perceptually *know* of the barn that it has the property of being a barn.

In the dachshund-wolf case, S = Oscar, b = Dack the dachshund, and F = being a dog. The first several conditions are again met. Is 3C met as well? There is a relevant alternative state of affairs in which Wiley the wolf is believed by Oscar to be a dog, but lacks that property. This state of affairs doesn't violate 3C, however, since it isn't a *perceptual equivalent* of the actual situation relative to being a dog. So this alternative doesn't disqualify Oscar from knowing Dack to be a dog.

Is there another alternative that *is* a perceptual equivalent of the actual situation (relative to being a dog)? We can imagine a DOE relation in which fancy devices between Wiley and Oscar distort the light coming from Wiley and produce in Oscar a Dack-like visual percept. The question here, however, is whether this perceptual equivalent is *relevant*. Relevance is determined not only by the hypothetical object and its properties, but also by the DOE relation. Since the indicated DOE relation is highly unusual, this will count (at least for a nonskeptic) against the alternative's being relevant and against its disqualifying Oscar from knowing.[15]

The following "Gettierized" example, suggested by Marshall Swain, might appear to present difficulties. In a dark room there is a candle several yards ahead of S which S sees and believes to be ahead of him. But he sees the candle only indirectly, via a system of mirrors (of which he is unaware) that make it appear as if he were seeing it directly.[16] We would surely deny that S knows the candle to be ahead of him. (This case does not really fit our intended analysandum, since the believed property F is relational. This detail can be ignored, however.) Why? If we say, with Harman, that all perceptual belief is based on inference, we can maintain that S infers that the candle is ahead of him from the premise that he sees whatever he sees *directly*. This premise being false, S's knowing is disqualified on familiar grounds.

My theory suggests another explanation, which makes no unnecessary appeal to inference. We deny that S knows, I suggest, becuase the system of mirrors draws our attention to a perceptual equivalent in which the candle is *not* ahead of S, i.e., a state

15. It is the "unusualness" of the DOE relation that inclines us not to count the alternative as relevant; it is not the mere fact that the DOE relation differs from the actual one. In general, our analysis allows knowledge to be defeated or disqualified by alternative situations in which the DOE relation differs from the DOE relation in the actual state of affairs. Our analysis differs in this respect from Fred Dretske's analysis in "Conclusive Reasons" [Chapter 1 in this volume]. Dretske's analysis, which ours resembles on a number of points, considers only those counterfactual situations in which everything that is "logically and causally independent of the state of affairs expressed by P" (p. 50) is the same as in the actual situation. (P is the content of S's belief.) This implies that the actual DOE relation cannot be counterfactualized, but must be held fixed. (It may also imply—depending on what P is—that one cannot counterfactualize the perceived object nor the full set of properties J.) This unduly narrows the class of admissible alternatives. Many *relevant* alternatives, that do disqualify knowledge, involve DOE relations that differ from the actual DOE relation.

16. Harman has a similar case, in *Thought*, pp. 22–23. In that case, however, S does not see the candle; it is not a cause of his percept. Given our causal requirement for perceptual knowledge, that case is easily handled.

of affairs where the candle is behind S but reflected in a system of mirrors so that it appears to be ahead of him. Since the actual state of affairs involves a system of reflecting mirrors, we are impelled to count this alternative as relevant, and hence to deny that S knows.

Even in ordinary cases, of course, where S sees a candle directly, the possibility of reflecting mirrors constitutes a perceptual equivalent. In the ordinary case, however, we would not count this as relevant; we would not regard it as a "serious", possibility. The Gettierized case impels us to take it seriously because there the actual state of affairs involves a devious system of reflecting mirrors. So we have an explanation of why people are credited with knowing in ordinary perceptual cases but not in the Gettierized case.

The following is a more serious difficulty for our analysis. S truly believes something to be a tree, but there is a relevant alternative in which an electrode stimulating S's optic nerve would produce an equivalent percept, which would elicit the same belief. Since this is assumed to be a relevant alternative, it ought to disqualify S from knowing. But it doesn't satisfy our definition of a perceptual equivalent, first because the electrode would not be a perceptual cause of the percept (we would not say that S *perceives* the electrode), and second because S would not believe *of the electrode* (nor *of* anything else) that it is a tree. A similar problem arises where the alternative state of affairs would involve S's having a hallucination.

To deal with these cases, we could revise our analysis of perceptual knowledge as follows. (A similar revision in the definition of perceptual equivalence would do the job equally well.) We could reformulate 3C to say that there must neither be a relevant perceptual equivalent of the indicated sort (using our present defintion of perceptual equivalence) *nor* a relevant alternative situation in which an equivalent percept occurs and prompts a *de dicto* belief that something has F, but where there is nothing that *perceptually* causes this percept and nothing *of* which F is believed to hold. In other words, knowledge can be disqualified by relevant alternative situations where S doesn't

perceive anything and doesn't have any *de re* (*F*) belief at all. I
am inclined to adopt this solution, but will not actually make
this addition to the analysis.

Another difficulty for the analysis is this. Suppose Sam's
"schemata" of Judy and Trudy have hitherto been indistinct, so
Judy-caused percepts sometimes elicit Judy-beliefs and sometimes Trudy-beliefs, and similarly for Trudy-caused percepts.
Today Sam falls down and hits his head. As a consequence a
new feature is "added" to his Judy-schema, a mole-associated
feature. From now on he will believe someone to be Judy only
if he has the sort of percept that would be caused by a Judy-like
person with a mole over the left eye. Sam is unaware that this
change has taken place and will remain unaware of it, since he
isn't conscious of the cues he uses. Until today, neither Judy
nor Trudy has had a left-eyebrow mole; but today Judy happens to develop such a mole. Thus, from now on Sam can discriminate Judy from Trudy. Does this mean that he will *know*
Judy to be Judy when he correctly identifies her? I am doubtful.

A possible explanation of Sam's not knowing (on future occasions) is that Trudy-with-a-mole is a relevant perceptual
equivalent of Judy. This is not Trudy's actual condition, of
course, but it might be deemed a relevant possibility. I believe,
however, that the mole case calls for a further restriction, one
concerning the *genesis* of a person's propensity to form a certain belief as a result of a certain percept. A merely fortuitous
or accidental genesis is not enough to support knowledge. I do
not know exactly what requirement to impose on the genesis of
such a propensity. The mole case intimates that the genesis
should involve certain "experience" with objects, but this may
be too narrow. I content myself with a very vague addition to
our previous conditions, which completes the analysis:

   (4) *S*'s propensity to form an *F*-belief as a result of percept
       P has an appropriate genesis.

Of course this leaves the problem unresolved. But the best I
can do here is identify the problem.

IV

A few words are in order about the intended significance of my analysis. One of its purposes is to provide an alternative to the traditional "Cartesian" perspective in epistemology. The Cartesian view combines a theory of knowledge with a theory of justification. Its theory of knowledge asserts that S knows that p at t only if S is (fully, adequately, etc.) justified at t in believing that p. Its theory of justification says that S is justified at t in believing that p only if either (A) p is self-warranting for S at t, or (B) p is (strongly, adequately, etc.) supported or confirmed by propositions each of which is self-warranting for S at t. Now propositions about the state of the external world at t are not self-warranting. Hence, if S knows any such proposition p at t, there must be some other propositions which strongly support p and which are self-warranting for S at t. These must be propositions about S's mental state at t and perhaps some obvious necessary truths. A major task of Cartesian epistemology is to show that there is some such set of self-warranting propositions, propositions that support external-world propositions with sufficient strength.

It is impossible to canvass all attempts to fulfill this project; but none have succeeded, and I do not think that any will. One can conclude either that we have no knowledge of the external world or that Cartesian requirements are too demanding. I presuppose the latter conclusion in offering my theory of perceptual knowledge. My theory requires no justification for external-world propositions that derives entirely from self-warranting propositions. It requires only, in effect, that beliefs in the external world be suitably caused, where "suitably" comprehends a process or mechanism that not only produces true belief in the actual situation, but would not produce false belief in relevant counterfactual situations. If one wishes, one can so employ the term 'justification' that belief causation of *this* kind counts as justification. In this sense, of course, my theory does require justification. But this is entirely different from the sort of justification demanded by Cartesianism.

My theory protects the possibility of knowledge by making Cartesian-style justification unnecessary. But it leaves a door open to skepticism by its stance on relevant alternatives. This is not a failure of the theory, in my opinion. An adequate account of the term 'know' should make the temptations of skepticism comprehensible, which my theory does. But it should also put skepticism in a proper perspective, which Cartesianism fails to do.

In any event, I put forward my account of perceptual knowledge not primarily as an antidote to skepticism, but as a more accurate rendering of what the term 'know' actually means. In this respect it is instructive to test my theory and its rivals against certain metaphorical or analogical uses of 'know.' A correct definition should be able to explain extended and figurative uses as well as literal uses, for it should explain how speakers arrive at the extended uses from the central ones. With this in mind, consider how tempting it is to say of an electric-eye door that it "knows" you are coming (at least that *something* is coming), or "sees" you coming. The attractiveness of the metaphor is easily explained on my theory: the door has a reliable mechanism for discriminating between something being before it and nothing being there. It has a "way of telling" whether or not something is there: this "way of telling" consists in a mechanism by which objects in certain DOE relations to it have differential effects on its internal state. By contrast, note how artificial it would be to apply more traditional analyses of 'know' to the electric-eye door, or to other mechanical detecting devices. How odd it would be to say that the door has "good reasons," "adequate evidence," or "complete justification" for thinking something is there; or that it has "the right to be sure" something is there. The oddity of these locutions indicates how far from the mark are the analyses of 'know' from which they derive.

The trouble with many philosophical treatments of knowledge is that they are inspired by Cartesian-like conceptions of justification or vindication. There is a consequent tendency to overintellectualize or overrationalize the notion of knowledge.

In the spirit of naturalistic epistemology,[17] I am trying to fashion an account of knowing that focuses on more primitive and pervasive aspects of cognitive life, in connection with which, I believe, the term 'know' gets its application. A fundamental facet of animate life, both human and infra-human, is telling things apart, distinguishing predator from prey, for example, or a protective habitat from a threatening one. The concept of knowledge has its roots in this kind of cognitive activity.

17. Cf. W. O. Quine, "Epistemology Naturalized," in *Ontological Relativity and Other Essays* (New York: Columbia University Press, 1969).

An early version of this paper was read at the 1972 Chapel Hill Colloquium. Later versions were read at the 1973 University of Cincinnati Colloquium, and at a number of other philosophy departments. For comments and criticism, I am especially indebted to Holly Goldman, Bruce Aune, Jaegwon Kim, Louis Loeb, and Kendall Walton.

9

Knowledge: Undefeated Justified True Belief

KEITH LEHRER *and* THOMAS D. PAXSON, JR.

If a man knows that a statement is true even though there is no other statement that justifies his belief, then his knowledge is basic. Basic knowledge is completely justified true belief. On the other hand, if a man knows that a statement is true because there is some other statement that justifies his belief, then his knowledge is nonbasic. Nonbasic knowledge requires something in addition to completely justified true belief; for, though a statement completely justifies a man in his belief, there may be some true statement that *defeats* his justification. So, we must add the condition that his justification is not defeated. Nonbasic knowledge is undefeated justified true belief. These analyses will be elaborated below and subsequently defended against various alternative analyses.[1]

Reprinted from *The Journal of Philosophy*, 66.8 (1969), 225–237, by kind permission of the authors and editor.
1. This analysis of knowledge is a modification of an earlier analysis proposed by Keith Lehrer, "Knowledge, Truth and Evidence," *Analysis*, 25.5 (1965), 168–175. It is intended to cope with objections to that article raised by Gilbert H. Harman in "Lehrer on Knowledge," *Journal of Philosophy*, 63.9 (1966), 241–247, and by Alvin Goldman, Brian Skyrms, and others. Criticisms of various alternative analyses of knowledge are given in Lehrer's earlier article, and the reader is referred to that article; such discussion will not be repeated here. The distinction between basic and nonbasic knowledge that is elaborated here was suggested by Arthur Danto in "Freedom and Forebearance," in *Freedom and Determinism* (New York: Random House, 1965), pp. 45–63.

I

We propose the following analysis of basic knowledge: S has basic knowledge that h if and only if (i) h is true, (ii) S believes that h, (iii) S is completely justified in believing that h, and (iv) the satisfaction of condition (iii) does not depend on any evidence p justifying S in believing that h. The third condition is used in such a way that it entails neither the second condition nor the first. A person can be completely justified in believing that h, even though, irrationally, he does not; and a person can be completely justified in believing that h, even though, unfortunately, he is mistaken.[2] Furthermore, the third condition does not entail that there is any statement or belief that justifies S in believing that h. The analysis, then, is in keeping with the characterization of basic knowledge given above. In basic knowledge, S is completely justified in believing that h even if it is not the case that there is any statement or belief that justifies his believing that h.

There are cases in which a person has some, perhaps mysterious, way of being right about matters of a certain sort with such consistency that philosophers and others have said that the person knows whereof he speaks. Consider, for example, the crystal-ball-gazing gypsy who is almost always right in his predictions of specific events. Peter Unger suggests a special case of this.[3] His gypsy is always right, but has no evidence to this effect and, in fact, believes that he is usually wrong. With respect to each specific prediction, however, the gypsy impulsively believes it to be true (as indeed it is). Whether or not the predictive beliefs of the ordinary gypsy and Unger's gypsy are cases of knowledge depends, we contend, on whether they are cases of basic knowledge. This in turn depends on whether the gypsies are completely justified in their beliefs. It is plausible to

2. Harman's criticism of Lehrer's earlier article rested on his interpreting Lehrer as saying that a person can be completely justified in believing something only if he does believe it. This interpretation leads to problems and is repudiated here.
3. "Experience and Factual Knowledge," *Journal of Philosophy*, 64.5 (1967), 152–173, esp. pp. 165–167; see also his "An Analysis of Factual Knowledge," ibid., 65.6 (1968), 157–170, esp. pp. 163–164.

suggest that these are cases of knowledge, but this is only because it is also plausible to think that the gypsies in question
have some way of being right that completely justifies their
prognostications. We neither affirm nor deny that these are
cases of knowledge, but maintain that, if they are cases of
knowledge, then they are cases of *basic* knowledge.

It is consistent with our analysis of knowledge to admit that a
man knows something even though no statement constitutes
evidence that completely justifies his believing it. Philosophers
have suggested that certain memory and perceptual beliefs are
completely justified in the absence of such evidential statements. We choose to remain agnostic with respect to any claim
of this sort, but such proposals are not excluded by our analysis.

II

Not all knowledge that p is basic knowledge that p, because
sometimes justifying evidence is essential. Consider the following
analysis of nonbasic knowledge: (i) h is true, (ii) S believes that
h, and (iii*) p completely justifies S in believing that h. In this
analysis, p is that (statement) which makes S completely justified in believing that h. Note that (iii*), like (iii), does not entail (ii) or (i).

This analysis of nonbasic knowledge is, of course, defective.
As Edmund Gettier has shown, there are examples in which
some false statement p entails and hence completely justifies S
in believing that h, and such that, though S correctly believes
that h, his being correct is mostly a matter of luck.[4] Consequently, S lacks knowledge, contrary to the above analysis.
Other examples illustrate that the false statement which creates
the difficulty need not *entail* h. Consider, for example, the case
of the pyromaniac described by Skyrms.[5] The pyromaniac has
found that Sure-Fire matches have always ignited when struck.
On the basis of this evidence, the pyromaniac is completely justified in believing that the match he now holds will ignite upon

4. "Is Justified True Belief Knowledge?" *Analysis,* 23.6 (1963), 121–123.
5. "The Explication of 'X knows that p'," *Journal of Philosophy,* 64.12 (1967),
373–389.

his striking it. However, unbeknownst to the pyromaniac, this match happens to contain impurities that raise its combustion temperature above that which can be produced by the friction. Imagine that a burst of Q-radiation ignites the match just as he strikes it. His belief that the match will ignite upon his striking it is true and completely justified by the evidence. But this is not a case of knowledge, because it is not the striking that will cause the match to ignite.

Roderick Chisholm has pointed out that justifications are defeasible.[6] In the examples referred to above, there is some true statement that would defeat any justification of S for believing that h. In the case of the pyromaniac, his justification is defeated by the true statement that striking the match will not cause it to ignite. This defeats his justification for believing that the match will ignite upon his striking it.

Thus we propose the following analysis of nonbasic knowledge: S has nonbasic knowledge that h if and only if (i) h is true. (ii) S believes that h, and (iii) there is some statement p that completely justifies S in believing that h and no other statement defeats this justification. The question we must now answer is—what does it mean to say that a statement defeats a justification? Adopting a suggestion of Chisholm's, we might try the following: when p completely justifies S in believing that h, this justification is defeated by q if and only if (i) q is true, and (ii) the conjunction of p and q does not completely justify S in believing that h.[7] This definition is strong enough to rule out the example of the pyromaniac as a case of knowledge. The statement that the striking of a match will *not* cause it to ignite, which is true, is such that when it is conjoined to any statement that completely justifies the pyromaniac in believing that the match will ignite, the resultant conjunction will fail to so justify him in that belief. Given this definition of defeasibility, the analysis of nonbasic knowledge would require that a man who

6. *Theory of Knowledge* (Englewood Cliffs, N.J.: Prentice-Hall, 1966), p. 48.

7. Chisholm, "The Ethics of Requirement," *American Philosophical Quarterly*, 1.2 (1964), 147–153. This definition of defeasibility would make our analysis of nonbasic knowledge very similar to one Harman derives from Lehrer's analysis and also one proposed by Marshall Swain in "The Analysis of Non-Basic Knowledge" (unpublished).

has nonbasic knowledge that h must have some justification for his belief that is not defeated by any true statement.

However, this requirement is somewhat unrealistic. To see that the definition of defeasibility under consideration makes the analysis of nonbasic knowledge excessively restrictive, we need only notice that there can be true statements that are misleading. Suppose I see a man walk into the library and remove a book from the library by concealing it beneath his coat. Since I am sure the man is Tom Grabit, whom I have often seen before when he attended my classes, I report that I know that Tom Grabit has removed the book. However, suppose further that Mrs. Grabit, the mother of Tom, has averred that on the day in question Tom was not in the library, indeed, was thousands of miles away, and that Tom's identical twin brother, John Grabit, was in the library. Imagine, moreover, that I am entirely ignorant of the fact that Mrs. Grabit has said these things. The statement that she has said these things would defeat any justification I have for believing that Tom Grabit removed the book, according to our present definition of defeasibility. Thus, I could not be said to have nonbasic knowledge that Tom Grabit removed the book.

The preceding might seem acceptable until we finish the story by adding that Mrs. Grabit is a compulsive and pathological liar, that John Grabit is a fiction of her demented mind, and that Tom Grabit took the book as I believed. Once this is added, it should be apparent that I did know that Tom Grabit removed the book, and, since the knowledge must be nonbasic, I must have nonbasic knowledge of that fact. Consquently, the definition of defeasibility must be amended. The fact that Mrs. Grabit said what she did should not be allowed to defeat any justification I have for believing that Tom Grabit removed the book, because I neither entertained any beliefs concerning Mrs. Grabit nor would I have been justified in doing so. More specifically, my justification does not depend on my being completely justified in believing that Mrs. Grabit did *not* say the things in question.

To understand how the definition of defeasibility must be amended to deal with the preceding example, let us consider an example from the literature in which a justification deserves to be defeated. Suppose that I have excellent evidence that completely justifies my believing that a student in my class, Mr. Nogot, owns a Ford, the evidence consisting in my having seen him driving it, hearing him say he owns it, and so forth. Since Mr. Nogot is a student in my class who owns a Ford, someone in my class owns a Ford, and, consequently, I am completely justified in believing that someone in my class owns a Ford. Imagine that, contrary to the evidence, Mr. Nogot does not own a Ford, that I have been deceived, but that unknown to me Mr. Havit, who is also in my class, does own a Ford. Though I have a completely justified true belief, I do not know that someone in my class owns a Ford. The reason is that my sole justification for believing that someone in my class does own a Ford is and should be defeated by the true statement that Mr. Nogot does not own a Ford.

In the case of Tom Grabit, the true statement that Mrs. Grabit said Tom was not in the library and so forth, should not be allowed to defeat my justification for believing that Tom removed the book, whereas in the case of Mr. Nogot, the true statement that Mr. Nogot does not own a Ford, should defeat my justification for believing that someone in my class owns a Ford. Why should one true statement but not the other be allowed to defeat my justification? The answer is that in one case my justification depends on my being completely justified in believing the true statement to be false while in the other it does not. My justification for believing that Tom removed the book does not depend on my being completely justified in believing it to be false that Mrs. Grabit said Tom was not in the library and so forth. But my justification for believing that someone in my class owns a Ford does depend on my being completely justified in believing it to be false that Mr. Nogot does not own a Ford. Thus, a defeating statement must be one which, though true, is such that the subject is completely justified in believing it to be false.[8]

8. In Skyrms' example of the pyromaniac cited earlier, the defeating statement is not one which the pyromaniac need believe; Skyrms suggests that the pyromaniac neither believes nor disbelieves that striking the match will cause it

The following definition of defeasibility incorporates this proposal: when p completely justifies S in believing that h, this justification is defeated by q if and only if (i) q is true, (ii) S is completely justified in believing q to be false, and (iii) the conjunction of p and q does not completely justify S in believing that h.

This definition of defeasibility, though basically correct, requires one last modification to meet a technical problem. Suppose that there is some statement h of which S has nonbasic knowledge. Let us again consider the example in which I know that Tom Grabit removed the book. Now imagine that there is some true statement which is completely irrelevant to this knowledge and which I happen to be completely justified in believing to be false, for example, the statement that I was born in St. Paul. Since I am completely justified in believing it to be false that I was born in St. Paul, I am also completely justified in believing to be false the conjunctive statement that I was born in St. Paul and that q, whatever q is, because I am completely justified in believing any conjunction to be false if I am completely justified in believing a conjunct of it to be false. Therefore, I am completely justified in believing to be false the conjunctive statement that I was born in St. Paul and Mrs. Grabit said that Tom Grabit was not in the library and so forth. Moreoever, this conjunctive statement is true, and is such that, when it is conjoined in turn to any evidential statement that justifies me in believing that Tom Grabit removed the book, the resultant extended conjunction will not completely justify me in believing that Tom Grabit removed the book. Hence, any such justification will be defeated.[9] Once again, it turns out that I do not have nonbasic knowledge of the fact that Tom is the culprit.

In a logical nut, the problem is that the current definition of defeasibility reduces to the preceding one. Suppose there is a

---

to ignite. Nevertheless, the pyromaniac would be completely justified in believing that striking the Sure-Fire match will cause it to ignite. Hence the statement that striking the match will *not* cause it to light is defeating.

9. A similar objection to Lehrer's earlier analysis is raised by Harman, p. 243.

true statement q such that, for any p that completely justifies S in believing h, the conjunction of p and q does not completely justify me in believing that h. Moreoever, suppose that I am not completely justified in believing q to be false, so that, given our current definition of defeasibility, q does not count as defeating. Nevertheless, if there is any true statement r, irrelevant to both p and q, which I am completely justified in believing to be false, then we can indirectly use q to defeat my justification for believing h. For I shall be completely justified in believing the conjunction of r and q to be false, though in fact it is true, because I am completely justified in believing r to be false. If the conjunction of q and p does not completely justify me in believing that h, then, given the irrelevance of r, neither would the conjunction of r, q and p justify me in believing that h. Hence, my justifications for believing h would be defeated by the conjunction r and q on the current definition of defeasibility as surely as they were by q alone on the preceding definition.

The defect is not difficult to repair. Though S is completely justified in believing the conjunction of r and q to be false, one consequence of the conjunction, q, undermines my justification but is not something I am completely justified in believing to be false, while another consequence, r, is one that I am completely justified in believing to be false but is irrelevant to my justification. To return to our example, I am completely justified in believing to be false the conjunctive statement that I was born in St. Paul and that Mrs. Grabit said that Tom was not in the library and so forth. One consequence of this conjunction, that Mrs. Grabit said that Tom was not in the library and so forth, undermines my justification but is not something I am completely justified in believing to be false, while the other consequence, that I was born in St. Paul, is something I am completely justified in believing to be false but is irrelevant to my justification. The needed restriction is that those consequences of a defeating statement which undermine a justification must themselves be statements that the subject is completely justified in believing to be false.

We propose the following definition of defeasibility: if p completely justifies S in believing that h, then this justification is defeated by q if and only if (i) q is true, (ii) the conjunction of p and q does not completely justify S in believing that h, (iii) S is completely justified in believing q to be false, and (iv) if c is a logical consequence of q such that the conjunction of c and p does not completely justify S in believing that h, then S is completely justified in believing c to be false.

With this definition of defeasibility, we complete our analysis of nonbasic knowledge. We have defined nonbasic knowledge as true belief for which some statement provides a complete and undefeated justification. We previously defined basic knowledge as true belief for which there was complete justification that did not depend on any justifying statement. We define as knowledge anything that is either basic or nonbasic knowledge. Thus, S knows that h if and only if S has either basic or nonbasic knowledge that h.

10

Knowledge and Defeasibility

DAVID ANNIS

In a recent article Keith Lehrer and Thomas Paxson, Jr.,
suggested that nonbasic knowledge is undefeated justified true
belief.[1] Their specific analysis of defeasibility however has been
shown to be defective.[2] In what follows I offer an alternative
account of defeasibility.

Knowledge that h is to be defined as:

S knows that h if and only if (i) h is true, (ii) S believes that
h, and (iii) there is a set of statements A that fully justifies S
in believing that h and there is no statement that defeats
this justification.

The third condition is crucial.

A set of statements A fully justifies S in believing that h if
and only if A justifies S in believing h and for every statement j, if j is a member of A, then S believes that j and is
justified in this belief; and for every such j there is a subset
Aj of the set A that justifies S in believing that j.[3]

Reprinted from *Philosophical Studies*, 24 (1973), 199–203, by kind permission
of the author and publisher. Copyright © 1973 by D. Reidel Publishing Company, Dordrecht, Holland.

1. Keith Lehrer and Thomas Paxson, Jr., 'Knowledge: Undefeated Justified
True Belief' [Chapter 9 in this volume].
2. Ernest Sosa, 'Two Conceptions of Knowledge', *Journal of Philosophy*, 67
(1970), 59–66. See also J. R. Kress, 'Lehrer and Paxson on Nonbasic Knowledge', *Journal of Philosophy*, 68 (1971), 78–82. In a later article Lehrer rejected
his earlier account of defeasibility. See Keith Lehrer 'The Fourth Condition of
Knowledge: A Defense', *Review of Metaphysics*, 24 (1970), 122–128.
3. Ernest Sosa offers a similar definition in 'Propositional Knowledge', *Philosophical Studies*, 20 (1969), 33–43. Compare Michael Clark, 'Knowledge and
Grounds: A Comment on Mr. Gettier's Paper', *Analysis*, 24 (1963), 46–48.

Some statement p may justify S in believing that h and what justifies S in believing that p may be the statement that q. Furthermore what justifies S in believing that q may be the statement that r. The set of statements that fully justifies S in believing that h will include p, q, and r. When considering whether a person is fully justified in believing that h, we should take into account the entire chain of justification. When S is justified in believing that j and this justification does not depend on any statement i, then the subset of A that justifies S in believing that j is the empty set. This allows justification to terminate. It also enables our definition to cover both basic and nonbasic knowledge.

Now how is defeasibility to be defined? One suggestion is:

(D1) When a set of statements A fully justifies S in believing that h, this justification is defeated by a statement q if and only if (i) q is true, and (ii) for some statement j, where j is a member of A or j is h, and for the corresponding subset Aj that justifies S in believing that j, the conjunction of the members of Aj and q does not justify S in believing that j.

The problem with this characterization of defeasibility is that it makes our definition of knowledge too strong. To take a familiar example, suppose that Jones is justified in believing both

p_1 Mr. Nogot, who is in the office, owns a Ford

and

p_2 Mr. Havit, who is in the office, owns a Ford.

Statements p_1 and p_2 justify Jones in believing

h_1 Someone in the office owns a Ford.

Suppose p_1 is false although p_2 is true. In this situation Jones knows that h_1. The set A that fully justifies Jones in believing h_1 includes p_1, p_2, and the statements justifying him in believing p_1 and p_2. But according to (D1), the justification A provides for h_1 is defeated. There is a true statement q such that for some j, where j is a member of A, the conjunction of the members of Aj and q does not justify Jones in believing that j. Whatever set of statements Aj justifies Jones in believing p_1, the conjunction of the members of Aj and the true statement that p_1 is false does not justify Jones in believing p_1.

The above situation can be characterized as follows. There is
a set of statements A that fully justifies S in believing h. There
are also two subsets of A that fully justify S in believing that h.
With regard to one of the subsets, there is a q that defeats the
justification this subset provides h, but there is no defeating q
for the other subset. In such a situation S knows that h. Whenever there are fully justifying subsets of A, in order for S to
know that h, there must be at least one fully justifying subset A'
such that there is no q that defeats the justification A' provides
h. Thus defeasibility is defined as:

> (D2) When a set of statements A fully justifies S in believ-
> ing that h, this justification is defeated if and only if
> for every fully justifying subset A', there is a state-
> ment q such that (i) q is true, and (ii) for some state-
> ment j, where j is a member of A' or j is h, and for
> the corresponding subset Aj' that justifies S in believ-
> ing j, the conjunction of the members of Aj' and q
> does not justify S in believing that j.

There are still problems with the notion of defeasibility. Suppose p justifies S in believing that h. Should any true q such that
the conjunction of p and q does not justify S in believing h be
allowed to defeat the justification p provides h? (D2) requires
this.[4] But consider the following example. Suppose that Smith,
whom Jones knows to be reliable and honest, tells Jones that he
just bought a new Ford from the local dealer. Jones is then justified in believing that he did make the purchase. Imagine however that the local dealer, who is also reliable and honest, asserts that Smith did not purchase a Ford. The statement that
the dealer asserted this defeats Jones's justification for believing
that Smith did make such a purchase. But suppose that the
dealer confused Smith with Brown and that Smith did purchase a new Ford from the dealer. Assume further that Jones is
not aware of what the dealer said. Even though there is a defeating q according to (D2), there is a strong inclination to say

---

4. To simplify the discussion, it will be carried on in terms of q defeating the
justification p provides h instead of the defeasibility of a fully justifying set of
statements.

that Jones does know that Smith bought a Ford.[5] If this is a case of knowledge, then not every true q such that the conjunction of p and q does not justify S in believing h should be allowed to defeat S's justification for believing h.

In the above example there is a true statement that is misleading evidence. But misleading evidence should not be allowed to defeat a person's justification. Let us say that

a defeating statement q is defective with respect to p, h, and S if and only if there is a true statement r which explains why q is misleading evidence with respect to p and h such that the conjunction of p, q, and r justifies S in believing h but r alone does not justify S in believing h.

The true statement r is restricted to explaining why q is misleading evidence and must not provide a new justification for believing h. In our dealer example, the true statement

   r The local dealer confused Smith with Brown

explains why

   q The local Ford dealer, who is reliable and honest, asserted that Smith did not purchase a Ford

is misleading evidence with respect to

   p Smith, who is reliable and honest, told Jones that he just bought a new Ford from the local dealer

and

   h Smith purchased a new Ford from the local Ford dealer.

The conjunction of p, q, and r justifies Jones in believing h but r alone does not justify Jones in believing h. Since the defeating statement q is defective with respect to p, h, and Jones, it is not allowed to defeat the justification p provides h. We must then add the following clause (iii) to our definition of defeasibility:

   (iii) q is not defective with respect to Aj', j, and S.

Only nondefective defeating statements are allowed to defeat a person's justification.

It should be noted that not all philosophers would agree that in our above example Jones does have knowledge.[6] And there

5. Lehrer and Paxson discuss a similar example. See 'Knowledge: Undefeated Justified True Belief', p. 150.
6. Peter D. Klein, 'A Proposed Definition of Propositional Knowledge', *Journal of Philosophy*, 68 (1971), 471–482.

is even less agreement about the following example. Suppose that in our dealer example a number of people know what the dealer said. They also know what Smith said. Surely these people do not know that Smith made the purchase. But, it is claimed, if these people do not have knowledge then we cannot grant knowledge to Jones. After all these people have all the evidence Jones has plus additional evidence.[7] Now it is true that these people do have additional evidence. But it is *misleading* evidence and their total evidence does not justify the belief that Smith bought a Ford. Additional evidence which is misleading may result in a person not knowing something he might otherwise have known. However Jones's evidence is not misleading and it does justify his belief about Smith. If we grant that Jones does have knowledge in the above two examples, then clause (iii) of the definition of defeasibility is required. If we decide that these are not cases of knowledge, then only clauses (i) and (ii) are needed.

7. Sosa, 'Two Conceptions of Knowledge', p. 62. See also Gilbert Harman's discussion of such examples in his 'Knowledge, Inference, and Explanation', *American Philosophical Quarterly,* 5 (1968), 164–173, and his paper 'Induction,' in *Induction, Acceptance, and Rational Belief,* ed. Marshall Swain (Dordrecht, Holland: D. Reidel Publishing Company, 1970), pp. 83–99.

11

Epistemic Defeasibility

MARSHALL SWAIN

In the recent literature of both ethics and epistemology the concept of defeasibility has played an important role. In ethical contexts, for example, it is hardly possible to make sense of the distinction between prima facie and absolute obligation without a clear notion of defeasibility.[1] Similarly, in epistemological contexts a distinction between prima facie and absolute justification has been used to advantage by a number of authors.[2] Unfortunately, the conditions under which a given obligation or justification is defeasible have not been specified in a way that meets with unanimous approval.

One of the more interesting applications of the concept of epistemic defeasibility concerns the perplexing problem of analyzing the concept of knowledge. It is well known that it is not sufficient for a man's having knowledge that he have justified true belief; it is also well known that the problem of specifying what else is necessary is exceedingly difficult. One suggestion concerning the "fourth" condition of knowledge which has received a good deal of attention is that for a man to have knowl-

Reprinted from *The American Philosophical Quarterly*, 11.1 (1974), 15–25, by kind permission of the editor.

1. A classic use of this distinction occurs in W. D. Ross, *The Right and the Good* (Oxford: Oxford University Press, 1930). For a precise treatment of the distinction and further references see Roderick Chisholm, "The Ethics of Requirement," *American Philosophical Quarterly*, 1 (1964), 147–153.

2. One recent example is John Pollock, "Perceptual Knowledge," *Philosophical Review*, 80 (1971), 287–319.

edge his justification must be indefeasible.[3] Even though no adequate characterization of indefeasibility has been provided, I am now convinced that this approach to the problem of knowledge is the correct one. In any event, I shall assume here that the analysis of knowledge in terms of indefeasible justification is the one to be adopted. Granted this assumption, we can specify a partial criterion for an adequate explication of the concept of defeasibility:

> (C) An explication of defeasible justification is adequate only if for any person S, and any proposition h, if (1) h is true and (2) S is justified in believing h and (3) S believes that h on the basis of his justification, then S knows that h if and only if his justification for h is indefeasible in accordance with that explication.

Given (C) we can "test" a proposed analysis of defeasibility by checking various agreed upon cases of knowledge and nonknowledge. A natural protest to this procedure is that to "test" an explication of defeasibility we shall need some independent way of deciding whether a man has knowledge in addition to merely having justified true belief, and we have no way of doing this. In general I would agree that it is a poor criterion indeed that directs us to test a proposed explication of one murky concept in terms of an equally difficult one. But, in this particular instance, I believe that the criterion (C) can be useful. There is a remarkable amount of agreement among philos-

3. Each of the following is an attempt to construct what I am calling a "defeasibility" analysis of knowledge, even though not all of the authors of these papers explicitly characterize their views in terms of defeasibility: Ernest Sosa, "The Analysis of 'Knowledge that *p*'," *Analysis*, 25 (1964), 1–8; Keith Lehrer, "Knowledge, Truth and Evidence," *Analysis*, 25 (1965), 168–175; Keith Lehrer and Thomas Paxson, "Knowledge: Undefeated Justified True Belief" [Chapter 9 in this volume] Ernest Sosa, "Propositional Knowledge," *Philosophical Studies*, 20 (1969), 33–43 and "Two Conceptions of Knowledge," *Journal of Philosophy*, 67 (1970), 59–66; Gilbert Harman, "Induction" in Marshall Swain, ed., *Induction, Acceptance, and Rational Belief* (Dordrecht: Reidel, 1970), pp. 83–100; Keith Lehrer, "The Fourth Condition of Knowledge: A Defense," *Review of Metaphysics*, 23 (1970), 122–128; Peter D. Klein, "A Proposed Definition of Propositional Knowledge," *Journal of Philosophy*, 68 (1971), 471–482; Marshall Swain, "Knowledge, Causality, and Justification" [Chapter 4 in this volume] and "An Alternative Analysis of Knowing," *Synthese*, 23 (1972), 423–442; Risto Hilpinen, "Knowledge and Justification," *Ajatus*, 33 (1971), 7–39.

ophers and others concerning those kinds of situations that are to be called instances of knowledge and those that are not. With appropriate reservations, I see no great harm in relying upon such widespread intuitions with respect to knowledge in order to generate an analysis of defeasibility.

In what follows I shall consider, and reject, a number of proposed explications of the concept of defeasible justification. I shall then present what I think is an acceptable explication of that concept. I shall rely upon the criterion (C) as an aid in judging the adequacy of various proposals.[4]

I

Let us begin by considering a proposal made by Roderick Chisholm in his paper "The Ethics of Requirement."[5] Chisholm provides us with an explication of the ethical concept of defeasibility, but suggests that an analogous explication can be given for the epistemic notion of defeasible justification. Taking the expression "p requires q" as primitive, and letting 'p', 'q', and 's' stand for events or states of affairs, Chisholm first defines the ethical notion of overriding:

(DI)   There is a requirement for the state of affairs q which has been overridden = df. There are states of affairs p and s such that (i) p occurs and p requires q and (ii) s occurs and the joint occurrence of p and s does not require q.

Then, Chisholm gives us the following definition of ethical defeasibility:

(D2)   A requirement for the state of affairs q is defeasible = df. There is a state of affairs p such that p requires q and this requirement may be overridden.

To obtain the epistemic analog of these definitions, we can take

4. In this criterion, and in the remainder of the paper, the question of what *constitutes* a man's justification is left open to interpretation. In some of the proposals to be considered (specifically, those in Sect. II) a man's justification for a proposition h is limited to some body of evidence e that he possesses. In the remaining proposals, there is allowance for the possibility that a man may have a justification for h even though his justification does not consist of some body of evidence.

5. Chisholm, *op. cit.*, especially pp. 147–149.

as primitive the expression "*e* justifies *h*," where '*e*' and '*h*' stand for propositions. Then we can say:

> (3) There is a justification for *h* which has been overridden = df. There is a body of evidence *e* and a body of evidence *e'* such that (i) *e* is true and *e* justifies *h* and (ii) *e'* is true and the conjunction of *e* and *e'* does not justify *h*.

We can then say that a justification for *h* is defeasible as follows:

> (D4) A justification for *h* is defeasible = df. There is a body of evidence *e* such that *e* is true and *e* justifies *h* and this justification may be overridden.

In opposition to those justifications that are defeasible are justifications that are indefeasible. It seems natural, given (D4), to define this concept in the following way:

> (D5) A justification for *h* is indefeasible = df. There is a body of evidence *e* such that *e* is true and *e* justifies *h* and this justification cannot be overridden.

But the notorious word "cannot" presents us (as usual) with a problem. Presumably, to say that a justification for *h* cannot be overridden is just to say that there cannot be any body of evidence *e'* such that *e'* in conjunction with the justifying body of evidence *e* fails to justify *h*. But how are we to understand the requirement that there cannot be any such body of evidence *e'*? We might take this to mean that it is not logically possible that there is such a body of evidence. However, criterion (C) shows us that this conception of indefeasibility is not satisfactory. The analysis of knowledge associated with this conception would be the following:

> (D6) *S* knows that *h* iff (i) *h* is true, (ii) *S* is justified in believing that *h* (that is, there is a true body of evidence *e* such that *S* is justified in believing *e* and *e* justifies *h*), (iii) *S* believes that *h* on the basis of his justification and (iv) *S*'s justification for *h* is indefeasible (that is, it is not logically possible that there is a body of evidence *e'* such that the conjunction of *e* and *e'* fails to justify *h*).

Rather obviously, (D6) is too strong. One way of seeing this is as follows. If *h* is a contingently true proposition, then it is logically possible that h is false. But if it is logically possible that h is false, then it is logically possible that there is some body of evidence e' such that the conjunction of e and e' fails to justify h. For, the denial of h would constitute such evidence—it is clear that the conjunction of e with not-h would fail to justify h. So, (D6) will have the result that we can only have knowledge of noncontingent propositions. This is not a happy result.

Another way in which we might interpret "cannot" in (D5) is to say that it is not physically possible that there should be a defeating body of counter-evidence e'. We could then revise our definition of knowledge (D6) by replacing (iv) with

    (iva) S's justification for h is indefeasible (that is, it is not physically possible that there is a body of evidence e' such that the conjunction of e and e' fails to justify h).

However, this analysis of knowing suffers from defects similar to the previous one. Suppose h is the proposition that there is a red ball in front of me. It is surely not physically impossible that h is false—the conjunction of the denial of h with the Laws of Nature would not yield a contradiction. Hence, any justification I might have for believing that h is true would be defeasible, and I could never know of any red ball (nor of anything else) that it is in front of me. The sceptic would enjoy this conclusion, but I do not.

Yet another way in which we might interpret "cannot" in (D5) is to say that there is *in fact* no true body of defeating counterevidence e'. That is, we can say that a man's justification for h is indefeasible just in case there is in fact nothing about the world that overrides that justification. This is compatible with saying that it is physically possible that there should be such counterevidence and that it is logically possible that there should be. To incorporate this suggestion, we can replace (iv) with

    (ivb) S's justification for h is indefeasible (that is, there is no true body of evidence e' such that the conjunction of e and e' fails to justify h).

The resulting definition of knowledge has a great deal to recommend it. For one thing, this definition is immune to the recalcitrant problems raised by Edmund Gettier in his paper

"Is Justified True Belief Knowledge?"[6] Gettier provides examples that prove the "traditional" analysis of knowing as justified true belief to be too weak. It is readily established that in each of his examples, and in any situation having the structure of his examples, the replacement of condition (iv) by (ivb) in the definition (D6) renders it strong enough to avoid the problem. For, in each of his cases there is some true body of evidence e' such that the conjunction of e' with S's evidence e fails to justify h.

Despite this meritorious feature, an analysis of knowing incorporating (ivb) will not suffice, for it is too strong. Hence, criterion (C) will lead us to reject this proposal. The following example will make this clear. Suppose that S attends a wedding ceremony in which two friends of his become married. The ceremony is performed by the Bishop and is performed without any errors. It would certainly seem that S knows, after having witnessed the ceremony, that his friends are married. But we can easily imagine the world being such that S's justification is defeasible in accordance with (ivb). Imagine, for example, that at the time the ceremony is performed, but unknown to anyone involved in the ceremony (including S), the Cardinal goes insane. He has long harbored a suppressed hatred of the Bishop, and in his insanity falsely denounces the Bishop as a fraud who is not authorized to marry anyone. There will then be a true body of counterevidence e' (namely, the statement "The Cardinal says that the Bishop is a fraud") such that e' in conjunction with S's evidence e would fail to justify the proposition that the people are married. This suffices to show that the analysis of knowing incorporating (ivb) is too strong. Since (1), (2), and (3) of criterion (C) are clearly satisfied here, we should reject (ivb) as an explication of indefeasibility.

One thing we may notice about this example is that the presence in the world of the defeating counterevidence e' is an entirely unexpected fact. That is, S's evidence e does not seem to

6. Edmund Gettier, "Is Justified True Belief Knowledge?," *Analysis*, 23 (1963), 121–123. Reprinted in A. Phillips Griffith, ed., *Knowledge and Belief* (Oxford, 1967), and in Roth and Galis, eds., *Knowing: Essays in the Analysis of Knowledge* (New York, 1970).

give support one way or the other to the proposition that the
Cardinal is, or is not, saying insanely that the Bishop is a fraud.
If this is too strong, we can at least say that S's evidence e does
not *justify* either e' or its denial. Perhaps, then, we can weaken
the defeasibility condition (ivb) by restricting the range of ad-
missable defeating counterevidence to those true propositions
for which the evidence e is strongly negative. If we revise the
definition by incorporating this restriction the resulting analysis
is essentially the same as one considered by Keith Lehrer and
Thomas Paxson.[7] The revision can be effected by exchanging
(ivb) for:

    (ivc) S's justification for h is indefeasible (that is, there is
          no true body of evidence e' such that (a) e justifies S
          in believing that e' is false and (b) the conjunction of e
          and e' fails to justify h).

Unfortunately, this straightforward way of incorporating the
restriction does not work. Lehrer and Paxson show that (ivc)
reduces to (ivb).[8] Suppose there is some statement r such that e
completely justifies S in believing r to be false, and in believing
h to be true, but r is utterly irrelevant to the justification of h by
e. Then, let q be any true statement whatever such that the conjunction of e and q fails to justify h but such that S is *not* justified in believing q to be false on the basis of e. Then, consider
the conjunction of r and q. Since S is completely justified in believing r to be false, he is completely justified in believing the
conjunction of r and q to be false. But, since r is utterly irrelevant to the justification of h by e, the conjunction of r and q and
e fails to justify h. So, there will be a true body of evidence e'
(namely, q & r) such that e justifies S in believing e' to be false
but such that the conjunction of e and e' fails to justify h. This
will hold, moreover, for *any* q that satisfies the conditions on e'
in (ivb). We can handle this kind of problem by revising (ivc):

    (ivd) S's justification for h is indefeasible (that is, there is
          no true body of evidence e' such that (a) e justifies S
          in believing e' to be false and (b) the conjunction of e
          and e' fails to justify h and (c) if q is a logical conse-

7. Lehrer and Paxson, *op. cit.*, especially p. 152.
8. Ibid., pp. 152–153.

quence of e' such that the conjunction of q and e fails to justify h then e justifies S in believing q to be false.) [9]

In the above, q is a logical consequence of $(q \& r)$ but S is not justified in believing q to be false. Hence the conjunction of r and q will not qualify as an instance of defeating counterevidence e'. This seems an appropriate result.

The analysis of knowledge that incorporates (ivd) is a promising one, since it avoids not only the Gettier examples but also the wedding example above. Hence, in accordance with criterion (C), we have some reason to think that (ivd) can serve as an explication of defeasibility. Unfortunately, this analysis of knowing is both too weak and too strong.

To see that this analysis is too strong, we can consider the following: Suppose that S has just thrown a rock at a window. It is a large rock, an ordinary window, and S can see that the rock is going to hit the window. Moreover, the rock is going to hit the window, and when it does the window will break as a result. It seems clear that S knows the window will break. For one thing, there does not appear to be any true defeating counterevidence available. We can, however, imagine some additional bizarre circumstances such that there would be defeating counterevidence in accordance with (ivd). We can note, first, that since S is justified by his evidence in believing that the window will break, he is also justified in believing that he will see the window break and hear it break. Now, suppose that S has a peculiar nervous disease hitherto unknown to the human race. This disease has never before manifested any symptoms in S, but he is about to be afflicted with some symptoms, namely, total visual and auditory paralysis. Let us also suppose that S will be afflicted by these symptoms at the instant the window breaks. So, S will neither see nor hear the window break—let us call this e'. It seems clear that e' in conjunction with S's evidence e fails to justify belief that the window will break, S is justified in believing e' to be false, and we may suppose that every logical consequence of e' satisfies condition (c) of (ivd). Thus,

9. This is the definition of defeasibility proposed by Lehrer and Paxson, ibid., pp. 153–154.

we should conclude that S does not know that the window will break, contrary to the fact that he does know that it will break. The fact that he will be afflicted with sensory paralysis has no effect whatever on his knowing this.[10]

The following example structure suffices to show that the analysis of knowing incorporating (ivd) is also too weak. Suppose that S has some body of evidence e such that e justifies h. But suppose that even though h is true and S believes that h he does not know h because there is some true counterevidence e' such that S is justified in believing e' to be false and e' overrides his justification. Then, suppose there is *also* some true counterevidence e'' available such that e'' in conjunction with e fails to justify h but S is *not* justified in believing e'' to be false. Consider then, the disjunction of e' with e''. This is a logical consequence of e', and since each disjunct in conjunction with e fails to justify h the disjunction as a whole in conjunction with e fails to justify h. So, in accordance with (ivd), S will have to be completely justified in believing the disjunction of e' with e'' to be false. But, for any disjunction, S is completely justified in believing it to be false if and only if he is justified in believing, of *each* disjunct, that it is false. We have already assumed that S is not justified in believing e'' to be false. Examples exhibiting this structure are not at all difficult to find, so we may conclude that the analysis of knowing incorporating (ivd) is too weak—it fails to exclude a case of nonknowledge. In each of these examples, clauses (1), (2), and (3) of criterion (C) are satisfied. So, the problem in each case has to do with the proposed explication of indefeasible justification, and we may conclude that (ivd) is inadequate.

II

We can give an intuitive characterization of what is wrong when a man's justification is defeasible by saying that he is less than "ideally situated" with respect to the evidence bearing upon h. The notion of being *ideally* situated is, of course, a pipe-dream. In any full sense of the term, anyone who falls

10. This example, and the following one, are similar to some examples given by Sosa in "Two Conceptions of Knowledge," pp. 60–62.

short of omniscience is thereby less than ideally situated. Nevertheless, we can make perfectly good sense out of the idea that at some times we are better off than at others with respect to the evidence we have for various propositions. In contexts of inquiry and investigation it is normal and natural to speak of the investigator as improving his evidential base. Let us imagine that a man has some evidence *e* which is strong enough to justify *h,* and let us suppose that over a period of time his evidential position with respect to *h* constantly improves (or, approaches some ideally situated state). He comes to know more and more evidence bearing upon *h.* It seems intuitively appealing to say that if his justification is indefeasible, then this improvement of his evidential position would never result in a weakening of his (present) justification for *h.* The problem is, can we make this intuitively appealing, but vague notion precise?

Recently, Risto Hilpinen[11] and Peter Klein[12] have independently proposed virtually the same analysis of defeasibility, and this analysis is very much in line with the intuitively appealing idea expressed above. I shall concentrate here on Hilpinen's proposal, but I believe that very similar remarks can be made about Klein's proposal.

In constructing his characterization of defeasibility, Hilpinen refers to a principle put forth by Jaakko Hintikka. Hilpinen calls this the "extendability thesis." This principle states that if a man genuinely knows some proposition *h,* then no matter what else he might come to know, he will not lose the knowledge that *h* as a result. Hintikka puts the matter in the following way:

> If somebody says "I know that *p*" in this strong sense of knowledge, he implicitly denies that any further information would have led him to alter his view. He commits himself to the view that he would still persist in saying that he knows *p* is true—or at the very least persist in saying that *p* is in fact true—even if he knew more than he now knows.[13]

11. Hilpinen, "Knowledge and Justification."

12. Klein, "A Proposed Definition of Propositional Knowledge." Although Klein does not explicitly characterize his "fourth" condition as a defeasibility condition, I believe that, given the context of his discussion, it is reasonable to interpret his definition as a defeasibility definition.

13. Jaakko Hintikka, *Knowledge and Belief: An Introduction to the Logic of the Two Notions* (Ithaca: Cornell University Press, 1962), pp. 20–21.

Leaving aside the dubious parts about what men would persist in saying, we can express the extendability thesis as follows:

(ET) If S knows that h, then for any true proposition q, S would know h even if he knew more than he now knows by knowing that q.

According to (ET), then, the corpus of propositions of which a man has genuine knowledge is always extendable to new instances of knowledge without detriment to any "previous" members of the corpus. Hilpinen suggests that the extendability thesis be adopted as ". . . a condition of adequacy for the definition of defeasibility."[14] That is, any characterization of defeasibility that we come up with must be such that if knowledge is indefeasibly justified true belief, then any instance of knowledge in accordance with our defeasibility analysis must satisfy the extendability thesis.

Let us consider, however, whether (ET) is a principle that we wish to accept. To begin, (ET) is vaguely formulated, as is often the case when a subjunctive clause is used. We are not told by (ET) what *else* is permitted to happen to S in the event that he should know more than he now knows by coming to know q. What does the expression "more than" in (ET) allow for? We might interpret this as saying that S knows more at t_2 than he knew at t_1 if and only if at t_2 S knows everything that he knew. at t_1 and knows at least one thing that he did not know at t_1. We can interpret the extendability thesis in accordance with this sense of "knowing more than" as follows:

(ET1) If S knows that h, then for any true proposition q, S would know h even if he knew everything that he now knows and also knew q.

(ET1) is a trivial analytic truth, however, for it says that if S knows h, then he would still know h even if he continued to know h and knew something else as well. This is not a very interesting principle. Any analysis of defeasibility would satisfy its demands.

A more interesting way of interpreting "more than" is to say

14. Hilpinen, *op. cit.* It should be pointed out that (ET) is not the version of the extendability thesis that Hilpinen uses. For his version, see (ET3) and footnote 15 below.

that S knows more at t_2 than he knew at t_1 if and only if at t_2 the sum total of S's information about the world is greater than it was at t_1. The phrase "sum total of S's information" is not intended to express any very technical sense of information. If we assume that some rough measure of the cognitive content of sentences in natural languages is available, then the sum total of S's information would simply be the measure assigned to the conjunction of everything that he knows. Clearly, the sum total of S's information could increase over a period of time even if the items of information that he has were to change; that is, it is compatible with (S2) that S should come to know more than he now knows even though he loses some of his present knowledge. Hence, we get the following nontrivial interpretation of the extendability thesis:

> (ET2) If S knows that h, then for any true proposition q, S would know h even if the sum total of his information about the world were to increase as a result of his coming to know q.

It is not difficult to see, however, that (ET2) is too strong. The reason why it is too strong is that it fails to specify any epistemic *connection* between the supposed increase in (true) information, and the question whether S would still know h were that increase to occur. If I forget something, and also learn a number of new things, then (ET2) gives the result that I never did know the thing I have forgotten, which is absurd. It seems clear that the intent of the extendability thesis is to specify that if a man knows something, then his coming to have more information about the world would not result on epistemic grounds in his losing the previous knowledge. If he does lose the previous knowledge (through mere forgetting, for example) this will be for other reasons. Perhaps we can capture this idea in the following way:

> (ET3) If S knows that h, then for any true proposition q, if the sum total of S's information about the world were to increase as a result of his coming to know q, then he would not lose his knowledge that h as an epistemic result of his coming to know q.

I suspect that the condition formulated here is pretty close to

what Hilpinen has in mind.[15] Unfortunately, even this formulation of the extendability thesis places restrictions on an analysis
of knowing that are too strong. We earlier imagined a man who
had just thrown a rock at a window, and who was about to suffer sensory paralysis. A careful study of that example will reveal that (ET3) is not satisfied, even though the man knows that
the window will break.

Assuming that (ET3), or something like it, is the intended interpretation of the extendability thesis, these criticisms show
that we are under no constraints to limit our analysis of defeasibility to one that satisfies the extendability thesis. It is not surprising that the defeasibility condition proposed by Hilpinen
(which is virtually the same as the one proposed independently
by Klein) turns out to be too strong. The condition proposed
by Hilpinen, which demonstrably satisfies the extendability thesis, is this:

> (ive) S's justification for h is indefeasible (that is, for any
> true proposition q, S would be completely justified in
> believing h, even if he were completely justified in be-
> lieving q).

The example of the rock thrower shows this to be too strong,
just as it shows (ET3) to be too strong.

I have construed the intuitive idea behind the approach of
Hilpinen and Klein in terms of approaching an ideally situated
state with respect to the evidence bearing upon some proposition. From a given epistemic position a man might approach
such an ideal state to any of a variety of degrees. He might pick
up a bit of information here, and a bit there, in piecemeal fashion. Ironically, a man will sometimes wind up in a position that
is worse than the one from which he began, even though he

---

15. Hilpinen derives his defeasibility condition from his formulation of the
extendability thesis: "If a knows that h on the basis of e, then for any true proposition q, a would be completely justified in believing that h even if he knew that
q" (*op. cit.*, p. 31). This is vague in just the way (ET) is. On the basis of personal
correspondence, I believe that (ET3) is close to the interpretation of the
extendability thesis that Hilpinen wants, although I am not sure he would
approve of my addition of the phrase "if the sum total of S's information about
the world were to increase. . . ." Even if that phrase were dropped, the resulting thesis would still be too strong—as would (ive).

has moved closer to an ideally situated position by acquiring some new information.

The proposals of Hilpinen and Klein fail precisely because they allow for the possibility that a man's justification might be defeated by acquisition of an arbitrary limited portion of the evidence that he does not already possess. Given criterion (C) this leniency proves undesirable. The acquisition of such a limited portion of available new evidence is, we might say, one extreme on the continuum of ways in which a man could move toward a more ideally situated position. The other extreme is the acquisition of all the additional available information, but this extreme is only an epistemologist's pipe dream. We need something in between. In what follows I shall develop the idea that, of the possible ways in which a man might move toward a more ideally situated position with respect to justification, only some of those ways are relevant to the question whether his justification is defeasible.

III

When we talk about what would happen if a man were to become more ideally situated with respect to the evidence bearing upon some hypothesis, we are talking about how things might have been, or might come to be otherwise epistemically for him. I find it fruitful to characterize this kind of situation in terms of what I have elsewhere called *epistemic frameworks* and *alternatives* to epistemic frameworks.[16] An epistemic framework (abbreviated "Fs") is a set of epistemic descriptions of the forms "S believes that p," "S knows that p," "S is justified in believing that p," and so forth, such that the set completely describes the epistemic state of affairs of the person S at a given time. An alternative to an epistemic framework is another set of epistemic descriptions whose membership is determined in one of a variety of ways relative to the membership of the epistemic framework to which it is an alternative. In the interesting cases, a defined type of alternative to an epistemic framework will characterize an epistemic state of affairs of the person S which is

16. Marshall Swain, "The Consistency of Rational Belief," in *Induction, Acceptance, and Rational Belief*, pp. 27–32, and "An Alternative Analysis of Knowing."

possible but in fact quite different from the state of affairs actually described by his epistemic framework.

There are many subsets of an epistemic framework that are of interest. One of these is the subset consisting of all true expressions of the form "*S* is justified in believing——," and other expressions that characterize *S*'s evidential situation. This set of expressions corresponds to what is usually called *S*'s evidential base, or body of evidence; accordingly, I shall call this subset the *evidence component* of *S*'s epistemic framework. The question whether an epistemic description of the form "*S* is justified in believing——" is a member of *S*'s evidence component is to be decided by proper explication of the concept of justification. Such an explication will yield a set of rules governing the admissability of these expressions into an epistemic framework. These rules are called rules of epistemic inference. A number of plausible rules of epistemic inference have been suggested,[17] but a great deal of work needs to be done in this difficult area.

Assuming the availability of an adequate set of epistemic inference rules, we can specify the conditions under which a man, *S*, is justified in believing something as follows:

S is justified in believing that *h* if and only if the expression "*S* is justified in believing that *h*" is derivable from the other members of *S*'s evidence component in accordance with the rules of epistemic inference.

Let us suppose, then, that our subject *S* is justified in believing that *h*. We are concerned with the question whether his justification is indefeasible. This question can now be recast in the following way. Suppose we have defined a type of alternative to *S*'s epistemic framework such that if that alternative had obtained (or will obtain) then *S* would be more ideally situated evidentially than he in fact is; relative to the evidence component of such an alternative would *S* still be justified in believing that

17. For some remarks about epistemic inference rules see the two papers referred to in footnote 16. See also Roderick Chisholm, *Theory of Knowledge* (Englewood Cliffs, 1966), chs. 2 and 3, and "On the Nature of Empirical Evidence," Chap. 15 in the present volume. See also Herbert Heidelberger, "Chisholm's Epistemic Principles," *Nous*, 3 (1969), 73–82.

h? If so, then his justification is indefeasible; if not, then his justification is defeasible. The critical question is, can we define a type of alternative to an epistemic framework such that the defeasibility or indefeasibility of a man's justification rests upon what would be the case if that alternative were actualized?

To see what kind of alternative we need, we can reflect again on the examples of defeasible and indefeasible justification raised earlier. In some of those examples, such as the rock-thrower example, even though there is "available" some negative counterevidence, the defeating effect of this counterevidence is itself overridden. In the other cases the defeating effect of the counterevidence is not overridden, and the man's justification is defeated. In all of these examples, where there is some negative counterevidence it consists of some proposition or set of propositions that the person *S* is *in fact* justified in believing to be *false*. The wedding ceremony example shows us, indeed, that we must hold it to be a necessary condition of a proposition's being a defeating proposition that it be one the person *S* is justified in believing to be false. If we do not impose this requirement we allow for the possibility that a man's justification can be overridden by some bit of evidence that is available as a result of accident. In most cognitive situations, we are justified in believing a number of false propositions along with the true propositions that we are justified in believing. Hence, one way in which a man might approach an ideally situated evidential position is that it should become evident for him that some (that is, at least one) of the false propositions that he is justified in believing to be true are in fact false. We could define a type of alternative to a man's epistemic framework which describes a possible situation of this sort. To make defeasibility dependent upon what would happen if this kind of alternative were actualized would not, however, differ essentially from the proposals of Hilpinen and Lehrer and Paxson. Our earlier discussion of those proposals shows that this type of alternative will not serve our purposes.

A more promising approach is to consider what would happen if a man were to become justified in believing to be true *all* of those true propositions that he is in fact justified in believing to be false, and where the remainder of his epistemic situation changes only in some minimal way required to preserve consistency. We can specify what such a situation would look like by defining a type of alternative, which I shall call an *evidence-restricted* alternative:

(D8) Fs* is an evidence-restricted alternative to an epistemic framework Fs if and only if (i) for every true proposition q such that "S is justified in believing not-q" is a member of the evidence component of Fs, "S is justified in believing q" is a member of the evidence component of Fs*, (ii) for some subset C of members of Fs such that C is maximally consistent epistemically with the members generated in (i), every member of C is a member of Fs*, and (iii) no other propositions are members of Fs* except those that are implied epistemically by the members generated in (i) and (ii).

In this definition, there are two technical expressions that need to be explained. The expression "is epistemically consistent with" is to be understood as follows: Relative to a given set of rules of epistemic inference, two epistemic descriptions E and E' are epistemically consistent just in case neither of them implies epistemically the denial of the other. The notion of maximal consistency can be defined in this context in the following way: A subset C of members of Fs is maximally consistent epistemically with the members generated by (i) if and only if (a) the union of the set of members generated by (i) with the members of C is epistemically consistent and (b) for any other subset C' of Fs such that C is a proper subset of C', the union of the set of members generated by (i) with C' is epistemically inconsistent.

An evidence-restricted alternative is, then, a complete description of how things might change for S if his body of evidence were purged of all false members, each of these being replaced by its denial. Such an alternative describes one very carefully circumscribed way in which a man's epistemic position can improve. We can make defeasibility dependent upon what would happen if one's epistemic position were to improve in just this carefully defined way by replacing our earlier condition (ive) with:

  (ivf) S's justification for h is indefeasible (that is, there is an evidence-restricted alternative Fs* to S's epistemic framework Fs such that "S is justified in believing that h" is epistemically derivable from the other members of the evidence component of Fs*).

If (ivf) is used to construct an analysis of knowing, then the result will avoid the various problems we have considered so far. I shall consider two cases in illustration of the merits of (ivf).

First, let us consider one of the cases proposed by Gettier. Suppose that Jones has recently been told by his employer that he will be the next vice-president. The employer has in the past been honest and reliable. Moreover, suppose Jones knows that he has ten coins in his pocket, having just counted them. These facts plus background evidence constitute his evidence e. Jones recognizes that his evidence e justifies him in believing that q, namely, "Jones has ten coins in his pocket and will be the next vice-president." He also recognizes that q entails h, namely, "The man who will be the next vice-president has ten coins in his pocket." He concludes that h is justified for him since h is entailed by the justified proposition q. Moreover, h is true, but not for the reasons that Jones thinks it is true. The employer has untypically made a mistake. It is Smith, not Jones, who will be the next vice-president, and Smith coincidentally has ten coins in his pocket. So, Jones does not know that h even though he has justified true belief. And, the reason he does not know h is that his justification is defeasible. If Jones were to become ideally situated in the manner specified in the definition of an evidence-restricted alternative, it would no longer be the case that h is justified for him, relative to the other members of his evidence component. Let us see why this is so. In the example, there are a number of false propositions that Jones is justified in believing. Some crucial ones are:

  (1) The employer has spoken the truth.
  (2) Jones will be the next vice-president.

According to the definition of an evidence-restricted alternative, we first list as evident for Jones the denials of all those false propositions that Jones is in fact justified in believing to be true. Thus, among the members of the evidence component of the alternative will be:

> (1') Jones is justified in believing that the employer has not spoken truly.
>
> (2') Jones is justified in believing that he will not be the next vice-president.

The next step in the formula is to add to the alternative all those statements in some subset C of members of Fs that is maximally consistent with the members generated by the first step. One subset will include the following:

> (3) Jones is justified in believing that the employer told him he would be the next vice-president.
>
> (4) Jones is justified in believing that he has ten coins in his pocket.
>
> (5) Jones is justified in believing that the employer has in the past been honest and reliable.

However, since (1') and (2') are already members of the alternative, we cannot consistently add that (1) and (2) are justified for Jones. It is quite clear that given the membership of the alternative evidence component in this example, the proposition that the man who will get the job has ten coins in his pocket is not justified for Jones under that alternative. Moreover, there does not appear to be any other maximally consistent set of members of Fs, relative to (1') and (2'), such that S will be justified in believing h relative to the evidence-restricted alternative including that set. Hence, Jones's justification is defeasible by (ivf) and he does not know h. This is the desired result.

Let us now consider the rock-thrower example used against Hilpinen's proposal above. It will be recalled that this is a case where we would say S knows that h, but where the other conceptions of defeasibility give us the wrong result. I shall now argue that S's justification is indefeasible in this example, according to (ivf).

In the rock-thrower case, as in the previous example, there are a number of false propositions that S is justified in believing. The important members of S's epistemic framework in this regard are:

(6) S is justified in believing that he will see the window break.

(7) S is justified in believing that he will hear the window break.

(8) S is justified in believing that his sensory mechanisms will continue to function properly.

Since each of these justified things is false, we first include the following in the evidence-restricted alternative:

(6') S is justified in believing that he will not see the window break.

(7') S is justified in believing that he will not hear the window break.

(8') S is justified in believing that his sensory mechanisms will not continue to function properly.

We then add to the alternative some subset of members of S's epistemic framework that are maximally consistent with (6')–(8'). One subset will include virtually all of S's *original* evidence, such as:

(9) S is justified in believing that the rock will hit the window.

(10) S is justified in believing that the window is a normal window

but will not include (6), (7), or (8). It is clear that in the alternative so generated, it will still be the case that S is justified in believing that the window will break. For, even though the evidence component of the alternative contains the potentially defeating (6') and (7'), it also contains (8'), which nullifies the defeating effect of those other members. Hence, we can conclude that S's justification here is indefeasible, and that he has knowledge. Again, we get the desired result.

The proposal embodied in (ivf) is essentially the same as one that I originally suggested in my paper "An Alternative Analysis of Knowing." [18] The examples just considered and the ones

18. See "An Alternative Analysis of Knowing."

considered in the earlier paper show that an analysis of knowing incorporating this proposal is capable of dealing with many of the problems that have been raised in the literature. However, I now believe that (ivf) is inaccurate, for it fails to take into account an important aspect of the notion of defeasibility. I suggested above that the difference between the Gettier case and the case of the rock-thrower is that in that latter S's justification is indefeasible because the defeating effect of the available counterevidence is in turn overridden, whereas in the Gettier cases this is not so. These facts become clear when we consider the relevant evidence-restricted alternatives. Unfortunately, I have now found variations on the Gettier cases wherein the defeating effect of the available counterevidence is also overridden, according to (ivf), even though S does not have knowledge. All that (ivf) requires for indefeasibility is that in some evidence-restricted alternative it be true that S is justified in believing h—there is no specification that his justification in the alternative be the *same* as the justification that he actually has. But it is clearly essential that this be so. Consider the following variation on the Gettier case above. Suppose everything is as before, except that for some reason Jones happens to know that Smith (the man who is really going to get the job) has ten coins in his pocket. If so, then in the relevant evidence-restricted alternative to Jones's epistemic framework it will be evident for Jones that Smith will get the job (since it is *in fact* evident for him that Smith will not get the job) and *also* evident for him that Smith has ten coins in his pocket. But this renders it evident for him (in the alternative) that the man who will get the job has ten coins in his pocket. According to (ivf), Jones's justification for h would be indefeasible, and he would have knowledge. But neither of these things is so.

This argument against (ivf) brings out the fact that it is always a particular justification that is defeasible or indefeasible. The fact that if a man were to become more ideally situated in the manner specified by the notion of an evidence-restricted alternative then he might have some *other* justification for h is irrelevant to the question whether *the* justification he in fact has is defeasible or not. We need to require that a justification be indefeasible only if that justification *itself* would continue to hold under the process of becoming more ideally situated epistemically. In the rock-thrower case it is clear that even if the man became more ideally situated by coming to know that he would suffer sensory paralysis, etc., the justification that he has for believing that the window will break would remain essentially the same. But, in the revised Gettier case just considered the justification S has would be replaced by another in the evidence-restricted alternative.

We must be cautious, however, about requiring that a justification be *exactly* preserved as we move to some evidence-restricted alternative if that justification is to be indefeasible. We shall have to allow for some slight changes here and there. First, it has been effectively argued in the literature[19] that sometimes a man's justification can involve some false evidence, provided this false evidence is not central to his justification. A man might, for example, have two evidential beliefs, each of which is sufficient to justify belief that h, but one of which is false. Provided that he fully bases his belief that h on both bits of evidence, there is no prima facie reason why his justification could not be indefeasible. In such a case, however, when we move to the evidence-restricted alternative the false evidence that he has will no longer form part of his justification. Secondly, in many cognitive situations, particularly those in which a man's justification is indefeasible, the justification that he would have under the alternative will be augmented by new information. Hence, we can say that his justification changes when we move to the alternative; but notice that it does not change in the sense of being *replaced* by a new line of justification.

To rule out the latest counterexample while allowing for the facts just discussed, I shall revise (ivf) as follows:

(ivg) S's justification for h is indefeasible (that is, there is an evidence-restricted alternative Fs* to S's epistemic framework Fs such that (i) "S is justified in believing

---

19. See Keith Lehrer, "Knowledge, Truth and Evidence." See also Roderick Chisholm, "The Nature of Empirical Evidence," pp. 119–122.

that h" is epistemically derivable from the other
members of the evidence component of Fs* and (ii)
there is some subset of members of the evidence
component of Fs* such that (a) the members of this
subset are also members of the evidence component
of Fs and (b) "S is justified in believing that h" is epistemically derivable from the members of this subset).

In the revised Gettier case above, even though S is justified in
believing that h under the evidence-restricted alternative, there
is no part of the justification that he in fact has which "carries
over" to the alternative and which is alone sufficient to justify h.
This, I believe, is the force of saying that his justification is replaced by a new one in the alternative. Hence, by clause (ii) of
(ivg) this example is eliminated.

However, (ivg) allows for the desired kind of changes in S's
justification when we move to the evidence-restricted alternative. It is compatible with clause (ii) of (ivg) that any false parts
of the justification that S in fact has will be eliminated in the alternative—part (b) of clause (ii) requires that that part of his
justification that *does* carry over to the alternative must be sufficient to justify h. This is the force of saying that the central
part of his justification is preserved in moving to the alternative. It is also compatible with clause (ii) that S's justification
changes under the alternative in the sense of being augmented
by new information. Even though clause (ii) requires that the
subset which "carries over" be sufficient to justify h, there is no
stipulation that this subset constitutes the total body of justifying evidence that S has under the alternative. Of course, any
additional evidence that S has in the alternative must be such
that clause (i) of (ivg) is satisfied.

I submit that (ivg) is, therefore, adequate as an analysis of
epistemic defeasibility. My argument for this claim rests heavily
on the criterion (C) introduced at the beginning of this paper.
It is perhaps a bit hasty to rest such a large conclusion on the
fact that the proposal works in one limited area, namely, the
problem of analyzing knowledge. The real test of my proposal

will be whether it also works in the other areas where epistemic defeasibility plays a role.[20]

20. A short version of this paper was read at the Eastern Division meetings of the American Philosophical Association, December 29, 1972. Ernest Sosa was the commentator. I am indebted to Sosa, and to a referee of this journal for helpful suggestions. In his commentary, Sosa argued that (D8) needs revision because, given (ivg), it has the result that if S's evidence E renders some false statement F evident, then in the evidence-restricted alternative it will be evident that not-F, which is incompatible with its also being evident in the alternative that E, which in turn implies that E is not in fact known by S. This problem can be dealt with by revising (D8) to guarantee that in the alternative there is some R such that R is evident for S and such that R confers evidence upon not-F as well as upon E. I regret that space limitations prohibit my giving a more detailed response to Sosa's problem at this time.

12

How Do You Know?

ERNEST SOSA

Despair of knowing what knowledge is dates back to Plato's *Theaetetus*. Most recently, the trinitarian view of knowledge as justified true belief has been refuted, and a multitude of problems has appeared. Progress on this question is perhaps fated to be asymptotic. But such progress as can now be made depends, in my opinion, on a careful study of the conditions within which a correctly believed proposition is a bit of knowledge. In what follows I hope to enhance our knowledge of knowledge by contributing to such a study.

I

An accepted truth is knowledge only if evident. What then is it for something to be evident? One short answer is this: a proposition is evident to someone provided he is (theoretically) justified in believing it.[1] But under what further circumstances is the truth of a proposition evident to someone? This is our first main question.

To begin with, there are two general situations where it is evident to someone S that p. First, there is the situation where it is self-evident to S that p, i.e., where from the fact that S correctly believes that p we may infer that it is evident to S that p. Our in-

Reprinted from *The American Philosophical Quarterly*, 11.2 (1974), 113–122, by kind permission of the author and editor.

1. The parenthetical qualification is meant to rule out as irrelevant whatever practical reasons there might be for having a belief, such as those of a sick man whose belief that he will recover is essential to his recovery.

ference here cannot be logically valid as it stands, however, since logic alone will not enable us to infer that anything is evident just from the fact that it is correctly believed. Some extralogical princples must be invoked to invalidate such an inference.

Such principles are clearly needed, in any case, provided we want to account for (and not deny) our empirical knowledge. Accordingly, they have long been recognized and accepted. The Greek Sceptics perceived the problems involved clearly and made some definite suggestions.[2] Descartes and Hume were in fundamental agreement about epistemic principles: There is first the self-evident, which includes some obvious general truths and some particular claims, mainly about one's subjective states; anything else that is evident must be made so by being deduced from the self-evident. This much, it seems to me, they both accepted, even if it led them in very different directions: Descartes to his baroque system, and Hume to his desert landscape. Coming to more recent philosophy, the principles underlying the "criteria" of Wittgenstein and others seem best understood as epistemic principles.[3] Discussion of epistemic principles and epistemic scales is to be found in Chisholm's writings.[4] Finally, the third of Sellars' Matchette Lectures, delivered at the University of Texas, is a discussion of "Epistemic Principles."[5] (Among the correlates of such principles in Sellars' philosophy are his principles of "trans-level inference."[6]

2. Thus the theory of Carneades of Cyrene is presented by Sextus Empiricus in his *Outline of Pyrrhonism* and in his *Against the Logicians*. This theory is discussed by Roderick M. Chisholm in his *Theory of Knowledge* (Englewood Cliffs, 1966), pp. 41–44.
3. Cf. Norman Malcolm, *Knowledge and Certainty* (Englewood Cliffs, 1963), pp. 113–117.
4. See *Perceiving: A Philosophical Study* (Ithaca, 1957); and *Theory of Knowledge*. For more recent developments see "On the Nature of Empirical Evidence" [Chapter 15 in this volume].
5. The lectures were delivered in 1970 but are as yet unpublished.
6. See *Science, Perception, and Reality* (London, 1963), p. 88. Trans-level inference is also discussed in "Empiricism and the Philosophy of Mind," in *Minnesota Studies in the Philosophy of Science*, Vol. I, ed. Herbert Feigl and Michael Scriven (Minneapolis, 1956). This essay is also Chapter 5 of *Science, Perception, and Reality*.

What would such epistemic principles look like? What would be some examples? Let us introduce the schematic letter 'p' to be replaced by declarative clauses. The following might then be a correct epistemic principle schema: "If S correctly believes that it occurs to him that p, then it is evident to S that it occurs to him that p."

Other examples of correct principle schemata yielding self-evident propositions are those corresponding to basic a priori truths, such as "If S believes that either p or it is false that p, then it is evident to S that either p or it is false that p." Here again from S's mere correct belief of a proposition that p (e.g., that either it is snowing or it is false that it is snowing) we may infer that it is evident to S that p, and hence such propositions count as self-evident for S. Moreover, as distinguished from the group about propositional attitudes the present group of propositions are self-evident-if-evident for every person. That either it is snowing or it is not snowing is self-evident-if-evident for everyone, but it is self-evident-if-evident only to Tom that it occurs to him that snow is white since it is true only of Tom that if he correctly believes that proposition, we can infer that it is evident to him.

We have seen how the first general situation where it is evident to S that p is one where it is self-evident to S that p. But obviously there are known facts that are not self-evident. Hence if a fact can't be known without being evident, there must be facts that are evident but not self-evident. And, more generally, there are propositions that are evident but not self-evident. This is of course the *second* general situation where it is evident to someone S that p. Now when it is evident to S that p but not self-evident to S that p, then that S correctly believes that p is not sufficient to establish it as evident to S that p, even with the help of the epistemic principles. What then *is* thus sufficient?

The answer I wish to propose is, in first approximation, that in such circumstances what makes it evident to S that p is a non-empty set of propositions α such that α validates the proposition that it is evident to S that p. Vaguely put, the idea is simply that if you know that p, but it is not self-evident to you that p, then you must have grounds for believing that p, and these grounds must make it evident to you that p. But to give your grounds for believing that p is not necessarily to give a complete epistemic explanation of how it comes to be evident to you that p. For often grounds that you have for believing that p cannot be groundless but require grounds of their own, and these may require grounds in turn, and so on. A complete epistemic explanation will not stop until it has adduced the grounds for every ground that has grounds.

It therefore appears that we need more than just the idea of a set of grounds that grounds the proposition that p for S. We need the idea of a set of grounds that *fully* grounds the proposition that p for S, the idea of a set that gives a complete epistemic explanation of how it comes to be evident to S that p.

But how are we to define this idea of a set's fully grounding a proposition for a subject at a time? Shall we say that α fully grounds x (for S at t) when for every ground y in α there is a subset α' of α such that α' grounds y? But what if $\alpha = \{$that the triangular card is approximately equilateral, that the triangular card is approximately equiangular$\}$ and $x =$ that each of the card's angles has approximately 60°? This appears to fulfill the conditions specified and yet α can hardly be said to provide a complete epistemic explanation for how it comes to be evident that each of the card's angles has approximately 60°. For instance, how do we know that there is a triangular card at all, or that it is approximately equilateral in the first place?

Adapting an idea of Frege's, shall we say that α fully grounds x iff α is the class of ancestral grounds of x? (Here y is an ancestral ground of x iff $(\forall\alpha)\{[x \in \alpha$ & $(\forall z)(\forall w)[(w \in \alpha)$ & $(z$ is a ground of $w)] \supset (z \in \alpha)] \supset y \in \alpha\}$; i.e., y is an ancestral ground of x iff y is a member of every class containing x and all grounds of members.)

The main problem with this definition derives from cases of epistemic over-determination. In such cases the class of ancestral grounds of x will contain superfluous grounds. This will turn out to be unfavorable to our purposes, mainly because a defective ground—say a false ground—surely need not flaw every fully grounding class, not if it's a superfluous ground.

And yet, according to the Fregean idea, there is only *one* fully grounding class, and it *will* contain *every* ancestral ground, superfluous or not.

My suggestion is therefore this: α fully grounds x for S at t if and only if there is a set of subsets of α which form a sequence $C_1, \ldots, C_n$, such that (i) C_1 grounds x, (ii) for each member y of any subset C_i, such that y requires grounds, the successor of C_i, C_{i+1}, grounds y and (iii) the last subset, C_n, contains no ground that requires grounds.

We are finally in a position to answer our first main question. A proposition x is evident to someone S in either of two general situations: *either* x is self-evident to S *or* there is a set of propositions that fully grounds x for S. But we may consider the first of these a special case of the second, if we allow that the null set fully grounds self-evident propositions. Thus we may conclude that *a proposition x is evident to S if and only if there is a set of propositions that fully grounds x for S.*

If I am right thus far, the well-known triadic account of knowledge as correct, evident belief is then equivalent to an account (1) according to which S knows that p provided that both (a) S correctly believes that p, and (b) there is a set of propositions that fully grounds that p for S.

Supposing this account correct, every bit of knowledge would be supported by a pyramid such as the following.

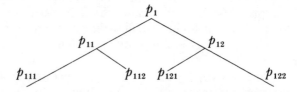

Each node of such a pyramid is a proposition. Thus the *apex* node is the-proposition-that p_1, and the first *terminal* node from the left is the-proposition-that-p_{111}.

Such "epistemic pyramids" must satisfy certain requirements:
   1. (Let us call node x a "successor" (i.e., a *direct* successor) of node y relative to pyramid P provided there are A and B such that (i) A stands for x on P and B stands for

y on P; (ii) A and B are connected by a straight line on P; (iii) B is closer to the apex node than A; and (iv) there is no C such that C stands for a proposition on P, and A, B, and C are connected by a straight line and B is closer to the apex node than C, and C is closer to the apex node than A.) The set of all nodes that (directly) succeed a given node must ground that node.

2. Each node must be a proposition that is evident to S.
3. If a node n is not a proposition that is self-evident to S then it must have successors, it must be succeeded by further nodes that ground the proposition n.
4. Each branch of an epistemic pyramid must terminate.

It follows that to each set that fully renders x evident to S there corresponds at least one epistemic pyramid for S and x. And we thus have a second account of knowledge that is also a close equivalent of the traditional account:

(2) S knows that p iff
    (a) it is true that p;
    (b) S believes that p; and
    (c) there is an epistemic pyramid for S and the proposition that p.

However, it is a well-known fact that the traditional account of propositional knowledge is inadequate. Therefore, if the above account is really equivalent to the traditional account, it should be similarly inadequate. And so it is.

Consider the following pyramid (schema) for S and the proposition that $p \lor q$.

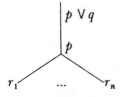

Supposing that S correctly believes that $p \lor q$, the three clauses in our account are satisfied. And yet S may not know that $p \lor q$, nevertheless. For it may be false that p, and the preceding diagram may be the *only* kind of epistemic pyramid available

190   Ernest Sosa

for S and the proposition that $p \lor q$, any other such pyramid being simply an "expansion" of the above, i.e., a pyramid obtainable by correctly adding further nodes. (Obviously, if there were another kind of pyramid, where instead of p we found q, then S might still know that $p \lor q$, in spite of the falsity of p.) [7]

A further restriction on pyramids immediately suggests itself: *to support knowledge epistemic pyramids must be non-defective, i.e., must contain only true nodes.*

According to Keith Lehrer the new requirement still leaves our account open to an interesting objection. Consider the following statements:

P_1: Mr. Nogot, who is in my office, owns a Ford;

P_2: Mr. Havit, who is in my office, owns a Ford; and

H: Someone in my office owns a Ford.

And imagine ". . . that I have seen Mr. Nogot drive a Ford on many occasions and that I now see him drive away in it. Moreover, imagine that he leaves his wallet at my house and that I, being curious, examine its contents. Therein I discover a certificate asserting that Mr. Nogot owns the Ford I have just seen him drive away. This would supply me with evidence E consisting of true statements, which would completely justify my believing P_1, and, therefore, H. But now imagine that . . . P_1 is false (due to some legal technicality), and P_2 is true, though I have no evidence for P_2. In this case, I do not know H, but all of Mr. Sosa's requirements for knowledge might well be met." [8]

7. I have here translated the objection raised originally by Edmund L. Gettier against the traditional account of propositional knowledge. See his "Is Justified True Belief Knowledge?" *Analysis*, 23 (1963), 121–123 (reprinted in the Bobbs-Merrill reprint series).

8. Keith Lehrer, "Knowledge, Truth and Evidence," reprinted in *Knowing*, ed. M. D. Roth and L. Galis (New York, 1970), p. 171. The requirements to which Lehrer refers were made in my "Analysis of 'Knowledge that p,'" *Analysis*, 25.1 (1964), 1–8 (reprinted in the Bobbs-Merrill reprint series). These requirements featured, in different terminology, the one now under review, viz., the requirement that for S to know that p there must be a nondefective pyramid of knowledge for S and the proposition that p. Indeed, the account of knowledge as correct belief buttressed by a nondefective pyramid is virtually my earlier account pruned of several inessential and confusing elements. I believe that the present account also enables us to deal with other difficulties reviewed in "Two Conceptions of Knowledge," *Journal of Philosophy*, 67 (1970), esp. pp. 63–66. The core idea involved has also been defended by Gilbert Har-

However, it is in general false that if one is justified in believing p and p entails q, then one is justified in believing q. I can surely believe the axioms of a theory and yet lack sufficient justification for believing many of the theorems. For many of the theorems may as yet be unproved.

Consequently, we must reject the general principle that if e provides good (inductive or deductive) grounds for p, and p entails q, then e provides good grounds for q. The point can also be put like this: even if your justifiably believing e and your believing p on the basis of your belief of e would together imply that your believing p is justified, and even if p entails q, it still would *not* follow that your justifiably believing e and your believing q on the basis of your belief of e would together imply that your believing q is justified. (Moreover, this would not follow even on the assumption that you do believe q and believe it on the basis of your belief of e.)

Thus I am puzzled by Lehrer's statement that E ". . . would completely justify my believing P_1, and, *therefore*, H." (My emphasis.) I see no reason for accepting this inference. Would my believing E and my believing H on the basis of E imply that my believing H is justified? Not necessarily, for whether I am justified surely depends on whether I see a connection between E and H.[9] If I believe axioms of a theory and believe a theorem on their basis I still may not be justified in believing that theorem. For I may believe the theorem on the basis of the axioms mistakenly and without having seen a real connection.

Normally, we would establish a connection between E and H by way of the likes of P_1 or P_2. Suppose that from among such

man, who argues that a condition for knowledge is that the lemmas be true, i.e., that one not reason *via* a falsehood. (See, e.g., "The Inference to the Best Explanation," *Philosophical Review*, 74.1 (1965), 88–95; and "Knowledge, Reasons, and Causes," *Journal of Philosophy*, 67 (1970), 841–856.) A recent defense of our core idea is "Knowledge without Paradox," by Robert G. Meyers and Kenneth Stern (*Journal of Philosophy*, 70 (1973), 147–160, which contains an interesting discussion of Lehrer's argument.

9. For particularly strong requirements on the structure of such a connection, see James W. Lamb's "Knowledge and Justified Presumption," *Journal of Philosophy*, 69 (1972), 123–127. This has been discussed by William Edward Morris in "Knowledge as Justified Presumption," *Journal of Philosophy*, 70 (1973), 161–165.

statements only P_1 is evident to you in some normal case. In that case you could make no connection between E and H except by way of a falsehood. Put another way, in that case there would be no non-defective pyramid for you and H. Therefore, our requirement would not be met by Lehrer's example after all. To be sure, there may be ways of connecting E and H without involving P_1. Perhaps there is some such way that does not violate the requirement, but I confess that I can't think of one.[10]

II

Despite the merits of the present account, however, I believe it can be shown to be too narrow. For it allows as determinants of what one knows only what one correctly believes with rational justification. But reflection will reveal much else that is equally relevant.

In the first place, what one is rationally justified in believing obviously depends on the data in one's possession. But what data one has can depend on how much and how well one investigates. Consider, therefore, the following possibility. What if A is rationally justified in believing x given his body of data D_1 whereas B is not rationally justified in believing x given his body of data D_2, where D_2 includes D_1 but is much more extensive as a result of A's irresponsible negligence and B's commendable thoroughness? The present account might unfortunately grant A knowledge while denying it to B, for A's neglect so far has no bearing on any epistemic pyramid.

We have considered a situation where someone lacks knowledge owing to his misuse of his cognitive equipment, either by letting it idle when it should be functioning or by busily employing it dysfunctionally. Another situation where someone

10. In favor of this reply to Lehrer's example, I would also urge that the proviso that one must not "reason" via a falsehood gives us the simplest, most natural solution to the Gettier problem, and that we should therefore let it fall only under the impact of a forceful counterexample. For a further defense of the proviso, see my papers "On Our Knowledge of Matters of Fact," *Mind*, 83 (1974), 388–405, and "Standard Conditions," *Modality, Morality, and Other Problems of Sense and Nonsense* (Gleerup and Co., 1974), a volume in honor of Soren Hallden edited by the Philosophy Department of the University of Lund.

lacks knowledge despite having rationally justified correct belief might be called the Magoo situation—where S lacks adequate equipment to begin with (relative to the question in
hand: whether p).[11] It is because of this type of lack that despite
his extensive experience with cable cars, Mr. Magoo does not
know that his cable car will arive safely when, unknown to him,
bombs are raining all around it. Of course, even if you have
less than 20–20 vision you can still know that there is an ele-
phant in front of you when you see one there. So not just any
defect will make your equipment inadequate for a judgment on
the question whether p. I would venture that it must be a defect
that prevents you from acquiring information that (i) a normal
inquirer in the epistemic community would acquire in that situation *and* (ii) makes a difference to what you can reasonably
conclude on the question whether p (or at least to how reasonably you can draw the conclusion).

The possibility of inadequate cognitive equipment requires a
further and more striking departure from the traditional conception of knowledge. Earlier we considered a situation where,
despite having warranted correct belief, someone lacks knowledge owing to his neglectful data-collection. There lack of
knowledge could be traced back to epistemic irresponsibility, to
substandard performance blamed on the investigator. In the
present example, blame is out of place. By hypothesis, Magoo
conducts impeccable "inquiry" both in arriving at his data and
on the basis of his data. But he still falls short of knowledge,
despite his warranted, correct belief. His shortcoming is substandard equipment, for which we may suppose him to be
blameless. Hence something other than epistemic justification
or correct belief can help determine what one knows or does
not know. Even if one correctly believes that p with full rational
justification and free of irrational or neglectful unbelief, one
may still be in no position to know, because of faulty cognitive
equipment.

In all of the foregoing cases, someone misses or is liable to

11. Thanks are due Jerome Shaffer for suggesting the problem posed by the
Magoo situation—the situation of that unfortunate deaf and blind cartoon
character who fortunately escapes disaster at every turn.

miss available information which may be highly relevant and important and may make a difference to what he can conclude on the question in hand. In each case, moreover, he seems culpable or discredited in some sense: he would seem less reliable than otherwise for his role in any such case. But there appear to be situations where again someone misses available information with no culpability *or* discredit. Harman gives an example where S reads in a newspaper that some famous person has been assassinated, but does not read the next edition, where all reports of the assassination are denied by highly authoritative and trustworthy people. If practically the whole country reads the next edition and people don't know what to believe, does S alone know of the assassination, provided the next edition is in fact a pack of lies?[12] I suppose we would be inclined to say that he does not know (especially if had he read the next edition, *he* would not have known what to believe). But what if only two or three people get a chance to read the next edition before it is recalled by the newspaper? Should we now say that out of the millions who read the first story and mourn the loved leader not one knows of his death? I suppose we would be inclined to say that the fake edition and the few deceived by it make no difference concerning what everybody else knows. It seems plausible to conclude that knowledge has a further "social aspect," that it cannot depend on one's missing or blinking what is generally known.

Our departures from the traditional conception of knowledge put in relief the relativity of knowledge to an epistemic community. This is brought out most prominently by the requirement that inquirers have at least *normal* cognitive equipment (e.g., normal perceptual apparatus, where that is relevant). But our new requirement—that inquirers not lack or blink generally known relevant information—also brings out the relativity. A vacationer in the woods may know that p well enough for an average vacationer, but he won't have the kind of knowledge his guide has. A guide would scornfully deny

12. Gilbert Harman, "Induction," in Marshall Swain, ed., *Induction, Acceptance, and Rational Belief* (Reidel, 1970), esp. Sect. IV, pp. 95–97. Cf. "The Analysis of 'Knowledge that p'," *op cit.*, p. 5.

that the tenderfoot really knows that *p*. Relative to the epistemic community of guides (for that area) the tenderfoot lacks relevant generally known information, and misses relevant data that the average guide would grasp in the circumstances.

(Understanding of these departures from the traditional account may perhaps be enhanced if we reflect that the honorific term "knowledgeable" is to be applied only to those who are reliable sources of information, surely an important category for a language-using, social species.)

We have now taken note of two types of situation where correct, fully warranted belief falls short of knowledge owing to no neglect or faulty reasoning or false belief. Despite commendable thoroughness and impeccable reasoning unspoiled by falsehood, one may still fail to be "in a position to know," owing either to faulty cognitive equipment or to missed generally known information. I am not suggesting that these are the only ways to be out of position to know. I have no complete list of epistemic principles describing ways of arriving at a position to know or of being blocked from such a position. My suggestion is only that there are such principles, and that in any case we must go beyond the traditional emphasis by epistemologists on warrant and reasoning as determinants of knowledge. Despite the importance of warranted correct belief in determining what we know, the Gettier examples show that it is not alone enough to guarantee knowledge. What is more, warranted correct belief supported by reasoning *unspoiled by falsehood* seems immune to Gettier examples, but it may still fall short of knowledge. We have considered several types of such shortfalling.

My conclusion is that to understand knowledge we must enrich our traditional repertoire of epistemic concepts with the notion of *being in a position to know (from the point of view of a K, e.g., a human being)*. Thus a proposition is evident (from the point of view of a *K*) to a subject only if *both* he is rationally justified in believing it *and* he is in a position to know (from the *K* point of view) whether it is true. It may *be* (and not just appear) evident to Magoo from *his* point of view that he will reach the other side safely, but it seems wrong to say of Magoo as he steps into the cable car with bombs raining all around that it *is*

196   Ernest Sosa

quite evident to him that he will arrive safely. It seems wrong
for whom to say this? For one of us, naturally; that is, for a normal human from *his* point of view. And since a normal human
could not help seeing and hearing the bombs, from the human
point of view Magoo is not in a position to know that he will arrive safely, inasmuch as he is missing relevant information that
a normal human would gather in the circumstances. Hence
Magoo does not have *human* knowledge that he will arrive
safely, for it is not evident to him from the human point of
view that he will so arrive.

Our latest account was this:

> (3) *S* knows that *p* iff
>> (a) it is true that *p*;
>> (b) *S* believes that *p*; and
>> (c) there is a non-defective epistemic pyramid for *S*
>> and the proposition that *p*.

It will be recalled that every node of such a pyramid must be
true *and* evident. And for every node *n* that has successors, the
successors must serve as grounds that give the subject *S* rational
warrant for believing *n*. What now seems too narrow about this
account emerges with the explanation of what a pyramid of
knowledge is, and of what the evident is. For in this explanation what is evident to *S* is identified with what *S* is rationally
justified in believing. But it now seems plain that for *x* to be evident to *S*, *two* conditions must be satisfied: (i) that *S* be rationally justified in believing *x*, and (ii) that *S* be in a position to
know whether *x* is true. And we must also take note of the relativity of knowledge to an epistemic community. Let us therefore replace (3) with the following:

> (4) *S* knows (from the *K* point of view) that *p* iff
>> (a) it is true that *p*;
>> (b) *S* believes that *p*; and
>> (c) there is a non-defective epistemic pyramid (from
>> the *K* point of view) for *S* and the proposition that
>> *p*.

Every node of such a pyramid must now be true and evident
from the *K* point of view.

Normally when epistemologists discuss knowledge (of the

colors and shapes of surrounding objects, of one's own or one's neighbor's mental states, and so on), they plainly do so from the *human* point of view. But other points of view are possible even in ordinary conversation. The expert/layman distinction is replicable in many different contexts, and with each replication we have a new epistemically relevant distinction in points of view, with expert knowledge on one side and layman knowledge on the other.

Neither Magoo nor the newspaper reader who alone has not seen the new edition is in a position to know (from the human point of view) about the relevant subject matter. Thus we can understand their ignorance and, by parity of reasoning, the ignorance of all those who are out of position to know that p because they lack either adequate cognitive equipment or relevant information that is generally known to those who have taken an epistemic stand on the question whether p (where to suspend judgment *is* to take an epistemic stand, whereas to be totally oblivious to the matter is not).

But the new account, with its broader conception of the evident, seems blatantly circular. For x must be evident to you if you are to know that x is true. But now x is evident to you only if you are in a position to know whether x is true. And what is it to be in a position to know except to be in a position such that if you believe correctly then you do *know*? Is there any defense against this charge of circularity? Let us begin by conceding— what is in fact questionable—that you are in a position to know if and only if you are in a position such that you have only to believe correctly in order to know. All the same, this need not be offered as an analysis but only as a truth. If that is not the analysis of being in a position to know, however, what is? Our account escapes the noose of circularity only to face a pit of obscurity.

A defense can be given in two stages. In the first place, if our account seems obscure at first sight, the traditional account seems equally obscure. What is the "rational justification" of which it speaks? This is particularly puzzling because it must be understood as a *sui generis* type of intellectual or theoretical justification, so as to rule out whatever practical considerations may militate for or against belief. In the second place, insofar as rational justification may be clarified it surely must be in terms of the principles of reasoning or epistemic principles that define its area of application. And the same may be done for being-in-a-position-to-know. Hence insofar as our account seems vague or obscure, the traditional account seems equally so, and insofar as the traditional account allows of clarification our account does so as well.

Thus S is in a position to know that p if it is self-evident to S that $p, \ldots$, and so on, drawing the content of our explanation from the relevant epistemic principles. Two such principles have been suggested as solutions to as many problems: (a) that to be in a position to have human knowledge whether p you must not miss any crucial information that a normal human in your situation would gather; and (b) that to be in a position to have human knowledge whether p you must not miss any crucial information that is generally known to those who have taken an epistemic stand on the question whether p. (Information is crucial relative to your knowing whether p provided that adding that information to your evidence base would induce a fall in the epistemic status of your belief either that p or that not-p to such an extent that where previously that belief was rationally justified it no longer is so.) It is such principles that give content to the idea of being in a position to know.

Doubtless we cannot hope here for such precision as is attainable in explaining, e.g., what it is to be a chess bishop. But chess is defined by a set of articicial conventions, whereas it is doubtful that epistemic principles are either artificial or conventional. At present, in any case, our understanding of what it is to be rationally justified or of what it is to be in a position to know is about as vague as our understanding of what it is to be moral, or well-mannered, or to speak grammatically. It would be very difficult to remove such vagueness, and it might turn out to be impossible.[13] In that case, Russell's view that knowledge is an inherently vague notion would have been vindicated. Meanwhile it is surely wise to elicit as much precise content as possi-

---

13. Cf. Malcolm, *op. cit.*, pp. 114–115.

ble from our epistemic practice, for content unelicited is missed understanding.

III

What it is for S's belief that p to be fully grounded had been explained earlier by means of our epistemic pyramids. That answer points in the right direction, but it needs to be made more precise. (Perhaps the main requirement is clarifying the grounding relation.) Moreover, we have found that a fully grounded correct belief is not necessarily knowledge, and this for at least two reasons: (i) it may rest directly or indirectly on some false ground, and (ii) the believer may not be in a position to know.

We have tried to allow for these possibilities by broadening epistemic pyramids, by making room for our new epistemic notion of being-in-a-position-to-know, and by noting that to support knowledge epistemic pyramids must be non-defective, i.e., must contain no false nodes. But pyramids are objectionable for other reasons as well: (i) they may mislead by suggesting that terminal nodes provide a "foundation" in one or another undesirable sense, or by suggesting that terminal nodes must come first in time, so that one may later build on them; (ii) more seriously, there is an unacceptable vagueness in the very idea of such a pyramid, which derives mainly from the vagueness of the "grounding" relation in terms of which pyramids were defined. What follows is an attempt to solve these problems by switching pyramids upside down into trees, and by providing a more precise definition of such trees. To achieve greater precision, however, we must first enrich our conceptual resources. Each of the three main concepts to be defined—(I), (II), and (III),—seems to me a source of light, and by this light we shall then trim our trees to a more precise outline.

(I) α *fully validates* S-epistemic proposition e if and only if there is a set of subsets of α that form a sequence, C_1, . . . , C_n, such that (i) C_1 validates e, (ii) each S-epistemic member of any subset C_i is validated by the immediate successor of C_i, $C_i + {}_1$, and (iii) no member of the last subset, C_n, is S-epistemic.

This account of full validation makes use of a battery of technical concepts. Among them are *validation* and *S-epistemic proposition,* each of which requires explanation.

(II) *S-epistemic propositions:* of these (i) some are to the effect that some other proposition x has some epistemic status relative to S (i.e., to the effect that S believes x and how reasonably); and (ii) others are to the effect that S is in a position to know whether a certain proposition is true. (i) and (ii) are the varieties of "positive S-epistemic propositions." Logical compounds of such propositions are also S-epistemic, but no other propositions are S-epistemic.

(III) *Epistemic validation.* Let $A,B,$ B, and C be sets of propositions.

    1. *A epistemically implies* that p if and only if A and the epistemic principles together logically imply that p, but neither does so alone.

    2. *A absolutely validates* S-epistemic proposition e if and only if A has only true members and epistemically implies e.

    3. *A confirms* S-epistemic proposition e if and only if (a) A is a set with only true members, and (b) supposing the true, positive S-epistemic propositions are at most those entailed or absolutely validated by A, e follows epistemically from this together with A.

    4. *A validates* S-epistemic proposition e if and only if A confirms e, A has only true members, and for every B with none but true members, such that $A \cup B$ does not confirm e, there is a C with none but true members such that $A \cup B \cup C$ does confirm e.[14]

(Note that 3 is included only for convenience, since *A confirms p* if and only if $A \cup$ {that the true, positive S-epistemic proposi-

14. The notion of epistemic validation makes the present proposal a "defeasibility analysis of knowledge," in Marshall Swain's terminology. Swain finds the earliest such use of defeasibility in "The Analysis of 'Knowledge that p'," *op. cit.* [see M. Swain, "Knowledge, Causality, and Justification," Chapter 4, above, n. 2]; and he traces its use through a dozen papers on knowledge in his "Epistemic Defeasibility," Chapter 11 above. Most recent developments include

tions are at most those entailed or absolutely validated by A} *absolutely validates p.*)

That completes the explanation of full validation (defined above). Note that what is fully validated by a set is always an S-epistemic proposition; and that the propositions in the validating set need not all be S-epistemic and that indeed perhaps none is S-epistemic. For example, some may be "self-certifying" or "self-discrediting" by specifying, with respect to a proposition x, that S correctly believes x, where this is sufficient for x to have a certain (positive or negative) epistemic status for S, given the epistemic principles; other *non*-epistemic members of a validating set may specify S's perceptual or cognitive basis for a belief he has; others may certify the adequacy of S's cognitive equipment relative to the epistemic community; and others yet may guarantee that S is not missing relevant generally known information.

(For convenience, in what follows let us terminologically stipulate that α (fully) validates that a proposition is evident, certain, reasonable, etc., for a subject when and only when the set α "(fully) renders certain, reasonable, etc.," that proposition for that subject; and that α (fully) validates that S is in a position to know that p when and only when α "(fully) puts S in a position to know that p.")

There is some simple reasoning behind the definition of full validation and behind the idea that if S knows that p then there must be a set that fully validates that it is evident to A that p. The reasoning boils down to this: Supposing that both circular justification and infinite regress are ruled out, it would seem that a chain of justification must eventually reach a last link that either is self-validating or helps validate further links without itself requiring validation.

Let us emphasize, however, that this will not commit one to a picture of knowledge according to which there is a bedrock of

Swain's "Alternative Analysis of Knowing," *Synthese* 23 (1972), 423–442, and "Epistemic Defeasibility." Finally, I have found R. M. Chisholm's "On the Nature of Empirical Evidence" especially helpful in thinking about epistemic validation. It appeared originally in *Experience and Theory,* ed. Lawrence Foster and J. W. Swanson (Amherst, 1970); and a revised version appears in *Empirical Knowledge,* ed. R. Chisholm and R. J. Swartz (New York, 1973). [Also reprinted in this volume as Chapter 15.]

self-evident propositions. It is perfectly consistent with the present theory that part of what makes *any* proposition evident be its coherence with a network of mutually supporting propositions. Since there is bound to be a multitude of such coherent networks, however, a non-arbitrary narrowing of the field must be supported by something other than coherence. And this is where the last subset in the sequence of subsets of a fully validating set may be invoked. However, it is not required that the last subset include any self-evident belief; for example, it may contain some merely self-certifying correct belief, i.e., a proposition specifying that some other proposition x is correctly believed, where this suffices for x to have *some* positive epistemic status, however lowly: acceptability, for instance (i.e., being such that not believing it is *not* preferable to believing it).

The concepts recently defined enable us to construct an account (5) according to which S knows that p provided that both (a) S correctly believes that p,[15] and (b) there is a set of propositions that fully and nondefectively renders it evident to S that p (where a set "nondefectively renders it evident to S that p" if and only if it does so without attributing to S any false belief).[16]

Supposing this account correct, every bit of knowledge has a tree such as the following, the "ranks" of which (RI, RII, and

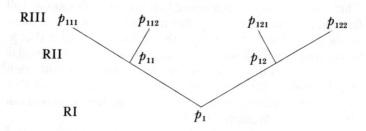

15. Whether knowledge entails belief at all is of course a vexed question of long standing, but there is no room for it here. A helpful and interesting discussion is found in Keith Lehrer's "Belief and Knowledge," *Philosophical Review*, 77 (1968), 491–499.

16. Here, in the account of concepts (I)–(III) above, and in what follows, the relativity of knowledge to an epistemic community is left implicit, as it normally is in ordinary thought and speech.

RIII) correspond to our epistemic subsets discussed above (in the definition of full validation).

Note that each node of such a tree is a proposition. Thus the "root" node is the-proposition-that-p_1, and the first terminal node (from the left) the-proposition-that-p_{111}.[17]

There is an important difference between these trees and our earlier pyramids. Except for terminal nodes, every node of a tree is an S-epistemic proposition, whereas not a single node of a pyramid need be epistemic at all. Pyramids display propositions that are evident to A (*not* propositions that such and such other propositions are evident to S), and they also show which propositions ground (for S) any proposition for which S has grounds. Trees display true epistemic propositions concerning S and they also show what "makes these propositions true" *via* epistemic principles (i.e., what successors "validate" these propositions). Trees do this for *every* epistemic proposition that constitutes one of its nodes. That is to say, trees contain no epistemic terminal nodes. It is in this sense that trees provide *complete* epistemic explanations of the truth of their root nodes.

The following requirements flow from the fact that trees are intended to correspond to the fully validating sets defined by (I) above, and from the fact that the ranks of trees are to correspond to the subsets $C_1, \ldots, C_n$ of (I).

1. (Let us call node x a "successor" (i.e., a *direct* successor) of node y relative to tree T provided there are A and B such that (i) A stands for x on T and B stands for y on T; (ii) A and B are connected by a straight branch on T; (iii) B is closer to the root node than A; and (iv) there is no C such that C stands for a proposition on T, and A, B, and C are connected by a straight branch and B is closer to the root node than C, and C is closer to the root node than A.) The set of all nodes that (directly) succeed a given node must validate that node.

2. If a node n is an S-epistemic proposition, then n must have

---

17. Strictly speaking, what we have here is obviously a *partial tree schema*. For convenience, however, I speak of trees even when I mean partial tree schemata. Also, it should not be thought that every tree must have exactly three ranks (RI, RII, and RIII). On the contrary, a tree may have any number of ranks, so long as it has more than one.

successors, it must branch out into a set of further nodes that validate n. (Trees are supposed to correspond to sets that fully validate S-epistemic propositions, and any such set is to provide, in a sense, a "complete" explanation of how the S-epistemic proposition comes to be true.)

3. The proposition that $-p_1$ must be S-epistemic.

4. Each branch of a complete tree of evidence must terminate. (And in some cases the terminal node specifies that S correctly believes x, and is the sole successor of its immediate predecessor, which is to the effect that x has a certain epistemic status for S.)

5. A non-defective tree of evidence for S must attribute no false belief to S. This applies not only to terminal nodes but also to non-terminal nodes. We know that a non-terminal node must be an S-epistemic proposition, given the nature of the consequents of epistemic principles and the fact that it is S's knowledge that is in question.[18] That is to say, each non-terminal node must be a proposition concerning a certain other proposition (or certain other propositions) and either (i) to the effect that it is (they are) believed by S and how reasonably, or (ii) to the effect that S is in a position to know whether it is (they are) true, or (iii) some logical compound of propositions of types (i) or (ii). Propositions of types (i) or (iii) may attribute belief to S. If the tree is to be non-defective, no such belief can be false.

Finally, if the root node of a non-defective tree of evidence is the proposition that it is evident to S that p, let us call such a tree not just a tree of evidence, but a *tree of knowledge* for S and the proposition that p.

In conclusion, we may now be sure that to each set that fully renders it evident to S that p there corresponds at least one tree of knowledge for S and the proposition that p. And we thus have an equivalent for our account of knowledge (5) as correct belief in what has been fully and nondefectively rendered evident:

18. But it should be noted that terminal nodes are not restricted to the last (or top) rank of a tree. On the contrary, any number of them may appear in any rank.

S knows that p iff
   (a) S correctly believes that p; and
   (b) there is a tree of knowledge for S and the proposition that p. [19]

19. I am indebted to Roderick M. Chisholm, Jaegwon Kim, Alvin I. Goldman, Robert Merrihew Adams, Stephen Leeds, and Robert J. Swartz. Work on this paper was supported in part by NSF Grant GS-2953.

13

Selections from *Thought*

GILBERT H. HARMAN

3. *Gettier Examples and Probabilistic Rules of Acceptance*

In any Gettier example we are presented with similar cases in which someone infers h from things he knows, h is true, and he is equally justified in making the inference in either case. In the one case he comes to know that h and in the other case he does not. I have observed that a natural explanation of many Gettier examples is that the relevant inference involves not only the final conclusion h but also at least one intermediate conclusion true in the one case but not in the other. And I have suggested that any account of inductive inference should show why such intermediate conclusions are essentially involved in the relevant inferences. Gettier cases are thus to be explained by appeal to the principle

> P Reasoning that essentially involves false conclusions, intermediate or final, cannot give one knowledge.

It is easy to see that purely probabilistic rules of acceptance do not permit an explanation of Gettier examples by means of principle P. Reasoning in accordance with a purely probabilistic rule involves essentially only its final conclusion. Since that conclusion is highly probable, it can be inferred without reference to any other conclusions; in particular, there will be no intermediate conclusion essential to the inference that is true in one case and false in the other. . . .

The trouble is that purely probabilistic rules are incompatible with the natural account of Gettier examples by means of principle P. The solution is not to attempt to modify P but rather to modify our account of inference.

1. Knowledge and Explanation: A Causal Theory

Goldman suggests that we know only if there is the proper sort of causal connection between our belief and what we know. For example, we perceive that there has been an automobile accident only if the accident is relevantly causally responsible, by way of our sense organs, for our belief that there has been an accident. Similarly, we remember doing something only if having done it is relevantly causally responsible for our current memory of having done it. Although in some cases the fact that we know thus simply begins a causal chain that leads to our belief, in other cases the causal connection is more complicated. If Mary learns that Mr. Havit owns a Ford, Havit's past ownership is causally responsible for the evidence she has and also responsible (at least in part) for Havit's present ownership. Here the relevant causal connection consists in there being a common cause of the belief and of the state of affairs believed in.

Mary fails to know in the original Nogot-Havit case[1] because the causal connection is lacking. Nogot's past ownership is responsible for her evidence but is not responsible for the fact that one of her friends owns a Ford. Havit's past ownership at least partly accounts for why one of her friends now owns a Ford, but it is not responsible for her evidence. Similarly, the man who is told something true by a speaker who does not believe what he says fails to know because the truth of what is said is not causally responsible for the fact that it is said.

1. "Mary's friend Mr. Nogot convinces her that he has a Ford. He tells her that he owns a Ford, he shows her his ownership certificate, and he reminds her that she saw him drive up in a Ford. On the basis of this and similar evidence, Mary concludes that Mr. Nogot owns a Ford. From that she infers that one of her friends owns a Ford. . . . However, as it turns out in this case, Mary is wrong about Nogot. His car has just been repossessed and towed away. . . . On the other hand, Mary's friend Mr. Havit does own a Ford, so she is right in thinking that one of her friends owns a Ford . . . but she does not know that one of her friends owns a Ford" (*Thought*, p. 121).

General knowledge does not fit into this simple framework. That all emeralds are green neither causes nor is caused by the existence of the particular green emeralds examined when we come to know that all emeralds are green. Goldman handles such examples by counting logical connections among the causal connections. The belief that all emeralds are green is, in an extended sense, relevantly causally connected to the fact that all emeralds are green, since the evidence causes the belief and is logically entailed by what is believed.

It is obvious that not every causal connection, especially in this extended sense, is relevant to knowledge. Any two states of affairs are logically connected simply because both are entailed by their conjunction. If every such connection were relevant, the analysis Goldman suggests would have us identify knowledge with true belief, since there would always be a relevant "causal connection" between any state of true belief and the state of affairs believed in. Goldman avoids this reduction of his analysis to justified true belief by saying that when knowledge is based on inference relevant causal connections must be "reconstructed" in the inference. Mary knows that one of her friends owns a Ford only if her inference reconstructs the relevant causal connection between evidence and conclusion.

But what does it mean to say that her inference must "reconstruct" the relevant causal connection? Presumably it means that she must infer or be able to infer something about the causal connection between her conclusion and the evidence for it. And this suggests that Mary must make at least two inferences. First she must infer her original conclusion and second she must infer something about the causal connection between the conclusion and her evidence. Her second conclusion is her "reconstruction" of the causal connection. But how detailed must her reconstruction be? If she must reconstruct every detail of the causal connection between evidence and conclusion, she will never gain knowledge by way of inference. If she need only reconstruct some "causal connection," she will always know, since she will always be able to infer that evidence and conclusion are both entailed by their conjunction.

I suggest that it is a mistake to approach the problem as a

problem about what else Mary needs to infer before she has knowledge of her original conclusion. Goldman's remark about reconstructing the causal connection makes more sense as a remark about the kind of inference Mary needs to reach her original conclusion in the first place. It has something to do with principle *P* and the natural account of the Gettier examples.

Nogot presents Mary with evidence that he owns a Ford. She infers that one of her friends owns a Ford. She is justified in reaching that conclusion and it is true. However, since it is true, not because Nogot owns a Ford, but because Havit does, Mary fails to come to know that one of her friends owns a Ford. The natural explanation is that she must infer that Nogot owns a Ford and does not know her final conclusion unless her intermediate conclusion is true. According to this natural explanation, Mary's inference essentially involves the conclusion that Nogot owns a Ford. According to Goldman, her inference essentially involves a conclusion concerning a causal connection. In order to put these ideas together, we must turn Goldman's theory of knowledge into a theory of inference.

As a first approximation, let us take his remarks about causal connections literally, forgetting for the moment that they include logical connections. Then let us transmute his causal theory of knowing into the theory that inductive conclusions always take the form *X causes Y,* where further conclusions are reached by additional steps of inductive or deductive reasoning. In particular, we may deduce either *X* or *Y* from *X causes Y.*

This causal theory of inferring provides the following account of why knowledge requires that we be right about an appropriate causal connection. A person knows by inference only if all conclusions essential to that inference are true. That is, his inference must satisfy principle *P*. Since he can legitimately infer his conclusion only if he can first infer certain causal statements, he can know only if he is right about the causal connection expressed by those statements. First, Mary infers that her evidence is a causal result of Nogot's past ownership of the Ford. From that she deduces that Nogot has owned a Ford. Then she infers that his past ownership has been causally responsible for present ownership; and she deduces that Nogot owns a Ford. Finally, she deduces that one of her friends owns a Ford. She fails to know because she is wrong when she infers that Nogot's past ownership is responsible for Nogot's present ownership.

2. Inference to the Best Explanatory Statement

A better account of inference emerges if we replace "cause" with "because." On the revised account, we infer not just statements of the form *X causes Y* but, more generally, statements of the form *Y because X* or *X explains Y*. Inductive inference is conceived as inference to the best of competing explanatory statements. Inference to a causal explanation is a special case.

The revised account squares better with ordinary usage. Nogot's past ownership helps to explain Mary's evidence, but it would sound odd to say that it caused that evidence. Similarly, the detective infers that activities of the butler explain these footprints; does he infer that those activities caused the footprints? A scientist explains the properties of water by means of a hypothesis about unobservable particles that make up the water, but it does not seem right to say that facts about those particles cause the properties of water. An observer infers that certain mental states best explain someone's behavior; but such explanation by reasons might not be causal explanation.

Furthermore, the switch from "cause" to "because" avoids Goldman's *ad hoc* treatment of knowledge of generalizations. Although there is no causal relation between a generalization and those observed instances which provide us with evidence for the generalization, there is an obvious explanatory relationship. That all emeralds are green does not cause a particular emerald to be green; but it can explain why that emerald is green. And, other things being equal, we can infer a generalization only if it provides the most plausible way to explain our evidence.

We often infer generalizations that explain but do not logically entail their instances, since they are of the form, *In circumstances C, X's, tend to be Y's.* Such generalizations may be inferred if they provide a sufficiently plausible account of observed instances all things considered. For example, from the fact that doctors have generally been right in the past when they have said that someone is going to get measles, I infer that doctors can normally tell from certain symptoms that someone is going to get measles. More precisely, I infer that doctors have generally been right in the past because they can normally tell from certain symptoms that someone is going to get measles. This is a very weak explanation, but it is a genuine one. Compare it with the pseudo-explanation, "Doctors are generally right when they say someone has measles because they can normally tell from certain symptoms that someone is going to get measles."

Similarly, I infer that a substance is soluble in water from the fact that it dissolved when I stirred it into some water. That is a real explanation, to be distinguished from the pseudo-explanation, "That substance dissolves in water because it is soluble in water." Here too a generalization explains an instance without entailing that instance, since water-soluble substances do not always dissolve in water.

Although we cannot simply deduce instances from this sort of generalization, we can often infer that the generalization will explain some new instance. The inference is warranted if the explanatory claim *that X's tend to be Y's will explain why the next X will be Y* is sufficiently more plausible than competitors such as *interfering factor Q will prevent the next X from being a Y*. For example, the doctor says that you will get measles. Because doctors are normally right about that sort of thing, I infer that you will. More precisely, I infer that doctors' normally being able to tell when someone will get measles will explain the doctor's being right in this case. The competing explanatory statements here are not other explanations of the doctor's being right but rather explanations of his being wrong—e.g., because he has misperceived the symptoms, or because you have faked the symptoms of measles, or because these symptoms are the result of some other disease, etc. Similarly, I infer that this sugar will dissolve in my tea. That is, I infer that the solubility of sugar in tea will explain this sugar's dissolving in the present case. Com-

peting explanations would explain the sugar's not dissolving—
e.g., because there is already a saturated sugar solution there,
because the tea is ice-cold, etc.

4. Statistical Inference

Statistical inference, and knowledge obtained from it, is also
better explicated by way of the notion of statistical explanation
than by way of the notion of cause or logical entailment.

1. Evidence One Does Not Possess: Three Examples

EXAMPLE (1). While I am watching him, Tom takes a library
book from the shelf and conceals it beneath his coat. Since I am
the library detective, I follow him as he walks brazenly past the
guard at the front door. Outside I see him take out the book
and smile. As I approach he notices me and suddenly runs
away. But I am sure that it was Tom, for I know him well. I saw
Tom steal a book from the library and that is the testimony I
give before the University Judicial Council. After testifying, I
leave the hearing room and return to my post in the library.
Later that day, Tom's mother testifies that Tom has an identical twin, Buck. Tom, she says, was thousands of miles away at
the time of the theft. She hopes that Buck did not do it; but she
admits that he has a bad character.

Do I know that Tom stole the book? Let us suppose that I am
right. It was Tom that took the book. His mother was lying
when she said that Tom was thousands of miles away. I do not
know that she was lying, of course, since I do not know anything about her, even that she exists. Nor does anyone at the
hearing know that she is lying, although some may suspect that
she is. In these circumstances I do not know that Tom stole the
book. My knowledge is undermined by evidence I do not possess.[2]

EXAMPLE (2). Donald has gone off to Italy. He told you ahead
of time that he was going; and you saw him off at the airport.
He said he was to stay for the entire summer. That was in June.
It is now July. Then you might know that he is in Italy. It is the

2. Lehrer and Paxson.

sort of thing one often claims to know. However, for reasons of his own Donald wants you to believe that he is not in Italy but in California. He writes several letters saying that he has gone to San Francisco and has decided to stay there for the summer. He wants you to think that these letters were written by him in San Francisco, so he sends them to someone he knows there and has that person mail them to you with a San Francisco postmark, one at a time. You have been out of town for a couple of days and have not read any of the letters. You are now standing before the pile of mail that arrived while you were away. Two of the phony letters are in the pile. You are about to open your mail. I ask you, "Do you know where Donald is?" "Yes," you reply, "I know that he is in Italy." You are right about where Donald is and it would seem that your justification for believing that Donald is in Italy makes no reference to letters from San Francisco. But you do not know that Donald is in Italy. Your knowledge is undermined by evidence you do not as yet possess.

EXAMPLE (3). A political leader is assassinated. His associates, fearing a coup, decide to pretend that the bullet hit someone else. On nationwide television they announce that an assassination attempt has failed to kill the leader but has killed a secret service man by mistake. However, before the announcement is made, an enterprising reporter on the scene telephones the real story to his newspaper, which has included the story in its final edition. Jill buys a copy of that paper and reads the story of the assassination. What she reads is true and so are her assumptions about how the story came to be in the paper. The reporter, whose by-line appears, saw the assassination and dictated his report, which is now printed just as he dictated it. Jill has justified true belief and, it would seem, all her intermediate conclusions are true. But she does not know that the political leader has been assassinated. For everyone else has heard about the televised announcement. They may also have seen the story in the paper and, perhaps, do not know what to believe; and it is highly implausible that Jill should know simply because she lacks evidence everyone else has. Jill does not know. Her knowledge is undermined by evidence she does not possess.

214   Gilbert H. Harman

These examples pose a problem for my strategy. They are
Gettier examples and my strategy is to make assumptions about
inference that will account for Gettier examples by means of
principle *P*. But these particular examples appear to bring in
considerations that have nothing to do with conclusions essential to the inference on which belief is based.

Some readers may have trouble evaluating these examples.
Like other Gettier examples, these require attention to subtle
facts about ordinary usage; it is easy to miss subtle differences
if, as in the present instance, it is very difficult to formulate a
theory that would account for these differences. We must compare what it would be natural to say about these cases if there
were no additional evidence one does not possess (no testimony
from Tom's mother, no letters from San Francisco, and no
televised announcement) with what it would be natural to say
about the cases in which there is the additional evidence one
does not possess. We must take care not to adopt a very skeptical attitude nor become too lenient about what is to count as
knowledge. If we become skeptically inclined, we will deny
there is knowledge in either case. If we become too lenient, we
will allow that there is knowledge in both cases. It is tempting
to go in one or the other of these directions, toward skepticism
or leniency, because it proves so difficult to see what general
principles are involved that would mark the difference. But at
least some difference between the cases is revealed by the fact
that we are *more inclined* to say that there is knowledge in the
examples where there is no undermining evidence a person
does not possess than in the examples where there is such evidence. The problem, then, is to account for this difference in
our inclination to ascribe knowledge to someone.

2. Evidence Against What One Knows

If I had known about Tom's mother's testimony, I would not
have been justified in thinking that it was Tom I saw steal the
book. Once you read the letters from Donald in which he says
he is in San Francisco, you are no longer justified in thinking
that he is in Italy. If Jill knew about the television announcement, she would not be justified in believing that the political

leader has been assassinated. This suggests that we can account for the preceding examples by means of the following principle.

> One knows only if there is no evidence such that if one knew about the evidence one would not be justified in believing one's conclusion.

However, by modifying the three examples it can be shown that this principle is too strong.

Suppose that Tom's mother was known to the Judicial Council as a pathological liar. Everyone at the hearing realizes that Buck, Tom's supposed twin, is a figment of her imagination. When she testifies no one believes her. Back at my post in the library, I still know nothing of Tom's mother or her testimony. In such a case, my knowledge would not be undermined by her testimony; but if I were told only that she had just testified that Tom has a twin brother and was himself thousands of miles away from the scene of the crime at the time the book was stolen, I would no longer be justified in believing as I now do that Tom stole the book. Here I know even though there is evidence which, if I knew about it, would cause me not to be justified in believing my conclusion.

Suppose that Donald had changed his mind and never mailed the letters to San Francisco. Then those letters no longer undermine your knowledge. But it is very difficult to see what principle accounts for this fact. How can letters in the pile on the table in front of you undermine your knowledge while the same letters in a pile in front of Donald do not? If you knew that Donald had written letters to you saying that he was in San Francisco, you would not be justified in believing that he was still in Italy. But that fact by itself does not undermine your present knowledge that he is in Italy.

Suppose that as the political leader's associates are about to make their announcement, a saboteur cuts the wire leading to the television transmitter. The announcement is therefore heard only by those in the studio, all of whom are parties to the deception. Jill reads the real story in the newspaper as before. Now, she does come to know that the political leader has been assassinated. But if she had known that it had been announced that he was not assassinated, she would not have been justified in believing that he has, simply on the basis of the newspaper story. Here, a cut wire makes the difference between evidence that undermines knowledge and evidence that does not undermine knowledge.

We can know that h even though there is evidence e that we do not know about such that, if we did know about e, we would not be justified in believing h. If we know that h, it does not follow that we know that there is not any evidence like e. This can seem paradoxical, for it can seem obvious that, if we know that h, we know that any evidence against h can only be misleading. So, later if we get that evidence we ought to be able to know enough to disregard it.

A more explicit version of this interesting paradox goes like this.[3] "If I know that h is true, I know that any evidence against h is evidence against something that is true; so I know that such evidence is misleading. But I should disregard evidence that I know is misleading. So, once I know that h is true, I am in a position to disregard any future evidence that seems to tell against h." This is paradoxical, because I am never in a position simply to disregard any future evidence even though I do know a great many different things.

A skeptic might appeal to this paradox in order to argue that, since we are never in a position to disregard any further evidence, we never know anything. Some philosophers would turn the argument around to say that, since we often know things, we are often in a position to disregard further evidence. But both of these responses go wrong in accepting the paradoxical argument in the first place.

I can know that Tom stole a book from the library without being able automatically to disregard evidence to the contrary. You can know that Donald is in Italy without having the right to ignore whatever further evidence may turn up. Jill may know that the political leader has been assassinated even though she would cease to know this if told that there was an

3. Here and in what follows I am indebted to Saul Kripke, who is, however, not responsible for any faults in my presentation.

announcement that only a secret service agent had been shot.

The argument for paradox overlooks the way actually having evidence can make a difference. Since I now know that Tom stole the book, I now know that any evidence that appears to indicate something else is misleading. That does not warrant me in simply disregarding any further evidence, since getting that further evidence can change what I know. In particular, after I get such further evidence I may no longer know that it is misleading. For having the new evidence can make it true that I no longer know that Tom stole the book; if I no longer know that, I no longer know that the new evidence is misleading.

Therefore, we cannot account for the problems posed by evidence one does not possess by appeal to the principle, which I now repeat:

> One knows only if there is no evidence such that if one knew about the evidence one would not be justified in believing one's conclusion.

For one can know even though such evidence exists.

3. A Result Concerning Inference

When does evidence one does not possess keep one from having knowledge? I have described three cases, each in two versions, in which there is misleading evidence one does not possess. In the first version of each case the misleading evidence undermines someone's knowledge. In the second version it does not. What makes the difference?

My strategy is to account for Gettier examples by means of principle *P*. This strategy has led us to conceive of induction as inference to the best explanation. But that conception of inference does not by itself seem able to explain these examples. So I want to use the examples in order to learn something more about inference, in particular about what other conclusions are essential to the inference that Tom stole the book, that Donald is in Italy, or that the political leader has been assassinated.

It is not plausible that the relevant inferences should contain essential intermediate conclusions that refer explicitly to Tom's mother, to letters from San Francisco, or to special television programs. For it is very likely that there is an infinite number of ways a particular inference might be undermined by misleading evidence one does not possess. If there must be a separate essential conclusion ruling out each of these ways, inferences would have to be infinitely inclusive—and that is implausible.

Therefore it would seem that the relevant inferences must rule out undermining evidence one does not possess by means of a single conclusion, essential to the inference, that characterizes all such evidence. But how might this be done? It is not at all clear what distinguishes evidence that undermines knowledge from evidence that does not. How is my inference to involve an essential conclusion that rules out Tom's mother's testifying a certain way before a believing audience but does not rule out (simply) her testifying in that way? Or that rules out the existence of letters of a particular sort in the mail on your table but not simply the existence of those letters? Or that rules out a widely heard announcement of a certain sort without simply ruling out the announcement?

Since I am unable to formulate criteria that would distinguish among these cases, I will simply *label* cases of the first kind "undermining evidence one does not possess." Then we can say this: one knows only if there is no undermining evidence one does not possess. If there is such evidence, one does not know. However, these remarks are completely trivial.

It is somewhat less trivial to use the same label to formulate a principle concerned with inference.

> Q One may infer a conclusion only if one also infers that there is no undermining evidence one does not possess.

There is of course an obscurity in principle Q; but the principle is not as trivial as the remarks of the last paragraph, since the label "undermining evidence one does not possess" has been explained in terms of knowledge, whereas this is a principle concerning inference.

If we can explain "undermining" without appeal to knowledge, given Q, we can use principle P to account for the differences between the two versions of each of the three examples described above. In each case an inference involves essentially the claim that there is no undermining evidence one does not possess. Since this claim is false in the first version of each case and true in the second, principle P implies that there can be knowledge only in the second version of each case.

So there is, according to my strategy, some reason to think that there is a principle concerning inference like principle Q. That raises the question of whether there is any independent reason to accept such a principle; and reflection on good scientific practice suggests a positive answer. It is a commonplace that a scientist should base his conclusions on all the evidence. Furthermore, he should not rest content with the evidence he happens to have but should try to make sure he is not overlooking any relevant evidence. A good scientist will not accept a conclusion unless he has some reason to think that there is no as yet undiscovered evidence which would undermine his conclusion. Otherwise he would not be warranted in making his inference. So good scientific practice reflects the acceptance of something like principle Q, which is the independent confirmation we wanted for the existence of this principle.

Notice that the scientist must accept something like principle Q, with its reference to "undermining evidence one does not possess." For example, he cannot accept the following principle,

> One may infer a conclusion only if one also infers that there is no evidence at all such that if he knew that evidence he could not accept his conclusion.

There will always be a true proposition such that if he learned that the proposition was true (and learned nothing else) he would not be warranted in accepting his conclusion. If h is his conclusion, and if k is a true proposition saying what ticket will win the grand prize in the next New Jersey State lottery, then *either k or not h* is such a proposition. If he were to learn that it is true that *either k or not h* (and learned nothing else), *not h* would become probable since (given what he knows) k is antecedently very improbable. So he could no longer reasonably infer that h is true.

There must be a certain kind of evidence such that the scientist infers there is no as yet undiscovered evidence of that kind against h. Principle Q says that the relevant kind is what I have been labelling "undermining evidence one does not possess." Principle Q is confirmed by the fact that good scientific practice involves some such principle and by the fact that principle Q together with principle P accounts for the three Gettier examples I have been discussing.

If this account in terms of principles P and Q is accepted, inductive conclusions must involve some self-reference. Otherwise there would be a regress. Before we could infer that h, we would have to infer that there is no undermining evidence to h. That prior inference could not be deductive, so it would have to be inference to the best explanatory statement. For example, we might infer that the fact that there is no sign of undermining evidence we do not possess is explained by there not being any such evidence. But, then, before we could accept that conclusion we would first have to infer that there is no undermining evidence to *it* which one does not possess. And, since that inference would have to be inference to the best explanation, it would require a previous inference that there is no undermining evidence for its conclusion; and so on *ad infinitum*.

Clearly, we do not *first* have to infer that there is no undermining evidence to h and only then infer h. For that would automatically yield the regress. Instead, we must at the same time infer both h and that there is no undermining evidence. Furthermore, we infer that there is not only no undermining evidence to h but also no undermining evidence to the whole conclusion. In other words, all legitimate inductive conclusions take the form of a self-referential conjunction whose first conjunct is h and whose second conjunct (usually left implicit) is the claim that there is no undermining evidence to the whole conjunction.

1. Conclusions as Total Views: Problems

[We have seen] that we could use principle P to account for many Gettier examples if we were willing to suppose that induction always has an explanatory statement as its conclusion. On that supposition reasoning would have to take the form of a series of inductive and deductive steps to appropriate intermediate conclusions that therefore become essential to our inference. However, certain difficulties indicate that this conception of inference is seriously oversimplified and that our account of Gettier examples must be modified.

[I have] already mentioned a minor complication. There is a self-referential aspect to inductive conclusions. Instead of saying that such conclusions are of the form *Y because X* we must say that they are of the form *Y because X and there is no undermining evidence to this whole conclusion.*

Another difficulty, . . . the "lottery paradox," poses a more serious problem. . . . This paradox arises given a purely probabilistic rule of acceptance, since such a rule would have us infer concerning any ticket in the next New Jersey lottery that the ticket will not win the grand prize. We might suggest that the paradox cannot arise if induction is inference to the best explanatory statement, since the hypothesis that a particular ticket fails to win the grand prize in the next New Jersey lottery does nothing to explain anything about our current evidence. However, there are two things wrong with such a suggestion. First, the paradox will arise in any situation in which, for some large number N, there are N different explanations of different aspects of the evidence, each inferable when considered apart from the other explanations, if we also know that only $N - 1$ of these explanations are correct. So, the paradox can arise even when we attempt to infer explanations of various aspects of one's evidence.

Furthermore, inference to the best explanatory statement need not infer explanations of the evidence. It can infer that something we already accept will explain something else. That is how I am able to infer that the sugar will dissolve when stirred into my tea or that a friend who intends to meet me on a corner in an hour will in fact be there. Moreover, we can sometimes infer explanatory statements involving statistical explanations; and, if a particular ticket does fail to win the grand prize, we can explain its not winning by describing this as a highly probable outcome in the given chance set-up. So, if induction is inference to the best explanatory statement, we should be able to infer of any ticket in a fair lottery that the conditions of the lottery will explain that ticket's failing to win the grand prize; the lottery paradox therefore arises in its original form. But before attempting to modify the present conception of inference in order to escape the lottery paradox, let us consider a different sort of problem involving that conception.

Our present conception of reasoning takes it to consist in a series of inductive and deductive steps. We have therefore supposed that there are (at least) two kinds of inference, inductive inference and deductive inference; and we have also supposed that reasoning typically combines inferences of both sorts. But there is something fishy about this. Deduction does not seem to be a kind of inference in the same sense in which induction is. Induction is a matter of inductive acceptance. On our current conception of inference, we may infer or accept an explanatory statement if it is sufficiently more plausible than competing statements, given our antecedent beliefs. On the other hand, deduction does not seem in the same way to be a matter of "deductive acceptance." So called deductive rules of inference are not plausibly construed as rules of deductive acceptance that tell us what conclusions we may accept, given that we already have certain antecedent beliefs. For example, although the deductive rule of *modus ponens* is sometimes stated like this, "From *P* and *If P*, then *Q*, infer *Q*," there is no plausible rule of acceptance saying that if we believe both *P* and *If P*, then *Q*, we may always infer or accept *Q*. Perhaps we should stop believing *P* or *If P, then Q* rather than believe *Q*.

A contradiction logically implies everything; anything follows (deductively) from a set of logically inconsistent beliefs. Although this point is sometimes expressed by saying that from a contradiction we may deductively infer anything, that is a particular use of "infer." Logic does not tell us that if we discover that our beliefs are inconsistent we may go on to infer or accept anything and everything we happen to think of. Given the discovery of such inconsistency in our antecedent beliefs, inference should lead not to the acceptance of something more but to the rejection of something previously accepted.

This indicates that something is wrong in a very basic way with our current conception of inference. We have been supposing that inference is simply a way to acquire new beliefs on the basis of our old beliefs. What is needed is a modification of that conception to allow for the fact that inference can lead as easily to rejection of old beliefs as to the acceptance of new beliefs. Furthermore, we want to avoid the supposition that deduction is a kind of inference in the same sense in which induction is inference, and we want to avoid the lottery paradox.

2. Inference to the Best Total Explanatory Account

Influenced by a misleading conception of deductive inference, we have implicitly supposed that inductive inference is a matter of going from a few premises we already accept to a conclusion one comes to accept, of the form X *because* Y (*and there is no undermining evidence to this conclusion*). But this conception of premises and conclusion in inductive inference is mistaken. The conception of the conclusion of induction is wrong since such inference can lead not only to the acceptance of new beliefs but also the rejection of old beliefs. Furthermore, the suggestion that only a few premises are relevant is wrong, since inductive inference must be assessed with respect to everything one believes.

A more accurate conception of inductive inference takes it to be a way of modifying what we believe by addition and subtraction of beliefs. Our "premises" are all our antecedent beliefs; our "conclusion" is our total resulting view. Our conclusion is not a simple explanatory statement but a more or less complete explanatory account. Induction is an attempt to increase the explanatory coherence of our view, making it more complete, less ad hoc, more plausible. At the same time we are conservative. We seek to minimize change. We attempt to make the least change in our antecedent view that will maximize explanatory coherence.

The conception of induction as inference to the best total explanatory account retains those aspects of our previous conception that permitted an account of Gettier examples, although that account must be modified to some extent. On the other hand, the new conception does not suppose that there is deductive inference in anything like the sense in which there is inductive inference, since deductive inference is not a process of changing beliefs. Furthermore, the new conception accounts for the fact that inference can lead us to reject something previously accepted, since such rejection can be part of the least change that maximizes coherence.

Finally, the new conception avoids the lottery paradox. Inference is no longer conceived of as a series of steps which together might add up to something implausible as a whole. Instead, inference is taken to be a single step to one total conclusion. If there can be only one conclusion, there is no way to build up a lottery paradox.

Consider the case in which there are N explanations of various aspects of the evidence, each very plausible considered by itself, where however it is known that only $N - 1$ are correct. Competing possible conclusions must specify for each explanation whether or not that explanation is accepted. A particular explanation will be accepted not simply because of its plausibility when considered by itself but only if it is included in an inferable total explanatory account. We will not be able to infer that all N explanations are correct since, I am assuming, that would greatly decrease coherence.

Similarly, we will be able to infer that a particular ticket will fail to win the grand prize in the next New Jersey lottery only if there is a total resulting view containing this result that is to be preferred to alternative total views on grounds of maximizing coherence and minimizing change. The claim that a particular ticket fails to win will be part of an inferable total view only if that claim adds sufficiently more coherence than do claims that other tickets fail to win. Otherwise that total view will not be any better than a different total view that does not contain the claim that the first ticket fails to win.

This is a rather complicated matter and depends not only on the probabilities involved but also on how we conceive the situation and, in particular, on what claims we are interested in.[4] We can see this by considering the conditions under which we can make inferences that give us knowledge. For example, if

4. Levi.

we are simply interested in the question of whether a particular ticket will win or fail to win, we cannot include in our total view the conclusion that the ticket will fail to win, since it would not be correct to say that in such a case we know the ticket will lose. On the other hand, if we are primarily interested in a quite different question whose answer depends in part on an answer to the question of whether this ticket fails to win, we may be able to include the conclusion that it does fail in our total view, since we can often come to have relevant knowledge in such cases. Thus, we might infer and come to know that the butler is the murderer because that hypothesis is part of the most plausible total account, even though the account includes the claim that the butler did not win the lottery (for if he had won he would have lacked a motive). Or we might infer and come to know that we will be seeing Jones for lunch tomorrow even though our total view includes the claim that Jones does not win the lottery (e.g., because if he won he would have to be in Trenton tomorrow to receive his prize and would not be able to meet us for lunch).

However I am unable to be very precise about how our interests and conception of the situation affect coherence or indeed about any of the factors that are relevant to coherence.

5. *Inference and Knowledge*

Having seen that induction is inference to the best total explanatory account, we must now modify our account of knowledge and of the Gettier examples.

One problem is that we want to be able to ascribe several inferences to a person at a particular time so as to be able to say that one of the inferences yields knowledge even though another does not. Suppose that Mary has evidence both that her friend Mr. Nogot owns a Ford and that her friend Mr. Havit owns a Ford. She concludes that both own Fords and therefore that at least one of her friends owns a Ford. Nogot does not own a Ford; but Havit does. We want to be able to say that Mary can know in this case that at least one of her friends owns a Ford, because one inference on which her belief is based satisfies principle P even if another inference she makes does not.

But, if inference is a matter of modifying one's total view, how can we ascribe more than a single inference to Mary?[5]

Principle P seems to be in trouble in any event. It tells us that one gets knowledge from an inference only if all conclusions essential to that inference are true. Since one's conclusion is one's total resulting view, principle P would seem to imply that one gains no knowledge from inference unless the whole of one's resulting view is true. But that is absurd. A person comes to know things through inference even though some of what he believes is false.

A similar point holds of premises. It is plausible to suppose that one comes to know by inference only if one already knows one's premises to be true. However, one's total view is relevant to inference even though it always contains things one does not know to be true.

The key to the solution of these problems is to take an inference to be a change that can be described simply by mentioning what beliefs are given up and what new beliefs are added (in addition to the belief that there is no undermining evidence to the conclusion). Mary might be described as making all the following inferences. (1) She rejects her belief that no friend of hers owns a Ford. (2) In addition she comes to believe that one of her friends owns a Ford and accepts a story about Nogot. (3) As in (2), except that that she accepts a story about Havit rather than one about Nogot. (4) She does all the preceding things. All the inferences (1)–(4) might be ascribed to Mary by an appropriate reasoning instantiator F.[6] Mary knows because inference (3) adds nothing false to her view.

5. Lehrer.
6. "Words like 'reasoning,' 'argument,' and 'inference' are ambiguous. They may refer to a process of reasoning, argument, or inference, or they may refer to an abstract structure consisting of certain propositions as premises, others as conclusions, perhaps others as intermediate steps. A functional account of reasoning says how a mental or neurophysiological process can *be* a process of reasoning by virtue of the way it functions. That is, a functional account says how the functioning of such a process allows it to be correlated with the reasoning, taken to be an abstract inference, which the process instantiates.

To be more precise, the relevant correlation is a mapping F from mental or neurophysiological processes to abstract structures of inference. If x is a process in the domain of F, then $F(x)$ is the (abstract) reasoning that x instantiates. Such

Given Mary's antecedent beliefs, there is a single maximal inference she makes, (4), which is the union of all the inferences she makes. An inference is warranted only if it is included in the maximal warranted inference. That is why the lottery paradox does not arise even though we allow for the possibility that Mary makes more than one inference.

In order to handle the problem about premises we must require, not that the actual premises of the inference (everything Mary believes ahead of time) be known to be true but only that the inference remain warranted when the set of antecedent beliefs is limited to those Mary antecedently knows to be true and continues to know after the inference. More precisely, let (A, B) be an inference that rejects the beliefs in the set A and adds as new beliefs those in the set B; let $B \cup C$ be the union of the sets B and C, containing anything that belongs either to B or to C or to both; and let Φ be the empty set that contains nothing. Then principle P is to be replaced by the following principle $P*$, which gives necessary and sufficient conditions of inferential knowledge.

$P*$ S comes to know that h by inference $(A, B$ if and only if (i) the appropriate reasoning instantiator F ascribes (A,B) to S, (ii) S is warranted in making the inference (A,B) given his antecedent beliefs, (iii) there is a possibly empty set C of unrejected antecedent beliefs not antecedently known by S to be true such that the inference $(\Phi, B \cup C)$ is warranted when antecedent beliefs are taken to be the set of things S knows (and continues to know after the inference (A,B) is made), (iv) $B \cup C$ contains the belief that h, (v) $B \cup C$ contains only true beliefs.[7]

Reference to the set C is necessary to cover cases in which S comes to know something he already believes. Part (v) of $P*$ captures what was intended by our original principle P.

-----

a mapping F is a *reasoning instantiator*. . . . To ascribe reasoning r to someone is to presuppose the existence of a reasoning instantiator F and to claim that his belief resulted from a process x such that $F(x) = r$" (*Thought*, pp. 48–49).

7. I have made substantive changes in the discussion of principle Q and in the statement of $P*$ in response to comments by Ernest Sosa.

Principle P must give way to principle $P*$, which says that we
know by inference only if one of our inferences remains warranted and leads to the acceptance only of truths when restricted in premises to the set of things we know ahead of time
to be true.

14

Foundational versus Nonfoundational Theories of Empirical Justification

JAMES W. CORNMAN

Is an empirical statement known only if some particular set of statements forms the evidential foundation which provides the ultimate justification for the statement? For many philosophers over many years, the answer to this question has been almost dogmatically affirmative. Recently, however, strong and diverse attacks have been launched against a foundational theory of justification by a wide variety of philosophers. At present, R. M. Chisholm stands out, almost alone, as the embattled defender of foundationalism. One of my primary aims in this paper is to examine that part of Chisholm's defense that consists in an attack on all nonfoundational theories. Before this examination, however, I must identify the basic foundational thesis and its major non-foundational opponents. I shall begin by characterizing the minimal version of each sort of thesis. This is important because a thesis is refuted only if its minimal version is refuted. Thus we need the two minimal theses in order to evaluate both Chisholm's objections to alternatives to foundationalism, and attacks of others on foundationalism. It will also, however, help us classify more precisely the theories of philosophers, such as Quine and Sellars, who are all too quickly described as nonfoundationalists.

Reprinted from *The American Philosophical Quarterly*, 14.4 (1977), by kind permission of the author and editor.

Chisholm's Thesis and Minimal Foundationalism

Because we shall consider Chisholm as a paradigm of a foundationalist, let us begin our search for a characterization of minimal foundationalism with a view he endorses that he calls "thesis *A*":

> *A* Every [empirical] statement, which we are justified in thinking that we know, is justified in part by some [empirical] statement which justifies itself.[1]

To see whether thesis *A* adequately characterizes minimal foundationalism we should unpack two phrases: '*x* justifies *y* in part,' and '*x* justifies itself.' In both cases I shall assume phrases are to be relativized to a person and time, and in the first case I shall assume that *x* must be a needed part of the justification of *y*. Thus:

> *D1* *x* justifies *y* in part (at least) for person *s* at time *t* = Df. there is evidence, *e*, that is a set of statements which justifies *y* for *s* at *t*, and *e* would not justify *y* if it did not contain *x* either as an element or as a conjunct of a statement that is logically equivalent to an element.

In the second case, it might seem we need only require that *x* is justified even if nothing else is, but this will not do because self-justifying statement, *x*, might justify another by entailing it. Then it would not be possible that *x* alone is justified. Let us use, then, the following:

> *D2* *x* is self-justifying (justifies itself) for *s* at *t* = Df. *x* is justified for *s* at *t*, and it is false that it would be justified for *s* at *t*, only if it were to be justified by some relationship it has to some other statement or group of statements.[2]

Note that *D2* is consistent with the view that a sentence is self-justifying for a person only at times when certain conditions are met. That is, *D2* does not require that a sentence be self-justifying under all conditions and at all times. The crucial point is whether or not some other statement is needed to jus-

1. R. Chisholm, "Theory of Knowledge," in R. Chisholm et al., *Philosophy:* (Englewood Cliffs, N.J.: Prentice-Hall, 1964), p. 263.
    2. Ibid., p. 273, for Chisholm's different definition.

tify it for a person at that time. For example, it might be that the report, 'I am now having a visual experience of my holding something large and heavy,' is self-justifying for s at t only if it does not conflict with any other report that s believes at t, such as 'I am not now having a tactual experience of something large and heavy.'[3]

Let us now use $D1$ and $D2$ to replace A by the following:

> $F1$ Any empirical statement, p, is justified for s at time t, *if and only if* either p is self-justifying for s at t; or (i) some evidence, e, justifies p for s at t, and (ii) e contains some empirical statement, x, other than p, that is self-justifying for s at t, and e without x does not justify p for s at t.

Note that $D2$ and $F1$ require that x be a statement, and they allow that something other than statements—for example, a certain experience—is required to justify a self-justifying statement. Should a statement justified only by an experience be called self-justifying? We could change $D2$ so statement x would be self-justifying only if nothing of any sort should be needed to justify it. I propose, however, that we should leave $D2$ unchanged for the minimal foundational thesis. I believe all foundational views require there to be self-justifying statements in someone's evidence, but the view that a statement is self-justifying only if *nothing* at all is needed to justify it, is too strong to express a necessary condition for the minimal view. What is required by clause (ii) in $F1$, when unpacked by $D2$, is strong enough.

I find that $F1$ states neither a necessary nor a sufficient condition for any foundational theory, and so it is not the minimal thesis. There are three reasons why it is not sufficient. First, on the assumption that $F1$ is a material bi-conditional, it would follow from universal skepticism about justification. But skepticism should not be allowed to justify the thesis. Second, $F1$ allows some statements to be justified for someone without any recourse to self-justifying statements. According to $F1$, a person need only have available *some* set of evidence for p that requires him to rely on a self-justifying statement. But he need

3. For a more detailed discussion of related points, see my "On the Certainty of Reports about What Is Given," *Nous* (forthcoming).

not use it to justify p. Such a situation is inconsistent with every foundational theory, because each one requires a person to have recourse to some self-justifying statement at some stage of his justification. Third, *F1* requires that some set of statements, e, which justifies p for s, contains a self-justifying statement. But consider a series of sets of statements, e_1 through e_n, where each e_i in the series justifies e_{i-1}, but only e_i justifies p. Any foundational theory should require that *some* e_i in any such chain of justification for p contains a self-justifying statement, but it need not require that, in at least one of thse series, a self-justifying statement is a member of e_1, the set of statements that justifies p.

To amend *F1* appropriately, let us use the concept of "evidential series" characterized as follows:

> *D3* E is an evidential series (E-series) for p = Df. E is a series of evidence sets, e_1, e_2, e_3, . . . such that: (1) e_1 justifies p; and (2) for any e_i in series E, e_i justifies e_{i-1} in E.

In other words, any such a chain of justifiers, from e_1 to some first justifier or *ad infinitum* is an E-series for p. And we can use this notion of an E-series to define another term that will be useful later:

> *D4* x is an evidential ancestor (E-ancestor) of p = Df. there is an E-series, E, for p, such that for some set e_i in E, e_i would not justify e_{i-1} if it did not contain x either as an element or as a conjunct of a statement that is logically equivalent to an element of e_i.

That is, roughly, x is an essential part of some evidence in a chain of justification that ends with evidence justifying p.

We can now amend *F1* to give us the following replacement:

> *F2* Any empirical statement, p, would be justified for s at time t *if and only if* it would be true that: either p is self-justifying for s at t; or (i) there is an E-series for p that justifies p for s at t, and (ii) all of s's E-series that justify p for s at t contain some empirical statement that is self-justifying for s at t.

I believe that *F2* is minimal, that is, all and only theories that satisfy it are foundational. Of course *F2* is not sufficient for many species of foundational theory. Chisholm, for example, seems to hold a Cartesian-like foundational theory which states that, of empirical statements, only those exclusively about either what is phenomenally given or about certain psychological attitudes are self-justifying.[4] Such a theory implies, but is not implied by *F2*.

The Minimal Nonfoundational Theory

The basic opponent of foundational theories is often called the coherence theory of justification. But I think it better to view the coherence theory as just one of many nonfoundational theories, rather than its minimal version. I also believe that the minimal nonfoundational theory, should require no more than that no self-justifying statements are *needed* for justification, so that it does not matter whether there are self-justifying statements. However, the minimal thesis should apply to every non-self-justifying statement. Thus we can rule out the contradictory of *F2*, which is true if merely *one* non-self-justifying empirical statement should be justified without reliance on self-justifying statements. The minimal doctrine should state that no justified, non-self-justifying empirical statements require justification by a self-justifying statement. Let us try then:

   N Any empirical statement, *p*, that is not self-justifying for
        s at *t* would be justified for *s* at *t*, *if and only if*, it would
        be true that there is an E-series that: (1) justifies *p* for *s*
        at *t*; and (2) contains no empirical statement that is self-
        justifying for *s* at *t*.

Thesis *N* allows there to be self-justifying statements, and it allows them to justify other statements. It only requires that none of them are needed to justify non-self-justifying statements. It may be objected, however, that no nonfoundational theory should allow self-justifying statements to justify other statements. It might seem, then, that we should add to the right hand side of *N* that none of *s*'s E-series contain any empirical statement that is self-justifying for *s* and that justifies *p* in part for *s*. Nevertheless, I propose *N* as the minimal theory, because

4. Ibid., pp. 273–285.

any theory stating that every empirical justification would be accomplished without self-justifying statements—so it does not matter whether there are self-justifying statements—would be a nonfoundational theory. If so, then the minimal thesis should be no stronger than N. And it surely should be no weaker than N. And as N, the minimal thesis conflicts with the minimal foundational thesis, $F2$, in the sense that either N or $F2$ is false if some non-self-justifying empirical statement is justified.

Objections to Nonfoundational Theories

With it settled that N is the basic alternative to $F2$, we can turn to Chisholm's attempt to show that the main nonfoundational alternatives to his thesis A should be rejected. I shall reconstruct his procedure as an attack on the chief varieties of N. There are two species of N: first, each justified non-self-justifying statement is justified by an E-series containing only justified E-ancestors but no self-justifying statement; and, second, each of these is justified by some series containing an E-ancestor that is not justified in any way, perhaps even unjustified in the sense of its denial being reasonable. But we can ignore E-series with such unjustified statements, because no series requiring an unreasonable statement justifies anything.

The first species allows two important varieties. If we followed Chisholm, one would not permit any statement in the relevant E-series for p to be partly justified by p, and the other would allow some of these statements to be partly justified by p. The first is supposed to lead to an infinite regress and the second to a circularity.[5] As stated, however, the first does not guarantee an infinite regress. According to it, each justified non-self-justifying statement, p, requires a series, E, of justified non-self-justifying statements, excluding p. Thus each statement in any e_i in E must in turn be justified by a set, e_{i+1}, of justified non-self-justifying statements that does not contain p. But this does not generate an infinite regress. Assume that p is justified by e_1 containing statements q_1, q_2, q_3, which are justified non-self-justifying statements that are different from p. As-

5. Chisholm, p. 264.

sume also that q_1 justifies q_2, q_2 justifies q_3, and q_3 justifies q_1. Here is a case that satisfies the first thesis without an infinite regress. Of course, it is bothersome that q_1, q_2, and q_3 are each E-ancestors of themselves, but that is allowed by this statement of the first variety of the first species. In other words, this version allows a certain sort of circularity which might better be included in the second variety. Consequently, to rule out any sort of circularity and to guarantee an infinite regress, the first variety should be stated so it allows neither p nor any E-ancestor of p in the series to be one of its own E-ancestors. Then the second would allow both sorts of E-ancestors.

Three Varieties of Nonfoundationalism

We have three main varieties of N. First:

> *N1* Any empirical statement, p, that is not self-justifying for s at t would be justified for s at t, *if and only if* it would be true that there is an E-series that: (1) justifies p for s at t; (2) contains no empirical statement that is self-justifying for s at t; (3) contains only E-ancestors of p that are justified for s at t; and (4) contains no empirical statement that is itself (or is analytically equivalent to) one of its own E-ancestors.

Second:

> *N2* Any empirical statement, p, that is not self-justifying for s at t would be justified for s at t, *if and only if* it would be true that there is an E-series that: (1) justifies p for s at t; (2) contains no empirical statement that is self-justifying for s at t; (3) contains only E-ancestors of p that are justified for s at t; and (4) contains some empirical statement that is itself (or is analytically equivalent to) one of its own E-ancestors.

Third:

> *N3* Any empirical statement, p, that is not self-justifying for s at t would be justified for s at t, *if and only if* it would be true that there is an E-series that: (1) justifies p for s at t; (2) contains no empirical statement that is self-justifying for s at t; and (3) contains some E-ancestor of p that is not justified for s at t.

We can reconstruct Chisholm's reasons for rejecting the main alternative to his *A,* as reasons to reject the three preceding theses. That is, he would reject *N1* because it leads to an unacceptable infinite regress of justification. He notes that this can be avoided by making "blind posits" or guesses. But to do this is to desert *N1* for *N3,* which he would reject because it fails to distinguish "between knowledge, on the one hand, and a lucky guess, on the other."[6] Finally, it seems he would reject *N2* because it requires circular justification.[7]

An Objection to the First Variety: Justification and Infinitely Long E-Series

It is clear that *N1* requires an infinitely long series of E-ancestors for every justified non-self-justifying empirical statement. It also seems, initially, as Chisholm requires, that the regress is vicious, in the sense that whatever requires such a regress is unacceptable. Recently, however, B. Aune has argued that the required regress is not vicious, because only an unreasonable thesis about justification would make it vicious. As applied to *N1* it would be:

A series of E-ancestors of *p* justifies *p* for *s only if s actually* justifies, individually, every statement in the series that is not self-justifying for *s.*[8]

Contrast this with the thesis that requires only that *s* be *able* to justify, individually, any such statement in the series. The first thesis, conjoined with *N1,* leads to a vicious regress, because it assigns an impossible task to *s.* But the second thesis requires of *s* neither an impossible nor even an implausible task. He must merely be able to justify any particular statement in the series. He need not, then, either be able to justify or actually justify individually the whole set of statements in the series. Thus, according to Aune, the regress is not vicious, if, as he maintains, the first thesis about justification can be rejected for the second.

I agree with Aune in rejecting the first thesis. No more

6. Chisholm, p. 268.
7. Chisholm, p. 264.
8. See B. Aune, "Remarks on an Argument by Chisholm," *Philosophical Studies,* 23.5 (1972), 329.

should be required of s than what the second thesis states. Furthermore, it seems plausible that if s actually justifies a significant sample of E-ancestors of p by other statements, and he does so in a way that gives reason to conclude he is able to justify non-circularly any one in the series by another, then it is reasonable to conclude that each statement in the series is justified by another, and that s is able to show this for any particular one of them. However, finding the infinite series of $N1$ innocent of viciousness does not solve the main problem confronting $N1$, namely, that it seems to allow infinite E-series to justify sets of statements, where it is clear that some members of the sets should not be justified.

For any statement we can generate an infinite E-series that meets the requirements (2) through (4) of $N1$. And for any set, e_i, in the series we can easily formulate a set that justifies the statements in e_i. Consider the singular statement Pa, where a is not a number. This is justified for s at t by $e_1 = \{Q_1a, (x)(Q_1x \supset Px)\}$. Then the statements in e_1 are justified by $e_2 = \{Q_2a, (x)(Q_2x \supset Q_1x), (x),[(Q_2a \cdot Q_1x) \supset Px]\}$. And those in e_2 are justified by $e_3 = \{Q_2a, (x)(Q_3x \supset Q_2x), (x)(Q_3a \cdot Q_2x)) \supset q_1x], (x)[(Q_3a \cdot Q_2a \cdot Q_1x) \supset Px]\}$. This series, E_1, goes on to infinity, because we have an infinite number of predicates of the form Q_ix. For example, we can let $Q_ix = x$ is either not a number or is greater than the number i. This series contains no statement that is its own E-ancestor, and, we can assume, it contains no self-justifying statements. Thus E_1 meets requirements (2) through (4) of $N1$, and so, if meeting those requirements is sufficient for E_1 to justify p, then, by $N1$, Pa is justified for s at t. But should Pa be justified in this way?

To see the problem E_1 raises for $N1$, consider the requirement:

R A theory of justification is acceptable only if it does not yield that both a sentence and its denial are justified for the same person at the same time.

If a theory violates what R requires of acceptable theories, then it yields that some sentence and its denial are both justified. Thus each would be more reasonable than its denial. But this implies that each of these is also less reasonable than its denial,

because each is the denial of the other. So a theory that violates
R should be rejected.

The main problem for $N1$ is that if it allows its conditions (2),
(3), and (4) to be sufficient for (1), then $N1$ violates R. Consider
Pa and its denial, $\sim Pa$. We can construct an infinite E-series,
E_2, for $\sim Pa$ just by substituting $\sim Px$ for Px throughout E_1.
Thus, contrary to what R requires, both Pa and $\sim Pa$ would be
more reasonable than their denials for s at t, if requirements (2)
through (4) are sufficient for justification. Of course, the problem would be avoided if $N1$ could be amended to state a fourth
condition as needed for an E-series to justify p for s at t. But
what might it be? Might it restrict s to the use of just one of
each pair like E_1 and E_2? But it should not merely allow s to
choose whichever one he wants. This would permit him to justify whatever he wants by substituting appropriately throughout E_1. Obviously, an $N1$-theorist cannot rely either on un-
covering the presence of self-justifying statements in justifying
E-series, or on making blind posits of statements in the E-series
he desires to justify some statements. And there seems to be no
plausible coherence feature that would be found only in the
justifying infinite E-series required by $N1$. However, $N1$ might
be amended, in accordance with R, so that an E-series does not
justify a statement, p, if there is no reason to pick that series instead of its analogue that would justify the denial of p. But
then, I suggest, we will find that few, if any, statements will
have justifying E-series according to $N1$, because few E-series
would meet all five requirements of $N1$ as amended. Consequently, because at present there seems to be no plausible
way to amend $N1$, we should reject the sort of justification it
requires—at least until someone proposes a viable emendation.

Objection to a Second Variety: Blind Posits
and Justification

With $N1$ in doubt, two sorts of theses that avoid foundationalism remain. If Chisholm is right, that sort which allows
some justifying statements not to be justified by anything at all,
that is, $N3$, should be rejected because it involves "blind posits"
and so fails to distinguish between knowledge and lucky

guesses. It is not clear, however, that this criticism is accurate when directed at *N3*. It is true that if *N3* is correct, then each statement, p, that is justified for someone, s, rests in part on at least one statement that is a "mere guess," in the sense that it is no more reasonable for s than its denial. But this does not show that s has no evidence at all for p, as would be true if s were merely guessing about the truth of p. Thesis *N3* allows some evidence and reasoning for and against p. It merely requires that some E-ancestor of p be not justified. Of course, if circular justification and infinite E-series are prohibited, then, sooner or later, some E-series for p ends with a final set of statements, none of which are justified. But *N3* by itself does not require this.

The crucial question for *N3* is not whether a statement justified according to *N3* is a mere guess or blind posit, but whether any statement, q, that is not justified for s is an immediate E-ancestor of a statement, r, in an E-series that justifies a statement p, for s. When the question is put this way, it seems that the answer is negative and *N3* should be rejected. When we consider q merely as one of many remote E-ancestors of p, it is not clear that the lack of justification of q has any ill effects. But this impression changes once we realize that to be one of many remote E-ancestors of p is to be, probably, one of only a few immediate E-ancestors of r. And that raises the question of whether any statement can be justified by a set of statements containing and requiring a statement such as q.

Consider the following argument about such a q and r. For r, in a set e_i, to be justified for a person, s, by a set, e_{i+1}, *of its immediate ancestors, its relationship to the members of* e_{i+1} must be one of two kinds: either that of conclusion to premises, or that of a statement that is probable relative to evidence. If the relationship is the first sort, then r is a conclusion that is inferred, either deductively or inductively, from several premises, one of which, q, is required but is not justified for s. But then the set of premises do not justify r for s, and s cannot justify anything else using r in set e_i. Consequently, no series which contains such a q as a remote ancestor of p is an E-series that justifies p, contrary to *N3*.

On the other hand, if such a q is considered to be contained in a set, e_{i+1}, of s's evidence relative to which this r is probable [that is, $PR(r/e_{i+1}) > .5$], the question arises about what else, if anything, is needed for r to be justified for s by the set e_{i+1}. Some people require that the probability of the conjunction, c, of the members of the set e_{i+1} be 1, but I think that this is too restrictive. Yet, surely, at minimum this conjunction must be probable [that is, $Pr(c) > .5$]. Nothing is justified for someone by evidence, even if its probability relative to that evidence is very high, if the evidence itself is not probable for him.[9] Given this, and that c is a conjunction of s's evidential statements, $f_1, f_2, f_3, \ldots, f_m$, then, because $Pr(c) = Pr(f_1 \cdot f_2 \cdots f_m)$, the following is true by the probability calculus:

$$Pr(c) = Pr(f_1) \times Pr(f_2/f_1) \times Pr(f_3/f_1 \cdot F_2) \times \cdots \times Pr(f_m/f_1 \cdot f_2 \cdots f_{m-1}).$$

But, letting $q = f_1$, then for s, $Pr(c) \leq .5$, because q is no more reasonable than its denial for s. Thus again e_{i+1} does not justify r for s. Consequently, for both relationships that a justified statement has to the set of its immediate E-ancestors, every member of that ancestral set is more reasonable for s than its denial, that is, it is justified for s. But if every immediate E-ancestor of each set of E-ancestors of a justified statement must be justified, then, contrary to $N3$, no E-series for any statement contains one of its E-ancestors that is not justified. Thus, $N3$, like $N1$ should be rejected.

Objections to the Third Variety: Coherence and Justification

I think that few nonfoundationalists would mourn the demise of $N1$ and $N3$, because most of them probably subscribe to some sort of coherence theory of justification and this requires $N2$. Such theories are often associated with coherence theories of truth, and often rejected because they require a circularity of justification. But it would be a mistake to think that a coherence theory of justification has important implications for theories of truth, or conversely, and it is clearly debatable

9. I discuss this in "On Acceptability without Certainty," *Journal of Philosophy* 74.1 (1977), 29–47.

whether the required circularity is vicious, that is, whether any
theory implying it should be rejected. Consider, for example,
what I take to be the minimal coherence theory of justification:

> N2a Any empirical statement, p, that is not self-justifying
> for s at t would be justified for s at t, if and only if it
> would be true that there is an E-series such that: (a)
> clauses (1), (2), (3), and (4) of N2 are true; and (b) for
> p and every statement in this E-series, either they are
> justified for s at t by being in a justifying set of state-
> ments, J, for s at t, or they are justified by the set J for
> s at t.

Like N1 and N3, N2a allows foundational sorts of justification,
but it requires there to be a coherence justification for every
justified, non-self-justifying statement. It is also compatible with
a variety of theories of truth, including what is rather vaguely
dubbed the "correspondence" theory. Our concern with N2a,
however, is to discover whether it should be rejected. If it
should be rejected, then we have reason for dismissing N2,
because, I find, N2a is its most plausible variety.

An Explanatory Coherence Theory of Justification. One way to approach the problem of evaluating N2a is to find a clear example of a coherence theory, and use it as a paradigm case. Although there have been few attempts to formulate such
theories clearly, it is fortunate that K. Lehrer has recently provided a statement of such a theory. It is an explanatory coherence theory (EC-theory), which he and many others attribute to
Sellars and Quine. For our purposes we can use a version that
is simpler than the one Lehrer considers. It uses the following
principle to determine whether a set is a justifying set for N2a:

> EC The set J is a justifying set for s at t, if and only if the
> members of J are:
> (1) the nonredundant explaining members of some sys-
> tem of statements, C, that has maximum explanatory
> coherence among those systems understood by s at t
> (that is, C is a "maximal" system for s at t), and
> (2) the statements explained by C.[10]

10. See K. Lehrer, *Knowledge* (Oxford: Oxford University Press, 1974),
p. 165.

Crucial to *EC* is the notion of maximum explanatory coherence which we can define in much the way Lehrer does:[11]

> *D5* System *C* has maximum explanatory coherence among the set of systems, *B* = Df. (1) *C* is consistent; and (2) for any system, *x*, in *B*, if *x* is consistent but incompatible with *C*, then (a) *C* explains at least as much as *x*, and (b) it is false that *x* explains at least as much as *C* and also explains more things better than *C* does.

Even with definition *D5*, much remains unclear about maximum explanatory coherence. One problem is to determine conditions for when one system explains better than another, but let us ignore that problem except for noting two points. First, as used here, '*x* explains *y*' does not imply that either *x* or *y* is true, and truth is not a test for deciding which of two systems explains better. Second, "systemic" tests are relevant to how well a system explains. Following Quine, we can list some of these tests as refutability, simplicity, familiarity or principle, scope ("implies a wider array of testable consequences"), and fecundity ("successful further extensions of theory are expedited").[12]

A different unclarity in *D5* is, however, too important to ignore. It concerns what it is for *x* to explain at least as much as *y*. I find three initially plausible construals:

    (a) *x* explains at least as many statements as *y* does;

    (b) *x* explains at least the statements *y* explains;

    (c) *x* explains at least as many statements that are to be explained as *y* does, and at most as many that are not to be explained as *y* does.

Interpretation (a) should be rejected. On some plausible theories of explanation, if a system explains *p*, then it explains infinitely many other statements, because it also explains $p \vee q_1$, and $p \vee q_1 \vee q_2$, and so on. Thus on such a view, any system that explains at least one statement explains as many as any other system.

11. Ibid.

12. W. Quine, *The Ways of Paradox and Other Essays* (New York: Random House, 1966), p. 234.

Interpretation (b) seems to be the view that many scientifically oriented coherence theorists would accept, but it makes *EC* too strong even if the explanatory systems for someone are, implausibly, limited to scientific theories. At present there is no one scientific theory that explains at least what every other one explains, not even if we consider only those theories currently in vogue. If it be replied that we should conjoin all these theories to get the maximal system, one problem is that the result may well be inconsistent, at least in its theoretical implications. But more importantly, there are many individually consistent scientific theories, such as Newtonian mechanics, which, although not in vogue, are not eliminated by *D5* using (b), and clearly no consistent system explains what Newton's theory explains and also what Einstein's theory explains. Thus, if nothing of what each theory explains is eliminated, then no statements are justified for anyone who understands both theories, because no system is maximal for him. This is surely too strong. The only reply is to say that one of the theories has been refuted, and so no maximal system is required to explain all that each explains. But then the problem for an *EC*-theorist is to show that one of the theories explains something that is not to be explained. It is clear, then, that (b) must be amended so it considers only those statements explained by *y* that are to be explained.

As stated, (c) does not require such an amendment, but it does require that there be some way to determine which statements are to be explained. A person should not be allowed to decide this arbitrarily, because, as Lehrer notes, he can limit the statements that require explanation to exactly those his favorite system explains very well.[13] Thus for both (c), (b), and, I find, any plausible construal of *D5*, the crucial problem for an *EC*-theorist is to find a nonarbitrary way to restrict the statements that are to be explained. Too see how difficult this task is, consider one plausible way he might begin. He might begin by limiting the statements to singular, categorical observation statements. He can do this either by identifying observation

13. Lehrer, p. 170.

predicates and singular referring terms and, thereby, observation statements, or, as Quine does, by considering a sentence to be "observational insofar as its truth value, on any occasion, would be agreed to by just about any member of the speech community witnessing the occasion."[14] The latter technique allows many statements that seem very theoretical to be observational. But the resulting set is still too large. He might next divide this set into maximally consistent subsets, but this leaves him with many conflicting sets, not all of which are to be explained. The natural way to eliminate further is not available to an EC-theorist. That is, he cannot limit the set to those statements that are confirmed by observation, individually and independently of any explaining theory. Such statements would be self-justifying, contrary to what $N2$ requires.

He might propose, instead, that the desired set include all and only true observation statements. But then the following objection arises. Let us assume that either Newton's theory or Einstein's theory (but not both) explains only true observation statements. If this present version of EC-theory is correct, then for all we can determine, the Newtonian theory and what it explains might be justified for us, because it explains only what is true. Most of us, following what scientists tell us, would believe—mistakenly and with no means for discovering our mistake—that Einstein's theory is justified. And anyone who doggedly has maintained the Newtonian theory would be justified in his belief even though he has no way to support his view except to say that what his theory explains is true. This is surely an objectionable feature of a theory of empirical justification, and it should be avoided. It seems, then, that an EC-theorist needs something more than the mere (lucky) truth of observation statements in order to limit the set of statements to be explained. He needs some nonarbitrary means that is more reliable than a mere guess or dogmatic assertion for choosing which of such conflicting theories is more reasonable.

I can think of just one other way an EC-theorist might proceed. He might try to base his elimination on agreement rather

14. W. Quine, *The Roots of Reference* (La Salle, Ill.: Open Court, 1974), p. 39.

than truth. For example, he might propose the following Quine-like principle:

> *OE* An empirical statement, e_i, of language L is to be explained on occasion, O_i, if and only if it is a singular observation statement and almost all members of speech community M (e.g., scientists who speak L) would assent to the truth of e_i on witnessing occasion O_i.

But is the right-hand side of *OE* more accessible than mere truth for an *EC*-theorist?

Consider a person, s, who uses *OE* to justify the acceptance of an observation statement, e_1, that is explained by Einstein's theory but denied by Newton's. To succeed, he must verify a general statement, such as:

> *G1* Many members of class M would assent to e_1 on witnessing occasion O_1.

Since *G1* is empirical but not a singular observation statement, it would be justified for s, according to this *EC*-theory, if and only if either it is a nonredundant explanatory part of a system that is maximal for s, or it is justified by set J. But how is an *EC*-theorist to justify that *G1* has either status?

I have found only one procedure available for an *EC*-theorist who relies solely on agreement via *OE* to justify what is to be explained on each occasion. He can first assume *G1* and some of its kin, then use the set of observation sentences which they and *OE* pick out to determine which explanatory systems are maximal, and, finally, discover whether *G1* either is in a maximal system, or is justified by a justifying set, J, or is neither in nor justified by J. If *G1* is in or justified by J, then it is justified and so is the claim that e_1 is to be explained. If *G1* is neither in nor justified by J, then neither *G1* nor the claim that e_1 is to be explained is justified. However, our *EC*-theorist can always supply *G1* an explanatory role, and thus justification, by using *G1*, on occasion O_1, to help explain e_2: Scientist, a, assents to e_1. Of course, it must be justified that e_2 is to be explained on occasion O_1, but this can be achieved by assuming *G2* which is like *G1* except that *G2* contains 'e_2' instead of 'e_1.' And then *G2* can be justified by having it explain e_3: Scientist, b, assents to e_2. And this goes on *ad infinitum*.

The preceding procedure for justifying $G1$ requires infinitely many explaining sentences and sentences to be explained. But that is not its problem. Like the problem for $N1$, its problem is that it is unjustifiably arbitrary. We need only substitute '$\sim e_1$' for 'e_1' in $G1$ and e_2, and, keeping all else the same, $\sim e_1$ is justified for s at t, instead of e_1. But, as was noted previously, any procedure should be rejected, if it allows someone to justify whichever one of a statement and its denial he desires to justify. Consequently, like the problem he faces if he relies on mere truth, an EC-theorist who proposes principles like OE that rely solely on agreement has no nonarbitrary way to justify that some set from among the many conflicting maximally consistent sets of observation statements is to be explained. Thus he does not excape the preceding objection to his theory by substituting agreement for truth.

Conclusion about Explanatory Coherence Theories. I believe that the serious problem facing an EC-theorist who relies on truth or on agreement is not unique. That is, I believe that any other way to justify the elimination of certain statements will have similar problems. It is clear, however, that I have not established this more general claim. Instead let me offer a challenge to any EC-theorist: refute the following dilemma or reject your theory. An EC-theorist must find a procedure for selecting a set of statements that are to be explained. He has but two alternatives: allow a person to restrict the set arbitrarily, or provide nonarbitrary but accessible particular restrictions. But the first alternative is objectionable, because it allows a person to pick just those statements that his favorite theory explains. And, as just indicated, it seems an EC-theorist has no way to realize the second alternative.[15] Consequently, all EC-theories

15. N. Rescher argues for a coherence theory of truth in *The Coherence Theory of Truth* (London: Oxford University Press, 1973), and it might be thought that he provides a coherence theory of justification. What is relevant is his attempt to eliminate all but one of the maximally consistent subsets of what he calls "truth-candidates" or "data" (pp. 53–70), so that the remaining one is justified as the set of true propositions. However, in chapter V, where he suggests five ways to eliminate competing sets, the most plausible ways depend on independently establishing claims about probabilities, or plausibilities, or specially designated theses. But if what I argue in this paper is correct, some sort of foundational theory of justification is needed to establish such claims.

should be rejected, either for a less objectionable theory or for skepticism.

I conclude that we should reject all *EC*-theories until this challenge is met. Of course, someone may prove me wrong, but my confidence in my conclusion is strengthened by another objection from Lehrer.[16] Even if being a nonredundant explanatory member of a system that is maximal for s, is sufficient for being justified for s, it is quite implausible that if s has no such explanatory system, then no empirical statements are justified for him. It surely seems that some of s's observation statements and certain of his psychological reports are justified, whether or not they are explained for s.

Lehrer raises a third objection that should be noted.[17] As stated above, *D5* allows several incompatible systems to be maximal, and so, Lehrer would claim, wherever this occurs, an *EC*-theory results in incompatible statements being justified for one person at one time. But that is wrong. Furthermore, if Quine is (or at least used to be) right in claiming that scientific theory is underdetermined, then there always are two conflicting, maximal systems, even when each explains exactly what is to be explained.[18] Thus if Lehrer and Quine are both right, there is another objection sufficient to refute *EC*-theories. And, we might note, this objection is the analogue of the crucial objection that supposedly defeats the coherence theory of truth. I think, however, that neither of these objections is decisive.

On Coherence Theories of Justification and Coherence Theories of Truth

The defect in *N2a*, as spelled out by *EC* and *D5*, that gives rise to the preceding objection can be easily corrected by adding a clause to *N2a* to the effect that a person may use at most one of his justifying sets at any one time. It may be objected

16. Lehrer, pp. 178–80.
17. Lehrer, pp. 181–82.
18. See W. Quine, *Word and Object* (Cambridge, Mass.: M.I.T. Press, 1960), pp. 21–22. I discuss this in "Reference and Ontology: Inscrutable but not Relative," *Monist* (July, 1976). For Quine's later views where he expresses doubts about underdetermination, see his "On Empirically Equivalent Systems of the World," *Erkenntnis* (1975), 313–328.

that this gives a person too much leeway. But, since each set includes only one maximal system and what it explains, it seems reasonable to allow *s* to choose whichever one he wants, because no such choice would ever result in *s* rejecting one justificatory system for another that is less reasonable. But, although this reply helps *EC*-theories, it is of no use to coherence theories of truth. Not only is it most implausible to allow someone's desires to decide what is true, but also, because different people have different maximal systems and different desires, determining truth in this way would probably result in some statements and their denials being true, unless truth is relativized to persons. But although justification should be so relativized, truth surely should not.

On a Coherence Theory of Truth with a Foundational Theory of Justification

It might seem that we have found a place where coherence theories of justification are superior to such theories of truth. However, I believe a "truth-coherence" theorist can begin a solution of his problem in a way that allows him to avoid the two crucial objections to "justification-coherence" theories, namely, they have no way to justify any particular restriction on what is to be explained, and explanation is not a necessary condition of justification. Thus his thesis may turn out to be the more plausible of the two. Once it is realized that explanation is one, but only one, important means of justification, it is quite natural and very tempting to adopt a theory of justification that goes, very roughly, as follows. Singular, categorical observation reports (such as 'I see something brown') and, I would suggest, psychological reports (such as 'I am hurting' and 'I believe I see a table') can be tested individually and either confirmed or disconfirmed by observing or experiencing what occurs on the appropriate occasion. Those that are so confirmed are to be explained. Then the empirical sentences that are justified for a person *s* are those singular observation and psychological reports he has confirmed, plus any universal and statistical observational generalizations inductively confirmed by these singular statements, plus the sentences of one explanatory system that is maximal in sense (c) for s regarding these first two sets, plus what these three sets jointly justify. Of course, what results is not a coherence theory. It is instead foundational, but that by itself is no cause for alarm, not even for a "truth-coherence" theorist.

A truth-coherence theorist can adopt the preceding foundational theory of justification and combine it with a coherence theory of truth. In this way he avoids the two objections to EC-theories. And he might begin to avoid the preceding objection to his theory of truth by adopting something like the following rough thesis. The true empirical statements include those observation reports and psychological reports that would be individually confirmed at each moment by an all-perfect perfect being, plus the nonredundant members of the explanatory system that would best explain all these reports for an all-perfect being, plus whatever is entailed by the first two sets of statements. Such a thesis would not be trouble-free, but it might be refined to avoid damaging objections, such as the previous one that no coherence theory of truth specifies exactly one consistent set of sentences as true. To avoid this crucial objection, this first, rough thesis about truth must be supplemented by some procedure for picking out exactly one member from each partition of empirical sentences that are not in the first three sets specified for an all-perfect being. Of course, if explanatory theory would be underdetermined for an all-perfect being, then the objection becomes even more difficult to answer. However, it is not clear that this would be true. If, as Quine says, familiarity of principle is one test of deciding among explanatory systems, then, even for us imperfect beings, it seems likely that at any one time, if several systems are maximal, except for familiarity, then one of these will be most familiar and thereby maximal. And would not there be, for an all-perfect being, just one system that does consist, and always has consisted of eternally familiar principles:

Quine and Sellars as Foundationalists

I find the preceding theory of justification that supplements a foundational thesis with explanatory coherence to be quite attractive. Furthermore, I believe that, contrary to most opinions, it is somewhat plausible to interpret both Quine and Sellars as holding some form of this combined thesis, in spite of some things they say which at first glance seem to imply a rejection of foundationalism. For example, Quine says:

Any statement can be held true come what may, if we make drastic enough adjustments elsewhere in the system. Even a statement very close to the periphery can be held true in the face of recalcitrant experience by pleading hallucination or by amending certain statements of the kind called logical laws. Conversely, by the same token, no statement is immune to revision.[19]

And Sellars states:

Our aim [is] to manipulate the three basic components of a world picture: (a) observed objects and events, (b) unobserved objects and events, and (c) nomological connections, so as to achieve a world picture with a maximum of 'explanatory coherence.' In this reshuffle, no item is sacred.[20]

In spite of these quotations, however, Quine and Sellars can be foundationalists if, as is plausible, we take their main thesis to be that no particular set of statements is immune to refutation and so none is irrevocably at the foundation of empirical justification. That is, empirical justification does not have "*the* given" at its foundation. Sellars is opposed to observation statements being given and thus unalterably at the foundation, because he claims that, in the scientific millennium, singular theoretical statements will provide the most accurate and comprehensive picture of what there is. Thus he wants to be able to justify the ultimate rejection of all nontheoretical, observation statements. But none of this requires that he reject foundationalism. Indeed, his rejection of "the" given is not a rejection of foundationalism:

To reject the myth of the given is to not commit oneself to the idea that empirical knowledge as it is now constituted has no rock bottom level of observation predicates proper. It is to commit oneself rather to

19. W. Quine, *From a Logical Point of View* (New York: Harper & Row, 1961), p. 43.
20. W. Sellars, *Science, Perception and Reality* (New York: Humanities Press, 1963), p. 356.

the idea where even if it does have a rock bottom level, it is *still* in principle replaceable by another conceptual framework in which these predicates do not, *strictly speaking*, occur. It is in this sense, and in this sense *only*, that I have rejected the dogma of given-ness with respect to observation predicates.[21]

Quine's views are amazingly similar. He seems to hold that observation statements are individually verifiable and are the tests of explanatory systems. He says that his view of the relationship of observation sentences

to our knowledge of what is true, is very much the traditional one: observation sentences are the repository of evidence for scientific hypotheses. . . . Sentences higher up in theories have no empirical consequences they can call their own; they confront the tribunal of sensory evidence only in more or less inclusive aggregates. The observation sentence, situated at the sensory periphery of the body scientific, is the minimal verifiable aggregate; it has an empirical content all its own and wears it on its sleeve.[22]

This surely seems to be a foundational thesis, indeed, one quite similar to the sort it is plausible to ascribe to Sellars. That is, both men seem to hold a foundational theory of justification that utilizes explanatory coherence but avoids "the" given. Yet, it might be objected, Quine and Sellars differ importantly, because Quine keeps observation statements at the foundation, but Sellars wants to depose them. But there is no disagreement here, because, as Quine characterizes observation sentences, they include the very singular, categorical "theoretical" statements that Sellars wishes to place finally at the foundation.

Conclusion: A Foundational Theory with Explanatory Coherence

Is it reasonable to attribute this "explanatory-coherence" foundational theory of empirical justification to Quine and Sellars? And is this theory I attribute to them reasonable? I shall leave the fist question for others to answer, preferably Quine and Sellars. Regarding the second, I shall make only three

21. W. Sellars, *Philosophical Perspectives* (Springfield, Ill,: Charles C. Thomas, 1967), p. 353.
22. W. Quine, *Ontological Relativity and Other Essays* (New York: Columbia University Press, 1969), pp. 88–89.

points here. First, this theory avoids the usual objections to foundational theories because it does not require an incorrigible given, does not restrict the sentences at the foundation to those solely about "the given," and does not limit inferential justification to deduction and induction by enumeration.[23] Second, if, as it seems plausible to expect, the notion of maximum explanatory coherence can be successfully clarified and the conditions for when a report is confirmed or disconfirmed by experience can be specified plausibly, then I find no damaging objections to the theory. Third, because of the first two points, and because in this paper we have seen some evidence that its main nonfoundational opponents are implausible, there is some reason to draw the tentative conclusion that this theory is a prime candidate for the most reasonable theory of empirical justification.[24]

23. However, for an objection to foundational theories that: (1) statements at a foundation must have a probability of 1, and (2) only logical truths have that probability, see Lehrer, pp. 150–51. I have argued against (1) in "On Acceptability without Certainty," and against (2) in "On the Certainty of Reports about What Is Given."

24. I wish to thank Jaegwon Kim and Ernest Sosa for their very helpful comments.

15

On the Nature
of Empirical Evidence

RODERICK M. CHISHOLM

The present paper[1] is divided into five parts. The first is a
sketch of what I take to be the basic concepts and principles of
epistemic logic; the second is an attempt to characterise in
terms of these epistemic concepts those propositions that may
be said to be basic to a man's knowledge at any given time; the
third is concerned with the notion of evidential support or justification; the fourth is concerned with the problem of defining
knowledge; and the fifth is an attempt to formulate criteria of
application for some of the concepts of the theory of evidence.
Much of what I have to say is by way of correction and emendation of what was said in my book *Theory of Knowledge* (Englewood Cliffs, N.J., 1966). I choose this occasion to make these
corrections and emendations, since the topic is basic to the
question of "Experience and Theory" and since I wish to deal
with problems that have been pointed out by Professor Gettier
and Professor Heidelberger of the University of Massachusetts.[2]

Originally published, in an earlier version, in *Experience and Theory,* edited by
Lawrence Foster and J. W. Swanson, copyright © 1970 by the University of
Massachusetts Press. Reprinted by kind permission of the author and the publisher.
  1. I am indebted to Herbert Heidelberger, Ernest Sosa, Robert Swartz, Edmund Gettier, Robert Keim, and Mark Pastin for criticisms of earlier versions
of this paper.
  2. See Edmund L. Gettier, "Is Justified True Belief Knowledge?" *Analysis,*
23.6 (1963), 121–123, and Herbert Heidelberger, "Chisholm's Epistemic Principles," *Nous,* 3.1 (1969), 73–82.

I

We may think of the theory of evidence as a branch of the theory of preference, or, more accurately, of the theory of *right* preference, or preferability. Let us take *epistemic preferability* as our undefined epistemic concept. Thus we begin with the locution, "*p* is epistemically preferable to *q* for S at *t*," where the expressions occupying the place of "*p*" and "*q*" are terms referring to states of affairs (or propositions) and where "S" and "*t*," respectively, refer to a particular person and to a particular time.

We may set forth the following seven principles as axioms of epistemic preferability. (1) Epistemic preferability, like other types of preferability, is such that, for any states of affairs *p* and *q*, if *p* is preferable to *q* for S at *t*, then it is not the case that *q* is preferable to *p* for S at *t*. (2) Again like other types of preferability, epistemic preferability is such that, for any states of affairs, *p*, *q*, and *r*, if it is not the case that *p* is preferable to *q*, and if it is not the case that *q* is preferable to *r*, then it is not the case that *p* is preferable to *r*. (3) For any propositions *h* and *i*, believing *h* is epistemically preferable to believing *i* for S at *t*, if and only if, believing *not-i* is epistemically preferable to believing *not-h* for S at *t*.[3] (4) For any proposition *h*, if withholding *h* (that is, neither believing *h* nor believing *not-h*) is *not* epistemically preferable to believing *h*, then believing *h* is epistemically preferable to believing *not-h*. "If agnosticism is not epistemically preferable to theism, then theism is epistemically preferable to atheism." (5) For any propositions *h* and *i*, withholding *h* is the same in epistemic value as withholding *i* for S at *t*, if and only

3. I have called the terms of the relation of epistemic preferability "propositions or states of affairs" and I have used the letters "*p*," "*q*," and "*r*" as variables designating such terms. I have called the objects of such attitudes as believing "propositions" and have used the letters "*h*," "*i*," and "*j*" to designate such objects. I believe, however, that the entities which are called in the one case "propositions or states of affairs" and in the other "propositions" are one and the same, but this belief is not essential to any of the points of the present paper. Some further defense of it may be found in my paper, "Language, Logic, and States of Affairs," in Sidney Hook, ed., *Language and Philosophy* (New York, 1969), pp. 241–248, and in "Events and Propositions," *Nous*, 4 (1970).

if, either believing h is the same in epistemic value as believing i for S at t or believing *not-h* is the same in epistemic value as believing i for S at t. (To say that one state of affairs is "the same in epistemic value" as another is to say that neither one is epistemically preferable to the other.) (6) For any propositions h and i, if believing i is epistemically preferable to believing h for S at t and also epistemically preferable to believing *not-h* for S at t, then withholding h is epistemically preferable to withholding i for s at t. And finally (7) withholding a proposition is the same thing as withholding its negation.[4]

In order to explicate the basic concepts of the theory of epistemic preferability, let us consider what is involved in asking, for any given proposition and any given subject and any given time, which is epistemically preferable: believing the proposition, disbelieving the proposition (that is, believing the negation of the proposition), or withholding the proposition (neither believing nor disbelieving the proposition). We may consider six different stages of affairs which, together with their negations, give us twelve possibilities.

a) The proposition may be such that believing it is epistemically preferable to withholding it (for the particular subject at the particular time). In this case, we may say that the proposition (for that subject at that time) is one that is *beyond reasonable doubt*, or, as we may put it more briefly, one that is *reasonable*. The propositions falling within the negation of this category are those which are such that believing them is *not* epistemically preferable to withholding them. Let us say that such propositions are epistemically *gratuitous*.[5]

4. These axioms are used in "A System of Epistemic Logic" by Roderick M. Chisholm and Robert Keim, *Ratio*, 15 (1973). The last three were proposed by Mr. Keim. Versions of the others may be found in: *Theory of Knowledge*, p. 22n; Roderick M. Chisholm, "The Principles of Epistemic Appraisal," in *Current Philosophical Issues: Essays in Honor of Curt John Ducasse*, ed. F. C. Dommeyer (Springfield, Ill., 1966), pp. 87–104, and "On a Principle of Epistemic Preferability," *Philosophy and Phenomenological Research*, 30 (1969); and Roderick M. Chisholm and Ernest Sosa, "On the Logic of 'Intrinsically Better,'" *American Philosophical Quarterly*, 3 (1966), 244–249.

5. If we use "reasonable" as short for "beyond reasonable doubt," we should avoid using "unreasonable" as short for "not beyond reasonable doubt." For "unreasonable" suggests "unacceptable," to be defined below, rather than "gratuitous."

b) The proposition may be such that believing it is epistemically preferable to disbelieving it (believing its negation). Let us say that a proposition of this sort is one that has *some presumption in its favor*. The phrase "more probable than not" is sometimes used to express this concept. Our principles imply that whatever is thus beyond reasonable doubt also has some presumption in its favor, but they do not imply the converse. Propositions falling within the negation of this second category—propositions which are such that believing them is not epistemically preferable to disbelieving them—will be such as to have no presumption in their favor.

c) The proposition may be such that withholding it is epistemically preferable to believing it. Let us say that a proposition of this sort is one that is *unacceptable*. Hence any proposition not such that withholding it is epistemically preferable to believing may be said to be *acceptable*. Our principles imply that any acceptable proposition is a proposition that has some presumption in its favor, but they do not imply the converse. They also imply that any proposition that is beyond reasonable doubt is one that is acceptable, but again they do not imply the converse. Hence we have the beginnings of an epistemic hierarchy. (The hierarchy may be illustrated as follows. If the police are justified in detaining you, then the proposition that you did the deed should be one which, for them, has some presumption in its favor. If the state is justified in bringing you to trial, then that proposition should be one which, for it, is acceptable. And if the jury is justified in finding you guilty, then the proposition should be one which, for it, is beyond reasonable doubt.)

d) The proposition may be such that withholding it is epistemically preferable to disbelieving it. Hence any proposition falling within this category is one having an unacceptable negation. And any proposition falling within the negation of this category—any proposition such that withholding it is not epistemically preferable to disbelieving it—is one that has an acceptable negation.

e) The proposition may be such that disbelieving it is epistemically preferable to believing it. In this case, the negation of the proposition is such that there is some presumption in its favor. And any proposition falling within the negation of this category will be one such that there is no presumption in favor of its negation.

f) Finally, the proposition may be such that disbelieving it is epistemically preferable to withholding it. In this case, the negation of the proposition will be beyond reasonable doubt and the proposition itself, therefore, will be unacceptable. A proposition falling within the negation of this category will be one that has a gratuitous negation.

If we use "*Bh*" for "believing *h*," "*B ~h*" for "believing *not-h*" (or "disbelieving *h*"), "*Wh*" for "withholding *h*," and "——— *P* . . ." for "———is epistemically preferable to . . . for *S* at *t*," then the following formulae will illustrate the categories just discussed:

a) $(Bh)P(Wh)$ *d*) $(Wh)P(B \sim h)$
b) $(Bh)P(B \sim h)$ *e*) $(B \sim h)P(Bh)$
c) $(Wh)P(Bh)$ *f*) $(B \sim h)P(Wh)$

We may use the letters, "*a*," "*b*," "*c*," "*d*," "*e*," and "*f*," respectively, as further abbreviations for these six formulae, and "*~a*," "*~b*," "*~c*," "*~d*," "*~e*," and "*~f*," respectively, as abbreviations for their negations.

Some of the consequences of our first and fourth axioms may now be abbreviated as follows:

a implies: *b*, *~c*, *d*, *~e*, *~f*   *f* implies: *~a*, *~b*, *c*, *~d*, *e*
b implies: *d*, *~e*, *~f*   *~b* implies: *~a*, *c*
c implies: *~a*   *~c* implies: *b*, *d*, *~e*, *~f*
d implies: *~f*   *~d* implies: *~a*, *~b*, *c*, *e*
e implies: *~a*, *~b*, *c*   *~e* implies: *d*, *~f*.

These formulae thus exhibit some of the relations holding among the various epistemic concepts defined above. For example, since *~c* implies *d* (that is, since any proposition which is such that withholding it is not epistemically preferable to believing it is also one which is such that withholding it is preferable to disbelieving it), we may say that if a proposition is acceptable then it has an unacceptable negation. Hence any proposition is such that either it or its negation is unacceptable.

Making use of some of the terms just defined, we may introduce still other epistemic categories. Thus we may say that a proposition is *counterbalanced* if there is no presumption in its favor and also no presumption in favor of its negation. In other words, a proposition is counterbalanced, for *S* at *t,* if believing it is not epistemically preferable to disbelieving it for *S* at *t* and if disbelieving it is not epistemically preferable to believing it for *S* at *t.* In still other words, *h* is counterbalanced if believing *h* and believing *not-h* are the same in epistemic value. We may say that a proposition *ought to be withheld* provided that both it and its negation are unacceptable. Our principles imply the Pyrrhonistic thesis according to which any proposition that is counterbalanced is also one that ought to be withheld.

The term "indifferent" is sometimes taken in the present sense of the term "counterbalanced"; in the book, *Theory of Knowledge,* I defined it in this way. But "indifferent" is sometimes taken, in analogy with one of its uses in ethics and deontic logic, to suggest that, if a proposition is thus indifferent to a man, then the doxastic attitude (believing, disbelieving, or withholding) that he may take toward the proposition is one that "does not matter." If we are right in saying that every proposition is such that either it or its negation is unacceptable, then, although there are many propositions that might be said to be "indifferent" in the first sense, there are no propositions that may be said to be "indifferent" in the second. Hence we shall avoid the term in the present discussion.

Two further concepts that are essential to the theory of empirical evidence are the concept of the *certain* and the concept of the *evident.* We could say that a proposition is *certain* provided only it is beyond reasonable doubt and it is at least as reasonable as any other proposition. And we could say that a proposition is *evident* if it is beyond reasonable doubt and such that any proposition that is more reasonable than it is one that is certain.

We now formulate somewhat more exactly a number of the definitions that have been proposed.

   (D1) *h* is beyond reasonable doubt for *S* = Df. Accepting
        h is epistemically preferable for *S* to withholding *h.*
   (D2) *h* has some presumption in its favor for *S* = Df. Ac-

cepting *h* is epistemically preferable for *S* to accepting not-*h*.

(D3) *h* is counterbalanced for *S* = Df. Accepting *h* is not epistemically preferable for *S* to accepting not-*h*, and accepting not-*h* is not epistemically preferable for *S* to accepting *h*.

(D4) *h* is acceptable for *S* = Df. Withholding *h* is not epistemically preferable for *S* to accepting *h*.

(D5) *h* is certain for *S* = Df. *h* is beyond reasonable doubt for *S*, and there is no *i* such that accepting *i* is more reasonable for *S* than accepting *h*.

(D6) *h* is evident for *S* = Df. *h* is beyond reasonable doubt for *S;* and for every *i*, if accepting *i* is more reasonable for *S* than accepting *h*, then *i* is certain for *S*.

II

We now consider briefly a somewhat different type of epistemic concept. Certain propositions may be said to be *directly evident,* or as we will say, *basic,* for a man at any given time. Of the propositions that are thus directly evident, or basic, some may be said to empirical and others *a priori.* Leibniz referred to these two types of directly evident proposition as "the first truths of fact" and "the first truths of reason," respectively.[6]

We will say that directly evident propositions of the first sort are propositions which are "self-presenting" for the person to whom they are evident, and that directly evident propositions of the second sort are *"a priori."* In defining them, we will make use of the concepts of *necessity* and *truth,* as well as that of the *evident,* defined above.

The term "self-presenting" was used by Meinong and suggested by Brentano.[7] We will construe a self-presenting propo-

6. G. W. Leibniz, *New Essays Concerning Human Understanding,* Book IV, Chapter 9. Compare Franz Brentano, *The True and the Evident* (London: Routledge & Kegan Paul, 1966), English edition edited by Roderick M. Chisholm, esp. pp. 123–132.

7. Compare A. Meinong, *Über emotionale Präsentation* (Vienna: Kais. Akademie der Wissenschaften, 1917), p. 31f., and Franz Brentano, *Psychologie vom empirischen Standpunkt* (Hamburg: Felix Meiner, 1955), Vol. 1, pp. 176–180.

sition as being a proposition which is such that, whenever it is true, it is evident. Because of the "whenever," we make the temporal reference explicit in the following definition:

(D7) h is *self-presenting* for S at $t =$ Df. (i) h is true at t and (ii) necessarily if h is true at t then h is evident for S at t.

(For those who cannot accept the presupposition that a proposition may be true at one time and not true at another the expression "is true" may be replaced by "occurs or obtains" and "h" construed as referring to an event or state of affairs.)

Among the propositions which are thus self-presenting for a man at a given time are propositions about his state of mind at that time—his thinking certain thoughts, entertaining certain beliefs, his sensing in certain ways. For it is impossible for a man to think such thoughts, have such beliefs, or sense in such ways unless it is then *evident* to him that he is thinking those thoughts, entertaining those beliefs, or sensing in those ways. We will return to this concept in Section V below.

What now of the *a priori*? It is traditional to say that an *a priori* proposition is a proposition that is "independent of experience" and such that "if you understand it then you can see that it is true." To get at what is intended by these descriptions, let us first say what it is for a proposition to be *axiomatic* for a person at a given time:

(D8) h is *axiomatic* for $S =$ Df. (i) S accepts h, (ii) necessarily h is true, and (iii) necessarily if S accepts h then h is evident for S.

The second clause tells us the sense in which an axiomatic proposition is "independent of experience," the third tells us the sense in which an axiomatic proposition is such that "if you understand it then you see that it is true," and the first and third together tell us that the man for whom the proposition is axiomatic does thus "see that it is true." We next define the somewhat broader concept of the *a priori*:

(D9) h is *a priori* for $S =$ Df. There is an e such that (i) e is axiomatic for S and (ii) the proposition that e entails h is also axiomatic for S.

Now we may define a basic proposition as one which is either self-presenting or *a priori*:

(D10) *h* is *basic* for *S* = Df. Either *h* is self-presenting for
        S or *h* is *a priori* for *S*.
Instead of "*h* is basic for *S*," we may also say "*h* is *directly evident*
for *S*."

III

The epistemic concepts defined up to now pertain to the
epistemic status a single proposition may have for a given subject at a given time. There is also a family of epistemic concepts
pertaining to the relations that may hold between two propositions when one of the propositions may be said to confer some
epistemic status upon another. Thus one proposition may be
said to *confer evidence* upon another, or to make the other evident. Or it may confer a lower epistemic status—that of being
beyond reasonable doubt, or that of having some presumption
in its favor. In the latter case, where one proposition confers
upon another the status of having some presumption in its
favor, the one proposition may be said to *confirm* the other
proposition. We will call these various relations "justifying relations" for they exemplify different ways in which one proposition may be said to *justify* another.[8]

Our major concern in this section will be to say what it is for
one proposition to *make evident* another proposition for a given
subject at a given time. It is one of the tasks of epistemology to
show ways in which a man's basic propositions at any time may
make evident to him other propositions at that time. We will
express the relation we wish to define in the locution "*e* makes *h*
evident for *S*." Let us first consider some of the things we wish
to be able to say about this relation.

Presumably we will want to say that, if *e* makes *h* evident for
S, then *e* as well as *h* is evident for *S*. But there will be many
propositions *e* and *h* which are evident for *S* (e.g. "There is a
sheep" and "There is a stone") which will not be such that either one of them makes evident the other for *S*. We will want

8. One proposition may also confer negative epistemic status upon another;
it may render the other nonevident, for example, or unacceptable. What may
be said about the positive cases may also be said *mutatis mutandis* about the negative cases.

to be able to say that an evident proposition may make evident some of the propositions it entails. But an evident proposition need not make evident every proposition it entails. Hence for an evident proposition e to make evident a proposition h for S, it will not be sufficient that e entail h.

Nor will it be necessary. Any adequate theory of evidence must provide for the fact that a proposition e may make evident a proposition h for a subject S even though e does not entail h. We reject the sceptical view according to which there is no reason to believe that the premises of an inductive argument ever confer evidence upon the conclusion. If this sceptical view were true, then we would know next to nothing about the world around us. We would not know, for example, such propositions as are expressed by "There are 9 planets," "Jones owns a Ford," and "The sun will rise tomorrow."[9]

In order to define the concept of *making evident*, we will first say what it is for one proposition to serve as a basis for another:

(D11) e is a basis of h for $S =$ Df. e is self-presenting for S; and necessarily, if e is self-presenting for S, then h is evident for S.

And now we may say what it is for one evident proposition to confer evidence upon another proposition:

(D12) e makes h evident for $S =$ Df. e is evident for S; and every b such that b is a basis of e for S is a basis of h for S.

If e makes h evident for S and also entails h, then we may say that e *demonstratively*, or *deductively*, makes h evident for S. But if e makes h evident for S and does not entail h, then we may say that e *inductively* makes h evident for S.

It may be noted in passing that we are now in a position to define the confirmation relation where this is considered as an absolute relation—a relation that holds eternally between propositions and involves no reference to a particular subject. This

9. ". . . in common discourse we readily affirm, that many arguments from causation exceed probability, and may be received as a superior kind of evidence. One would appear ridiculous who would say, that it is only probable that the sun will rise tomorrow, or that all men must die: though it is plain we have no further assurance of these facts than what experience affords us." David Hume, *A Treatise of Human Nature*, ed. L. A. Selby-Bigge (Oxford, 1888), Bk. 1, Pt. 3, Sec. XI, p. 124.

relation has been expressed in various ways; for example, as "*h* is more probable than not in relation to *e*." We will express it as "*e* tends to confirm *h*" and define it in the following way:

    (D13) *e* tends to confirm *h* = Df. Necessarily, for every *S*, if *e* is evident for *S* and if everything evident for *S* is entailed by *e*, then *h* has some presumption in its favor for *S*.

This sense of "*e* tends to confirm *h*" might be expressed, somewhat loosely, by saying: "If *e* were the only thing you knew, or the only relevant evidence you had, then you would also have some reason for accepting *h*."[10] We may also express this relation, more simply, as "*e* confirms *h*."

Let us now turn to the concept of knowledge.

IV

The traditional definition of knowledge may be put as follows:

    S knows at *t* that *h* is true = Df. *h* is true, *S* believes at *t* that *h* is true, and *h* is evident for *S* at *t*.

In countenancing the possibility that a proposition *e* may inductively confer evidence upon a proposition *h*, we also countenance the possibility that *e* is true and *h* is false and therefore that there are some propositions that are both evident and false. But Professor Gettier has shown that, if there are propositions that are both evident and false, then the traditional definition of knowledge is inadequate. It is necessary, therefore, to revise the traditional definition. I wish now to suggest that we can revise the traditional definition in terms of the vocabulary that we have introduced here.

What Gettier has shown is that the traditional definition is in-

10. Our account of confirmation may be compared with the following informal explication by Carnap of a closely related concept: "To say that the hypothesis *h* has the probability *p* (say 3/5) with respect to the evidence *e*, means that for anyone to whom this evidence but no other relevant knowledge is available, it would be reasonable to believe in *h* to the degree *p* or, more exactly, it would be unreasonable for him to bet on *h* at odds higher than *p*: (1-*p*)." Rudolph Carnap, "Statistical and Inductive Probability," in Edward Madden, ed., *The Structure of Scientific Thought* (Boston, 1960), pp. 269–279; the quotation appears on page 270. Compare Carnap's *Logical Foundations of Probability* (Chicago, 1950), p. 164. In the latter passage Carnap refers to a subject who "knows *e*, say, on the basis of direct observations, and nothing else."

adequate to the following situation. (i) There is a set of propositions e such that e inductively confers evidence for S upon a certain false proposition f; (ii) S accepts the false but evident f; (iii) f confers evidence for S upon a true proposition h; and (iv) S accepts h. The traditional definition, in application to this situation, would require us to say that S knows that h is true. But it is clear that, in such a situation, S may not know that h is true.

Gettier cites the following example. (i) There is a set of propositions e such that e inductively confers evidence for Smith upon the false proposition f that Jones owns a Ford. We may suppose that e contains such propositions as these: "Jones has at all times in the past within Smith's memory owned a car, and always a Ford" and "Jones has just offered Smith a ride while driving a Ford."[11] (ii) Smith accepts the false but evident f ("Jones owns a Ford"). (iii) We may assume that f deductively confers evidence upon the disjunctive proposition h that either Jones owns a Ford or Brown is in Barcelona. And we will suppose that, as luck would have it and entirely unsuspected by Smith, Brown is in Barcelona. Therefore h ("Either Jones owns a Ford or Brown is in Barcelona") is true. And (iv) Smith, who sees that f, which he believes to be true, entails h, also believes that h is true. Hence the proposition "Either Jones owns a Ford or Brown is in Barcelona" is a proposition which is such that: it is true, Smith believes that it is true, and it is evident for Smith. But our description of the situation does not warrant our saying that Smith knows it to be true.

---

11. Some authors, I believe, have been misled in two respects by Gettier's example: (a) He has used "justify" where I have used "confer evidence upon." But "justify" may also be taken to mean the same as the weaker "confer reasonability upon" or even "confirms." The example given would not be counter to the traditional definition of knowledge, if e could be said, only in one of these weaker senses, to justify h; it is essential that e confer evidence upon h. (b) The two propositions which Gettier cites as members of e ("Jones has at all times in the past within Smith's memory owned a car and always a Ford" and "Jones has just offered Smith a ride while driving a Ford") are not themselves sufficient to confer evidence for Smith upon the false proposition f ("Jones owns a Ford"). At the most, they justify f only in the weaker sense of making f reasonable. In discussing the example, however, we will imagine that e contains still other propositions and that it does confer evidence upon f for Smith.

What has gone wrong? Is it that the evidence e that Smith has for h also confers evidence upon a false proposition? This isn't quite the difficulty. For we may assume that e itself is a proposition that S knows to be true; but e confers evidence upon a false proposition; therefore whatever confers evidence upon e also confers evidence upon a false proposition; and so a proposition can be known even though what confers evidence upon it confers evidence upon a false proposition. The problem might seem to be, rather, that e confers evidence upon a false proposition f and that h does *not* confer evidence upon that false proposition f. To repair the traditional definition of knowledge, we must add a qualification roughly to the effect that, if S knows h to be true, then the evidence he has for h itself confers evidence upon f. But just how shall we formulate the qualification? Of the possibilities that first come to mind, some exclude too much and others exclude too little.

Shall we say, for example: "If a man knows a proposition h to be true, then *nothing* that confers evidence upon h for him confers evidence upon a false proposition f unless h also confers evidence upon f;"? This would exclude too much. Consider some proposition k that the Smith of Gettier's example does know to be true and suppose that Smith accepts the conjunction of k and f, where f is the false but evident "Jones owns a Ford." Since the conjunction, k and f, confers evidence upon k for Smith and also upon the false proposition f, the proposed qualification would require us to say that Smith does not know that k is true.

Should we say: "If a man knows a proposition h to be true, then *something* that confers evidence upon h for him is such as not to confer evidence upon a false proposition f unless h confers evidence upon f"? This would exclude too little. Suppose that the h of Gettier's example ("Jones owns a Ford or Brown is in Barcelona") does not confer evidence upon any false proposition for Smith. Then there will be something which deductively confers evidence upon h for Smith and which confers evidence upon no false proposition; this something could be h itself as well as the conjection of h with various other evident propositions that do not confer evidence upon false propositions. Hence the proposed qualification would require us to say that the Smith of Gettier's example does know h to be true.

Should we say: "If a man knows a proposition h to be true, then something that *inductively* confers evidence upon h for him is such as to confer evidence upon no false proposition f unless h itself confers evidence upon f"? This too, would exclude too little. Consider the disjunction, e or h, where e is the set of propositions that inductively confers evidence upon h for Smith. Like e itself, the disjunction, e or h, inductively confers evidence upon h for Smith. And if it is such as to confer evidence upon no false proposition, then, once again, the proposed qualification would require us to say that Smith knows h is true.

Should we say: "If a man knows a proposition h to be true, then something that inductively confers evidence upon h for him is such that (i) h does not confer evidence upon *it* for him and (ii) it confers evidence upon no false proposition f for him unless h confers evidence upon f for him"? This, too, excludes too little. Suppose Smith accepts the disjunction, "e or (h and p)," where p is any other proposition. If this disjunction confers evidence upon no false proposition, we will still be committed to saying that Smith knows that h is true.[12]

Have we construed "e confers evidence upon h" too broadly? We began by considering a single "h-evidencer"—a single set of propositions e which conferred evidence upon h for S. But we have seen that even our simple example involves many additional *h-evidencers. In addition to e* there are: h itself; the disjunction "h or e"; the disjunction "(h and p) or e," where p is any proposition; the disjunction "(e and p) or h"; the conjunction "e and k," where k is any other evident proposition: thus also the conjunction "e and f," where f is a false but evident proposition; and such disjunctions as "(e and f) or h" and "(h and p) or (e and k)."[13]

12. I am indebted to Professor Gettier for the points made in this paragraph and the one that precedes it.

13. Still other h-evidencers for S may be constructed by disjoining any of the h-evidencers above with certain propositions e' which confer evidence in the absolute sense upon h. Suppose, for example, e' is "Jones has just bought a car from the local Ford dealer; the Registry of Motor Vehicles and other reliable

Though we thus seem able to construct h-evidencers *ad indefinitum,* some of them would seem to be parasitical upon others. If we had a way of marking off the parasitical h-evidencers from the nonparasitical ones, then we could formulate the desired qualification in terms merely of S's nonparasitical h-evidencers. A nonparasitical h-evidencer would be one which, so to speak, did not derive any of its epistemic force from any of S's other h-evidencers. What, then, would be an instance of such a nonparasitical h-evidencer?

The answer is obvious: S's nonparasitical h-evidencers are to be found among those *basic propositions* which make h evident for S. And so we might say:

> (D14) h is nondefectively evident for S = Df. Either h is certain for S, or h is evident for S and is entailed by a conjunction of propositions each having for S a basis which is not a basis of any false proposition for S.

Then the desired definition of knowledge would be this:

> (D15) h is known by S = Df. h is accepted by S; h is true; and h is nondefectively evident for S.

V

What now of the applicability of our various epistemic terms—"evident," "beyond reasonable doubt," "confirmed," and so on? In considering this question we turn from epistemic logic to epistemology. To answer it, we may attempt to formulate certain epistemic rules or principles—rules or principles describing the conditions under which a proposition may be said to be evident, or to be beyond reasonable doubt, or to be confirmed, and similarly for our other epistemic terms. In attempting to formulate these rules, we should proceed as we do in logic when we formulate rules of inference, or as we do in ethics when we formulate rules telling one the conditions under which a state of affairs may be said to be good, bad, or

---

and trustworthy authorities affirm that Jones owns a Ford; etc." Then, whether or not e' is true, and whether or not it is evident for S, the epistemic state of S may be such that such disjunctions as "e or e'" and "h or e'" also make h evident for him.

neutral, or an action may be said to be obligatory, or wrong, or permitted. The procedure is thus essentially Socratic. We begin with certain instances which the rules should countenance and with certain other instances which they should not countenance. And we assume that by reflecting upon these instances and asking ourselves, Socratically, "Just why should our rules countenance cases of the first sort and not countenance cases of the second sort?", we will arrive at certain general criteria.

It is sometimes said that such ethical theories as hedonism are theories telling us what sorts of characteristics are "good-making characteristics" or "better-making characteristics." One could say, analogously, that the attempt to formulate epistemic criteria of the sort described is an attempt to say what sorts of characteristics are "evidence-making characteristics," or "reasonability-making characteristics," or even "epistemically-better-making characteristics."

In the book *Theory of Knowledge*, I proposed "a sketch of a theory of empirical evidence" and formulated nine such principles. The set of principles was conceded to be incomplete and I noted that "corrections of detail may well be required." As a result of Professor Heidelberger's criticisms, in his article "Chisholm's Epistemic Principles," I now see that the latter observation was true and that the principles I had formulated should be modified in a number of respects.

In what follows, I shall describe briefly certain types of principles or rules which, I believe, are essential to any adequate theory of evidence. The reader who is interested in further details is referred to the original sketch and to Professor Heidelberger's paper. I shall describe eight different types of rule or principle.

1) The first type of principle was summarized in *Theory of Knowledge* as follows: "If there is a 'self-presenting state' such that S is in that state, then it is evident to S that he is in that state" (p. 44). The formula should be thought of as holding for any subject and any time. It should also be thought of as being an abbreviation for a large set of principles that are more specific—more specific with reference to the "self-presenting state"

that is involved. Meinong's technical term "self-presenting state" was used to refer to certain thoughts, attitudes, and experiences which were assumed to be such that it is evident to a man that he is thinking such a thought, taking such an attitude, or having such an experience if and only if he *is* thinking such a thought, taking such an attitude, or having such an experience.

Examples of the more specific principles of this first type would be: "Necessarily, for any S and any t, if S believes at t that Socrates is mortal, then it is evident to S at t that he then believes that Socrates is mortal"; "Necessarily, for any S and any t, if S thinks at t that he perceives something that is red, then it is evident to S at t that he then thinks he perceives something that is red." Other principles of this sort would refer to such intentional phenomena as hoping, fearing, wishing, wondering; for example, "Necessarily, for any S and any t, if S wonders at t whether the peace will continue, then it is evident to S at t that he then wonders whether the peace will continue." Still others would refer to certain ways of sensing or being appeared to. Thus there is a possible use of "is appeared to redly" which is such that, if we give the expression that use, then we may say: "Necessarily, for any S and any t, if S is appeared to redly at t, then it is evident to S then he is then appeared to redly."

2) To introduce the second set of principles, I shall begin with the earlier, inadequate formulation that appears in *Theory of Knowledge:* "If S believes that he perceives something to have a certain property F, then the proposition that he does perceive something to be F, as well as the proposition that there is something that is F, is one that is *reasonable* for S" (p. 43). The expression "S believes that he perceives something to have a certain property F" was used in a rather special sense to refer to what is sometimes called a "spontaneous act of perception." The expression "takes," or "perceptually takes," is sometimes used in a similar way. Thus if a man can be said to *take* something to be a dog, in this sense of "take," his act will be entirely spontaneous and not reached as the result of reflection, de-

liberation, or inference.[14] And if the man is rational and honest, then, in answer to the question, "What is your justification for thinking you know there is a dog here?", he will say that he *perceives* something to be a dog—that he sees, or hears, or smells, or feels there to be a dog. A man can thus take there to be a dog, in the present sense of the term "take," when in fact no dog is there to be taken.

Why not have the simpler rule: "If a man *perceives* there to be a dog then the proposition that a dog is there is one that is reasonable for him"? What this simpler rule states is, of course, true. But to apply it one would need a criterion for deciding when in fact one *does* perceive a dog. Our more complex rule, on the other hand, was intended to provide such a criterion; for the *taking* to which it refers is one of the "self-presenting states" with which the first set of rules is concerned.

The second rule, then, was designed to tell us of certain conditions under which we would say that, for a given subject, a proposition is beyond reasonable doubt. But the rule is much too permissive. For it countenances as being beyond reasonable doubt certain propositons which are hardly worthy of this epistemic status. The point was clearly made by Heidelberger:

As applied to a particular case, principle (B) tells us that if a man believes that he perceives a certain object to be yellow then the proposition that he does perceive that object to be yellow and the proposition that that object is yellow are reasonable for him. But let us suppose that the following facts are known by that man: there is a yellow light shining on the object, he remembers having perceived a moment ago that the object was white, and at that time there was no colored light shining on the object. Suppose that, in spite of this evidence, he believes that he perceives that the object is yellow. It would not be cor-

14. In *Perceiving: A Philosophical Study* (Ithaca, N.Y.: Cornell University Press, 1957), I have discussed "perceptual taking" in more detail; see pp. 75–77. "Taking" is preferable to "believing that one perceives," in the present context, for the latter expression, unlike the former, suggests a higher-order propositional attitude (believing) which has *another* propositional attitude (perceiving) as its object. If a man takes there to be a dog, in our present sense of "take," the object of his attitude is, not another propositional attitude, but simply the being of a dog. "Taking," in this sense, might be said to be related to "perceiving" in the way in which "believing" is related to "knowing." Perceiving (or "veridical perceiving") and unveridical perceiving are both species of the common genus that is here called "taking," or "thinking-that-one-perceives."

rect to say that for our man the proposition that the object is yellow is a reasonable one. Merely from the fact that a man believes that he perceives something to have a certain property F, it does not follow, accordingly, that the proposition that that something is F is a reasonable one for him; for, as in our example, he may have other evidence which, when combined with the evidence that he believes that he perceives something to have F, may make the proposition that something is F highly unreasonable. [Op. cit., p. 75]

Our rule was intended to give the senses their due, so to speak, but it gave them far more than they deserve. Clearly some kind of restraint is necessary.

In what sense, then, can we say that taking, or thinking-that-one-perceives, confers reasonability upon the proposition that one does in fact perceive? We could say this: if the only things that were evident to a man were the proposition that he does, say, take something to be yellow, along with various propositions this proposition entails, then, for such a man, the proposition that he does in fact perceive something to be yellow could be said to be beyond reasonable doubt. But this fact does not constitute a principle we could apply to any particular case, since there is no one whose evidence is thus restricted. In order to have a principle we can apply, I suggest we say this: the proposition that one perceives something to be yellow is made reasonable provided (i) the man takes, or thinks-he-perceives, something to be yellow and (ii), of the things that are evident to him, none is such that the conjunction of it and the proposition that he *takes* something to be yellow will *fail* to confirm the proposition that he perceives something to be yellow. (For simplicity, we here use "confirm" in place of the longer expression, "tends to confirm," defined in D9.)

Consider again the man to whom Heidelberger refers. He takes something to be yellow—he thinks he perceives something to be yellow. But he also happens to know that the following set of propositions i is true: "there is a yellow light shining on the object, he remembers having perceived a moment ago that the object was white, and at that time there was no colored light shining on the object." Although for the man who knows nothing else, taking, or thinking-that-he-perceives, confers reasonability upon the proposition that he does in fact perceive, the present man, as Heidelberger observes, is not one for whom the proposition that he is perceiving something yellow is thus beyond reasonable doubt. And, I would say, the reason that it is not beyond reasonable doubt lies in this fact: the man's independent information i is such that the conjunction of i and the proposition that he takes something to be yellow does not confirm the proposition that he does in fact perceive anything to be yellow. Thinking-that-one-perceives something to be yellow not only confirms but also makes reasonable the proposition that one does perceive that something is yellow; but thinking-that-one-perceives something to be yellow in conjunction with the proposition i referred to above does *not* confirm the proposition that one does perceive something to be yellow.

I suggest, then, that the members of our second set of epistemic principles might be put in the following form:

> Necessarily, for any S and any t, if (i) S at t believes himself to perceive something to be F, and if (ii) there is no proposition i such that i is evident to S and such that the conjunction of i and the proposition that S believes himself to perceive something to be F does not confirm the proposition that he does then perceive something to be F, then the proposition that he does then perceive something to be F, as well as the proposition that something is, or was, F, is one that is beyond reasonable doubt for S at t.

The letter "F" may be replaced by any predicate which is such that the result of replacing "F" by that predicate in "S takes something to be F," or "S thinks-he-perceives something to be F," where "takes" and "thinks-he-perceives" have the special use we have attempted to characterize here, is meaningful.

3) A third set of principles may be obtained from the second in the following way: (a) the predicates that can replace "F" in our formulation are restricted to those connoting sensible characteristics; and (b) the expression "is beyond reasonable doubt" in the final clause is replaced by "is evident."

Examples of sensible characteristics are: such visual characteristics as being blue, being green, being black; such auditory characteristics as sounding or making a noise; such somesthetic

characteristics as being rough, being smooth; those characteristics that were traditionally called "the common sensibles"; and
the relations that are connoted by such expressions as "is
louder than," "is similar in color to," and "is more fragrant
than."[15]

The third set of principles would tell us, then, that taking
something to have a certain sensible characteristic confers, not
only reasonability, but also evidence, upon the proposition that
one does in fact perceive something to have that characteristic.
Is this too permissive? I have argued elsewhere that, if we are
not to be sceptics with respect to our perception of the external
world, we must say that the spontaneous act of *taking* confers
evidence and reasonability.[16] Otherwise, I believe, we will not
be able to say of any synthetic proposition about a physical
thing that that proposition is evident to anyone.[17]

4) To be able to apply the members of our second and
third sets of principles, we must also be able to apply principles

15. See *Theory of Knowledge*, pp. 46–47, for a fuller list.
16. See *Perceiving: A Philosophical Study*, chap. 6 ("Some Marks of Evidence"),
and "'Appear,' 'Take,' and 'Evident,'" *Journal of Philosophy*, 53 (1956),
722–731, reprinted in Robert Swartz, ed., *Perceiving, Sensing, and Knowing* (Garden City, New York, 1965).
17. Heidelberger proposes what he calls the "traditional empirical" alternative to our third set of principles. This may be suggested by: "the proposition
that an object looks rectangular to a man makes evident the proposition that
the object is rectangular" (p. 82). I think this principle, too, is sound—provided
that "looks rectangular" is taken in that phenomenal or noncomparative sense
which is such that, if it has that sense in the sentence "All rectangular things
look rectangular under conditions that are optimum for viewing shape," then
the sentence is both true and synthetic. But the proposed principle has other
possible interpretations under which it would not be satisfactory. Thus it would
be inapplicable if "looks rectangular" were taken to mean the same as "looks
the way rectangular objects look under conditions such as those that now obtain" or "looks the way I remember rectangular objects to have looked when I
have perceived them in the past." And the proposed principle would be less
plausible than any of my third set of principles if "looks rectangular" were
taken to mean the same as "looks the way I think-I-remember rectangular objects having looked to me when I have thought-I-have-perceived them in the
past" (for surely the object of thinking-that-one-remembers-having-thought-
that-one-perceived is not *more* worthy of credence than that of thinking-that-
one-perceives). And although the proposed principle, when taken in its first
sense above, may be an alternative to my third set of principles pertaining to
sensible characteristics, it does not provide an alternative to the *second* set of
principles pertaining to other types of perceptual taking.

274 Roderick M. Chisholm

of still another sort. For the members of the second and third sets of principles each contain a *proviso*. They tell us that taking something to be *F* confers reasonability or evidence upon the proposition that one perceives something to be *F provided that* the following condition holds: there is no evident proposition *i* such that the conjunction of *i* and the proposition that one takes something to be *F fails* to confirm the proposition that one perceives something to be *F*. Hence our fourth set of principles should tell us what types of proposition *i* are such that the conjunction of *i* and the proposition that one takes something to be *F fails* to confirm the proposition that one perceives something to be *F*. How are we to specify such propositions *i*? I shall attempt only a general characterization.

Such propositions *i* would be propositions casting doubt upon the particular testimony of the senses. They could do this in two ways—either "internally" by constituting conflicting testimony, or "externally" by suggesting the possibility of some perceptual malfunction.

The "internal" case presents no problem. Consider a man who thinks-he-sees something to be the only object in his hand and to be round and who, at the same time, things-he-feels something to be the only object in his hand and to be rectangular. We may say that each of these takings casts doubt upon the intentional object of the other. The two takings in conjunction are such as to fail to confirm the proposition that there is just one object in his hand and that object is round, and they also fail to confirm the proposition that there is just one object in his hand and that object is rectangular.

What of the "external" case—those evident propositions *i* which suggest the possibility of perceptual malfunction? If it *were* evident to our subject that his senses were not functioning properly, then, of course, there would be an *i* of the sort described. But we have not yet specified any conditions under which such a proposition *i* might be evident to him. Can we describe such a proposition *i* without assuming that our subject has any evidence beyond that so far countenanced by our principles? Heidelberger's criticisms suggest that he might put the problem in the following way: Can we describe such propositions i without abandoning the "program of establishing as evident propositions about physical things entirely on the basis of subjective propositions" (p. 76), where "subjective propositions" are those propositions about "self-presenting states" referred to in our first set of principles?

Here we must distinguish at least two different questions. The first question would be: "Suppose we wish to describe conditions under which the proposition that a man is perceiving some object to be F is one that is evident or beyond reasonable doubt for him. Can we do this without assuming that some *other* proposition about a physical object is evident to the man?" The answer to *this* question would seem clearly to be affirmative. For our principles say merely that as long as propositions of a certain sort are *not* evident to the man, then, if he takes something to be F, it is evident or reasonable to him that something is F.

The second question would be: "Consider the situation of a man taking something to be F and his *not* being such that it is evident or reasonable to him that he is then perceiving something to be F. Can we describe this situation without assuming that some other proposition about a physical thing is evident or reasonable for him?" Here, too, I think the answer is affirmative. Consider a set of believings, takings, and seemings-to-remember of the following sort: the various propositions which are the intentional objects of the members of the set (the propositions that one believes, takes, or seems to remember to be true) are such that, in conjunction, they are consistent and logically *confirm* the proposition that one is *not* perceiving anything to be F. Consider this situation: a man takes something to be yellow; he seems to remember having had a sensory disorder causing him to mistake the colors of things; and he believes that the circumstances that now obtain are of the sort that have always misled him in the past. I suggest that the propositions which are the intentional objects of this seeming-to-remember and this believing are such that they logically confirm the proposition that he is not now perceiving anything to be yellow. And these propositions need not themselves be evident in order for the present testimony of the senses to be discredited. They need only be the objects of believing and of seeming-to-remember: and, by our first set of principles, if they are such objects, then it will be evident to the man that he does thus believe or seem-to-remember.

An adequate formulation of our fourth set of principles, then, would tell us what propositions would *confirm* the proposition that one is *not* perceiving anything to be F. And our principles will say that such propositions are of this sort: the proposition i asserting that one believes, takes, or seems-to-remember them to be true will be such that the conjunction of i and the proposition that one takes something to be F *fails to confirm* the proposition that one perceives something to be F.

We should remind ourselves that our principles are intended only to formulate *sufficient* conditions for the applicability of our epistemic terms. They are not intended to formulate *necessary* conditions. Thus, from the fact that a man takes something to be yellow under conditions where there is no i of the sort we have described, we may infer that it is evident to him that he is perceiving something to be yellow. But, from the fact that he takes something to be yellow under conditions where there is such an i, we may *not* infer that it is *not* evident to him that he is perceiving something to be yellow.

5) Our fifth set of principles, pertaining to "thinking-that-one-remembers," or "seeming-to-remember," will be analogous to our second set, pertaining to "thinking-that-one-perceives." But where our second set tells us that thinking-that-one-perceives confers *reasonability* upon the proposition that one does perceive, this fifth set will tell us that thinking-that-one-remembers confers some presumption in favor of the proposition that one does remember. I suggest that the members of this fifth set might be put in the following form:

Necessarily, for any S and any t, if (i) S at t believes himself to remember having at a certain time perceived something to be F, and if (ii) there is no proposition i such that i is evident to S and such that the conjunction of i and the proposition that S believes himself to remember having at that time perceived something to be F does not confirm the proposition that he does then remember having perceived something to be F, then the proposition that he does then remember having perceived something at that time to be F, as well as the proposition that he did perceive something at that time to be F and the proposition that something at that time was, or had been, F, is one that has some presumption in its favor for S at t.

6) Our sixth set of principles will be analogous to the third. Where the third describes conditions under which thinking-that-one-perceives confers evidence, the sixth will describe conditions under which thinking-that-one-remembers confers reasonability. The sixth may be obtained from the fifth as follows: (a) the predicates that replace "F" in our formulation are restricted to those connoting sensible characteristics; and (b) the expression "has some presumption in its favor" in the final clause of our formulation is replaced by "is beyond reasonable doubt." In short, thinking that one remembers having perceived something to have had a certain sensible characteristic not only confirms, but also confers reasonability upon the proposition that one does in fact remember having perceived something to have had that characteristic.

7) The seventh set of principles would be analogous to the fourth. The fourth set of principles, it will be recalled, tells of certain conditions under which taking something to be F fails to confer evidence or reasonability upon the proposition that one perceives something to be F. The seventh set, analogously, would specify conditions under which thinking-that-one-remembers having perceived something to be F fails to confirm or confer reasonability upon the proposition that one does remember having perceived something to be F. If it is possible to formulate an adequate set of principles of the fourth type, then, I think, it is also possible to formulate an adequate set of principles of this seventh type.

8) Our eighth set of principles would make use of the notion of *concurrence*, where this notion is defined as follows: any set of propositions that are mutually consistent and such that no one of them entails any other of them is concurrent provided only that each member of the set is confirmed by the conjunction of all the other members of the set. In *Theory of Knowledge*, I pro-

posed the following, somewhat over-simplified example of a set of concurrent propositions: (h) "There is a cat on the roof today"; (i) "There was a cat on the roof yesterday"; (j) "There was a cat on the roof the day before yesterday"; (k) "There was a cat on the roof the day before the day before yesterday"; and (l) "There is a cat on the roof almost every day."[18]

One example, then, of an epistemic principle making use of this concept of concurrence would be the following, which tells us, in effect, that every perceptual proposition belonging to a concurrent set of reasonable propositions is evident:

Necessarily, for any S and any t, if (i) S at t believes himself to perceive something to be F, if (ii) there is no proposition i such that i is evident to S and such that the conjunction of i and the proposition that S believes himself to perceive something to be F does not confirm the proposition that he does then perceive something to be F, and if (iii) the proposition that he does then perceive something to be F is a member of a set of concurrent propositions each of which is beyond reasonable doubt for S at t, then the proposition that he does then perceive something to be F, as well as the proposition that something is, or was F, is one that is evident for S at t.

Any adequate theory of empirical evidence would include canons of inductive logic and doubtless many other epistemic principles as well. But, I am certain, it would also include principles of the sort I have tried to describe.

18. The notion of concurrence is similar to what H. H. Price has called "coherence" and to what C. I. Lewis has called "congruence"; see Price's *Perception* (New York, 1933), p. 183, and Lewis' *An Analysis of Knowledge and Valuation* (La Salle, Ill., 1946), p. 338. Compare also Bertrand Russell, *An Inquiry into Meaning and Truth* (New York, 1940), pp. 201–202, and Roderick Firth, "Coherence, Certainty, and Epistemic Priority," *Journal of Philosophy,* 61 (1964), 545–557.

16

Modest Foundationalism
and Self-Warrant

MARK PASTIN

There are fundamental disagreements among epistemologists as to the form which a reconstruction of knowledge, an account of the conditions which a person would be
(epistemically) warranted in believing a proposition, should
take. These disagreements, particularly the disagreements between foundationalists and non-foundationalists and among
foundationalists, are often described in terms of notions of incorrigibility, absolute certainty, or infallibility.[1] However, I believe that what is essential to these disagreements can be better
described in terms of the notion of a proposition being *self-warranted* for a person at a time. Intuitively, a proposition which is
self-warranted for a person at a time is a proposition which the
person would be warranted to some degree, however slight, in
believing at the time, even if he had no inductive evidential
support for the proposition at the time. In this paper I shall
first indicate some of the ways in which the notion of self-warrant can be employed in describing fundamental disagreements
among epistemologists. Then I shall provide an account of this
notion which is compatible with its role in describing these disagreements and which will deepen our understanding of these
disagreements. In order to provide this account I shall outline

Reprinted from *The American Philosophical Quarterly*, monograph series
number 4, 141–149, by kind permission of the author and editor.
    1. For instance see the A.P.A. symposium on "The Experiential Element in
Knowledge" in which the participants were Hans Reichenbach Nelson Goodman, and C. I. Lewis, reprinted in *Philosophical Review*, 61 (1952), 147–175.

a partial framework for deliberation upon the reconstruction of a person's knowledge.

Perhaps the most important disagreement among epistemologists is the disagreement between foundationalists and non-foundationalists. This disagreement can be described in terms of self-warrant. Foundationalists hold that all empirical propositions which are warranted for a person at a time "ultimately derive" their warrant from a core class of empirical propositions which are self-warranted for the person at the time. Non-foundationalists hold that no empirical propositions are self-warranted for persons, or at least that not all empirical propositions which are warranted for a person at a time "ultimately derive" their warrant from a core class of empirical propositions which are self-warranted for the person at the time. Non-foundationalists may hold that empirical propositions which are warranted for a person at a time "ultimately derive" their warrant from their interrelationships or "coherence."[2] (I shall comment upon "deriving warrant" and "ultimately deriving warrant" shortly.)

Many foundationalists undoubtedly would hold that core propositions are not only self-warranted, but also absolutely certain, incorrigible, or infallible. I believe that we may regard this as following not from the foundationalism of these philosophers *per se*, but from their accepting some principle such as: If propositions in the empirical core were not absolutely certain (incorrigible, infallible), then no empirical proposition could be probable to any degree.[3] I shall call foundationalists who hold that core propositions need only be self-warranted "modest foundationalists," and foundationalists who accept some form of the above principle "radical foundationalists." I believe that

2. This seems to be Reichenbach's position in the symposium mentioned above. Keith Lehrer also seems to defend such a psoition in "Justification, Explanation, and Induction" in *Induction, Acceptance, and Rational Belief*, ed. Marshall Swain (Dordrecht, 1970) and in a series of later papers.

3. While a form of this principle is most closely associated with Lewis's views, Keynes and Russell among others have also accepted such a principle. See Lewis's *An Analysis of Knowledge and Valuation* (LaSalle, Ill., 1946), p. 186, Keynes' *Treatise on Probability* (London, 1921), pp. 16–17, and Russell's *Human Knowledge: Its Scope and Limits* (New York, 1948), p. 416.

many epistemologists, because they have failed to distinguish
these two types of foundationalism, have produced arguments
against radical foundationalism in the belief that they were arguing against foundationalism *per se*.

There are important disagreements which may arise among
modest foundationalists which can also be described in terms of
self-warrant. Modest foundationalists may disagree as to the
kinds of empirical propositions which can be self-warranted for
a person. Some modest foundationalists, the "Cartesian" modest foundationalists, may hold that the only empirical propositions which can be self-warranted for a person are propositions
about just the person's "immediate experience" at a given time.
Other modest foundationalists may hold that "observational"
propositions of various kinds can also, or exclusively, be self-
warranted for a person.[4] Modest foundationalists who agree as
to the kinds of empirical propositions which can be self-warranted for a person may disagree as to which of these propositions belong to the core from which all warranted empirical
propositions "ultimately derive" their warrant. For instance,
some "Cartesian" modest foundationalists may hold that only
propositions about a person's *sensory* immediate experiences
belong to this core, while other "Cartesian" modest foundationalists may hold that propositions about a person's *memory*
immediate experiences also belong to this core.

These are a few of the ways in which the notion of self-warrant can be employed in describing fundamental disagreements
among epistemologists. In the balance of this paper I shall attempt to provide an account of this notion which is compatible
with its role in describing these disagreements. If an account of
self-warrant is to be compatible with the role of this notion in
describing fundamental disagreements among epistemologists,
it should not presuppose the correctness of any of their positions. This might be put by saying that we are seeking a *theory-
of-evidence-independent* account of self-warrant, an account
which will enable us to say what propositions, if any, are self-

4. Epistemologists in the tradition of Descartes, Berkeley, Locke, and Lewis
are most likely to be "Cartesian" modest foundationalists, while philosophers of
science may be more likely to be "observational" modest foundationalists.

warranted *if* some epistemic viewpoint or other is correct. It is in order to provide this kind of account of self-warrant that I shall outline a partial framework for deliberation upon the reconstruction of a person's knowledge. In terms of this partial framework I shall also provide some indication as to how the notions of one proposition deriving warrant, or ultimately deriving warrant, from another proposition are to be understood.

Earlier I said that, intuitively, a proposition which is self-warranted for a person at a time is a proposition which the person would be warranted to some degree, however slight, in believing at the time, even if he had no inductive evidential support for the proposition at the time. It may seem that there is no need for any account of self-warrant beyond this "intuitive" account. However, I believe that unpacking the "counterfactual import" of this intuitive account will reveal an important structure of epistemic notions. I shall assume that we have an adequate grasp of the following notions: (i) the notion of a proposition being (epistemically, not ethically or otherwise) warranted for a person at a time, that is—the notion of a proposition being such that a person would be to some degree, however slight, warranted in believing it at a time, whether or not he in fact believes it at the time, (ii) the notion of a proposition providing deductive evidential support for another proposition for a person at a time, and (iii) the notion of a proposition providing inductive evidential support, construed broadly—as non-deductive evidential support, for another proposition for a person at a time. These notions have received considerable attention from epistemologists and inductive logicians. While the accounts of these notions currently available may not be fully satisfactory, there is no indication that these notions presuppose the notion of self-warrant.[5] Thus I shall take these notions as my starting point in providing an account of self-warrant.

One standard strategy for "unpacking" counterfactual statements is to express them in terms of logical necessity; in terms of statements of the form "Necessarily if . . . , then . . ."

5. For instance, see Chisholm's account of these notions in "On the Nature of Empirical Evidence" (Amherst, Mass., 1970), [Chapter 15 in this volume].

where "necessarily" means "in all logically possible worlds" or "in all metaphysically possible worlds." Employing this strategy in the present case leads to the following account of self-warrant:

> Proposition P is self-warranted for person S at time t: (i) P is warranted for S at t, and (ii) not necessarily if P is warranted for S at t, then S has inductive evidential support for P at t.

This account is unsatisfactory. In order to test whether an account of self-warrant is satisfactory, we must consider whether the positions of various epistemic viewpoints concerning different situations could be adequately described on the given account of self-warrant.

Let us consider the following situation: The proposition, call it P, *there is a pencil on the desk* is warranted for a person S at a time t. S reasons from P to the proposition, call it D, *there is a pencil on the desk or I am in pain* so that D is also warranted for S at t. I believe that most foundationalist viewpoints should be described as not holding that D is self-warranted for S at t in this situation. However, on the present account of self-warrant, any epistemic viewpoint according to which it is logically (or metaphysically) *possible* for D to be warranted for S at t without S having inductive evidential support for D at t, for instance—if S were to be in pain at t, must be described as holding that D is self-warranted for S at t in the above situation.

This problem indicates that the clause "even if the person had no inductive evidential support for the proposition at the time," as present in the intuitive account of self-warrant, presupposes that certain epistemically relevant conditions be held constant in evaluating what a person would be warranted in believing. But clause (ii) of the above account of self-warrant does not adequately capture this presupposition. I shall now outline a partial framework for deliberation upon the reconstruction of a person's knowledge in terms of which this presupposition can be adequately captured.

As a first step let us consider the notion of a set of propositions constituting an *epistemic system*. The elements of an epistemic system are propositions of the forms "P is warranted for

S at t" (abbreviated "$W(P, S, t)$"), "P provides inductive evidential support for Q for S at t" (abbreviated "$I(P, Q, S, t)$"), and "P
provides deductive evidential support for Q for S at t" (abbreviated "$D(P, Q, S, t)$"), where S and t are held constant. A set of
propositions R of the appropriate forms constitutes an epistemic system if, and only if, it is logically (or metaphysically)
possible that there be a person S and a time t such that for all
propositions P and Q: (i) $W(P, S, t) \epsilon R$ iff $W(P, S, t)$; (ii) $I(P, Q,
S, t) \epsilon R$ iff $I(P, Q, S, t)$; and (iii) $D(P, Q, S, t) \epsilon R$ iff $D(P, Q, S, t)$.
(This condition is formulated in terms of logical or metaphys-
ical possibility to assure that the supply of epistemic systems is
adequate for the deliberations of a very wide range of epistemologists.) An epistemic system R is the epistemic system of a
person S' at a time t' if, and only if, letting $S = S'$ and $t = t'$, all
the elements of R are true. Among the things which epistemologists concerned with the reconstruction of knowledge
deliberate upon are what sets of propositions constitute epistemic systems and what epistemic system is to be attributed to
a person at a time.

Next let us consider the notion of *one epistemic system R' being
a subsystem of another epistemic system R with respect to a specified element or set of elements E of R* (abbreviated "R' Subst R on E"). R'
Subst R on E if, and only if, R' can be obtained from R by first
eliminating E or the members of E from R and then eliminating $n \geq 0$ other elements of R. In deliberating upon the reconstruction of knowledge considering subsystems to a particular
epistemic system is important in several contexts, particularly in
determining what propositions derive warrant, or ultimately
derive warrant, from what other propositions in the system.
For instance, it is roughly the case that if $W(Q, S, t) \epsilon R$ and, for
every R' Subst R on $W(P, S, t)$, $W(Q, S, t) \notin R'$, then Q *derives
warrant* from P in R. Again, roughly, if $W(Q, S, t) \epsilon R$ and Q
derives warrant from a proposition P in R which does not
derive warrant from some other proposition in R, *then P ultimately derives warrant* from Q in R. Providing full accounts of
these notions, as well as of the closely related notions of deductive and inductive evidential support, is beyond the scope of
this paper.

In terms of the notions considered so far it is possible to provide the following tentative account of self-warrant:

> Proposition P is self-warranted for person S at time t: S's epistemic system at t, call it R, is such that: (i) $W(P, S, t) \in R$, and (ii) it is not the case that every subsystem R' of R with respect to the set of all propositions of the form "$I($, P, S, t)" is such that $W(P, S, t) \notin R'$.

The idea behind this account is that if P is self-warranted for S at T, and not otherwise, then $W(P, S, t)$ should remain in some subsystems of S's epistemic system at t with respect to the inductive evidence for P. The example which raised difficulties for the account of self-warrant considered earlier is not a problem for the present account. For the subsystem relation does not permit the addition of the proposition "I am in pain" to S's epistemic system at T. However, the present account of self-warrant is unsatisfactory in an important respect; it does not adequately take account of the features of a person's condition at a time in virtue of which he has a particular epistemic system at the time.

On some epistemic viewpoints it may be possible for the proposition "I feel warm," call it F, to be warranted for a person S at a time t *solely* on the basis of inductive evidential support which S has for F at t. While these epistemic viewpoints should not be described as holding that F is self-warranted for S at t, I believe that they must be so described on our current account of self-warrant. Let R be S's epistemic system at t. $W(F, S, t)$ is a member of R as well as propositions of the form "$I($, F, S, t)," the set of which constitute the inductive evidence in R for F. If there are subsystems R' of R with respect to the inductive evidence for F such that $W(F, S, t) \in R'$, then, on our current account of self-warrant, F is self-warranted for S at t. It is plausible to hold that there are such subsystems of R for the following reason: Eliminating the inductive evidence for F from R, with *no other changes in R* relevant to F, yields a new epistemic system. However, this new system is not one which would be attributable to S at t on the assumption that the only change in S's condition at t be that he has no inductive evidence for F. This system would be attributable to S at t only on the assumption that S's condition at t be further changed in some way, for instance by S's becoming aware of a sensation of warmth, which would support F's being warranted for S at t without inductive evidence. This underscores the fact that, while it is important for epistemologists concerned with the reconstruction of knowledge to consider "abstractly" various subsystems to a person's epistemic system at a time, the features of the person's condition at the time in virtue of which he might have one subsystem rather than another must also be considered.

The above example indicates that for the purposes of providing an account of self-warrant we should focus on those subsystems of a person S's epistemic system R at time t with respect to an element (or set of elements) E such that these systems would be attributable to S at t on the assumption that his condition at t be changed only as required on epistemic grounds by the fact that E (or the members of E) is eliminated from his epistemic system. I shall call such subsystems *minimal subsystems for S at t of R with respect to E*. Obviously what subsystems one considers minimal subsystems for S at t of R with respect to E will depend upon one's epistemic viewpoint. In terms of this notion of a minimal subsystem it is possible to provide the following account of self-warrant:

Proposition P is self-warranted for person S at time t: S's epistemic system at t, R, is such that: (i) $W(P, S, T) \in R$, and (ii) it is not the case that in every minimal subsystem R' for S at t of R with respect to the inductive evidence for P is such that $W(P, S, t) \notin R'$.

I believe that none of the problems considered for earlier accounts of self-warrant apply to this account.

This final account of self-warrant gives content to our earlier descriptions of fundamental disagreements among epistemologists. Of course to describe these disagreements is not to resolve them. However, I believe that distinguishing radical foundationalism from modest foundationalism may lead to some reconciliation. It is significant that in an important symposium in which Hans Reichenbach and Nelson Goodman criticize C. I. Lewis's claim that phenomenal reports provide an absolutely certain foundation for empirical knowledge, both

Goodman and Lewis make remarks indicating that they might accept modest foundationalism. The following comments by Goodman suggest that he might accept modest foundationalism:

Credibility may be transmitted from one statement to another through deductive or probability connections; but credibility does not spring from these connections by spontaneous generation. Somewhere along the line some statements, whether atomic sense reports or the entire system or something in between, must have initial credibility. . . . To say that some statements must be initially credible if any statement is even to be credible at all is not to say that any statement is immune from withdrawal.[6]

In responding to Reichenbach and Goodman, Lewis surprisingly indicates that he too might accept some form of modest foundationalism, rather than the radical foundationalism vigorously defended by him in his writings. He says:

I see no hope for such a coherence theory which repudiates data of experience which are simply given—or no hope unless a postulate be added to the effect that some synthetic statements are probable a priori; the postulate, for example, that every perceptual belief has *some* probability just on account of being a perceptual belief. (The emphasis is Lewis's.)[7]

Of course even if a number of epistemologists were to embrace modest foundationalism, this would be but a slight reconciliation. For, as Goodman's comments indicate, there are many ways to be a modest foundationalist.

In concluding I shall comment briefly upon the sort of account of self-warrant which I have provided here, an account in terms of a partial framework for deliberating upon the reconstruction of a person's knowledge. This partial framework is constituted by the notions of an epistemic system, an epistemic system being a person's epistemic system at a time, of one epistemic system being a subsystem of another system with respect to certain elements, and of one epistemic system being a minimal subsystem for a person at a time of another system

6. "Sense and Certainty," p. 163, which is Goodman's contribution to the symposium mentioned above.
7. "The Given Element in Empirical Knowledge," p. 173.

with respect to certain elements. These notions constitute a *partial* framework for deliberating upon the reconstruction of a person's knowledge in that these notions are essential for assessing various views as to a person's epistemic condition at a time, that is—various theories of evidence. To provide a *more complete* framework for such deliberations, at least the following three tasks would have to be undertaken: (1) To provide clear accounts of further notions for assessing various views as to a person's epistemic condition at a time; (2) To provide a "menu" of major types of theories of evidence from which one, perhaps composite, theory is to be selected; and (3) To provide a description of the conditions under which such deliberations should occur, e.g., the goals and interests of those undertaking the deliberations as well as the information which should be available to them might be specified.

The account of self-warrant presented here in terms of a partial framework for deliberation upon the reconstruction of knowledge gives the epistemologist undertaking such deliberations an important tool for assessing various theories of evidence in crucial respects. There is another task which might be called "providing an account of self-warrant" which I have not undertaken here. This is the task of determining what sort of empirical propositions, if any, can be self-warranted for a person and whether there is a core of these propositions which support all of a person's empirical knowledge. This task can be contrasted with the task undertaken here by describing it as the task of providing an epistemological account, rather than a meta-epistemological account, of self-warrant. With respect to this second task I believe that a "Cartesian" version of modest foundationalism is correct—but that is another story.[8]

8. I am indebted to both the writings of and private communications with Roderick Firth. Daniel Garber's criticisms of earlier drafts have been helpful as well as discussions with my colleagues in the Philosophy Department at Indiana University.

17

Systematic Justification:
Selections from *Knowledge*

KEITH LEHRER

The Circle of Belief

In whatever way a man might attempt to justify his beliefs, whether to himself or to another, he must always appeal to some belief. There is nothing other than one's belief to which one can appeal in the justification of belief. There is no exit from the circle of one's beliefs. This might not seem obvious. It might, for instance, seem that one can appeal directly to experience, or the testimony of others, to justify one's beliefs. But this is illusory. Sense experience, whether commonly casual or carefully controlled, always leaves open the question of what we are to believe. The prick of sense often elicits ready consent, but what we believe in the face of sensory stimulation depends on our antecedent convictions. For example, imagine we believe we see something red before us, and this belief arises so naturally and quickly that no other belief seems to be involved. But we are enmeshed in our beliefs. We believe our circumstances are those in which we may trust our senses and, consequently, that there is little chance of error. If we believed instead that the chance of error was great, we would resist responding with such perceptual belief. Thus the stimulation of the senses elicits belief through the mediation of a system of antecedent beliefs.

The example of perceptual belief reveals the system and re-

lation required for our theory of justification. Such beliefs
some philosophers consider self-justified. Chisholm, for instance, claims such beliefs are evident, or, in our terms, completely justified, whenever they arise, though he suggests such
justification is defeasible.[1] In general, men think there is very
little chance that such beliefs are erroneous. If I believe I see
something red just before me, and have no reason to doubt this
at all, then I shall believe there is so little chance that I am in
error that I readily repudiate any competing hypothesis and
claim complete justification for my belief. This simple belief
shows us the outline of a satisfactory theory of justification. It is
the relation of this belief to others that yields justification. The
belief does not depend on anything other than my beliefs for
complete justification. Among these beliefs is a belief about the
chances of error in such matters. I believe that there is comparatively little chance of such beliefs being in error. The chances
of error are thought to be less than for any competing hypothesis. These features account for the complete justification of
the belief. Indeed, they illustrate the system and relation
required for the complete justification of any belief.

The Doxastic System and Complete Justification

First, the system a man's beliefs must cohere with, in order to
be completely justified, consists of a set of statements articulating what he believes. The system will consist, not of the statements believed, but statements saying that the man believes
what he does. It is such a system that completely justifies a
man's belief. An example may be helpful. A distinguished
chemist who is a friend told me that isotopes differ in certain
chemical properties from paradigm elements. He then went on
to tell me about his research aimed at explaining these differences. Now I believe that I understood his words correctly
and that he is altogether reliable in such matters. What he said
is consistent with my understanding of chemistry. My believing
these things, about chemistry, about a man and about what he
has said, together with my belief that there is comparatively

1. R. M. Chisholm, *Theory of Knowledge,* 1st ed. (Englewood Cliffs: Prentice-
Hall, 1966), p. 48.

little chance of my believing these things and yet being incorrect in believing that some isotopes differ in chemical properties from paradigm elements, makes me completely justified in believing the latter. Thus, the system with which my belief must cohere is a system of statements to the effect that I believe these things: it is the justificatory system. I call such a system a *doxastic* system of a man. The doxastic system of a man, a set of subjective statements articulating what he believes, is what his beliefs must cohere with in order to be completely justified. It contains—not the statements believed by a man—but those statements to the effect that he believes what he does.

One additional qualification is required. If the doxastic system of a man is to completely justify a belief when truth is the objective of justification, then some beliefs must be purged from the doxastic system. A man may believe things because of the comfort it gives him, because of greed, because of hate, and so forth. Such beliefs may be totally irrelevant to the question of what the man is completely justified in believing. It is only those beliefs which he would retain in an impartial and disinterested search for truth that sustain justification aimed at veracity. Hence, for justification with truth as the objective, the doxastic system of a man must be suitably corrected.

Let us put the matter somewhat more precisely. The *doxastic* system of a person S, is a set of statements of the form, S believes that p, S believes that q, and so forth, which describes what S believes. The *corrected* doxastic system of S is that subset of the doxastic system resulting when every statement is deleted which describes S as believing something he would cease to believe as an impartial and disinterested truth-seeker. I shall hereafter refer to such impartial and disinterested truth-seekers as *veracious* inquirers.

It may be wondered how a man decides what statements are contained in his corrected doxastic system. How, that is, may a man decide what he would believe as an impartial and disinterested seeker after truth? We shall soon lay down some general criteria appropriate to an effective hunt for the verific, but an informal reply may be offered. The way for a man to find out what he would believe as a veracious inquirer is for him to strive for that ideal and see what he believes. In short, the test is in the trial.

Coherence and the Chance of Truth

Let us now turn to the matter of coherence. Suppose we agree that a corrected doxastic system of a man is the one with which a statement must cohere for him to be completely justified in believing it to be true. What does it mean to say that a statement *coheres* with such a system? The answer was suggested above. A statement coheres with a corrected doxastic system of a man if and only if the statement is believed within the system to have a good chance of being true. But how good is good enough for complete justification?

If any probability less than one is taken to completely justify believing a statement on the basis of some evidence, then, by appeal to lotteries, we can show that a man would be completely justified in believing a set of statements inconsistent with the evidence in question. A theory of probability is a theory of chance. Hence, if we suppose that a man is completely justified in believing some statement whenever the statement is believed to have a chance of being true less than one but of at least some fixed value, then, chances being probabilities, we would be led to the lottery paradox.[2] For example, if the fixed value in question was m/n, where m is less than n and both are integers, each ticket in a n ticket fair lottery with a single winner would have a chance of at least m/n of not being picked, and hence, if we know this much about the lottery, we would be completely justified in believing that each of the tickets is not the winner. From the completely justified conclusion that each ticket will not win it follows that lottery lacks a winning ticket. This conslusion is, of course, inconsistent with what we know. Therefore, we cannot claim that any fixed level of probability less than one is good enough for complete justification.

We shall offer a quite different theory of complete justifica-

2. See H. E. Kyburg, Jr., *Probability and the Logic of Rational Belief* (Middletown, Conn.: Wesleyan University Press, 1961), p. 197. A solution along somewhat different lines from those suggested here was proposed by the author in 'Induction, Reason and Consistency', in the *British Journal of the Philosophy of Science*, 21 (1970), 103–114.

tion in terms of the chance of truth. First, we shall not assume a *quantitative* measure of the chance of truth a man believes a statement to possess. A man may believe that one statement has a better chance of being true than another without believing either statement to have any precise numerical chance of being true. In our explication of complete justification we shall only presuppose comparisons and not quantities. Recent work in the theory of subjective probability suggests that under certain conditions we may derive a quantitative measure of subjective probability from the comparative beliefs, but our coherence theory of justification will assume no more than comparisons.[3] We shall assume that for any two statements a person believes to be relevant to each other in a way to be specified, one is believed to have a better chance of being true than the other or neither is believed to have a better chance of being true than the other, within the person's corrected doxastic system.

Problems concerning the ascertainment and justification of probability statements do not arise in the present context. One reason is that we shall not assume any quantitative measure of probability. The most important reason is that we do not require the comparisons in question to guarantee truth. If we claim that our believing one statement to have a better chance of being true than others *guaranteed* the truth of the former, we would require some justification for our beliefs about the comparative chances. Of course, if we explicated justified belief in terms of beliefs about the comparative chances of a statement being true, and then went on to require the latter to be antecedently justified, our project would become strikingly unilluminating. This is not our approach. Unlike defenders of the foundation theory, we do not suppose that we have any guarantees of truth. Our justification has truth as an objective, but rather than demanding some external guarantee of success, we construct our theory on the subjective integrity of a veracious inquirer and the internal relations among his beliefs. The belief that one statement has a better chance of being true than another need only belong to the corrected doxastic system of a

3. See, for example, Richard Jeffrey's *The Logic of Decision* (New York: McGraw-Hill, 1965), pp. 100–116.

man to provide justification in the quest for truth. We do not assume there to be any guarantee of the truth of these beliefs or those they serve to justify.

Justification and Competition

We shall now answer the central question before us. For a man to be completely justified in believing a statement to be true, the statement must be believed to have a better chance of being true than certain others within the corrected doxastic system of the man in question. Our problem is to designate those other statements. To rephrase our solution, a man is completely justified in believing a statement to be true when, within his corrected doxastic system, he believes the statement to have a better chance of being true than any statement with which it competes for that status. We conceive of a statement competing with others for the epistemic status of the completely justified and winning the competition by being believed to have a better chance of being true than its competitors. Putting the matter this way, we only need a method for determining the competitors of a statement to complete our analysis.

The lottery paradox illustrates the need to construe broadly the relation of competition. Each hypothesis to the effect that a certain ticket is a loser has a high probability, higher than its denial for example. Yet the total set of such statements taken in conjunction with the statement that the lottery has one winning ticket, is a logically inconsistent set of statements. The members of the set are related to each other in a very important way. Each statement is negatively relevant to each other. One statement is negatively relevant to a second if and only if the second statement has a lower chance of being true on the assumption that the first is true than otherwise. To illustrate, suppose there is some fixed number of tickets in the fair lottery, consecutively numbered, one of which is the winner. The hypothesis that the number two ticket is a loser is negatively relevant to the hypothesis that the number one ticket is a loser, because, assuming the truth of the latter statement, the former has less chance of being true than otherwise. If there are one thousand tickets in the lottery, the chances are 999/1,000 that the number one ticket is a loser. However, on the assumption that the number two ticket is a loser, the chances of the number one ticket being a loser are reduced to 998/999.

The foregoing suggests an explication of competition. A statement competes with all those statements believed to be negatively relevant to it within the corrected doxastic system of the man in question.[4] This proposal, however, requires modification. Suppose that there is some statement r which is negatively relevant to a statement p. Suppose that q is a statement that is quite irrelevant to p, that is, the chances of p being true are no better or worse on the assumption that q is true than otherwise. Nevertheless, the inclusive disjunction $(r$ or $q)$ may be negatively relevant to p simply because r is negatively relevant to p. The chances of that disjunction being true are at least as good as the chances of q being true, because the disjunction is true if q is true. Hence, by the suggested explication, a man is completely justified in believing that p only if he believes that there is a better chance that p is true than that q is true even though q is quite irrelevant to p. In short, if we so explicate competition that a statement competes with all those statements negatively relevant to it, we would obtain the result that a statement competes with many irrelevant statements. This is clearly unsatisfactory.

We must restrict the conception of competition to some stronger form of negative relevance. Consider again the disjunction $(r$ or $q)$ in which r is negatively relevant to p and q is irrelevant to p. It is tempting simply to exclude all such disjunctions as competitors of p. However, every statement that is negatively relevant to r is logically equivalent to some disjunction which has a disjunct that is irrelevant to p. Most simply, consider the disjunction of r and any contradictory statement c. Such a disjunction is logically equivalent to r, and, presumably, the contradictory disjunct, c, is irrelevant to p. Moreover, unless

<hr />

4. Construing competition as negative relevance was proposed to me by Marshall Swain a number of years ago but was rejected because of the difficulty mentioned below. Interpreting competition in this way yields very similar results to the way in which the author interpreted that notion in 'Induction and Conceptual Change', *Synthese*, 23 (1971), 206–225, and in 'Evidence and Conceptual Change', *Philosophia*, 2 (1972), 273–281.

r logically entails the falsity of p, we can find a disjunction logically equivalent to r with a disjunct that is relevant to p and non-contradictory. If r does not logically entail the falsity of p, then there will be some statement, s, such that the conjunction (r and s), is irrelevant to p because s offsets the negative relevance of r. But r is logically equivalent to the disjunction of that conjunction and the conjunction of r and $\sim s$, that is, to ((r and s) or (r and $\sim s$)). Hence we cannot rule out a statement as a competitor of p just because it is a disjunction or is logically equivalent to a disjunction which contains a disjunct irrelevant to p. Honest competitors of p are going to be logically equivalent to such disjunctions.

The solution to the problem is to find one disjunctive form of a statement that is suitable for evaluating the relevance of it to other statements. In Carnap's system, a disjunction of the state descriptions in the range of a statement provides such a disjunctive form.[5] However, the analysis of statements in terms of state descriptions rests on assumptions concerning logical theory that remain controversial. For our purposes what is important about state descriptions is that they constitute a partition, that is, a set of statements which are logically inconsistent in pairs and such that it is logically impossible for all of the statements in the set to be false. From any set of statements, $s1$, $s2$, and so forth to sn, we can readily construct a partition. The partition consists of the conjunction of this set of statements in numerical order and all other conjunctions formed by replacing one or more statements in that conjunction by its negation. These conjunctions will be logically inconsistent in pairs, and it will be logically impossible for all of the conjunctions to be false. The resulting partition may be inflated by conjunctions that are internally inconsistent. These are disregarded. Each of the original statements is logically equivalent to some disjunction of members of the resulting partition.

We may employ these logical considerations to construct a stronger conception of negative relevance appropriate to our theory of justification. Note that it is somewhat unrealistic to

5. R. Carnap, The Logical Foundations of Probability (Chicago: University of Chicago Press, 1950), pp. 70–80.

expect even the best-intentioned pursuer of truth to reflect on *every* other statement to decide whether it competes with a statement whose epistemic status is under scrutiny. Surely he is going to restrict his consideration to some set of statements which he, as a veracious man, believes to be germane to the statement in question. We shall speak of such a set as an *epistemic field.* For example, in considering whether a given ticket is the winner in a lottery, an appropriate field of statements would be those that concern the outcome of the lottery and not ones about planets, rulers, and pure mathematics. A man may change his mind about such matters. What a man deems epistemically pertinent at one time, he may not at another. Of course, if a man is veracious, his choice of an epistemic field will not be capricious or arbitrary but will conform to the interests of truth.

Once we elicit a set of statements constituting the epistemic field of a statement for a man, we obtain a partition by the method of forming conjunctions cited above. The members of the partition will be conjunctions. Using this partition, we can construct a standard disjunctive form for each statement in the epistemic field of a statement. Each statement in the epistemic field will be logically equivalent to a member, or to a disjunction in numerical order of all those members of the partition consistent with it. We may then require that a competitor of a statement, in addition to being negatively relevant to it, be one whose standard disjunctive form does not contain any disjunction irrelevant to the statement. Thus, if r is logically equivalent to a disjunction ($m1$ or $m2$ or $m3$ or $m6$ or $m9$) of members of the partition formed from the epistemic field of p for a person S, then, even if r is negatively relevant to p, r would not compete with p if the disjunction ($m2$ or $m9$) was irrelevant to p.

Let us call the partition formed from the epistemic field of a statement for a person the *epistemic partition* of that statement. Then we may define *strong* negative relevance. A statement r is strongly negatively relevant to p for S if and only if (i) r is negatively relevant to p and (ii) the disjunction of members in numerical order of the epistemic partition of p for S that is logically equivalent to r, is such that no disjunction of those members is irrelevant to p. In the lottery example, statements describing the possible winners of the lottery (or conjunctions equivalent to those statements) may be thought of as forming the epistemic partition for statements concerning winners and losers. The statement that the number one ticket is the loser is equivalent to a disjunction stating that either the number two ticket is the winner, or the number three ticket is the winner and so forth. None of those disjuncts or any disjunction of them is irrelevant to the statement that the number two ticket is a loser. Hence the statement that the number one ticket is a loser is strongly negatively relevant to the statement that the number two ticket is a loser.

Other gambling situations provide further illustration. Suppose you have drawn a marble from an urn you know to contain 60 per cent black marbles but have not looked at the colour. Consider the statement that the marble drawn is black. The statement that the marble is not black is strongly negatively relevant to this statement, and so is the statement that there are non-black marbles in the urn. If the statement that there are non-black marbles in the urn has a better chance of being true than the statement that the drawn marble is black, then the man is not completely justified in believing or claiming to know that the marble he has drawn is black. Thus, it is a consequence of the theory here espoused, that a man is not completely justified in believing that a randomly selected member of a class has a certain attribute unless it is more probable that the member in question has that attribute than that there are members of the class not having that attribute.

It may be useful to consider a non-mathematical example. Consider a perceptual belief, my belief that I see a red apple before me. Now not only do I believe this, I also believe that there is comparatively little chance that I am in error, that is, when I compare the statement that I see an apple with those with which it competes. For example, I believe that the statement has a better chance of being true than the statement that present circumstances or my own condition have somehow conspired to deceive me about the existence or the character of the object I believe I see before me. More particularly, I believe that there is a better chance that I see a red apple before me than that I see only a wax imitation of an apple, or that I see only a painting of an apple, and so forth. These statements are not only strongly negatively relevant to the statement that I see a red apple, they logically imply that I do not.

Other statements, for example, that I am hallucinating in such a way that I would not be able to tell whether or not I am seeing a red apple, or that there are such perfect wax imitations of red apples placed about in my vicinity that no one can tell them from the real thing by sight, do not logically imply that I do not see a red apple. But they too have strong negative relevance to the statement, and, therefore, I must believe that there is a better chance that I see a red apple than that each of these statements is true in order to be completely justified in believing I see a red apple before me. I do believe these things, and these are beliefs I would retain if I were interested in nothing but the truth in these matters and were not in any way swayed by hunger or apple lust. In short, I believe that there is a better chance that I see a red apple than that any statement is true which, if pressed by another as an objection to my claim to complete justification, would constitute a serious objection to my contention.

By contrast, general statements such as that people sometimes mistake one object for another, or that people sometimes have red apple hallucinations, are not competitors of the statement that I see a red apple. Such general statements are not serious objections to my contention. They are not strongly relevant either. In my corrected doxastic system such statements may be simply irrelevant to my perceptual belief. If they are negatively relevant, some disjunction of disjuncts in the standard disjunctive form of such statements may be irrelevant, for example, statements about the perceptual errors and hallucinations of people entirely unlike myself.

An Analysis of Complete Justification

The conception of strong relevance supplies the needed ingredient for our definition of competition. A statement competes with a second within the doxastic system of a man if and only if the first statement is believed to have strong negative relevance to the other within that system. With this definition we proceed directly to an analysis of complete justification. It is as follows:

(cj) S is completely justified in believing that p if and only if, within the corrected doxastic system of S, p is believed to have a better chance of being true than the denial of p or any other statement that competes with p.

The account of complete justification is a coherence theory in which the relation of coherence is explicated in terms of a statement being believed to have a better chance of truth than its competitors within a system of a specified sort. The system is a set of statements describing the beliefs a man would retain were he to purge his beliefs to bring them in line with an impartial and disinterested search for truth, that is, the beliefs he would retain as a veracious man.

We have not imposed any restrictions on how a man should go about the search for truth. He might, in seeking truth, be guided by experimental study or theoretical speculation, by the authority of others or the light of his reasoning, by considerations of explanatory coherence or predictive fecundity, and so forth. The diverse ways in which scientists and plain men have pursued the truth with integrity and success belies the idea that there is a single way with truth. Our epistemology, being doxastic, is at the same time pluralistic. It assumes the competence of man in his quest for truth.

The Rationality of Completely Justified Belief

It is time to turn from rhetoric to demonstration. We shall prove that it is reasonable for a man seeking truth to believe a statement if and only if he is completely justified in believing the statement in the sense explicated above. Our proof will be decision-theoretic, that is, it will be formulated in terms of the concept of expected value restricted to the values of a veracious man. To obtain such a proof, we shall initially assume a quantitative measure of the chance a man believes a statement to have of being true. We shall subsequently dispense with this assumption.

We shall let '$p(h)$' mean 'the chance S believes h to have of being true within his corrected doxastic system', and '$p(h,e)$' mean 'the chance S believes h to have of being true within his corrected doxastic system on the assumption that e is true'. We can then define the notions we introduced earlier as follows.

(i) r has strong negative relevance to h within the corrected doxastic system of S if and only if $p(h,r)$ is less than $p(h)$ and the disjunction d which is logically equivalent to h and contains as disjuncts members $m1$, $m2$, and so forth of the epistemic partition of h for S in numerical order, is such that no disjunction d' of any of those members can be formed where $p(h,d')=p(h)$.

(ii) r competes with h for S if and only if r has strong negative relevance to h within the corrected doxastic system of S.

(iii) S is completely justified in believing that h if and only if $p(h)$ is greater than $p(\sim h)$ and for any r, if r competes with h for S, then $p(h)$ is greater than $p(r)$.

With this somewhat more formal statement of our analysis, we can proceed to our decision-theoretic defence. We argued in an earlier chapter that if one seeks a guarantee of truth from justification, the expected value of believing some statement is at a maximum only if the probability of the statement is one. That result we said leads to scepticism. Now we are concerned with a man who without demanding any guarantee is nevertheless seeking truth in his beliefs.

A man may seek truth in two senses. First, he may seek truth in the sense that he seeks to believe *only* what is true. Second, he may seek truth in the sense that he seeks to believe *all* that is true. These two objectives are quite distinct. The first, believing only what is true, may be achieved most effectively by extreme circumspection, by believing almost nothing. The less one believes the less one is apt to believe what is not true. The second objective may be achieved most effectively by extreme boldness, by believing almost everything, because the more one believes

the less apt one is to miss believing what is true. Thus, a veracious man who aims at *both* believing only what is true, and at
believing all that is true, has some difficult choices to make. In
order to obtain both, he must not be so circumspect as to believe nothing and thus forego the chance to believe anything
true, nor so bold as to believe everything and thus fall into
error.

Consistency

The foregoing suggests a consistency restriction on corrected
doxastic systems. If a man believes a set of statements that are
inconsistent, then not all statements of those beliefs should be
included in his doxastic system. If a man believes p, believes q,
and so forth, when the statements p, q, and so forth are inconsistent, the statements affirming that he believes each of these
things will be consistent. No statements accurately describing
the beliefs of a man can be inconsistent even if the statements
he believes are inconsistent. Within a corrected doxastic system,
we shall require that the set of statements a man is described as
believing be consistent as well as the set of statements describing those beliefs. Hence a doxastic system must be shorn of
some statements, when the beliefs it describes are inconsistent,
to correct it so that it describes the beliefs of a veracious man.

Suppose, unrealistically, that a man believes only three contingent statements, p, q, and r, all of which are logically independent of each other. If the man adds the belief that at
least one of these three statements is false to his doxastic system, his beliefs would become inconsistent. It is also the case
that he would be certain of having at least one true belief. Believing the first three statements alone, he might be entirely in
error, that is, all three statements might be false. If he adds to
his beliefs the belief that at least one of the first three statements is false, then if the other beliefs are false, this one will be
true. He will be certain to bag at least one truth. A man interested in believing what is true may gain something by adding a
belief that makes his beliefs inconsistent.

However, the addition of such a belief is not worth the loss
measured in terms of the objective of believing *only* what is

true. By believing at least one of the three statements is false a man makes certain that at least one of the things he believes is erroneous. If the first three statements are all true, then the added belief will not be true. He has purchased the certainty of having one true belief at the price of ensuring that he has one false belief. The price is even more dear. By adding the belief that renders his beliefs inconsistent he automatically foregoes the chance of optimum success in the search for truth, that is, believing truths and only truths. Hence we impose the requirement of consistency of belief on corrected doxastic systems.

To ensure consistency among those statements a man is completely justified in believing the different epistemic partitions used by a veracious man must be independent of each other. Otherwise, inconsistency may result. For example, suppose a man used as an epistemic partition the two statements, 'the number one ticket is the winner', and 'the number one ticket is a loser'. On the basis of this epistemic partition, the second statement would only have to compete with the first for the status of being completely justified and would thus achieve that status. If the man proceeded to form such two-membered partitions for each of the statements describing a ticket as a winner or loser, he would be completely justified in believing that the number one ticket is a loser, the number two ticket is a loser, and so forth. We would thereby again obtain the lottery inconsistency.

Of course, we intended to block such a selection of epistemic partitions by requiring that the selection of an epistemic partition by a veracious man not be arbitrary or capricious. However, it is useful to specify a condition for the selection of epistemic partitions that will guarantee the consistency of the set of statements a man is completely justified in believing. We therefore impose the condition that the total set of epistemic partitions a veracious man uses at any one time should be such that we obtain a consistent set of statements by taking any single member from each of the epistemic partitions.

Since every statement we are completely justified in believing is logically equivalent to some member of an epistemic partition or some disjunction of such members, this condition provides consistency. Members of an epistemic partition logically entail all disjunctions of such members. Therefore, if any set of members drawn singly from those epistemic partitions is logically consistent, so are the entailed disjunctions of members of those epistemic partitions. The consistency condition is a condition requiring that epistemic partitions be strongly independent of each other. This means that the epistemic partitions a man uses must be broad enough to cover an entire field or subject-matter in sufficient detail so that no other epistemic partition encroaching on the area is needed to formulate the competitors for other statements.

Expected Utility

What would it be reasonable for a man to believe to obtain a maximum of expected value in the search for truth? As we noted in an earlier chapter, expected value is based on quantitative probabilities. We shall initially assume quantitative probabilities, and, subsequently in the argument, explain how our justification rests only on comparative probabilities. We have already discussed subjective probabilities. The theory of probability is the theory of chance. We assumed that within the corrected doxastic system of a man there are beliefs concerning the chances of statements being true. We also assumed that this set of beliefs is consistent. The theory of probability partially defines, at least implicitly, chances or probabilities. Therefore beliefs about the chances of statements being true must be consistent with the theory of probability. Hence beliefs about the chances of statements being true contained within in a corrected doxastic system may be construed as subjective probabilities.

Assuming quantitative subjective probabilities, we can offer a decision-theoretic defence of our theory of justification.[6] In the

6. The application of decision theory to epistemic problems was proposed by Hempel, and developed by Pietarinen, Hintikka, Levi, and Hilpinen. See C. Hempel, 'Deductive-Nomological vs. Statistical Explanation', *Minnesota Studies in the Philosophy of Science,* vol. 3, ed. Herbert Feigl and Grover Maxwell (Minneapolis: University of Minnesota Press, 1962), pp. 98–169; Jaakko Hintikka and J. Pietarinen, 'Semantic Information and Inductive Logic', in *Aspects of Inductive Logic,* ed. J. Hintikka and P. Suppes (Amsterdam: North-Holland

decision-theoretic model, reasonableness is determined by two factors. One is the value assigned to certain outcomes in terms of how they contribute to the attainment of one's objectives, and the other is the probability of those outcomes. Once the values are assigned and probabilities ascertained, we can calculate what is reasonable by applying the formula for expected value.

When a man seeks to believe all that is true and only what is true, we need only consider two outcomes of belief. If I believe that p, and have truth as my objective, then there are two relevant outcomes; namely, that I believe that p and am correct, and that I believe that p and am in error. Symbolically, then, we let '$vt(h)$' mean 'the value for S of believing that h when it is true that h', '$vf(h)$' mean 'the value for S of believing that h when it is false that h', and '$e(h)$' means 'the expected value for S of believing that h'. The formula for the calculation of expected value is:

$$e(h) = p(h)vt(h) + p(\sim h)vf(h).$$

This formula tells us that expected value is the sum of value of true belief times the probability of that outcome, plus the value of erroneous belief times the probability of that outcome. We have suppressed, for typographical simplicity, reference to time and subject. But the values and subjective probabilities are those of a person at a given time.

The Value of Truth and Error

Assuming subjective probabilities are given, we need only specify the values of outcomes to calculate expected value. Let

Publishing Co., 1968); Risto Hilpinen, *Rules of Acceptance and Inductive Logic* (Amsterdam: North-Holland Publishing Co., 1968); and I. Levi, *Gambling with Truth: An Essay on Induction and the Aims of Science* (New York: Knopf, 1967). The present work is greatly indebted to the results obtained by these authors. Application to the selection of evidence was proposed by the author in 'Evidence and Conceptual Change', op. cit., and more elaborately in 'Evidence, Meaning and Conceptual Change: A Subjective Approach', in G. Pearce and P. Maynard, eds., *Conceptual Change* (Dordrecht. Reidel, 1974). The earlier articles were concerned with the application of decision theory to the acceptance of statements by inductive inference. The latter two articles are the first attempt to apply such theories to the problem of the selection of statements of evidence.

us consider the value of erroneously believing some statement
to be true. Erroneous belief is what we seek to avoid in seeking
truth. Hence error has negative value, that is, it constitutes an
epistemic loss. We can measure this loss in terms of the probability of a strongest competitor of the statement in question. We
discussed the concept of competition above. A strongest competitor of a statement, h, is a statement, $h*$, which has as high
a probability as any competitor of h. Formally, this gives us the
equality.

$$vf(h) = -p(h*).$$

Intuitively, what this says is that the loss resulting from erroneously believing h to be true is equal to the highest chance
any competitor of h has of being true. In believing h to be true,
we pass up the opportunity to believe any competitor of h, and
hence our loss is equal to the greatest chance for truth we
passed up in believing what we did.

Specifying the value of erroneous belief in this way, the value
of correct belief is readily derived. Since we are equating gains
and losses with probabilities, the maximum gain is unity. The
gain resulting from correctly believing h to be true is equal to
the maximum gain, less the loss that would have resulted from
erroneously believing it. Formally, we obtain the equality

$$vt(h) = 1 - p(h*).$$

From the foregoing equalities together with the theorem

$$p(\sim h) = 1 - p(h)$$

we obtain by substitution in the equation for expected value

$$e(h) = p(h)\,(1 - p(h*)) + (1 - p(h))\,(-p(h*))$$

which by algebraic manipulation reduces to

$$e(h) = p(h) - p(h*).\text{[7]}$$

The latter formula tells us that the expected value for a man of
believing h to be true is positive if and only if the chance he

7. These results were obtained by the author in the two articles cited in the
previous footnote.

believes h to have of being true within his corrected doxastic system is better than the chance he believes the strongest competitor of h to have of being true.

Complete Justification and Positive Value

We relate this result to the explication of complete justification formulated as (i), (ii), and (iii) above by the addition of the following principle:

    (iv) h^* is a strongest competitor of h for S if and only if h^* competes with h for S and, for any k, if k competes with h for S, then $p(h^*)$ is at least as great as $p(k)$.

It follows from (iv) that $p(h)$ is greater than $p(h^*)$ if and only if, for any r that competes with h for S, the $p(h)$ is greater than $p(r)$. Thus we obtain the following final result:

    (v) S is completely justified in believing that h if and only if $e(h)$ is positive, that is, $p(h)$ is greater than $p(h^*)$.

Hence we have obtained the conclusion that a man is completely justified in believing a statement if and only if the expected value for him of believing the statement is positive.

This conclusion shows us how we may dispense with the assumption of a quantitative measure of subjective probability employed in the argument from expected value. Complete justification presupposes no more than comparisons of the chances we believe statements to have of being true. The equivalence of complete justification and positive expected utility shows that the comparison of the chances statements are believed to have of being true suffices for the determination of positive expected value. For our purposes, the assumption that there is a single correct quantitative measure of the chances we believe statements to have of being true is no more than a convenient fiction. Any arbitrarily selected quantitative measure compatible with the comparative chances is equally satisfactory for obtaining the decision-theoretic demonstration of rationality articulated above.

To complete our decision-theoretic demonstration of the rationality of believing exactly those statements one is completely justified in believing according to our analysis, we must argue for the rationality of believing exactly those statements having a positive expected value. The standard account of rationality in decision theory tells us that only an alternative having a *maximal* expected value is rational. Decision theory finds primary application in the case of action where the alternatives are logically disjoint, that is, where it is logically impossible to adopt more than one alternative. The rational course is to obtain as much expected value as you can, and therefore we have the rule to adopt an alternative having a maximum of expected value. However, in the present application, the alternatives are not disjoint. A man may believe all those statements whose expected value is positive; he is not logically limited to a single alternative. Hence, on the principle of obtaining as much expected value as one can, the rational course is to believe every statement when we obtain a gain in expected value by so doing. Seeking truth, it is rational to believe a statement just in case the expected utility of doing so is positive. This means that, as we have specified the values of truth and error, it is rational, on decision-theoretic grounds, for a person to believe a statement if and only if he is completely justified in believing it in terms of our analyses. This completes our demonstration of the rationality of our results.

18

Some Forms of
Epistemological Scepticism

GEORGE S. PAPPAS

We may think of scepticism generally as a thesis or claim concerning some group of statements, namely, that each of the members of the group is doubtful in some way and to some degree. Thus, one form of ethical scepticism would be the view that each ethical standard is doubtful in the sense that no ethical standard is justifiably acceptable. Or another form of ethical scepticism, more extensive than the latter, is the thesis that no ethical statements of any form are justifiably acceptable. Similar sceptical theses are readily formulated in areas related to ethics, such as aesthetics or political theory. Presumably, the expression 'justifiably acceptable' in such contexts is subject to a number of different interpretations, so that many different versions of ethical (aesthetic, political) scepticism are possible.

Epistemological scepticism may be thought of in the same fashion, that is, as a thesis concerning some group of statements. For instance, it might be held that each statement about the external physical world is doubtful in some way and to some degree, perhaps in the sense that no statement of that sort is known to be true. Or, again, some philosophers have alleged that there are good grounds for thinking that no person knows anything about the existence and character of another person's mental states. These versions of external physical world scepticism and other minds scepticism are *epistemological* since each is a thesis about different classes of putatively known statements.

To say that each of the statements in a given set is doubtful is not to say that each is, or ought to be, doubted. Typically, not even a proponent of scepticism does doubt the relevant statements, and it seems clear that for most sceptical positions, the sceptic need not actually doubt any of the statements in question. The term 'doubt' is here used solely to indicate that statements in a given set are suspect in some manner, that there are some considerations weighing against such statements. The nature and extent of these negative considerations will vary; hence, the choice of the vague and suitably neutral term 'doubtful' for expressing the basic idea ingredient in various scepticisms. These matters will be further clarified and illustrated below in the account of epistemological scepticism.

There are many different varieties of epistemological scepticism, so it will be useful to sort them into some admittedly rough, but helpful, categories. Broadly speaking, we may divide epistemological scepticism into three groups: knowledge epistemological scepticism or *KES;* (epistemic) justification epistemological scepticism or *JES;* and what I will call *meta-*epistemological scepticism, or *MES.* Under *KES* will be, for example, the sceptical thesis that no person knows any proposition to be true, and a version of *JES* would be the view that no propositions are epistemically justified for any person. Meta-epistemological scepticism, by contrast, is a sceptical view concerning the epistemological enterprise itself, or some portion of that enterprise, or perhaps concerning some way of conceiving of the epistemological enterprise. One example of *MES* would be the thesis, defended by L. Nelson,[1] that the theory of knowledge is *impossible* in some sense. And, given that we assume that a central task of epistemology is to provide an analysis or explication of factual knowledge, then the view that all such analyses are doomed to fail would be a more restrictive version of *MES.*[2]

1. L. Nelson, "The Impossibility of the Theory of Knowledge," in R. Chisholm and R. Swartz, eds., *Empirical Knowledge* (Englewood Cliffs: Prentice-Hall, 1973). Quine defends a more restrictive version of *MES* in "Epistemology Naturalized," in his *Ontological Relativity* (New York: Columbia University Press, 1969), reprinted in Chisholm and Swartz.

2. *Cf.* C. Radford, "Analysing 'Knows That'," *Philosophical Quarterly,* 20.80 (1970).

It was indicated above that epistemological scepticisms are theses concerning sets of statements. Thus, consider the set *M* of putatively known statements. Then one common version of *KES* would be the thesis that no member of *M* is in fact known to be true. Similarly, one common version of *JES* would be a thesis concerning the set of putatively epistemically justified statements, viz., that no statement in that set is in fact epistemically justified. Presumably, with some ingenuity we could construe *MES* as a group of sceptical views about sets of statements as well, perhaps about sets of statements describing different conceptions of the domain and tasks of epistemology.

Globality and Strength

To help make our classification more exact, we need to distinguish, first, between *global* and *local* versions of epistemological scepticism. Consider, again, the set *M* of putatively known statements.[3] Some versions of *KES* are global in the sense that they are doctrines concerning *every* member of *M*. Hence, the view defended by Lehrer[4] that no statements at all are known would be a global version of *KES*. And Unger's thesis[5] that hardly any statements are known would be just slightly less global than Lehrer's view. By contrast, the thesis that no statement about the external world is known would qualify as a form of local *KES*. It is a thesis about a proper subset of *M*, rather than about all of the members of *M*.

The distinguishing feature of local versions of *KES* (and *JES*) is that such doctrines are restricted to a given subject matter. Scepticisms regarding other minds, the past, the future, and the external world are each local versions of either *KES* or *JES*.[6] Global forms of *KES* and *JES*, though, are not restricted to specific subject matters. Still, there are degrees of globality. The most extreme form of *KES* will concern every statement in

3. We have to construe this expression timelessly. *M* is to include all statements putatively known at any time.

4. K. Lehrer, "Why Not Scepticism?" [Chapter 21 in this volume].

5. P. Unger, "In Defense of Scepticism" [Chapter 19 in this volume].

6. What we might call "KK-scepticism," viz., that no one knows that a person knows any statement to be true, is here reckoned a form of *local* epistemological scepticism.

M, of course. Traditionally, however, philosophers have excluded necessarily true statements; these were typically regarded as not subject to sceptical doubt. In addition, some philosophers have excluded certain first-person phenomenal statements, usually on the grounds that such statements are incorrigible or absolutely certain, and thus immune to sceptical threats.[7]

With respect to *MES*, Nelson's thesis alluded to above is perhaps the most global. Considerably less global is the view seemingly endorsed by Quine,[8] namely, that epistemology conceived in a certain manner is misdirected and mistaken, and that it should be replaced with scientific psychology.

Epistemological scepticisms may also differ in strength. Thus, consider *KES* again and, specifically, the very strong thesis that

(a) No statement is knowable, i.e., it is *impossible* for any statement to be known.

Claim (a) is at its strongest if 'impossible' means 'logically impossible,' but even if some weaker notion of impossibility is intended, (a) will be stronger than,

(b) No statement is in fact known.

Similarly with *JES*, the claim that

(c) No statement is epistemically justifiable

is considerably stronger than

(d) No statement is in fact epistemically justified.

It is unlikely that any philosopher has seriously entertained and defended either (a) or (c). But (b) and (d) have won support recently, with (b) defended by Lehrer and Unger, and (d) championed recently by Oakley and Kekes.[9]

Armed with the foregoing distinctions, we can classify a large number of forms of epistemological scepticisms. Consider, first, *KES*, in the following versions:

7. Chisholm seems to construe epistemological scepticism in this fashion. See *Theory of Knowledge*, 2d ed. (Englewood Cliffs: Prentice-Hall, 1976), p. 121.

8. W. V. O. Quine, "Epistemology Naturalized," *op. cit.*

9. Lehrer, "Why Not Scepticism?" and Unger, "In Defense of Scepticism;" I. Oakley, "An Argument for Scepticism concerning Justified Belief," *American Philosophical Quarterly*, 13.3 (1976) 221–228, and J. Kekes, "The Case for Scepticism," *Philosophical Quarterly*, 25.98 (1975), 28–39.

(a) No statement in the set M is knowable, i.e., it is logically impossible for any statement in M to be known.

(b) No statement in the set M is in fact knowable, i.e., it is empirically impossible for any statement in M to be known.

(e) No statement in M is in fact known.

(f) No statement in M is knowable with certainty, i.e., it is logically impossible for any statement in M to be known with certainty.

(g) It is empirically impossible for any statement in M to be known with certainty.

(h) No statement in M is in fact known with certainty.[10]

These main forms of *KES* are listed in order of decreasing strength. In fact, (f), (g), and (h) admit of a great many further variations, since the notion of certainty can be (and has been) explicated in many different ways.[11] It should be clear, furthermore, that each of these sceptical theses can be varied by changing the degree of globality, so that, for example, each deals solely with contingent statements or solely with contingent nonphenomenal statements. The result will be still more versions of *KES,* but with the overall classification based mainly on degree of globality and of strength.

Most of the above comments carry over to *JES* as well, but there is an added complication. Epistemic justification is a degree-concept in the sense that such justification can vary from very high or strong to very weak. Thus, additional variants of *JES* will result depending on degree of justification together with different combinations of globality and strength. We can illustrate these matters by considering the contrast between two versions of *JES:*

10. One version of (h) is defended by Lehrer, in "Scepticism and Conceptual Change," in R. Chisholm and R. Swartz, eds., *Empirical Knowledge.*

11. Cf., e.g., R. Firth, "The Anatomy of Certainty, *Philosophical Review,* (1967), reprinted in Chisholm and Swartz, *Empirical Knowledge.* I here include under 'certainty' such allied concepts as incorrigibility, indubitability, and the like. The stronger the notion of certainty used in variants of (h), the more likely it is that the variant is true—some would say truistic since the stronger notions of certainty used in (h) and its variants will yield very weak versions of *KES.*

(i) No statement is *at all* epistemically justified, i.e., no statement has any degree of justification for a person

(j) No statement is completely epistemically justified for a person.

If, as is plausible, we take the notion of complete justification as an unexplicated upper bound on degree of epistemic justification, then plainly (i) is a more radical form of *JES* than (j), even though they have the same strength and degree of globality.

The notion of complete epistemic justification can be explicated in a number of ways, just as the notion of certainty used in versions of *KES* may be. Indeed, it may be that some notion of certainty is needed to help explicate complete justification, and conversely. And, just as forms of *KES* which use strong notions of certainty are quite plausible, so forms of *JES* which put high demands on the notion of complete epistemic justification will be plausible as well. At least such doctrines will have more initial plausibility than forms of *JES* closer in spirit to the extreme form given in (i).

It should be clear that very many different combinations of strength and degree of globality, and different notions of certainty and complete epistemic justification, are available, and that in sheer numbers there are incredibly many forms of epistemological scepticism.[12] Such variety and complexity might ordinarily be cause for despair for the nonsceptical epistemologist with an interest in defusing sceptical positions. But, I believe, there are some reasons to believe that not all or even most forms of epistemological scepticism warrant careful scrutiny and counterargument.

Evaluating Epistemological Scepticism

Consider what we can call the *epistemic status* of a given sceptical doctrine. That is, apropos of some sceptical thesis, *S*, it might be claimed that *S* is epistemically justified, or perhaps that *S* is merely somewhat reasonable to believe. In general, the epistemic status of *S* can be scaled in a fashion similar to that

12. I here omit any comments on different forms of *MES*, but the above remarks on forms of *JES* and *KES* should give some idea of how to differentiate forms of *MES*.

indicated above for degrees of strength of forms of *KES* and *JES*. We can take the upper limit on the scale for epistemic status to be that of knowing with certainty (in a suitably strong sense of the latter notion), and the lower end of the scale to be that of having some slight reason in favor of *S*, or perhaps no reasons against *S* but none for it either.

Two things seem initially clear: First, it will be unreasonable to ascribe very high epistemic status (such as knowing with certainty) to a sceptical thesis. This is not a consequence of the sceptical thesis in question; it derives simply from the fact that virtually no hypothesis has that sort of epistemic status. Moreover, the claimed epistemic status of a given sceptical doctrine can be no greater than the strength of a specific global form of *KES* or *JES*. To see this, notice that the would-be sceptic is in no position to hold that it is *known* that

(b) No statement is in fact known

nor that it is *epistemically justified* for him that

(d) No statement is epistemically justified for a person.

Such claims in behalf of sceptical hypotheses are self-defeating in an obvious way. Something more moderate is needed, such as that it is reasonable to believe that (b),[13] and that there is some reason to believe that (d).

Moreover, some forms of global *KES* and *JES* have no initial plausibility. For instance,

(k) It is impossible (logically, empirically) for any statement to be known

need not be seriously considered, nor need we bother debating a thesis such as

(l) It is impossible (logically, empirically) for any statement to be epistemically justified for a person.

Only weaker forms of global *KES* and *JES* require careful scrutiny. But even with such weaker versions, there are qualifications.

Perhaps the most important qualification is that the weaker the version of global *KES* and *JES* the more likely it is that the

13. A point duly noted by Unger and Lehrer in the papers reprinted in this volume.

thesis is true *and acceptable to the nonsceptical epistemologist.* Thus, most philosophers in the latter group would completely agree that

(h) No statement in M is known with certainty

provided that the notion of certainty is explicated along customarily stringent lines. For (h) is consistent with

(m) Some statements in M are in fact known to be true

and it is the latter that a nonsceptical philosopher is most apt to defend. Similarly, a thesis such as

(n) No statement is completely epistemically justified

is likely to be perfectly acceptable to the nonsceptic if the notion of complete justification is set very high. The nonsceptic is interested, typically, in defending such a thesis as

(o) Some statements are epistemically justified for some persons

and (n) and (o) are consistent, at least for some interpretations of (n).

The foregoing brief remarks suggest in different ways that the task facing the nonsceptic is neither unending nor hopeless. For, there will be many forms of global *KES* and *JES* that will pose no threat to the contents of and arguments for many nonsceptical positions. They also suggest, I think, that dealing with epistemological scepticism is no special sort of problem. Like any other hypothesis, a given form of epistemological scepticism is to be judged comparatively reasonable or unreasonable in relation to its nonsceptical competition. And, given the intuitive initial implausibility of any sceptical hypothesis likely to be a threat to nonsceptical epistemologies, we have some slight reason to think that no important form of global epistemological scepticism, at least within *KES* and *JES,* is likely to prove acceptable.

19

A Defense of Skepticism

PETER UNGER

The skepticism that I will defend is a negative thesis concerning what we know. I happily accept the fact that there is much that many of us correctly and reasonably believe, but much more than that is needed for us to know even a fair amount. Here I will not argue that nobody knows anything about anything, though that would be quite consistent with the skeptical thesis for which I will argue. The somewhat less radical thesis which I will defend is this one: every human being knows, at best, hardly anything to be so. More specifically, I will argue that hardly anyone knows that 45 and 56 are equal to 101, if anyone at all. On this skeptical thesis, no one will know the thesis to be true. But this is all right. For I only want to argue that it may be reasonable for us to suppose the thesis to be true, not that we should ever know it to be true.

Few philosophers now take skepticism seriously. With philosophers, even the most powerful of traditional skeptical argument has little force to tempt them nowadays. Indeed, nowadays, philosophers tend to think skepticism interesting only as a formal challenge to which positive accounts of our common-sense knowledge are the gratifying responses. Consequently, I find it at least somewhat natural to offer a defense of skepticism.[1]

Reprinted from *The Philosophical Review*, 80 (1971), 198–218, by kind permission of the author and editor.
1. Among G. E. Moore's most influential papers against skepticism are "A Defense of Common Sense," "Four Forms of Scepticism," and "Certainty."

My defense of skepticism will be quite unlike traditional arguments for this thesis. This is largely because I write at a time when there is a common faith that, so far as expressing truths is concerned, all is well with the language that we speak. Against this common, optimistic assumption, I shall illustrate how our language habits might serve us well in practical ways, even while they involve us in saying what is false rather than true. And this often does occur, I will maintain, when our positive assertions contain terms with special features of a certain kind, which I call *absolute* terms. Among these terms, "flat" and "certain" are *basic* ones. Due to these terms' characteristic features, and because the world is not so simple as it might be, we do not speak truly, at least as a rule, when we say of a real object, "That has a top which is flat" or when we say of a real person, "He is certain that it is raining." And just as basic absolute terms generally fail to apply to the world, so other absolute terms, which are at least partially defined by the basic ones, will fail to apply as well. Thus, we also speak falsely when we say of a real object or person, "That is a cube" or "He knows that it is raining." For an object is a cube only if it has surfaces which are flat, and, as I shall argue, a person knows something to be so only if he is certain of it.

These papers are now available in Moore's *Philosophical Papers* (New York, 1962). More recent representatives of the same anti-skeptical persuasion include A. J. Ayer's *The Problem of Knowledge* (Baltimore, 1956) and two books by Roderick M. Chisholm: *Perceiving* (Ithaca, 1957) and *Theory of Knowledge* (Englewood Cliffs, N.J., 1966). Among the many recent journal articles against skepticism are three papers of my own: "Experience and Factual Knowledge," *Journal of Philosophy*, 64.5 (1967), "An Analysis of Factual Knowledge," *Journal of Philosophy*, 65.6 (1968) 157–170, and "Our Knowledge of the Material World," *Studies in the Theory of Knowledge, American Philosophical Quarterly Monograph* No. 4 (1970). At the same time, a survey of the recent journal literature reveals very few papers where skepticism is defended or favored. With recent papers which do favor skepticism, however, I can mention at least two. A fledgling skepticism is persuasively advanced by Brian Skyrms in his "The Explication of 'X knows that p,'" *Journal of Philosophy*, 64.12 (1967) 373–389. And in William W. Rozeboom's "Why I Know So Much More Than You Do," *American Philosophical Quarterly*, 4.4 (1967) 257–268, we have a refreshingly strong statement of skepticism in the context of recent discussion.

I. Sophisticated Worries about What Skepticism Requires

The reason contemporary sophisticated philosophers do not take skepticism seriously can be stated broadly and simply. They think that skepticism implies certain things which are, upon a bit of reflection, quite impossible to accept. These unacceptable implications concern the functioning of our language.

Concerning our language and how it functions, the most obvious requirement of skepticism is that some common terms of our language will involve us in error systematically. These will be such terms as "know" and "knowledge," which may be called the "terms of knowledge." If skepticism is right, then while we go around saying "I know," "He knows," and so on, and while we believe what we say to be true, all the while what we say and believe will actually be false. If our beliefs to the effect that we know something or other are so consistently false, then the terms of knowledge lead us into error systematically. But if these beliefs really are false, should we not have experiences which force the realization of their falsity upon us, and indeed abandon these beliefs? Consequently, shouldn't our experiences get us to stop thinking in these terms which thus systematically involve us in error? So, as we continue to think in the terms of knowledge and to believe ourselves to know all sorts of things, this would seem to show that the beliefs are not false ones and the terms are responsible for no error. Isn't it only reasonable, then, to reject a view which requires that such helpful common terms as "knows" and "knowledge" lead us into error systematically?

So go some worrisome thoughts which might lead us to dismiss skepticism out of hand. But it seems to me that there is no real need for our false beliefs to clash with our experiences in any easily noticeable way. Suppose, for instance, that you falsely believe that a certain region of space is a vacuum. Suppose that, contrary to your belief, the region does contain some gaseous stuff, though only the slightest trace. Now, for practical purposes, we may suppose that, so far as gaseous contents go, it is not important whether that region really is a vacuum or whether it contains whatever gaseous stuff it does contain. Once this is supposed, then it is reasonable to suppose as well that, for practical purposes, it makes no important difference whether you falsely believe that the region is a vacuum or truly believe this last thing—namely, that, for practical purposes, it is not important whether the region is a vacuum or whether it contains that much gaseous stuff.

We may notice that this supposed truth is entailed by what you believe but does not entail it. In other words, a region's being a vacuum entails that, for practical purposes, there is no important difference between whether the region is a vacuum or whether it contains whatever gaseous stuff it does contain. For, if the region *is* a vacuum, whatever gas it contains is nil, and so there is no difference at all, for any sort of purpose, between the region's being a vacuum and its having that much gaseous stuff. But the entailment does not go the other way, and this is where we may take a special interest. For while a region may not be a vacuum, it may contain so little gaseous stuff that, so far as gaseous contents go, for practical purposes there is no important difference between the region's being a vacuum and its containing whatever gaseous stuff it does contain. So if this entailed truth lies behind the believed falsehood, your false belief, though false, may not be harmful. Indeed, generally, it may even be helpful for you to have this false belief rather than having none and rather than having almost any other belief about the matter that you might have. On this pattern, we may have many false beliefs about regions being vacuums even while these beliefs will suffer no important clash with the experiences of life.

More to our central topic, suppose that, as skepticism might have it, you falsely believe that you *know* that there are elephants. As before, there is a true thing which is entailed by what you falsely believe and which we should notice. The thing here, which presumably you do not actually believe, is this: that, with respect to the matter of whether there are elephants, for practical purposes there is no important difference between whether you know that there are elephants or whether you are in that position with respect to the matter that you actually are in. This latter, true thing is entailed by the false thing you believe—namely, that you know that there are elephants. For if you do know, then, with respect to the matter of the elephants, there is no difference at all, for any purpose of any sort, between your knowing and your being in the position you actually are in. On the other hand, the entailment does not go the other way and, again, this is where our pattern allows a false belief to be helpful. For even if you do not really know, still, it may be that for practical purposes you are in a position with respect to the matter (of the elephants) which is not importantly different from knowing. If this is so, then it may be better, practically speaking, for you to believe falsely that you know than to have no belief at all here. Thus, not only with beliefs to the effect that specified regions are vacuums, but also with beliefs to the effect that we know certain things, it may be that there are very many of them which, though false, it is helpful for us to have. In both cases, the beliefs will not noticeably clash with the experiences of life. Without some further reason for doing so, then, noting the smooth functioning of our "terms of knowledge" gives us no powerful reason for dismissing the thesis of skepticism.

There is, however, a second worry which will tend to keep sophisticates far from embracing skepticism, and this worry is, I think, rather more profound than the first. Consequently, I shall devote most of the remainder to treating this second worry. The worry to which I shall be so devoted is this: that, if skepticism is right, then the terms of knowledge, unlike other terms of our language, will never or hardly ever be used to make simply, positive assertions that are true. In other words, skepticism will require the terms of knowledge to be isolated freaks of our language. But even with familiar, persuasive arguments for skepticism, it is implausible to think that our language is plagued by an isolated little group of troublesome freaks. So, by being so hard on knowledge alone, skepticism seems implausible once one reflects on the exclusiveness of its persecution.

II. Absolute Terms and Relative Terms

Against the worry that skepticism will require the terms of knowledge to be isolated freaks, I shall argue that, on the contrary, a variety of other terms is similarly troublesome. As skepticism becomes more plausible with an examination of the terms of knowledge, so other originally surprising theses become more plausible once their key terms are critically examined. When all of the key terms are understood to have essential features in common, the truth of any of these theses need not be felt as such a surprise.

The terms of knowledge, along with many other troublesome terms, belong to a class of terms that is quite pervasive in our language. I call these terms *absolute terms*. The term "flat," in its central, literal meaning, is an absolute term. (With other meanings, as in "His voice is flat" and "The beer is flat," I have no direct interest.) To say that something is flat is no different from saying that it is absolutely, or perfectly, flat. To say that a surface is flat is to say that some things or properties *which are matters of degree* are *not* instanced in the surface *to any degree at all*. Thus, something which is flat is not at all bumpy, and not at all curved. Bumpiness and curvature are matters of degree. When we say of a surface that it is bumpy, or that it is curved, we use the *relative terms* "bumpy" and "curved" to talk about the surface. Thus, absolute terms and relative terms go together, in at least one important way, while other terms, like "unmarried," have only the most distant connections with terms of either of these two sorts.

There seems to be a syntactic feature which is common to relative terms and to certain absolute terms, while it is found with no other terms. This feature is that each of these terms may be modified by a variety of terms that serve to indicate (matters of) degree. Thus, we find "The table is *very* bumpy" and "The table is *very* flat" but not "The lawyer is *very* unmarried." Among those absolute terms which admit such qualification are all those absolute terms which are *basic* ones. A basic absolute term is an absolute term which is not (naturally) defined in terms of some other absolute term, not even partially so. I suspect that "straight" is such a term, and perhaps "flat" is as well. But in its central (geometrical) meaning, "cube" quite clearly is not a basic absolute term even though it is an absolute term. For "cube" means, among other things, "having edges that are *straight* and surfaces which are *flat*": and "straight" and "flat" are absolute terms. While "cube" does not admit of qualification of degree, "flat" and "straight" do admit of such qualification. Thus, all relative terms and all basic absolute terms admit of constructions of degree. While this is another way in which these two sorts of terms go together, we must now ask: how may we distinguish terms of the one sort from those of the other?

But is there now anything to distinguish here? For if absolute terms admit of degree construction, why think that any of these terms is not a relative term, why think that they do not purport to predicate things or properties which are, as they now look to be, matters of degree? If we may say that a table is very flat, then why not think flatness a matter of degree? Isn't this essentially the same as our saying of a table that it is very bumpy, with bumpiness being a matter of degree? So perhaps "flat," like "bumpy" and like all terms that take degree constructions, is, fittingly, a relative term. But basic absolute terms may be distinguished from relatives even where degree constructions conspire to make things look otherwise.

To advance the wanted distinction, we may look to a procedure for paraphrase. Now, we have granted that it is common for us to say of a surface that it is pretty, or very, or extremely, flat. And it is also common for us to say that, in saying such things of surfaces, we are saying *how* flat the surfaces are. What we say here seems of a piece with our saying of a surface that it is pretty, or very, or extremely, bumpy, and our then saying that, in doing this, we are saying *how* bumpy the surface is. But, even intuitively, we may notice a difference here. For only with our talk about "flat," we have the idea that these locutions are only convenient means for saying how closely a surface approximates, or *how close it comes to being,* a surface which is (absolutely) flat. Thus, it is intuitively plausible, and far from being a nonsensical interpretation, to paraphrase things so our result with our "flat" locutions is this: what we have said of a surface is that it is pretty *nearly* flat, or very *nearly* flat, or extremely *close to being* flat and, in doing that, we have said, not simply how flat the surface is, but rather *how close* the surface is *to being* flat. This form of paraphrase gives a plausible interpretation of our talk of flatness while allowing the term "flat" to lose its appearance of being a relative term. How will this form of paraphrase work with "bumpy," where, presumably, a genuine relative term occurs in our locutions?

What do we say when we say of a surface that it is pretty bumpy, or very bumpy, or extremely so? Of course, it at least appears that we say *how* bumpy the surface is. The paraphrase has it that what we are saying is that the surface is pretty *nearly* bumpy, or very *nearly* bumpy, or extremely *close to being* bumpy. In other words, according to the paraphrase, we are saying *how close* the surface is *to being* bumpy. But anything of this sort is, quite obviously, a terribly poor interpretation of what we are saying about the surface. Unfortunately for the paraphrase, if we say that a surface is very bumpy it is entailed by what we say that the surface is bumpy, while if we say that the surface is very close to being bumpy it is entailed that the surface is *not* bumpy. Thus, unlike the case with "flat," our paraphrase cannot apply with "bumpy." Consequently, by means of our paraphrase we may distinguish between absolute terms and relative ones.

Another way of noticing how our paraphrase lends support to the distinction between absolute and relative terms is this: the initial data are that such terms as "very," which standardly serve to indicate that there is a great deal of something, serve with opposite effect when they modify terms like "flat"—terms which I have called basic absolute terms. That is, when we say, for example, that something is (really) very flat, then, so far as flatness is concerned, we seem to say less of the thing than when we say, simply, that it is (really) flat. The augmenting function of "very" is turned on its head so that the term serves to diminish. What can resolve this conflict? It seems that our paraphrase can. For on the paraphrase, what we are saying of the thing is that it is very *nearly* flat, and so, by implication, that it is *not* flat (but only very nearly so). Once the paraphrase is exploited, the term "very" may be understood to have its standard augmenting function. At the same time, "very" functions without conflict with "bumpy." Happily, the term "very" is far from being unique here; we get the same results with other augmenting modifiers: "extremely," "especially," and so on.

For our paraphrastic procedure to be comprehensive, it must work with contexts containing explicitly comparative locutions. Indeed, with these contexts, we have a common form of talk where the appearance of relativeness is most striking of all. What shall we think of our saying, for example, that one surface is not *as* flat as another, where things strikingly look to be a matter of degree? It seems that we must allow that in such a suggested comparison, the surface which is said to be the *flatter* of the two may be, so far as logic goes, (absolutely) flat. Thus, we should *not* paraphrase this comparative context as "the one surface is not as *nearly* flat as the other." For this form of paraphrase would imply that the second surface is not flat, and so it gives us a poor interpretation of the original, which has no such implication. But then, a paraphrase with no bad implications is not far removed. Instead of simply inserting our "nearly" or our "close to being," we may allow for the possibility of (absolute) flatness by putting things in a way which is only somewhat more complex. For we may paraphrase our original by saying: the first surface is *either not flat though the second is, or else it is* not as *nearly* flat as the second. Similarly, where we say that one surface is flatter than another, we may paraphrase things like this: the first surface is *either flat though the second is not or else it is closer to being flat* than the second. But in contrast to all this, with comparisons of bumpiness, no paraphrase is available. To say that one surface is not as bumpy as another is not to say either that the first surface is not bumpy though the second is, or else that it is not as nearly bumpy as the second one.

Our noting the availability of degree constructions allows us to class together relative terms and basic absolute terms, as against any other terms. And our noting that only with the absolute terms do our constructions admit of our paraphrase allows us to distinguish between the relative terms and the basic absolute terms. Now that these terms may be quite clearly distinguished, we may restate without pain of vacuity those ideas on which we relied to introduce our terminology. Thus, to draw the *connection* between terms of the two sorts we may now say this: every basic absolute term, and so every absolute term whatever, may be defined, at least partially, by means of certain relative terms. The defining conditions presented by means of the relative terms are negative ones; they say that what the relative term purports to denote is *not* present *at all,* or *in the least,* where the absolute term correctly applies. Thus, these negative conditions are logically necessary ones for basic absolute terms, and so for absolute terms which are defined by means of the basic ones. Thus, something is flat, in the central, literal sense of "flat," only if it is not at all, or not in the least, curved or bumpy. And similarly, something is a cube, in the central, literal sense of "cube," only if it has surfaces which are not at all, or not in the least, bumpy or curved. In noting these demanding *negative relative requirements,* we may begin to appreciate, I think, that a variety of absolute terms, if not all of them, might well be quite troublesome to apply, perhaps even failing consistently in application to real things.

In a final general remark about these terms, I should like to motivate my choice of terminology for them. A reason I call terms of the one sort "absolute" is that, at least in the case of the basic ones, the term may always be modified, grammatically, with the term "absolutely." And indeed, this modification fits so well that it is, I think, always redundant. Thus, something is flat if and only if it is absolutely flat. In contrast, the term "absolutely" never gives a standard, grammatical modification for any of our relative terms: nothing which is bumpy is absolutely bumpy. On the other hand, each of the relative terms takes "relatively" quite smoothly as a grammatical modifier. (And, though it is far from being clear, it is at least arguable, I think, that this modifier is redundant for these terms. Thus, it is at least arguable that something is bumpy if and only if it is relatively bumpy.) In any event, with absolute terms, while "relatively" is grammatically quite all right as a modifier, the construction thus obtained must be understood in terms of our paraphrase. Thus, as before, something is relatively flat if and only if it is relatively close to being (absolutely) flat, and so only if it is not flat.

In this terminology, and in line with our linguistic tests, I think that the first term of each of the following pairs is a relative term while the second is an absolute one: "wet" and "dry," "crooked" and "straight," "important" and "crucial," "incomplete" and "complete," "useful" and "useless," and so on. I think that both "empty" and "full" are absolute terms, while "good" and "bad," "rich" and "poor," and "happy" and "unhappy" are all relative terms. Finally, I think that, in the sense defined by our tests, each of the following is neither an absolute term nor a relative one: "married" and "unmarried," "true" and "false," and "right" and "wrong." In other plausible senses, though, some or all of this last group might be called "absolute."

III. On Certainty and Certain Related Things

Certain terms of our language are standardly followed by propositional clauses, and, indeed, it is plausible to think that wherever they occur they *must* be followed by such clauses on pain of otherwise occurring in a sentence which is elliptical or incomplete. We may call terms which take these clauses *propositional terms* and we may then ask: are some propositional terms absolute ones, while others are relative terms? By means of our tests, I will argue that "certain" is an absolute term, while "confident," "doubtful," and "uncertain" are all relative terms.

With regard to being certain, there are two ideas which are important: first, the idea of something's being certain, where that which is certain is *not* certain *of* anything, and, second, the idea of a being's being certain, where that which is certain *is* certain *of* something. A paradigm context for the first idea is the context "It is certain that it is raining" where the term "it" has no apparent reference. I will call such contexts *impersonal contexts*, and the idea of certainty which they serve to express, thus, the impersonal idea of certainty. In contrast, a paradigm context for the second idea is this one: "He is certain that it is raining"—where, of course, the term "he" purports to refer as clearly as one might like. In the latter context, which we may call the *personal* context, we express the personal idea of certainty. This last may be allowed, I think, even though in ordinary conversations we may speak of dogs as being certain; presumably, we treat dogs there the way we typically treat persons.

Though there are these two important sorts of context, I think that "certain" must mean the same in both. In both cases, we must be struck by the thought that the presence of certainty amounts to the complete absence of doubt, or doubtfulness. This thought leads me to say that "It is certain that *p*" means, within the bounds of nuance, "It is not at all doubtful that *p*." The idea of personal certainty may then be defined accordingly; we relate what is said in the impersonal form to the mind of the person, or subject, who is said to be certain of something. Thus, "He is certain that *p*" means, within the bounds of nuance, "*In his mind,* it is not at all doubtful that *p*." Where a man is certain of something, then, concerning that thing, all doubt is absent in that man's mind. With these definitions available, we may now say this: connected negative definitions of certainty suggest that, in its central, literal meaning, "certain" is an absolute term.

But we should like firmer evidence for thinking that "certain" is an absolute term. To be consistent, we turn to our procedure for paraphrase. I will exhibit the evidence for personal contexts and then say a word about impersonal ones. In any event, we want contrasting results for "certain" as against some related relative terms. One term which now suggests itself for contrast is, of course, "doubtful." Another is, of course, "uncertain." And we will get the desired results with these terms. But it is, I think, more interesting to consider the term "confident."

In quick discussions of these matters, one might speak indifferently of a man's being confident of something and of his being certain of it. But on reflection there is a difference between confidence and certainty. Indeed, when I say that I am certain of something, I tell you that I am not confident of it but that I am *more than* that. And if I say that I am confident that so-and-so, I tell you that I am *not so much as* certain of the thing. Thus, there is an important difference between the two. At least part of this difference is, I suggest, reflected by our procedure for paraphrase.

We may begin to apply our procedure by resolving the problem of augmenting modifiers. Paradoxically, when I say that I am (really) very certain of something, I say *less* of myself, so far as certainty is concerned, that I do when I say, simply, that I am (really) certain of the thing. How may we resolve this paradox? Our paraphrase explains things as before. In the first case, what I am really saying is that I am very *nearly* certain, and so, in effect, that I am not really certain. But in the second case, I say that I really am. Further, we may notice that, in contrast, in the case of "confident" and "uncertain," and "doubtful" as well, no problem with augmenting arises in the first place. For when I say that I am very confident of something, I say more of myself, so far as confidence is concerned, than I do when I simply say that I am confident of the thing. And again our paraphrastic procedure yields us the lack of any problems here. For the augmented statement cannot be sensibly interpreted as saying that I am very nearly confident of the thing. Indeed, with any modifier weaker than "absolutely," our paraphrase works well with "certain" but produces only a nonsensical interpretation with "confident" and other contrasting terms. For example, what might it mean to say of someone that he was rather confident of something? Would this be to say that he was rather close to being confident of the thing? Surely not.

Turning to comparative constructions, our paraphrase separates things just as we should expect. For example, from "He is more certain that p than he is that q" we get "He is either certain that p while not certain that q, or else he is more nearly certain that p than he is that q." But from "He is more confident that p than he is that q" we do *not* get "He is either confident that p while not confident that q, or else he is more nearly confident that p than he is that q." For he may well already be confident of both things. Further comparative constructions are similarly distinguished when subjected to our paraphrase. And no matter what locutions we try, the separation is as convincing with impersonal contexts as it is with personal ones, so long as there are contexts which are comparable. Of course, "confident" has no impersonal contexts; we cannot say "It is confident that p," where the "it" has no purported reference. But where comparable contexts do exist, as with "doubtful" and "uncertain," further evidence is available. Thus, we may reasonably assert that "certain" is an absolute term while "confident," "doubtful," and "uncertain" are relative terms.

IV. The Doubtful Applicability of Some Absolute Terms

If my account of absolute terms is essentially correct, then, at least in the case of some of these terms, fairly reasonable suppositions about the world make it somewhat doubtful that the terms properly apply. (In certain contexts, generally where what we are talking about divides into discrete units, the presence of an absolute term need cause no doubts. Thus, considering the absolute term "complete," the truth of "His set of steins is now complete" may be allowed without hesitation, but the truth of "His explanation is now complete" may well be doubted. It is with the latter, more interesting contexts, I think, that we shall be concerned in what follows.) For example, while we say of many surfaces of physical things that they are flat, a rather reasonable interpretation of what we do observe makes it at least somewhat doubtful that these surfaces actually *are* flat. When we look at a rather smooth block of stone through a powerful microscope, the observed surface appears to us to be rife with irregularities. And this irregular appearance seems best explained, not by being taken as an illusory optical phenomenon, but by taking it to be a finer, more revealing look of a surface which is, in fact, rife with smallish bumps and crevices. Further, we account for bumps and crevices by supposing that the stone is composed of much smaller things, molecules and so on, which are in such a combination that, while a large and sturdy stone is the upshot, no stone with a flat surface is found to obtain.

Indeed, what follows from my account of "flat" is this: that, as a matter of logical necessity, if a surface is flat, then there never is any surface which is flatter than it is. For on our paraphrase, if the second surface is flatter than the first, then either the second surface is flat while the first is not, or else the second is more nearly flat than the first, neither surface being flat. So if there is such a second, flatter surface, then the first surface is not flat after all, contrary to our supposition. Thus there cannot be any second, flatter surface. Or in other words, if it is logically possible that there be a surface which is flatter than a given one, then that given surface is not really a flat one. Now, in the case of the observed surface of the stone, owing to the stone's irregular composition, the surface is *not* one such that it is logically impossible that there be a flatter one. (For example, we might veridically observe a surface through a microscope of the same power which did not appear to have any bumps or crevices.) Thus it is only reasonable to suppose that the surface of this stone is not really flat.

Our understanding of the stone's composition, that it is composed of molecules and so on, makes it reasonable for us to suppose as well that any similarly sized or larger surfaces will fail to be flat just as the observed surface fails to be flat. At the same time, it would be perhaps a bit rash to suppose that much smaller surfaces would fail to be flat as well. Beneath the level of our observation perhaps there are small areas of the stone's surface which are flat. If so, then perhaps there are small objects that have surfaces which are flat, like this area of the stone's surface: for instance, chipping off a small part of the stone might yield such a small object. So perhaps there are physical objects with surfaces which are flat, and perhaps it is not now reasonable for us to assume that there are no such objects. But even if this strong assumption is not now reasonable, one thing which does seem quite reasonable for us now to assume is this: we should at least suspend judgment on the matter of whether there are any physical objects with flat surfaces. That there are such objects is something it is not now reasonable for us to believe.

It is at least somewhat doubtful, then, that "flat" ever applies to actual physical objects or to their surfaces. And the thought must strike us that if "flat" has no such application, this must be due in part to the fact that "flat" is an absolute term. We may

then do well to be a bit doubtful about the applicability of any
other given absolute term and, in particular, about the applicability of the term "certain." As in the case of "flat," our paraphrase highlights the absolute character of "certain." As a matter of logical necessity, if someone is certain of something, then
there never is anything of which he is more certain. For on our
paraphrase, if the person is more certain of any other thing,
then either he is certain of the other thing while not being certain of the first, or else he is more nearly certain of the other
thing than he is of the first; that is, he is certain of neither.
Thus, if it is logically possible that there be something of which
a person might be more certain than he now is of a given thing,
then he is not really certain of that given thing.

Thus it is reasonable to suppose, I think, that hardly anyone,
if anyone at all, is certain that 45 and 56 are 101. For it is reasonable to suppose that hardly anyone, if anyone at all, is so
certain of that particular calculation that it is impossible for
there to be anything of which he might be yet more certain.
But this is not surprising; for hardly anyone *feels* certain that
those two numbers have that sum. What, then, about something of which people commonly do feel absolutely certain—
say, of the existence of automobiles?

Is it reasonable for us now actually to believe that many people are certain that there are automobiles? If it is, then it is reasonable for us to believe as well that for each of them it is not
possible for there to be anything of which he might be more
certain than he now is of there being automobiles. In particular, we must then believe of these people that it is impossible
for any of them ever to be more certain of his own existence
than all of them now are of the existence of automobiles. While
these people *might* all actually be as certain of the automobiles
as this, just as each of them *feels* himself to be, I think it
somewhat rash for us actually to believe that they *are* all so certain. Certainty being an absolute and our understanding of
people being rather rudimentary and incomplete, I think it
more reasonable for us now to suspend judgment on the matter. And, since there is nothing importantly peculiar about the
matter of the automobile the same cautious position recom-

mends itself quite generally: so far as actual human beings go, the most reasonable course for us now is to suspend judgment as to whether any of them is certain of more than hardly anything, if anything at all.[2]

V. Does Knowing Require Being Certain?

One tradition in philosophy holds that knowing requires being certain. As a matter of logical necessity, a man knows something only if he is certain of the thing. In this tradition, certainty is not taken lightly; rather, it is equated with absolute certainty. Even that most famous contemporary defender of common sense, G. E. Moore, is willing to equate knowing something with knowing the thing with absolute certainty.[3] I am rather inclined to hold with this traditional view, and it is now my purpose to argue that this view is at least a fairly reasonable one.

To a philosopher like Moore, I would have nothing left to say in my defense of skepticism. But recently some philosophers have contended that not certainty, but only belief, is required for knowing.[4] According to these thinkers, if a man's belief meets certain conditions not connected with his being certain, that mere belief may properly be counted as an instance or a bit of knowledge. And even more recently some philosophers have held that not even so much as belief is required for a man to know that something is so.[5] Thus, I must argue for the traditional view of knowing. But then what has led philosophers to move further and further away from the

2. For an interesting discussion of impersonal certainty, which in some ways is rather in line with my own discussion while in other ways against it, one might see Michael Anthony Slote's "Empirical Certainty and the Theory of Important Criteria," *Inquiry*, 10 (1967). Also, Slote makes helpful references to other writers in the philosophy of certainty.

3. See Moore's cited papers, especially "Certainty," p. 232.

4. An influential statement of this view is Roderick M. Chisholm's, to be found in the first chapter of each of his cited books. In "Experience and Factual Knowledge," I suggest a very similar view.

5. This view is advanced influentially by Colin Radford in "Knowledge by Examples," *Analysis*, 27.1 (1966) 1–11. In "An Analysis of Factual Knowledge," and Especially in "Our Knowledge of The Material World," I suggest this view.

traditional strong assertion that knowing something requires being certain of the thing?

My diagnosis of the situation is this. In everyday affairs we often speak loosely, charitably, and casually; we tend to let what we say pass as being true. I want to suggest that it is by being wrongly serious about this casual talk that philosphers (myself included) have come to think it rather easy to know things to be so. In particular, they have come to think that certainty is not needed. Thus typical in the contemporary literature is this sort of exchange. An examiner asks a student when a certain battle was fought. The student fumbles about and, eventually, unconfidently say what is true: "The Battle of Hastings was fought in 1066." It is supposed, quite properly, that this correct answer is a result of the student's reading. The examiner, being an ordinary mortal, allows that student knows the answer; he judges that the student knows that the Battle of Hastings was fought in 1066. Surely, it is suggested, the examiner is correct in his judgment even though this student clearly is not certain of the thing; therefore, knowing does not require being certain. But is the examiner really correct in asserting that the student knows the date of this battle? That is, do such exchanges give us good reason to think that knowing does not require certainty?

My recommendation is this. Let us try focusing on just those words most directly employed in expressing the concept whose conditions are our object of inquiry. This principle is quite generally applicable and, I think, quite easily applied. We may apply it by suitably juxtaposing certain terms, like "really" and "actually," with the terms most in question (here, the term "knows"). More strikingly, we may *emphasize* the terms in question. Thus, instead of looking at something as innocent as "He knows that they are alive," let us consider the more relevant "He (really) *knows* that they are alive."

Let us build some confidence that this principle is quite generally applicable, and that it will give us trustworthy results. Toward this end, we may focus on some thoughts about definite descriptions—that is, about expressions of the form "the so-and-so." About these expressions, it is a tradition to hold that they require uniqueness, or unique satisfaction, for their proper application. Thus, just as it is traditional to hold that a man knows something only if he is certain of it, so it is also traditional to hold that there is something which is the chair with seventeen legs only if there is exactly one chair with just that many legs. But, again, by being wrongly serious about our casual everyday talk, philosphers may come to deny the traditional view. They may do this by being wrongly serious, I think, about the following sort of ordinary exchange. Suppose an examiner asks a student, "Who is the father of Nelson Rockefeller, the present Governor of New York State?" The student replies, "Nelson Rockefeller is the son of John D. Rockefeller, Jr." No doubt, the examiner will allow that, by implication, the student got the right answer; he will judge that what the student said is true even though the examiner is correctly confident that the elder Rockefeller sired other sons. Just so, one might well argue that definite descriptions, like "the son of X," do not require uniqueness. But against this argument from the everyday flow of talk, let us insist that we focus on the relevant conception by employing our standard means for emphasizing the most directly relevant term. Thus, while we might feel nothing contradictory at first in saying, "Nelson Rockefeller is the son of John D. Rockefeller, Jr., and so is Winthrop Rockefeller," we must confess that even initially we would have quite different feelings about our saying "Nelson Rockefeller is actually *the* son of John D. Rockefeller, Jr., and so is Winthrop Rockefeller." With the latter, where emphasis is brought to bear, we cannot help but feel that what is asserted is inconsistent. And, with this, we feel differently about the original remark, feeling it to be essentially the same assertion and so inconsistent as well. Thus, it seems that when we focus on things properly, we may assume that definite descriptions do require uniqueness.

Let us now apply our principle to the question of knowing. Here, while we might feel nothing contradictory at first in saying "He knows that it is raining, but he isn't certain of it," we would feel differently about our saying "He really *knows* that it is raining, but he isn't certain of it." And, if anything, this feeling of contradiction is only enhanced when we further emphasize, "He really *knows* that it is raining, but he isn't actually *certain* of it." Thus it is plausible to suppose that what we said at first is actually inconsistent, and so that knowing does require being certain.

For my defense of skepticism, it now remains only to combine the result we have just reached with that at which we arrived in the previous section. Now, I have argued that each of two propositions deserves, if not our acceptance, at least the suspension of our judgment:

> That, in the case of every human being, there is hardly anything, if anything at all, of which he is certain.

> That (as a matter of necessity), in the case of every human being, the person knows something to be so only if he is certain of it.

But I think I have done more than just that. For the strength of the arguments given for this position on each of these two propositions is, I think, sufficient for warranting a similar position on propositions which are quite obvious consequences of the two of them together. One such consequential proposition is this:

> That, in the case of every human being, there is hardly anything, if anything at all, which the person knows to be so.

And so this third proposition, which is just the thesis of skepticism, also deserves, if not our acceptance, at least the suspension of our judgment. If this thesis is not reasonable to accept, then neither is its negation, the thesis of "common sense."[6]

6. Ancestors of the present paper were discussed in philosophy colloquia at the following schools: Brooklyn College of the City University of New York, The University of California at Berkeley, Columbia University, The University of Illinois at Chicago Circle, The Rockefeller University, Stanford University, and The University of Wisconsin at Madison. I am thankful to those who participated in the discussion. I would also like to thank each of these many people for help in getting to the present defense: Peter M. Brown, Richard Cartwright, Fred I. Dretske, Hartry Field, Bruce Freed, H. P. Grice, Robert Hambourger, Saul A. Kripke, Stephen Schiffer, Michael A. Slote, Sydney S. Shoemaker, Dennis W. Stampe, Julius Winberg, and Margaret Wilson, *all* of whom remain at least somewhat skeptical. Finally, I would like to thank the Graduate School of The University of Wisconsin at Madison for financial assistance during the preparation of this defense.

20

In Reply to
"A Defense of Skepticism"

JAMES CARGILE

In his paper "A Defense of Skepticism"[1] Peter Unger argues that "every human being knows, at best, hardly anything to be so. More specifically, I will argue that hardly anyone knows that 45 and 56 are equal to 101, if anyone at all" (p. 317).

Unger's reason for this claim is that (1) knowing entails being certain, and (2) hardly anything is certain.

In connection with (1), Unger rejects such an example as that of a student who is credited with knowing the answer on an exam even though he is not certain his answer is right. Unger says, "In everyday affairs we speak loosely, charitably, and casually." But if Unger is right, we would also be merely charitable in saying that even the teacher knows that 45 plus 56 is 101, since, if he is right, even teachers are not certain of this. So if Unger were right about certainty, there would be much better examples suggesting that knowing does not entail being certain than is usually thought.

Unger stresses the claim that by attacking knowledge on the question of certainty he is avoiding "normative" questions and is boldly "picking on what is just about the easiest requirement of knowledge." He says:

one more difficult requirement might be that the knower be completely *justified* in being certain. . . . I wanted this defense to avoid the more difficult requirements because they rely on normative terms—

Reprinted from *The Philosophical Review*, 81 (1972), 229–236, by kind permission of the author and editor.
1. [Chapter 19 in this volume.]

for example, the term "justified." The application of normative terms presents problems which, while worked over by many philosphers, are still too difficult to handle at all adequately. [P. 217]

So Unger is suggesting that it is, as a matter of fact, extremely unusual for anyone to be certain of anything. To support this, he has the following formula: if I am more certain that p than I am that q, then I am not certain that q. He applies this formula to his suggestion that for virtually any proposition, there is some other proposition that is more certain, and gets his conclusion, that virtually nothing is certain.

In my opinion, both this formula and the suggestion to which it is applied are preposterous. The idea that there is, for me at least, any proposition more certain than that 45 plus 56 equals 101 is false. The idea that there is a *series* of propositions beyond this latter proposition, each more certain than the one before, is worse than false.

Unger calls "certain" and "flat" and various others "absolute terms." He says "something is flat if and only if it is absolutely flat" (p. 326) and he seems to assume that, similarly, something is certain if and only if it is absolutely certain. He says that calling something very flat is to imply that it is not really flat, but only close to being so. And I take him to imply that to call something very certain is to imply it is not really certain.

Now if someone asks me, "Is he really certain?" and I reply firmly, "Yes, he is very certain," my reply, which is surely a correct form of speech, would be contradictory, on Unger's account. Perhaps Unger would remind us that "In everyday affairs we speak loosely, charitably, and casually." But then Unger's formula may be a case of being "loose, charitable and casual" with skepticism. I can understand an Ungerian saying that western Kansas is not really flat, but an Ungerian can understand my saying that western Kansas is really flat. Which of us would be exercising the greater charity is a matter of opinion.

Unger does not offer any statistics to support his suggestion that virtually no proposition is absolutely certain. But he does say, "Is it reasonable for us now to actually believe that many people are certain that there are automobiles: . . . we must then believe of these people that it is impossible for any of them ever to be more certain of his own existence than all of them now are of the existence of automobiles" (p. 332). And the implication is clearly that, like as not, one is, or could be taught to be, more certain of one's own existence than one now is that there are automobiles.

Unger says nothing to support this assumption. One thing which has been said occasionally in favor of it is that it is logically impossible to think you exist and be mistaken, while it is logically possible that someone should think there are automobiles and be mistaken. But then it is also logically impossible that someone should think that 45 plus 56 is 101 and be mistaken, and yet Unger claims that this latter proposition is not certain either. If he considers his own existence more certain than truths of arithmetic, he might appeal to the Cartesian idea that the *Cogito* is superior in clarity and distinctness to arithmetical truths. It might be said that arithmetical truths are propositions of a *kind* about which I have been mistaken, since I have sometimes mistaken a false proposition about arithmetic for a truth, while I have never been mistaken about a proposition like the proposition that I exist, since this is such a special proposition.

Here, then, are two considerations which some philosophers have advanced for regarding one's existence as specially certain: first, that it is logically impossible to believe mistakenly the proposition; and second, that the proposition is not even of a kind which it is logically possible to be mistaken in believing. Perhaps these considerations have seemed to relate to certainty because they sound as if they involve ruling out ways of being mistaken, or kinds of mistake one could make, and it is natural to assume that the less room there is for error, the more certain one is entitled to be.

I think it is wrong to think that ruling out the logical possibility of error is always a case of leaving less "room" for error, or that not ruling out the logical possibility of error is automatically to leave "room" for error. But at any rate, in typical cases in which the question of certainty arises, these considerations are just irrelevant.

For example, suppose that I am laid up with a broken leg, and from my bedroom window I seem to hear (by the bell) that the cow is in the garden. I call my wife, and she rushes out of the kitchen, leaving dinner to burn, only to find that the cow is not in the garden, but tethered nearby. She is irritated by my error. A few days later, I look out the window and actually see the cow break loose and head into the garden. I shout down to my wife in the kitchen, where she is having a second try at the fancy concoction which burned a few days before, "The cow is in the garden!" My wife calls back, in an anguished tone, "Are you certain?" I reply, "Yes, I can see her plainly." Recognizing the overriding emergency, my wife lets the recipe go again and rushes out to save the food supply.

Now, this is a case in which I am perfectly correct in saying I am certain. It is logically possible I am mistaken in thinking the cow is in the garden. It is logically possible that elves have taken a stuffed replica of the cow into the garden, and that no harm is being done to the vegetables. But to regard this as a reason for demurring in response to my wife's "Are you *certain?*" would be idiotic. Nor would the situation be any different if the question were the less natural "Is it certain?" I am right in saying not only that I am certain, but that it is certain, that the cow is in the garden.

Unger offers some remarks which might be mistaken for a reply to this example. He distinguishes between what it is all right to say "for practical purposes," and what is strictly speaking true. He says:

even if you do not really know, still, it may be that for practical purposes you are in a position with respect to the matter . . . which is not importantly different from knowing. If this is so, then it may be better, practically speaking, for you to believe falsely that you know than to have no belief at all here. [P. 321]

It seems clear that this remark about the practical use of "know" would also apply to "certain."

Unger compares this strictly incorrect, but practically useful, use of "know," with the use of such a term as "vacuum." It may be all right for me to call a certain region a vacuum even if it contains some tiny amount of gaseous stuff, because the region is just like a vacuum for practical purposes. It might in some contexts be silly and pointless for me to insist that a certain region is not a vacuum when it is close enough to being one for the purpose at hand. But what I say may nonetheless be true. Similarly with skepticism.

In my opinion, this is a very poor analogy. It may be that nature abhors a vacuum, and that there are no perfect vacuums. And there are not, in the physical world, any mathematically flat surfaces. But "vacuum" and "flat" do have very clear (and I do not mean "close to clear") applications within idealized systems which are themselves of considerable interest and even practical importance. A Euclidean plane is flat, and geometry is of considerable interest. And in physical theory, the notion of a perfect vacuum has applications. The absence of actual, real-life occasions for applying such terms as "perfect vacuum" or "mathematically flat" is compensated by their clear roles in important idealized systems.

This is not the case with "know." Perhaps the skeptic who says that the term "know" has no applications, or virtually none, in real-life situations, will be willing to formulate some idealized setup in which the term does have a use. But there is no such system which is not of overwhelming insignificance by contrast with the ordinary use of the term. The physical theory of vacuums would be nice to know if I were going to be dealing with what are "for practical purposes" vacuums. But the skeptic's theory of knowledge is worthless in dealing with what is "for practical purposes" knowledge.

One correct feature of Unger's remarks is that for practical purposes there is no difference between something's being strictly true and its being close enough to strictly true to be treated as true for practical purposes. But this obvious truth is no basis for claiming that claims to knowledge or certainty are hardly ever strictly true. It is just that if we ever do find that, for reasons of theory, some term which is frequently applied in everyday use does not really apply truly very often, we can ease the conflict between the theory and everyday usage by explaining the everyday use as "close enough for practical purposes." But the merit of such a proposal depends on the theory.

As has been observed, Unger gives no reason for thinking that people might be, or become, more certain of their own existence than they now are that there are automobiles. He says that of course people *might* all be this certain there are automobiles and that "each of them *feels* himself to be" this certain. But he says:

I think it somewhat rash for us actually to believe that they *are* all so certain. Certainty being an absolute and our understanding of people being rather rudimentary and incomplete, I think it more reasonable for us now to suspend judgment on the matter. [P. 332]

The reaons offered for not accepting the fact that most people *feel* absolutely certain there are automobiles (along with any other favorable considerations) as proof they *are* certain are, first, that "certainty is an absolute" and, second, that "our understanding of people is rather rudimentary." To say that certainty is an absolute is just to hark back to the formula that if p is more certain than q, then q is not certain. It is to give no reason at all for thinking that people are wrong to deny that anything is more certain than that there are automobiles. To say people would not qualify as certain there are automobiles if they could be more certain of something else is not to give a reason for thinking, contrary to what they think, that they could be more certain of something else.

The other reason offered, that our understanding of people is rather rudimentary, is difficult to comprehend. Perhaps the idea is that people are unpredictable, and may come to claim they have become more certain they exist than that there are automobiles. In a few years, the *Cogito* might become a national fad, with crowds milling in the streets chanting, "I exist! I exist! Nothing else is as certain as this!" Holding it to be certain there are automobiles might become associated with a defeatist attitude toward environmental pollution.

In my opinion, it is possible for a person to determine whether he is certain there are automobiles, without having to consider the possibility of his succumbing to Cartesianism at some future date. Being certain is not like, say, being as happy as you can be. It is easy to see how someone might think he is as happy as he could be, and then find later that he is happier than that. But Unger's own definition of "certain" makes certainty a different matter.

Unger says: " 'He is certain that p' means, within the bounds of nuance, '*In his mind,* it is not at all doubtful that p' " (p. 328). He also holds that "certain" has the same meaning in the impersonal context "It is certain that p." Perhaps this is right; but it is worth noting that "It is certain that p" entails p while "He is certain that p" does not.

At any rate, if someone feels that he has no doubt that p, and shows no doubt or hesitation about p, then what sense is there in suspending judgment as to whether, for him, it is at all doubtful that p? Of course he may come to doubt that p, either for good reason or because he responds stupidly to some sophistical rigmarole; but what reason would this be for supposing the doubts he has acquired were with him all along? Here, to plead that our knowledge of people is "rather rudimentary" is false caution.

It might be said that if my life had to be put at stake, I would rest easier staking it on the proposition that I exist than I would on the proposition that there are automobiles. It is far from obvious how I would feel in such a vaguely specified situation, but in any case, how I would feel has nothing to do with how I feel now. By exercising my imagination, I can make myself angry, sad, frightened, and so forth. Perhaps I could make myself feel what I would call feelings of doubt. And perhaps this is easier to do with respect to the proposition that I exist. But being able to work up a feeling of doubt by mental exercises is not the same as doubting.

Besides being unconvincing, Unger's argument is not up to what he promised at the beginning of his essay. He began by saying that, while he could not, of course, claim to know that little is known, he would show it is reasonable to believe that little is known. But at the crucial step just criticized we find him arguing that it is reasonable to suspend judgment on the question whether much is certain. And this falls short of arguing that it is reasonable to believe that very little is certain. But then even this more limited argument ends up in a question-begging suggestion that we be careful about questions involving our understanding of people.

It is interesting to contrast Unger's definition of "certain" with the views of another philospher who regards certainty as very rare. H. A. Prichard says:

I, for example, might be, as we say, thinking without question that the thing in front of me is a table, or that to-day is Tuesday, or that so-and-so came to see me last week. Cook Wilson said of this state that it simulates knowledge since, as is obvious, in this state there is no doubt or uncertainty. But it obviously is not the same as *being certain*. In such states we are, of course, constantly being mistaken, and unless we distinguish such states from being certain, we are apt to take instances of them as instances of our being certain and yet mistaken. And once we have noticed the distinction, we are forced to allow that we are certain of very much less than we should have said otherwise.[2]

Note that Prichard grants it as obvious in everyday cases that "there is no doubt or uncertainty." So by Unger's definition he would be required to grant that certainty is equally common. In my opinion, this is a good feature of Unger's definition. It is only strange that while accepting this definition, Unger should think that cases of certainty are rare.

Prichard regards it as part of the meaning of "certain" that it is impossible for someone to be certain and yet be mistaken. It even seems that he goes further than this and assumes that being certain entails the logical impossibility of being wrong. This idea has already been criticized.

It is pretty clear what Prichard means by "certain," and thus clear what he means by denying that he is certain there is a table in front of him (in a case where there is a table in front of him). He means that it is logically possible that there really is no table there, in spite of his impressions to the contrary. Some philosophers might regard this claim as unclear. But I think it is comprehensible. And even though it is a high redefinition of the ordinary word "certain," we may at least be grateful for the comprehensibility and bear in mind that the redefinition could have been worse.

Prichard's procedure really could benefit from Unger's dis-

2. H. A. Prichard, *Knowledge and Perception* (Oxford, 1930), pp. 96–97.

tinction between strict truth and being close enough for practical purposes. Ordinary cases in which we use "certain" may be close enough to "really certain" to be treated as such for all practical purposes.

In this way, we could see Prichard's redefinition of "certain" in proper perspective, as an altogether trifling matter. Consider, for example, some great question concerning certainty: can we be certain God exists? It would be just as exciting to learn that we could be close enough to certain to treat it as certain for all practical purposes, as it would be to learn we can be certain. It is a small matter to allow Prichard his use of "certain."

The same cannot be said for Unger, however. He does not provide a high redefinition of "certain." Rather, he suggests mysteries. I cannot find in myself any doubt whatsoever that there are automobiles, or that 45 plus 56 is 101. Even Prichard would acknowledge this. But Unger tells us that our knowledge of people is "rather incomplete." Let us suspend judgment and allow that there may be a doubt lurking somewhere, which is a doubt of mine, though utterly undetected now! It appears that Unger's reason for suspending judgment on the question whether we know much is that we do not know enough about people to be in a position to say people are certain about much. But this particular lack of knowledge about people could be remedied by simply listening to what the people are telling us, that they are certain.

21

Why Not Scepticism?

KEITH LEHRER

The sceptic has been mistreated. Sophisticated epistemologies have been developed in defense of dogmatic knowledge claims. Recently, theories of ignorance have been so rare that the name for such theories, *agnoiology*, sounds like the antique it is. Actually, James F. Ferrier [1] introduced both the terms *epistemology* and *agnoiology* into the philosophical lexicon, but the latter has fallen into disuse through lack of denotation. Scepticism suffers from many defects, or so say the dogmatists. Some have contended that scepticism is contradictory, others that it is meaningless, and still others that it amounts to nothing more than an ingenious restatement of what we already believe. One problem with refutations of scepticism is that they are overly plentiful and mutually inconsistent. This should create some suspicion in the minds of the philosophically wary that some theory of ignorance, an agnoiology, might sustain the contentions of scepticism. I shall develop an agnoiology for the defense of scepticism against dogmatic knowledge claims. By so doing I hope to convince you of the tenability and importance of theories of rational belief and action based on probability without knowledge.

The form of scepticism I wish to avow is more radical than traditional sceptics have been wont to defend. Some philoso-

Reprinted from *The Philosophical Forum*, 2.3 (1971), 283–298, by kind permission of the author and editor.

1. James F. Ferrier, *Institutes of Metaphysics* (Edinburgh and London: William Blackwood & Sons, 1854).

phers have maintained that we do not know about anything
beyond some necessary truths and some truths about our own
subjective states. But they have not denied that we do know
about those matters. I wish to seriously consider a stronger
form of scepticism, to wit, that we do not know anything.

I

Some qualification is necessary to avoid misunderstanding
and to escape the burden of replying to overeasy refutations.
The form of scepticism that concerns me does not embody the
thesis that we know that we do not know anything. That thesis
is obviously self-refuting. Rather, the contention is that no one
knows anything, not even that no one knows anything. You
might feel a surge of confidence in the face of such contention
simply because the sceptic has admitted that he does not know
that he is correct, and hence, that he does not know that you
are incorrect when you affirm that you do know something.
But this confidence is misplaced because scepticism entails that,
just as the sceptic does not know that we do not know anything,
so we do not know that we do know anything, and, moreover,
that we do not know anything.

In setting out to develop an agnoiology, the sceptic looks as
though he must inevitably fall into embarrassment. For, in saying why he says what he does, must he not fall back on the
claim that he knows various things to be true which support his
conclusion? Again the answer is negative. The sceptic is not
prevented by his agnoiology from believing most of the same
things that we believe; indeed, all his position debars him from
is believing in such things as would entail that we have knowledge. About devils, dust, and delight, he may believe what he
wishes. He may even consider some beliefs to be more prudent
than others or more useful, and he surely may distinguish between what is true and what is false.

He affirms that we know nothing, but he believes most of
what most men believe. He affirms much else besides, only
here he must be careful not to mislead with his sceptical
speech. For often when a man speaks we take him to be claiming to know, though he does not say he knows. Indeed, it is

perhaps more common than not to attach such implications to
the acts of speech we confront. However, there is nothing inevitable or irreversible in this practice. When a man wishes to tell
us what he thinks has transpired but does not wish to be understood as making any pretense to knowledge in the matter
whereof he speaks, we may understand him without any confu-
sion or perplexity. The agnoiologist who is about to defend
scepticism must be understood as speaking in a similar manner.
The premisses of his agnoiology must not be understood as
claims to knowledge but only formulations of what he believes
and hopes we shall concede. Not even the claim that conclusion
follows from premiss would be taken as a claim to knowledge.
His words are addressed to us in the full conviction that they
are the truth but without any pretense to knowledge.

II

Before attempting to offer any argument for so general a
thesis as one affirming universal ignorance, it is essential to
include in our agnoiology an account of what knowledge entails. And here we immediately confront the problem that
whatever one philosopher has said knowledge is another philosopher has rejected. Hence it is impossible to avoid controversy. Having written elsewhere on this subject, I shall have
to rely on those results. I shall consequently assume that if a
man knows *that p,* then it is true *that p.* It has seemed evident to
most epistemologists that no one can know anything to be true
which is not true. Second, I shall assume that if a man knows
that p, then he believes *that p.* This has been controverted, but I
shall not undertake any defense of the assumption here.[2] Next,
I shall assume that if a man knows *that p,* then he is completely
justified in believing *that p.* A word of explanation. As I am
using the locution, "completely justified," it is logically possible
that a man should be completely justified in believing something even though he has no justificatory argument to support

2. A defense is contained in the author's "Belief and Knowledge," *Philosophical Review,* 76 (1968), 491–499.

his belief.[3] However, as an agnoiologist I shall deny the existence of such beliefs. Though completely justified true belief is a necessary condition of knowledge, it is not sufficient for reasons that might further aid the cause of scepticism.

III

We may best serve the purposes of scepticism by developing our agnoiology in an area where the dogmatist considers himself to be the most invulnerable, namely with respect to those claims to knowledge that he considers to be most certain and beyond doubt. Two classes of such claims are those concerning some logical and mathematical truths as well as those concerning some of our present conscious states. Let us consider necessary truths.

One argument against the sceptic in these matters is that such beliefs are ones where all possibility of error is excluded by logical necessity. This argument is worth a moment of consideration, because by so doing the first agnoiological stronghold of scepticism may be secured. It is logically impossible to be mistaken in believing any necessary truth. If I believe that the axiom of choice is independent of the continuum hypothesis, and if it is a necessary truth that the axiom of choice is independent of the continuum hypothesis, then it is impossible that I should believe that the axiom of choice is independent of the continuum hypothesis and also be in error. Of course, this is also true of more mundane beliefs like my belief that there is a natural number greater than two and less than five which is prime.

However, the above-mentioned fact, if it constituted any defense of dogmatism, would constitute equally good grounds for the wildest forms of speculation concerning the necessary and the impossible. For, it is logically impossible to be mistaken when one believes any statement which is a necessary truth no matter how speculative or groundless such a belief may be. If it is necessarily true *that p,* then the statement that I am mistaken

3. The intended use of this location is explained in the author's "Knowledge, Truth and Evidence," *Analysis,* 25.5 (1965) 168–175.

in believing *that p* would be equivalent to the conjunctive statement that I believe *that p* and it is false *that p*. If it is necessarily true *that p*, then the statement that it is false *that p* cannot possibly be true. Moreover, no conjunctive statement entailing that it is false *that p* could possibly be true either. Therefore, if it is necessarily true *that p*, then it cannot possibly be true that I am mistaken in believing *that p*. No one can possibly be mistaken in believing any necessary truth.

What the preceding proves is that if the dogmatist argues that a person knows that a statement is true whenever it is logically impossible for him to be mistaken in believing it, then he will be committed to the implausible conclusion that a person knows a mathematical statement to be true whenever he correctly believes it to be so no matter how foolish or groundless his belief. However, this violates our assumption that a belief must be completely justified as well as true or else we lack knowledge. Before any proof was forthcoming, someone might have believed that the axiom of choice was independent of the continuum hypothesis, but he did not know it. There is a distinction of justification between being right in mathematics and knowing that one is right. Of course, our agnoiology does not imply that anyone ever does know anything but it does imply that *if* anyone knows anything, then that person must not only have true belief, but complete justification as well.

Thus the preceding argument shows that we cannot assume a man knows whereof he believes simply because it is logically impossible that he should be mistaken in what he believes. For, he may have no proof or justification for believing what he does. Indeed, we might wish to say of the man that he could have been mistaken even though it was logically impossible that he should have been mistaken. What is the force of this *could* which defies logical possibility? In what sense could he have been mistaken? The answer is—he could have been mistaken in the sense that, for all he knows, what he believes is false. This, in turn, means that what he knows does not establish that what he believes is true. And, so, if he knows nothing, then he could have been mistaken even though it is logically impossible that he should be mistaken.

The logical impossibility of error in beliefs concerning the impossible and the necessary, that is, statements which if true are necessary and if false are impossible, is no bulwark against scepticism. The logical impossibility of error in such matters is perfectly consistent with complete ignorance. Thus our agnoiology shows that there is no refutation of scepticism to be built on such logical impossibility of false belief.

IV

Let us, however, leave the realm of the necessary and the impossible for that of the contingent. Suppose a man believes some contingent statement to be true, a statement which is neither logically necessary nor logically impossible. What if, in such a case, it is logically impossible for the man to believe falsely? Must not we concede that the man knows?

Before answering this question let us note how few beliefs have the character in question. Some philosophers have thought that beliefs about one's current psychological states were ones that excluded the logical possibility of error. But this is, I am convinced, mostly mistaken. Let me explain why.

First, there are almost no beliefs about one's own present states of consciousness that it is logically inconsistent to suppose should be false. The best candidates for such incorrigible beliefs are ones concerning one's present sensations or thoughts. But it is logically possible for such beliefs to be mistaken. Consider sensations first. Suppose it is affirmed that if a person believes that he is having sensation S, a pain for example, then it is logically impossible that such a belief should be mistaken. This is not so. One might believe one is having a sensation S, a pain for example, because one is having a different sensation, S*, an itch for example, and one has mistaken S* for S, that is, one has mistaken an itch for a pain. How could this happen? It might happen either because of some general belief, to wit, that itches are pains, which one has been led to believe by some authority, or one may simply be misled on this occasion because one has been told by some authority that one will experience a pain. In short, one might have some false belief which together with the sensation of an itch produces the belief that one is in pain. Beliefs about sensations can be inferential, and one can infer that one is in a conscious state that one is not in by inferring from some false belief that this is so. One might believe that sensation S* is S, just as with respect to thoughts, one might believe that some thought T* is T, and thus arrive at the mistaken conclusion that one is in state S or state T because one is in state S* or T*.[4]

The preceding argument might be bolstered by examples to please the fancy, but the argument is so simple as to render them superfluous. For all that I have assumed is that it is logically possible for a person, under the influence of authority, to mistake one conscious state for another and thus to believe that he is in a conscious state when in fact he is not in that state. The argument applies to almost all conscious states with a notable exception. If I believe that I believe something, then the first belief does seem to be one such that it is logically impossible that I should be mistaken. For, it is logically inconsistent to suppose both that I believe that I believe something and that I do not believe anything. It would be tempting to rid oneself of such troublesome cases by saying that it does not make sense to speak of believing that one believes, but I do not believe that such a contention is correct. So, I concede that the set of incorrigible beliefs about one's own conscious states is not null.

V

The preceding argument shows how little contingent knowledge we would need to concede to the dogmatist even if we conceded that we know those beliefs to be true which are such as to exclude the logical possibility of error. But the sceptic need not concede that we know even that. It is not the logical impossibility of error that could yield knowledge but rather our *knowledge* of the logical impossibility of error. Consider the mathematical case again. If I know that something is logically impossible, for example, if I know that it is contradictory to suppose that the axiom of choice and the continuum hypothesis are not independent, then I know that the axiom of choice

4. Cf. Kathryn Parsons, "Mistaking Sensations," *Philosophical Review*, 79 (1970), 201–213.

is independent of the continuum hypothesis. It is not the logical impossibility of error by itself that guarantees knowledge but only *knowledge* of the logical impossibility. *If* we know that it is logically impossible that certain of our beliefs are mistaken, then, no doubt, we know that those beliefs are true. But this *if* is the noose that strangles dogmatism. For, even if we agree it is logically impossible for certain contingent beliefs to be mistaken, still it does not follow that we *know* that it is logically impossible for those beliefs to be mistaken, and, hence it does not follow that we know that the beliefs are true. A sceptic may contend that we do not *know* that anything is logically impossible however strongly convinced we may be. And he may conclude that we do not know that those beliefs are true even where the logical possibility of error is excluded, because we do not know that the logical possibility of error is excluded.

VI

So far, I have argued for the logical consistency of scepticism. But you may have your doubts about whether scepticism makes any sense at all. There are familiar lingering doubts about the intelligibility of such matters which we have inherited from Wittgenstein and his followers. Let us put these doubts on the therapeutic couch. The sceptic says, "No one knows anything." Appalled you reply, "I know many things, that I see this paper for example." The sceptic says you do not know. Now if we imagine an ordinary situation, which this is not, where a man denies that you know that you see this paper, you would not understand. His speech act would not make sense to you. Notice, however, that this does not imply that you would not understand what he has said, or that he would have said nothing. On the contrary, you would understand what he has said, but you would not understand his saying it. You cannot understand why he said it. When a man denies that we know what we see right before our eyes, ordinarily we do not understand his behavior. But this is the *ordinary* case. In the extraordinary case in which men are not about their humdrum practical affairs but are engaged in intellectual speculation, we may well understand a man denying that we know things. We understand why

he said it. He said it because he is a sceptic showing his agnoiological goods.

From these considerations one can appreciate that we must
avoid the trap of refuting the sceptic by intentionally misunderstanding his behavior. If we treat his speech acts like those of a
man with more ordinary and less intellectual interests, we are
guilty of bad manners and bad philosophy. We know why he
utters the words he does, he utters them to affirm his agnoiology and to deny that we know what we say we know. Thus
we can understand his behavior, it does make sense, but a
doubt still lingers. Does what he says really make sense?

Very intelligent philosophers have held widely divergent
views on this matter. Some have thought that what he said is
meaningless. If this contention has no more content than to
imply that what the sceptic says is nonsense, then perhaps it is
correct, *if* the sceptic is mistaken. There is a sense of "nonsense" in which it is nonsense to say what is obviously false. If a
man says what is obviously false, we say, "Nonsense!" and that
is well said. However, this sort of remark is a compliment that
may be returned. When we say we know, the sceptic may re-
tort, "Nonsense!" and then we shall have both relieved our
frustrations without any notable philosophical illumination.
However, those who have maintained that what the sceptic says
is meaningless have implied that he utters words with the intent
of affirming or asserting the truth of something, but, in fact, he
has not succeeded in asserting or affirming the truth of anything! Negatively put, he intended to deny something by uttering the words he did, namely, that we know the things we think
we know, but he has failed because the words he utters are
without meaning.

The sceptic may surely regard it as a peculiar matter that
words should go about losing their meaning in this way. You
say you know, the sceptic says you do not know, and according
to the dogmatist, the words the sceptic utters suddenly have no
meaning. But this is implausible. We do understand what the
sceptic says precisely because we can tell that he has denied
what we have affirmed. No matter how hard one tries not to
understand, one cannot fail to understand that much. Thus,

because you understand what you affirm, you must understand what the sceptic denies. You might still think the sceptic is talking nonsense—but it is meaningful. Even a dogmatist must concede that the sceptic speaks meaningful nonsense.

VII

A related attempt to demolish the sceptic semantically is to aver that the systematic difference from ordinary practice in the use of the word "know" by the sceptic shows that he means something different by that term than we do. Here we have shifted from the position that he does not mean anything to the thesis that he means something different. The model for this argument is the foreigner who calls all and only blue things "red" and so we conclude that he means by the term "red" what we mean by the term "blue." The best explanation of the use that the foreigner makes of the word "red" is that what he means by "red" is what we mean by the word "blue", but a similar conclusion would be quite inappropriate in the case of the sceptic. We can easily explain why the sceptic uses the word "know" as he does without supposing that he means something different by the term. The way in which he uses the term is most readily and simply explained by supposing that he believes something different from the rest of us. This contrasts with the case of the foreigner, where the way in which he uses the word "red" is most readily and simply explained by supposing that he means something different by that term than we do. Thus, the correct conclusion to draw is that the sceptic means what we mean by the word "know", and the reason he says what he does is that he believes that nobody knows anything. What could be simpler?

In the last two sections I have argued that scepticism is logically consistent and that the words of the sceptic may be understood as having meaning. He denies what we assert and there is nothing inconsistent or semantically unacceptable in so doing. Language allows for such radical disagreement as that between the sceptic and his detractors. It is this resource of language that provides for possibility of speculation and innovation. Thus, the question to which we must now turn is this—if the

356   Keith Lehrer

position of scepticism is neither meaningless nor contradictory, then why not scepticism?

VIII

The most common answer stems from Thomas Reid. It is based on the assumption that some beliefs are completely justified, because they are beliefs of a special kind which are justified without any supporting justificatory argument.[5] Beliefs of this kind are *basic* beliefs. Thus, if a man believes *that p*, where this is a basic belief of kind K, then he is completely justified in believing *that p* without argument unless there is some good reason for believing *p* to be false. The kind K of basic beliefs may be specified differently by philosophers of different epistemic biases, which already offers succor to the sceptic, but dogmatists have generally agreed that at least some kinds of perceptual beliefs, memory beliefs, and beliefs concerning our conscious states are among them.

Now it is not at all difficult to conceive of some hypothesis that would yield the conclusion that beliefs of the kind in question are not justified, indeed, which if true would justify us in concluding that the beliefs in question were more often false than true. The sceptical hypothesis might run as follows. There are a group of creatures in another galaxy, call them Googols, whose intellectual capacity is 10^{100} that of men, and who amuse themselves by sending out a peculiar kind of wave that affects our brain in such a way that our beliefs about the world are mostly incorrect. This form of error infects beliefs of every kind, but most of our beliefs, though erroneous, are nevertheless very nearly correct. This allows us to survive and manipulate our environment. However, whether any belief of any man is correct or even nearly correct depends entirely on the whimsy of some Googol rather than on the capacities and faculties of the man. If you are inclined to wonder why the Googols do not know anything, it is because there is another group of men, call them Googolplexes, whose intellectual capacity is

5. Thomas Reid, *The Works of Thomas Reid, D.D.* (Edinburgh: Maclaugh and Steward, 1863), p. 234.

10^{100} that of the Googols, and who amuse themselves by sending out a peculiar wave that affects the brains of Googols in such a way that . . . I think you can see how the story goes from here. I shall refer to this hypothesis as the *sceptical hypothesis*. On such a hypothesis our beliefs about our conscious states, what we perceive by our senses, or recall from memory, are more often erroneous than correct. Such a sceptical hypothesis as this would, the sceptic argues, entail that the beliefs in question are not completely justified.

The reply of the dogmatist to such imaginings might be that we are not only justified in those basic beliefs, we are also justified in rejecting any hypothesis, such as the sceptical one, which conflicts with those beliefs. But the sceptic may surely intercede long enough to protest that he has been ruled out by fiat. The beliefs of common sense are said to be basic and thus completely justified without any justificatory arguments. But why, the sceptic may query, should the dogmatists' beliefs be considered completely justified without argument and his hypothesis be rejected without argument? Dogmatists affirm that the beliefs of common sense are innocent until proven guilty, but why, the sceptic might inquire, should his hypothesis not receive comparable treatment before the bar of evidence? Why not regard the sceptical hypothesis as innocent until proven guilty. Indeed, the sceptic might continue, why not regard all belief as innocent until proven guilty? And, he might add, where all is innocence, nothing is justified or unjustified, which is precisely the agnoiology of scepticism.

Some opponents of scepticism have been willing to concede that unless we hold some beliefs to be justified without argument, then we must surely accept the conclusion of scepticism. But, when replying to the sceptic, it will not do to say that we must regard the beliefs of common sense as justified or else we shall wind up on the road to scepticism. For that is precisely the route the sceptic would have us travel.

Let me clarify the preceding argument. In one passage, Bishop Berkeley replics to a dogmatist by appeal to the agnoiological precept that the burden of proof always lies with

the affirmative.[6] The precept could be doubted, and generally
arguments about where the burden of proof lies are unproduc-
tive. It is more reasonable to suppose that such questions are
best left to courts of law where they have suitable application.
In philosophy a different principle of agnoiology is appropriate, to wit, that no hypothesis should be rejected as unjustified
without argument against it. Consequently, if the sceptic puts
forth a hypothesis inconsistent with the hypotheses of common
sense, then there is no burden of proof on either side, but neither may one side to the dispute be judged unjustified in believing his hypothesis unless an argument is produced to show
that this is so. If contradictory hypotheses are put forth without
reason being given to show that one side is correct and the
other in error, then neither party may be fairly stigmatized as
unjustified. However, if a belief is completely justified, then
those with which it conflicts are unjustified. Therefore, if neither of the conflicting hypotheses is shown to be unjustified,
then we must refrain from concluding that belief in one of the
hypotheses is completely justified.

We have here an argument that does not prejudicially presuppose that the burden of proof rests on one side or the other
but instead takes an impartial view of the matter and refuses to
side with either party until some argument has been given.
Thomas Reid was wont to argue that the beliefs of common
sense had a right of ancient possession and were justified until
shown to be unjustified.[7] But such epistemology favors the sen-
timents of conservative defenders of the status quo in both philosophy and politics. And the principle that, what is, is justified,
is not a better principle of epistemology than of politics or
morals. It should be supplanted by the agnoiological principle
of impartiality. Thus, before scepticism may be rejected as unjustified, some argument must be given to show that the infamous hypotheses employed by sceptics are incorrect and the
beliefs of common sense have the truth on their side. If this is
not done, then the beliefs of common sense are not completely

6. George Berkeley, *Dialogues I* in *Principles, Dialogues and Correspondence.*
C. M. Turbayne, ed. (New York: Bobbs-Merrill, 1965), p. 146.
7. Ibid., p. 617.

justified, because conflicting sceptical hypotheses have not been shown to be unjustified. From this premiss it follows in a single step that we do not know those beliefs to be true because they are not completely justified. And then the sceptic wins the day.

IX

The preceding agnoiological argument can be extended to defeat a whole range of alleged refutations of scepticism. For example, some philosophers have rejected scepticism on the grounds that the sceptic is denying our standards of evidence or our criteria of justification or something of the sort. Now, of course, this may be trivially true; obviously the sceptic is denying that we are completely justified in certain beliefs which we consider to be completely justified, and if that constitutes rejecting our ordinary standards or criteria of evidence, then the sceptic is indeed denying them. But that is no argument against the sceptic; it is a restatement of his position. Unless we can show that the sceptical hypothesis is false, we cannot justly conclude that it is unjustified. In that case our beliefs, which contradict the sceptical hypotheses, are not completely justified. So much the worse for our standards or criteria of evidence.

Next, there are arguments claiming that the sceptic is making proposals which undermine our conceptual framework and change the very concepts we use to formulate our beliefs. The reply is twofold. Sometimes talking about changing concepts is a disguised way of talking about changing meaning of words. I have already argued that scepticism does not have that consequence. So I discount that contention. Other than that, the change of concepts implied by scepticism seems to me, to amount to no more than a change of belief, perhaps of very fundamental beliefs. The reply to this objection is that first, the agnoiology of the sceptic allows him to embrace most of the same beliefs we do. He need not *believe* the sceptical hypothesis to argue that if the sceptical hypothesis is true, then our more familiar beliefs are more often false than true. By thus employing the hypothesis, he has placed us in a position of either showing the hypothesis to be false, or else conceding that our beliefs are not completely justified. Thus the sceptic need not advocate ceasing to believe those fundamental hypotheses which constitute the assumptions, presuppositions, or what not of our conceptual framework. He only denies that we know those beliefs to be true.

Thus appeals to ancient rights, standards of evidence, and conceptual frameworks are all equally ineffective against the basic challenge of scepticism, to wit—either show that the sceptical hypothesis is false and unjustified or concede that beliefs inconsistent with that hypothesis are not completely justified!

X

We must now turn to a rather different sort of maneuver against the sceptic. It might be conceded that we cannot show that our beliefs are true and the sceptical hypothesis false, but contended that we can show that our beliefs are completely justified, not perhaps for the purpose of arriving at the truth, but for other epistemic ends. Thus it has been proposed that we believe whatever will facilitate explanation and increase our information. If a person is seeking to have beliefs which facilitate explanation and increase information, then he is completely justified in adopting beliefs contributing to those objectives. This argument against scepticism is, I believe, the very strongest that can be offered. For, even if we can offer no argument to show that our beliefs are true and the sceptical hypothesis false, still we may be completely justified in our beliefs in terms of objectives other than truth.

Finally, the move has an intuitive appeal. For, the sceptical hypothesis according to which most of our beliefs arise because of the deception of Googols yields results that would make it difficult to explain in a satisfactory manner what we believe to be the case and, it would make it even more difficult for us to increase our information about the world. Many generalizations about the world, and theories as well, would turn out to be incorrect on that hypothesis, thus making explanation difficult and complicated. Moreover, we would, by hypothesis, have no way of telling when our beliefs give us information about the world and when we are simply being misled by the Googols. All in all the sceptical hypothesis is quite unsatisfac-

tory from the standpoint of explaining things and increasing
our information; so unsatisfactory that anyone seeking to explain as much as possible and to increase his information as
much as possible would be completely justified in rejecting it.

Is there any reply to this line of argument? The sceptic might
reply that he is under no obligation to accept the ends of facili-
tating explanation and increasing information. But this will not
refute the claim that we who do accept such ends are completely justified in believing what we do for the sake of obtaining those objectives. There is a better line of reply available to
the sceptic, namely, that our disregard for truth will, in the
final accounting, destroy our assets. For agnoiology shows that
such pragmatic justification of belief ultimately depends on the
assumption that the beliefs are true. Suppose we adopt those
beliefs that are most full of explanatory power and informative
content, and those admirable beliefs turn out to be false. In
that case, by adopting those beliefs we shall have correctly explained nothing and increased our genuine information not at
all. For any belief to correctly explain or genuinely inform it
must first be true. Only what correctly explains or genuinely in-
forms can constitute knowledge. Therefore, we must be completely justified in believing what we do simply because by so
doing we shall obtain true beliefs, or else our beliefs are not
completely justified in the manner requisite for knowledge.

XI

The preceding line of argument leads to an inevitable conclusion. To meet the agnoiological challenge of scepticism, we
must provide some argument to show that the sceptical hypothesis is false and that the beliefs of common sense are correct.
And this leads to a second equally inescapable conclusion. The
challenge cannot be met. Many reasons may be given for not
believing the sceptical hypothesis. Indeed, a sceptic himself need
not believe the sceptical hypothesis, and he might agree that
there are practical disadvantages in believing such a hypothesis.
But he might justifiably insist that we are not completely justified in concluding that the hypothesis is *false*. The hypothesis
might seem silly, it might interfere with the attempt to explain

things, and it might make it very difficult to arrive at any sensible set of beliefs for conducting practical affairs and scientific investigations. There are perfectly cogent practical considerations, the sceptic might concede, for not believing the hypothesis. However, agnoiology rejects the premiss contending that inconvenient hypotheses are false. To suppose that would be to trip back into the clutches of a simplistic pragmatism from which we have been rescued all too recently.

The principal argument offered to show that sceptical hypotheses are false is simply that they conflict with our dogmatic beliefs. Since it is precisely the justification of the latter that is in question, this conflict cannot be taken to adjudicate against the sceptical hypothesis. We are not completely justified in rejecting the sceptical hypothesis, and thus we are not completely justified in believing the others. We do not know that the sceptical hypothesis is false, and thus we do not know that anything else is true. That is the agnoiology that sustains scepticism.

XII

In conclusion, let me remark that we need not mourn the passing of knowledge as a great loss. The assumption of dogmatists that some beliefs are completely justified and that they are true, is not a great asset in scientific inquiry where all contentions should be subject to question and must be defended on demand. Moreover, the sceptic is not deprived of those practical beliefs necessary to carrying on the business of practical affairs. Indeed, economists and philosophers have suggested that an analysis of rational choice requires only subjective probability, which is a coherent measure of belief, and the utilities we attach to various outcomes.

It might seem that to introduce an appeal to probabilities is to concede the day to scepticism because the probabilities must be based on observational evidence and the latter must be something we know to be true. But this objection is unsound. First, as Richard Jeffrey has shown, we may employ a concept of subjective probability in which no observation statement is assigned a probability of unity.[8] Moreover, we may reassign probabilities on the basis of sense experience without assigning the probability of unity to any such statement. Finally, even if we do assign a probability of unity to a statement, for example, to a tautology, we need not interpret this assignment as meaning that we know the statement to be true. To be sure, the statement must have a kind of subjective certainty, but this may be analyzed in terms of the betting preferences of the subject rather than as knowledge. If there is any statement of which a person feels so certain that he would prefer to bet the statement is true rather than false no matter what the odds, then the subjective probability of that statement for that man is unity. It does not follow that he knows the statement to be true.

Finally, I would contend that just as we can give an analysis of rational decision in terms of probabilities and practical values, so we can give an analysis of rational belief on the basis of probabilities and epistemic values. In the first case we maximize practical utilities and in the second case we maximize epistemic ones. Neither analysis requires the assumption that we know anything. We can instead regard practical action and scientific inquiry as aiming at the satisfaction of objectives appropriate to each sphere. We change our beliefs to better satisfy those objectives. Thus, we may, while remaining sceptics, contend that our beliefs and actions are rational even though we agree that such beliefs are not so completely justified as to constitute knowledge. As such, all beliefs, even those we consider rational, are subject to critical review. None can be exempted from evaluation on the grounds that it is known to be true without need of supporting argument. Such are the fruits of agnoiology.[9]

8. Richard Jeffrey, *The Logic of Decision* (New York: McGraw-Hill, 1965).

9. An earlier version of this paper was presented at the Pacific Coast Division Meetings of the American Philosophical Association in Los Angeles on May 28, 1971. Support by N.S.F. of related projects on inductive inference enabled me to find time to appreciate the merits of scepticism. So many philosophers have written about scepticism that to cite them all would result in more footnotes than content. Instead, I only footnote sources that are unfamiliar or specifically discussed. However, I should like to cite "A Defense of Scepticism" in the *Philosophical Review*, April 1971, by Peter Unger as an interesting bit of recent agnoiology [Chapter 19 in the present volume].

22

Why Scepticism?

DAN TURNER

In his article "Why Not Scepticism?"[1] Lehrer argues for two general claims. One is: Why not scepticism?, or, more perspicuously, that all of the standard arguments purporting to show scepticism false or untenable fail. The other is that scepticism is true. I shall be concerned in this paper with the other.

The type of scepticism Lehrer takes himself to be defending in his article is, as he admits, a very radical form. It is that no one knows anything. (347) (I believe Lehrer intends this thesis to be a statement of empirical fact, not a necessary truth.) As far as I can tell, his general argument (GA) for his radical form of scepticism is this:

(GA)

    (I) If someone S knows something (that p), then S is completely justified in believing that p.

    (II) No one is completely justified in believing anything.

Thus,

    (III) No one knows anything.

We can hardly evaluate (GA) unless we have some idea of what Lehrer means by complete justification. Lehrer does not tell us in his article; however, in a reply to Lehrer, Lesher[2] did some work on this notion and showed that for one way of construing Lehrer's remarks, (GA) fails. In this paper, I shall construe

1. Keith Lehrer, "Why Not Scepticism?" [Chapter 21 in this volume].
2. James Lesher, "Lehrer's Sceptical Hypothesis," *Philosophical Forum*, 4 (1973), 299–302.

Lehrer's remarks in another way, providing a different reconstruction of Lehrer's argument, and show that it fails, also.

We begin by trying to reconstruct Lehrer's argument for (II).
Lehrer argues for (II) by appealing to what he calls 'the sceptical hypothesis,' which is as follows (356).

There are a group of creatures in another galaxy, call them Googols,
whose intellectual capacity is 10^{100} that of men, and who amuse themselves by sending out a peculiar kind of wave that affects our brain in
such a way that our beliefs about the world are mostly incorrect. This
form of error infects beliefs of every kind, but most of our beliefs,
though erroneous, are nevertheless very nearly correct. This allows us
to survive and manipulate our environment. However, whether any
belief of any man is correct or even nearly correct depends entirely on
the whimsy of some Googol rather than on the capacities and faculties
of the man.

Lehrer then says that "such a sceptical hypothesis would . . .
entail that the beliefs in question are not completely justified."
(357) It appears that this claim is at least as strong as either

> (X) If the sceptical hypothesis is true, then no one is com-
> pletely justified in believing anything.

or

> (Y) If it is possible that the sceptical hypothesis is true, then
> no one is completely justified in believing anything.

(X) is certainly much less problematic (with respect to truth
value) than (Y). If we give Lehrer (X), then to get (II) from it in
any interesting way he must appeal to premises which support:

> (S) The sceptical hypothesis is true.

However, it is clear (and Lehrer would agree) that there is no
reason to believe (S). It is also clear that Lehrer does not intend
to argue for (II) via (X) and (S). This leaves (Y). Regarding (Y)
we shall only remark that the hypothesis that Lehrer intends to
argue for (II) via (Y) is the interpretation adopted by Lesher,
who impugns Lehrer's argument as so interpreted.

Let us then see if we can find a plausible third interpretation.
Toward this end consider the following remarks of Lehrer's
(358–359):

If a belief is completely justified, then those with which it conflicts are
unjustified.

. . . before scepticism may be rejected as unjustified, some argument must be given to show that the infamous hypotheses employed by sceptics are incorrect and the beliefs of common sense have truth on their side. If this is not done, then the beliefs of common sense are not completely justified, because conflicting sceptical hypotheses have not been shown to be unjustified.

These point the way to a third interpretation of Lehrer's argument for (II), as follows:

> (Z) If the sceptical hypothesis is not shown to be unjustified, then no one is completely justified in believing anything.
>
> (aZ) The sceptical hypothesis is not shown to be unjustified.

from which (II) follows by modus ponens.

Moreover, from the remarks of Lehrer's below, we can construct an argument for (aZ). The relevant passages are these (361, 362):

. . . we must be completely justified in believing what we do simply because by so doing we shall obtain true beliefs, or else our beliefs are not completely justified in the manner requisite for knowledge.

The preceding line of argument leads to an inevitable conclusion. To meet the agnoiological challenge of scepticism, we must provide some argument to show that the sceptical hypothesis is false and that the beliefs of common sense are correct. And this leads to a second equally inescapable conclusion. The challenge cannot be met.

The principal argument offered to show that sceptical hypotheses are false is simply that they conflict with our dogmatic beliefs. Since it is precisely the justification of the latter that is in question, this conflict cannot be taken to adjudicate against the sceptical hypothesis.

On the basis of these remarks and those previously quoted I construct the following argument for (aZ).

> (1) The sceptical hypothesis is shown to be unjustified only if there is some argument which shows it to be false.
>
> (2) All arguments which are offered in the attempt to show the sceptical hypothesis false beg the question against it.
>
> (3) If (2), then there are no arguments which show the sceptical hypothesis false.

Thus,

(4) There are no arguments which show the sceptical hypothesis false.

Thus,

(aZ) The sceptical hypothesis is not shown to be unjustified.

Now suppose we ask why anyone would believe (1). The most obvious reason seems to be that (1) is an instance of the more general claim:

(P1) An hypothesis is shown to be unjustified only if there is some argument which shows it to be false.

Read straightforwardly (P1) seems clearly problematic. For (P1) requires, if it has a chance of being true, a very strong (non-straightforward) sense of 'unjustified.' If 'sJp' is short for 's is justified in believing that p' then the sense of 'unjustified' required in (P1) is *not* the negation of 'sJp,' but rather the (non-straightforward) internal negation of 'sJp,' viz., 'sJ-p.' If the weaker (straightforward) sense of 'unjustified' is employed (P1) would be obviously false, for on the weaker sense no more is needed to show an hypothesis unjustified than to show that there is *no justification* for it; and this is clearly less demanding than to require the existence of an argument which shows the hypothesis false. To keep this clear, let us rewrite (P1) as follows:

(P1') Someone is justified in believing an hypothesis false only if there is some argument showing it to be false.

To remain consistent with (P1') we rewrite (1) and (aZ) (using the new names '(1')' and '(aZ'),' respectively). (We should also make corresponding changes in (Z).) Making the appropriate changes, the argument for (aZ') is:

(A1)

(1') Someone is justified in believing the sceptical hypothesis false only if there is some argument which shows it to be false.

(2) All arguments which are offered in the attempt to show the sceptical hypothesis false beg the question against it.

(3) If (2), then there are no arguments which show the sceptical hypothesis false.

Thus,

> (4) There are no arguments which show the sceptical
> hypothesis false.

Thus,

> (aZ') No one is justified in believing the sceptical hypoth-
> esis false.

We have already seen that (1') is an instance of the more general claim (P1'). (3) also appears to be justified, if at all, as an instance of a more general claim, viz.:

> (P3) If all arguments which are offered in an attempt to
> show an hypothesis false are question begging, then
> there are no arguments showing that hypothesis false.

With this observation we can impugn (A1) by constructing the following argument (A2), on analogy to (A1). Let H = "Every premise of every argument is false." Then we have

> (A2)
>
> (1a) Someone is justified in believing H false only if there
> is some argument which shows it to be false.
>
> (2a) All arguments which are offered in the attempt to
> show H false are question begging.
>
> (3a) If (2a), then there are no arguments which show H
> false.

Thus,

> (4a) There are no arguments which show H false.

Thus,

> (5a) No one is justified in believing H false.

Now I take it that (5a) is uncontroversially false.[3] Thus, since (A2) is valid at least one of its premises is false.

But (2a) is not false; or, at least, Lehrer is in no position to argue that it is. For consider any argument (A) which, let us suppose, is offered in the attempt to show H false. (A) works against H only if (A) has true premises. But H implies trivially that (A) does not have true premises. Thus, to offer an argument against H is to assume the truth of some premises, which

---

3. Notice that if (5a) said, "No one is *completely* justified in believing H false," then I would be begging a question against Lehrer when I say that (5a) is un-controversially false. But it does not say that, and so I do not see that I am begging any questions.

is to suppose the falsity of H, the view one is trying to impugn. To paraphrase a statement of Lehrer's quoted above, since it is precisely the truth value of H that is in question, the conflict between a supposition that some premise is true and H cannot be taken to adjudicate against H. Thus, it seems that the sense of "question-begging" on which Lehrer relies is equally applicable to the case of H as to the sceptical hypothesis, and so Lehrer should give us (2a).

This leaves (1a) or (3a) (or both), as being false. Notice that (1a) and (3a) are clear instances of the general principles (P1') and (P3), respectively. Thus (P1') or (P3) (or both) are false. Yet if one does not believe (P1') and (P3), why would one believe (1') and (3)? Moreover, as we have seen from the quoted passages, Lehrer seems to appeal to some such principles as (P1') and (P3) in his argument. In any case, if we accept (2a), as it seems Lehrer must, we must reject (P1') or (P3) and so what seems to be the basis for Lehrer's (1') or (3). There thus appears to be no reason to accept (A1), and hence, if we have fairly construed Lehrer's remarks, his argument for (II) fails and so also his argument that no one knows anything.

Selected Bibliography

The following list of books and articles is suggested for further reading. The selection was made from a compiled list of hundreds of books and articles that have been published in English primarily during the last decade, and does not include the works that have been reprinted in this volume. Considerable use has been made of an extensive bibliography compiled by William Edward Morris of the University of Cincinnati.

Books and Anthologies

Armstrong, D. M. *Belief, Truth and Knowledge*. London: Cambridge University Press, 1973.

Aune, Bruce. *Knowledge, Mind and Nature*. New York: Random House, 1967.

Ayer, A. J. *The Problem of Knowledge*. Baltimore: Pelican, 1956.

Chisholm, Roderick. *Perceiving: A Philosophical Study*. Ithaca: Cornell University Press, 1957.

———. *Theory of Knowledge*. Englewood Cliffs: Prentice-Hall, 1966.

———, and R. Swartz, eds. *Empirical Knowledge*. Englewood Cliffs: Prentice-Hall, 1973.

Danto, Arthur. *Analytical Philosophy of Knowledge*. London: Cambridge University Press, 1968.

Dretske, Fred I. *Seeing and Knowing*. Chicago: University of Chicago Press, 1969.

Ginet, Carl. *Knowledge, Perception, and Memory*. Dordrecht: Reidel, 1975.

Harman, Gilbert. *Thought*. Princeton: Princeton University Press, 1973.

Hintikka, Jaakko. *Knowledge and Belief: An Introduction to the Logic of the Two Notions*. Ithaca: Cornell University Press, 1962.

Lehrer, Keith. *Knowledge*. New York: Oxford University Press, 1974.

———, ed. *Analysis and Metaphysics*. Dordrecht: Reidel, 1975.

Lewis, C. I. *An Analysis of Knowledge and Valuation*. LaSalle, Ill.: Open Court, 1946.

Pollock, John. *Knowledge and Justification*. Princeton: Princeton University Press, 1974.

Quinton, Anthony. *The Nature of Things*. London: Routledge & Kegan Paul, 1973.

Roth, Michael D., and Leon Galis, eds. *Knowing: Essays in the Analysis of Knowledge*. New York: Random House, 1970.

Slote, Michael Anthony. *Reason and Scepticism*. London: George Allen and Unwin, 1970.

Swain, Marshall, ed. *Induction, Acceptance, and Rational Belief*. Dordrecht: Reidel, 1970.

Unger, Peter. *Ignorance*. London: Oxford University Press, 1975.

Articles

Alston, William. "Self-Warrant: A Neglected Form of Privileged Access." *American Philosophical Quarterly* 13.4 (1976), 257–272.

———. "Two Types of Foundationalism." *Journal of Philosophy*, 73 (1976), 165–185.

Aune, Bruce. "Remarks on an Argument by Chisholm." *Philosophical Studies*, 23.5 (1972), 327–334.

Barker, John. "What You Don't Know Won't Hurt You?" *American Philosophical Quarterly*, 13.4 (1976), 303–308.

———. "Knowledge and Causation." *Southern Journal of Philosophy*, 10 (1972), 313–321.

———. "Knowledge, Ignorance and Presupposition." *Analysis*, 33 (1974), 33–45.

Barnes, G. "Unger's Defense of Scepticism." *Philosophical Studies*, 24.2 (1973), 119–124.

Bonjour, Laurence. "The Coherence Theory of Empirical Knowledge." *Philosophical Studies*, 30.5 (1976), 281–312.

Chisholm, Roderick. "Epistemic Statements and the Ethics of Belief." *Philosophy and Phenomenological Research*, 16.4 (1956), 447–460.

———. "The Ethics of Requirement." *American Philosophical Quarterly*, 1.2 (1964), 147–153.

———. "Evidence as Justification." *Journal of Philosophy*, 58.24 (1961), 739–748.

———. "Knowledge and Belief: De Dicto and De Re." *Philosophical Studies*, 29.1 (1976), 1–20.

———. "Theory of Knowledge." In R. Chisholm et al., *Philosophy*, Englewood Cliffs: Prentice-Hall (1964), 235–344.

Clark, Michael. "Knowledge and Grounds: A Comment on Mr. Gettier's Paper." *Analysis*, 24.2 (1963), 46–48.

Coder, David. "Thalberg's Defense of Justified True Belief." *Journal of Philosophy*, 67.12 (1970), 424–425.

———. "Naturalizing the Gettier Argument." *Philosophical Studies*, 26.2 (1974), 111–118.

Collier, Kenneth. "Against the Causal Theory of Knowing." *Philosophical Studies*, 24 (1973), 350–351.

Cornman, James. "On the Certainty of Reports about What Is Given." *Nous*, forthcoming.

———. "On Acceptability without Certainty." *Journal of Philosophy*, 74. 1 (1977), 29–47.

Dreher, John. "Evidence and Justified Belief." *Philosophical Studies*, 25.6 (1974), 435–439.

Dretske, Fred. "Reasons and Consequences." *Analysis*, 28.5 (1968), 166–168.

———. "Epistemic Operators." *Journal of Philosophy*, 67.24 (1970), 1007–1023.

———. "Reasons, Knowledge, and Probability." *Philosophy of Science*, 38.2 (1971), 216–220.

Feldman, Richard. "An Alleged Defect in Gettier-Counterexamples." *Australasian Journal of Philosophy*, 52.1 (1974), 68–69.

Gettier, Edmund L. "Is Justified True Belief Knowledge?" *Analysis*, 23.6 (1963), 121–123. Reprinted in Roth and Galis, *op. cit.*, 35–38.

Harman, Gilbert. "The Inference to the Best Explanation." *Philosophical Review*, 74.1 (1965), 88–95.

———. "Enumerative Induction as Inference to the Best Explanation." *Journal of Philosophy*, 65.18 (1968), 529–533.

———. "Knowledge, Inference, and Explanation." *American Philosophical Quarterly*, 5.3 (1968), 164–173.

Hart, J., and R. Dees. "Paradox Regained: A Reply to Meyers and Stern." *Journal of Philosophy*, 71 (1974), 367–372.

Heidelberger, Herbert. "Chisholm's Epistemic Principles." *Nous*, 3.1 (1969), 73–82.

Hilpinen, Risto. "Knowledge and Justification." *Ajatus* 33.1 (1971), 7–39.

Hooker, Michael. "In Defense of a Principle of Deducibility for Justification." *Philosophical Studies*, 24 (1973), 402–406.

Johnsen, Bredo. "Knowledge." *Philosophical Studies*, 25.4 (1974), 273–282.

Kekes, J. "The Case for Scepticism." *Philosophical Quarterly*, 25.98 (1975) 28–39.

Klein, Peter D. "A Proposed Definition of Propositional Knowledge." *Journal of Philosophy*, 68.16 (1971), 471–482.

———. "Knowledge, Causality, and Defeasibility." *Journal of Philosophy*, 73.20 (1976), 792–812.

Lamb, James W. "Knowledge and Justified Presumption." *Journal of Philosophy*, 69.5 (1972), 123–127.

Lehrer, Keith. "Knowledge, Truth and Evidence." *Analysis,* 25.5 (1965), 168–175. Reprinted in Roth and Galis, *op. cit.,* 55–66.

——. "Scepticism and Conceptual Change." In R. Chisholm and R. Swartz, eds., *Empirical Knowledge, op. cit.*

——. "Truth, Evidence and Inference." *American Philosophical Quarterly,* 11.1 (1974), 79–92.

Lesher, James. "Lehrer's Sceptical Hypothesis." *Philosophical Forum,* 4 (1973), 299–302.

Lewis, C. I. "The Given Element in Empirical Knowledge." *Philosophical Review,* 61.2 (1952), 168–175.

Lucey, K. "Scales of Epistemic Appraisal." *Philosophical Studies,* 29.3 (1976), 169–179.

Lycan, William, and Mark McAll. "The Catastrophe of Defeat." *Philosophical Studies,* 28.2 (1975), 147–150.

Malcolm, Norman. "Knowledge and Belief." *Mind,* 61.242 (1952), 178–189. Reprinted in Malcolm, *Knowledge and Certainty,* Prentice-Hall, 1963, and in Roth and Galis, *op. cit.,* 17–32.

Martin, Raymond. "Empirical Conclusive Reasons and Skepticism." *Philosophical Studies,* 28.3 (1975), 215–217.

Meerbote, Ralf. "The Distinction between Derivative and Non-Derivative Knowledge." *Philosophical Studies,* 23.6 (1972), 131–137.

Meyers, Robert, and Kenneth Stern. "Knowledge without Paradox." *Journal of Philosophy,* 70 (1973), 147–160.

Morris, William. "Knowledge as Justified Presumption." *Journal of Philosophy,* 70 (1973), 161–165.

Oakley, I. "An Argument for Skepticism concerning Justified Belief." *American Philosophical Quarterly,* 13.3 (1976), 221–228.

Pappas, George. "Knowledge and Reasons." *Philosophical Studies,* 25.6 (1974), 423–428.

——. "Incorrigibility, Knowledge and Justification." *Philosophical Studies,* 25.3 (1974), 129–226.

Pastin, Mark. "Foundationalism Redux." *Journal of Philosophy,* 71 (1974), 709–710.

Pollock, John L. "Criteria and Our Knowledge of the Material World." *Philosophical Review,* 76.1 (1967), 28–60.

——. "What Is an Epistemological Problem?" *American Philosophical Quarterly,* 5.3 (1968), 183–190.

——. "Chisholm's Definition of Knowledge." *Philosophical Studies,* 19.5 (1968), 72–76.

——. "The Structure of Epistemic Justification." *American Philosophical Quarterly,* Monograph Series Number 4 (1970), 62–78.

Quinton, Anthony. "The Foundations of Knowledge." In Williams and Montefiore, eds., *British Analytical Philosophy,* London: Routledge & Kegan Paul (1966), 55–86.

Radford, Colin. "Knowledge—By Examples." *Analysis*, 27.1 (1966), 1–11. Reprinted in Roth and Galis, *op. cit.*, 171–185.

Rescher, Nicholas. "Foundationalism, Coherentism, and the Idea of Cognitive Systemization." *Journal of Philosophy*, 71 (1974), 695–708.

Rozeboom, William W. "Why I Know So Much More Than You Do." *American Philosophical Quarterly*, 4.4 (1967), 257–268.

Saunders, John Turk. "Thalberg's Challenge to Justification via Deduction." *Philosophical Studies*, 23 (1972), 358–364.

——, and Champawat Narayan. "Mr. Clark's Definition of 'Knowledge.'" *Analysis*, 25.1 (1964), 8–9.

Scott, R. "Swain on Knowledge." *Philosophical Studies*, 29 (1976), 419–424.

Sharpe, R. "On the Causal Theory of Knowledge." *Ratio*, 7.2 (1975), 206–216.

Skyrms, Brian. "The Explication of 'X knows that p'." *Journal of Philosophy*, 64.12 (1967), 373–389. Reprinted in Roth and Galis, *op. cit.*

Sosa, Ernest. "The Analysis of 'Knowledge that p.'" *Analysis*, 25.1 (1964), 1–8.

——. "Propositional Knowledge." *Philosophical Studies*, 20.3 (1969), 33–43.

——. "Two Conceptions of Knowledge." *Journal of Philosophy*, 67.3 (1970), 59–66.

——. "On Our Knowledge of Matters of Fact." *Mind*, 83.331 (1974), 388–405.

Steiner, Mark. "Platonism and the Causal Theory of Knowledge." *Journal of Philosophy*, 70 (1973), 57–66.

Stine, Gail. "Dretske on Knowing the Logical Consequences." *Journal of Philosophy*, 68.9 (1971), 296–299.

——. "Skepticism, Relevant Alternatives and Deductive Closure." *Philosophical Studies*, 29.4 (1976), 249–261.

Swain, Marshall. "Skyrms on Non-Derivative Knowledge." *Nous*, 3.2 (1969), 227–231.

——. "An Alternative Analysis of Knowing." *Synthese*, 23.4 (1972), 423–442.

——. "Defeasibility: A Reply to R. Scott." *Philosophical Studies*, 29 (1976), 425–428.

Thalberg, Irving. "In Defense of Justified True Belief." *Journal of Philosophy*, 66.22 (1969), 795–803.

——. "Is Justification Transmissible through Deduction?" *Philosophical Studies*, 25.5 (1974), 347–356.

Unger, Peter. "An Analysis of Factual Knowledge." *Journal of Philosophy*, 65.6 (1968), 157–170. Reprinted in Roth and Galis, *op. cit.*, 113–130.

——. "Two Types of Scepticism." *Philosophical Studies*, 25.2 (1974), 77–96.

Index

Absolute terms: applicability of, 330-333; basic, 322-323; Cargile on, 338-339; and propositional terms, 327; and relative terms, 322-327; Unger on, 322-327; *see also* "Certain"

Absolute validation, 200

Acceptability, 256

Agnoiology, 346

Almeder, R., 13n

Alternatives to epistemic frameworks, 173; evidence-restricted, 176

Ancestral grounds, 187

Annis, David, 27, 30, 31; on defeasibility, 155-159; on full justification, 155-156

A priori propositions, Chisholm on, 260

Armstrong, David, 21n, 100n, 129n

Aune, Bruce, 35, 236

Augustine, Saint, 37n

Axiomatic propositions, Chisholm on, 260

Ayer, A. J., 11

Barker, John, 100n

Basic beliefs, 356

Basic propositions, 33; Chisholm on, 259-261

Basic knowledge, 87, 146-148

Basing relation, the, 58-59

Basis of a proposition, 262

Berkeley, George, 357-358

Brentano, Franz, 259n

Cargile, James, 39; on absolute terms, 338-339; on Prichard, 344-345; on Unger, 337-345

Carnap, Rudolf, 296

Causal chains: with admixtures of logical connections, 81; alternative, 113-115; correct reconstruction of, 24, 25, 74-75, 208; defective, 110-119; and inference, 73; as a necessary condition for knowledge, 72; Pattern 1 and Pattern 2, 23, 77-78; significant alternatives to, 114-116; as sources of defeat, 95-97, 107-108

Causal theory of knowledge, the: and appropriate knowledge-producing processes, 82, 84; and causal sufficiency, 92-94, 102-103; and the causal theory of perception, 69-70; and common causal antecedents, 76-78; comparison with the traditional analysis of knowledge, 75-76, 83, 86; and explanation, 207-212; and extrasensory perception, 84; Goldman on, 67-86; and inference, 71-72; and knowledge of mental states, 84; and memory, 71; Swain on, 86-99, 109-119; and testimonial knowledge, 74-75; and universal facts, 82-92, 210-211

"Certain": as an absolute term, Unger on, 327-330; and "confident" distinguished, 328-329

Certain propositions: defined by Chisholm, 259; and foundationalism, 280-281; and noninferentially justified propositions, 33

Certainty, 315-345 *passim;* and absence of doubt, 328-343; absolute, 32-33,

Certainty *(cont.)*
38; comparative, 332-333, 338-339, 342; distinguished from confidence, 328-329; and the logical possibility of error, 339-340; as a requirement for knowledge, 333-336, 337

Champawat, Narayan, 78-80

Chisholm, Roderick, 11, 15n, 18, 31, 33, 89n, 90n, 149, 160n, 162, 185n, 201n, 229, 230, 233, 234, 236, 290, 318n, 333n; on the *a priori,* 260; on the axiomatic, 260; on basic propositions, 259-261; on certain propositions, 258, 259; on criteria of application, 267-278; on defining knowledge, 263-267; on the directly evident, 259-261; on epistemic logic, 254-259; on epistemic preferability, 254; on the evident, 258-259, 272-273; on evidential support, 261-263; on Gettier examples, 264-265; on Heidelberger, 270-272; on justifying relations, 261-263; on the nondefectively evident, 267; on the self-presenting, 259-260, 268-269

Clark, Michael, 67n, 68, 75-76, 78-80, 155n

Coherence theory of justification, the, 35; and the chance of truth, 292-294; and circular justification, 240-241; and coherence theories of truth, 247-248; Cornman on, 240-248; explanatory, 241-247; Lehrer on, 292-300; and minimal nonfoundationalism, 233; minimal version of, 241; and self-evidence, 201-202

Competition among statements, 294-300; analysis of, 301; and complete justification, 294; and epistemic partitions, 297; Lehrer on, 294-300; and the lottery paradox, 294; and negative relevance, 294; and strong negative relevance, 295-301

Complete justification, 39; as a condition for knowledge, 147-148; Lehrer on, 300

Conclusions as total views, Harman on, 220-225

Conclusive reasons: and the causal theory of knowledge, 23; Dretske on, 41-60; empirically, 56; and the giving of reasons, 58-59; knowledge defined in terms of, 56; logically, 55-56; Pappas and Swain on, 61-66; and the possibility of error, 20-22; and reasoning, 60; and scepticism, 56-57

Concurrence, 277-278

Cornman, James, 31, 34, 35; on Chisholm, 230, 233, 234-240 *passim;* on coherence theories of justification, 240-248; on coherence theories of truth, 247-252; on evidential series, 232; on Lehrer, 241-247; on minimal foundationalism, 232-233; on minimal nonfoundationalism, 233-234; on objections to nonfoundationalism, 234-247; on Quine, 249-252; on Sellars, 249-252

Danto, Arthur, 146n

Dees, R., 14n

Defeasibility, epistemic, 26-30; adequacy condition for the analysis of, 161; Annis on, 155-159; and ethical defeasibility, 160, 162; Goldman on, 123-124; Lehrer and Paxson on, 149-154; Sosa on, 200; Swain on, 88-89, 109-110, 160-183

Defective causal chains, 110-119; and objective likelihood, 113-115; and pseudo-overdeterminants, 111, 117-118

Descartes, René, 125, 143-145, 185

Doxastic systems: consistency restrictions on, 302-304; corrected, 291; Lehrer on, 291-292

Dretske, Fred, 22-23, 26, 61-66, 140n; on conclusive reasons, 41-60; on Goldman, 46-47; on Harman, 44-47; on knowledge, 41-60

Epistemic consistency, 176-178

Epistemic frameworks, 173; evidence component of, 174, 178; evidence-restricted alternatives to, 176-183

Epistemic implication, 174, 200
Epistemic inference rules, 174, 185-186
Epistemic overdetermination, 187
Epistemic preferability: axioms of, 254-255; basic concepts of, 255-256
Epistemic pyramids, 188-192, 199
Epistemic systems, 283-284; minimal subsystems of, 286; subsystems of, 284
Epistemic validation, 200
Epistemological scepticism, 35-40; Cargile on, 337-345; and claims to know, 347-348; and criteria of justification, 359-360; degrees of globality of, 36-38, 311-312; and epistemic goals, 360-361; epistemic status of, 314-316; and impartiality, 358; intelligibility of, 353-355; and language, 318; Lehrer on, 346-363; meta-, 310; Pappas on, 309-316; and scientific inquiry, 362; strength of, 37-38, 312-314; Turner on, 364-369; Unger on, 317-336
Evidential ancestor, 232
Evidential series, 232
Evident propositions: Chisholm on, 258, 259, 272-273; directly, 259, 261; nondefectively, 267; noninferentially, 33; self-, 184-185; Sosa on, 184-188
Expected utility: and complete justification, 307; Lehrer on, 304-308; and subjective probability, 304-305
Extendability thesis, 169-172

Feldman, Richard, 16n
Ferrier, James, 346
Firth, Roderick, 313n
Foundationalism: with a coherence theory of truth, 248-252; Cornman on, 232-234; minimal, 232; modest versus radical, 32-33, 280, 286-288; Pastin on, 279-288
Frege, Gottlob, 187-188
Fully justified propositions: and defeasibility, 157; defined, 155; and knowledge, 155
Full validation, Sosa on, 199-201

Gettier, Edmund, 11, 57n, 62, 67, 88, 148, 164-165, 253, 263, 266n
Gettier cases, 11-18, 26, 57n, 62, 67-68, 90-91, 148, 164-165, 177-178, 180, 206, 264-266
Goldman, Alvin, 23-24, 25, 46, 48n, 89n, 92, 100, 115-116, 146n, 207-212; on the causal theory of knowing, 67-86; on the causal theory of perception, 69-70; on Clark, 75-80; on discrimination and perceptual knowledge, 120-145; on Gettier's examples, 67-68; on inferential knowledge, 71-86; on knowledge of mental states, 84; on knowledge of universal facts, 81-82; on memory, 70-71; on Pattern 1 and Pattern 2 causal chains, 77-78; on perceptual equivalents, 130-136; on relevant alternatives, 124-128; on testimony, 74-75; on the traditional analysis of knowledge, 75, 83; on Unger, 123
Goodman, Nelson, 279n, 286-287
Grice, H. P., 69, 71n

Harman, Gilbert, 14n, 18, 24, 27, 28, 30, 31, 44, 47-48, 83n, 89n, 92n, 123, 140, 146n, 147n, 149n, 152n, 159n, 190n, 194; on conclusions as total views, 220-225; on Gettier examples, 206-207; on Goldman, 207-210; on inference to the best explanation, 210-212; on knowledge by inference, 225-228; on the lottery paradox, 221-222, 224; on unpossessed evidence, 212-220
Hart, J., 14n
Heidelberger, Herbert, 253, 268, 270, 272, 274; Chisholm on, 270-272
Hempel, Carl, 304n
Hilpinen, Risto, 63n, 169, 172, 175, 178, 304n
Hintikka, Jaakko, 130n, 169, 304n
Hooker, Michael, 18n
Hume, David, 185

Incorrigibility, 33, 279-280, 352
Inductive evidential support, 282
Inference: to best explanation, 210-211, 223-225; to causal expla-

Inference (*cont.*)
nation, 209-210; as a causal process, 73; and conscious reasoning, 71; epistemic rules of, 174, 185-186; and inductive acceptance, 222-223; inductive versus deductive, 222-223; and knowledge, 225-228; maximal warranted, 227; statistical 212
Infinite regress of justification, 31, 32, 234-237

Jeffrey, Richard, 293, 363
Justification: ancestral chain of, 32, 156; complete, 147-148, 300; defeasible, 26-30, 88-89, 109-110, 123-124, 149-154, 155-159, 160-183, 200; epistemic, 30-31; by experience, 230-231; foundational versus nonfoundational theories of, 30-35, 229-253, 280-281; full, 155-156; inductive, 13, 26, 28; inferential, 31-35; noninferential, 32-33; principle of deduction for, 17-18
Justifying relations, Chisholm on, 261-263

Keim, Robert, 255n
Kekes, J., 312
Klein, Peter D., 123n, 158n, 169, 172
Knowledge: based on testimony, 43-44, 74-75; basic, 87, 146-148; expert versus layman, 197; of mental states, 84, 351-352; of necessary truths, 260, 349-351; nonbasic, 88-89, 146; and the possibility of error, 56-58, 349-350; primary nonbasic, 87-99, 101, 106; and reliability, 43-44; secondary nonbasic, 88; *see also entries for individual authors*
Kress, J. R., 89n, 155n
Kyburg, Henry E., 292n

Lamb, James W., 191n
Lehrer, Keith, 15, 16, 17, 27, 29, 30, 31, 35, 36, 37, 38, 57n, 67n, 80, 88n, 123n, 146n, 147n, 149n, 152n, 155, 158n, 166, 175, 181n, 191, 192n, 202n, 226n, 241, 243, 247, 252n, 311, 312, 313n, 364, 368, 369; on basic knowledge, 147-148; on the circle of belief, 289-290; on coherence, 292-300; on competition, 294-300; on complete justification, 300; on corrected doxastic systems, 291-292; on defeasibility, 149-154; on doxastic systems, 291; on Googols, 356-357; on the lottery paradox, 294-295, 298; and Paxson on knowledge, 146-154; on the rationality of justified belief, 300-308; on refutations of scepticism, 359-362; on scepticism, 346-363; on strong negative relevance, 295-298
Leibniz, Gottfried Wilhelm von, 259
Leith, E. N., 69n
Lesher, James, 364n
Levi, Isaac, 304n
Lewis, C. I., 279n, 286-287
Loeb, Louis E., 117n
Lottery paradox: Harman on, 221-222, 224; Lehrer on, 294-295, 298

Malcolm, Norman, 185n, 200n
Meinong, Alexius, 259, 269
Memory: causal theory of, 70-71; schemata, 128
Meyers, Robert, 14n, 191n
Moore, G. E., 317n, 318n, 333
Morris, William Edward, 191, 370

Naturalistic epistemology, 144-145
Nelson, L., 310, 312
Nonbasic knowledge, 87, 88-89, 146
Nonfoundationalist theory of justification. *See* Foundationalism *and* Justification

Oakley, I., 40n, 312

Pappas, George S., 36-38; on evaluating sceptical views, 314-316; on forms of epistemological scepticism, 309-316; on global versus local scepticism, 311-312; on strength of sceptical theses, 312-314; and Swain on Dretske, 61-66
Parsons, Kathryn, 352n
Pastin, Mark, 31; on epistemic subsystems, 284; on epistemic systems, 283-284; on foundationalism versus nonfoundationalism, 280-281; on Goodman, 286-287; on Lewis,

Pastin, Mark (*cont.*)
   286-287; on minimal subsystems,
   286; on modest foundationalism,
   280-281; on Reichenbach, 286-287;
   on self-warrant, 279-288
Paxson, Thomas D., Jr., 25, 27, 29, 30,
   88n, 109, 110, 112, 123n, 155, 158n,
   166, 175; on basic knowledge,
   147-148; on defeasibility, 149-154;
   and Lehrer on knowledge, 146-
   154; on Swain, 100-105
Perceptual equivalents, Goldman on,
   130-136
Perceptual knowledge, Goldman on,
   69-70, 120-145
Pietarinen, J., 304n
Plato, 11, 184
Pollock, John, 160n
Posner, Michael I., 134
Prichard, H. A., on certainty, 344-345
Primary knowledge, 86-99, 109-119
Probabilistic rules of acceptance, 206

Quine, Willard van Orman, 229, 241,
   242, 244, 247, 310n, 312; Cornman
   on, 249-252

Radford, Colin, 310n, 333n
Reasonability, 255, 269-272, 277
Reasoning: through false premises,
   14-16; and the having of conclusive
   reasons, 27; instantiators, 226, 227
Reichenbach, Hans, 279n, 286-287
Reid, Thomas, 356, 358
Relative terms. *See* Absolute terms
Relevant perceptual alternatives, Gold-
   man on, 124-128
Reliability: of belief-governing mech-
   anism, 121, 138; of cognitive mech-
   anism, 120; and discrimination,
   120; and knowledge, 43-44; of per-
   ceptual mechanism, 120-121, 138;
   of reasoning mechanism, 121
Rescher, Nicholas, 246n
Ross, W. D., 160n
Rozeboom, William W., 318n
Russell, Bertrand, 67n, 125

Saunders, John, 18, 78-80
Scepticism. *See* Epistemological scepticism

Secondary knowledge, 88, 119
Self-justifying statements, 230
Self-presenting, Chisholm on the,
   259-260, 268-269, 275
Self-warrant, 33; Pastin on, 279-288
Sellars, Wilfrid, 185, 229, 241; Cornman on, 249-252
Sextus Empiricus, 185n
Shaffer, Jerome, 193n
Skyrms, Brian, 57n, 62n, 92, 146n,
   148, 151n, 318n; Swain on, 92-93
Slote, Michael Anthony, 333n
Sosa, Ernest, 27, 30, 31, 67n, 89n,
   155n, 159n, 183n, 225n, 227n; on
   being in a position to know, 195-198;
   on epistemic principles, 185-186; on
   epistemic pyramids, 188-192, 199;
   on epistemic trees, 199-205; on epistemic validation, 200; on the evident,
   184-188; on full validation, 199-201;
   on knowledge, 184-205; on non-
   defective trees, 204; on S-epistemic
   propositions, 200; on the self-
   evident, 185-186
Stern, Kenneth, 14n, 191n
Suppes, Patrick, 304n
Swain, Marshall, 24-25, 27, 30, 31, 62n,
   89, 100-108, 140, 149n, 200n; on
   Chisholm, 162-163; on defeasibility,
   88-89, 109-110, 160-183; on defective causal chains, 110-119; on defective pseudo-overdeterminants, 118;
   on evidence-restricted alternatives,
   176-183; on the extendability thesis,
   169-172; on Gettier's examples,
   90-91, 164-165, 177-178, 180; on
   Hilpinen, 169-173; on Hintikka,
   169; on Klein, 169-173; on Lehrer
   and Paxson, 166-168; and Pappas on
   Dretske, 61-66; on Paxson, 109, 110,
   112; on primary nonbasic knowledge, 86-99, 109-119; on Skyrms,
   92-93; on Tolliver, 109, 113-117

Thalberg, Irving, 17-18
Tolliver, Joseph T., 25, 109, 110, 113;
   Swain on, 109, 113-117; on Swain,
   106-108
Traditional analysis of knowledge, 11,
   67-68, 75, 83, 100, 122, 148, 165,
   184, 188-189, 197, 263-264

Truth as a necessary condition for
     justification, 13-18
Turner, Dan, 39; on Lehrer, 364-369

Unger, Peter, 19-20, 36-40, 100, 123,
     147, 311, 337-345; on absolute and
     relative terms, 322-327; on "certain"
     as an absolute term, 327-332; on

knowledge and certainty, 333-336;
     on scepticism, 317-336
Upatnieks, J., 69n

Veracious inquirers, 291, 301-302

Warrant, self-, 279, 283, 285, 286;
     Pastin on, 279-288
Wittgenstein, Ludwig, 185, 353

Library of Congress Cataloging in Publication Data
(For library cataloging purposes only)

Main entry under title:
Essays on knowledge and justification.

   Bibliography: p.
   Includes index.
   1. Knowledge, Theory of—Addresses, essays, lectures.
   2. Justification (Theory of knowledge)—Addresses, essays,
lectures. 3. Skepticism—Addresses, essays, lectures.
I. Pappas, George Sotiros, 1942- II. Swain, Marshall.
BD161.E7   121   77-10299
ISBN 0-8014-1086-X
ISBN 0-8014-9865-1 pbk.